NAKAMA 1

INTRODUCTORY JAPANESE: *COMMUNICATION, CULTURE, CONTEXT*

Third Edition

Yukiko Abe Hatasa
Hiroshima University

Kazumi Hatasa
Purdue University
The Japanese School, Middlebury College

Seiichi Makino
Princeton University

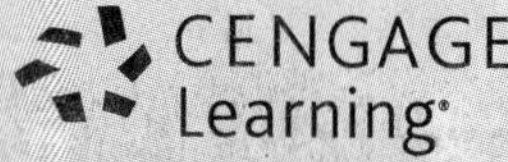

Australia • Brazil • Japan • Korea • Mexico • Singapore • Spain • United Kingdom • United States

Nakama 1: Introductory Japanese: Communication, Culture, Context
Third Edition
Yukiko Abe Hatasa, Kazumi Hatasa, Seiichi Makino

Product Director: Beth Kramer

Senior Product Managers: Nicole Morinon, Martine Edwards

Managing Developer: Katie Wade

Senior Content Project Manager: Lianne Ames

Content Coordinator: Gregory Madan

Product Assistant: Kimberley Hunt

Associate Media Developer: Patrick Brand

Executive Market Development Manager: Ben Rivera

Senior Art Director: Linda Jurras

Manufacturing Planner: Betsy Donaghey

Rights Acquisition Specialist: Jessica Elias

Production Service: Inari Information Services

Cover Designer: Wing Ngan

Cover Image: © Image Source/Alamy

Compositor: Inari Information Services

Library of Congress Control Number: 2013950679

Student Edition:
ISBN-13: 978-1-285-42959-5
ISBN-10: 1-285-42959-1

Loose-leaf Edition:
ISBN-13: 978-1-305-94637-8
ISBN-10: 1-305-94637-5

Cengage Learning
200 First Stamford Place, 4th Floor
Stamford, CT 06902
USA

Cengage Learning is a leading provider of customized learning solutions with office locations around the globe, including Singapore, the United Kingdom, Australia, Mexico, Brazil, and Japan. Locate your local office at: **international.cengage.com/region**

Cengage Learning products are represented in Canada by Nelson Education, Ltd.

For your course and learning solutions, visit **www.cengage.com**

Purchase any of our products at your local college store or at our preferred online store **www.cengagebrain.com**

Instructors: Please visit **login.cengage.com** and log in to access instructor-specific resources.

Printed in the United States of America
4 5 6 7 8 9 10 20 19 18 17 16

ABOUT THE AUTHORS

Professor Yukiko Abe Hatasa received her Ph.D. in linguistics in 1992 from the University of Illinois at Urbana-Champaign. She is known nationwide as one of the premier Japanese methodologists in the United States and as an experienced coordinator of large teacher-training programs. She has served as the coordinator of the Japanese language program at the University of Iowa and is currently professor and chair of the Department of Teaching Japanese as a Second Language at Hiroshima University, where her primary responsibilities are teacher training and SLA research.

Professor Kazumi Hatasa received his Ph.D. in education in 1989 from the University of Illinois at Urbana-Champaign. He is currently a professor at Purdue University and Director of the Japanese School at Middlebury College. He is recognized internationally for his work in the development of instructional software and online resources for the Japanese language. He has also been active in incorporating traditional performing art in language instruction.

Professor Seiichi Makino received his Ph.D. in linguistics in 1968 from the University of Illinois at Urbana-Champaign. He is an internationally prominent Japanese linguist and scholar, recognized throughout the world for his scholarship and for his many publications. Before beginning his tenure at Princeton University in 1991, he taught Japanese language, linguistics and culture at the University of Illinois while training lower-division language coordinators. He is an experienced ACTFL oral proficiency trainer in Japanese and frequently trains Japanese instructors internationally in proficiency-oriented instruction and in the administration of the Oral Proficiency Interview. Professor Makino has been the Academic Director of the Japanese Pedagogy M.A. Summer Program at Columbia University since 1996. He also directs the Princeton-in-Ishikawa Summer Program.

Chapter 6: Leisure Time

Chapter 7: Favorite Things and Activities

Chapter 8: Shopping

Chapter 9: Restaurants and Invitations

Chapter 10: My Family

Chapter 11: Seasons and Weather

Chapter 12: Annual Events

Reference Section

TO THE STUDENT

Nakama 1 is organized around the principle that learning another language means acquiring new skills, not just facts and information—that we learn by doing. To achieve this goal, *Nakama 1* systematically involves you in many activities that incorporate the language skills of listening, speaking, reading, and writing. We believe that culture is an integral component of language, too. To help you become familiar with Japanese culture, your text includes high-interest culture notes and relevant communication strategies. We have also created a storyline video, featuring a Japanese-American exchange student in Tokyo, to bring chapter dialogues to life.

ORGANIZATION OF THE TEXTBOOK

Nakama 1 consists of twelve chapters in two parts. In Chapter 1, you will learn the sounds of the Japanese language and a set of Japanese syllabary symbols called **hiragana**. You will also learn basic greetings and classroom instructions. A second Japanese syllabary called **katakana** is presented after Chapter 2. Chapters 2 through 12 each focus on a common communicative situation and contain the following features:

- Chapter Opener: Each chapter opens with a theme-setting photograph and chapter contents by section. Keeping in mind the objectives listed at the top of the opener will help you focus on achieving your learning goals.
- Vocabulary: Vocabulary is presented in thematic groups, followed by a variety of communicative activities and activities in context. Supplemental vocabulary is introduced throughout the chapter without demanding that you retain it. All active vocabulary is listed by function at the beginning of each chapter, except for Chapter 1. There the list appears at the chapter's end, where you can better make use of it after learning to read **hiragana**.
- Dialogue: The lively dialogues center on Alice Ueda, a Japanese-American college student, who is spending two years studying in Japan. Through the dialogue and accompanying video, you will get to know a series of characters and follow them through typical events in their lives. The video, related activities, and interactive online practice will all reinforce your understanding of the content, discourse organization, and use of formal and casual Japanese speech styles.
- Japanese Culture: Up-to-date culture notes in English explore social, economic, and historical aspects of Japanese life, knowledge of which is essential to effective communication.
- Grammar: Clear, easy-to-understand grammar explanations are accompanied by sample sentences and notes that help you understand how to use the grammar appropriately. In-class pair and group activities let you immediately practice what you've learned. As there is a high correlation between successful communication and grammar accuracy, this section is especially important.
- Listening: Useful strategies and pre-listening activities for general comprehension precede the section's main listening practice. Post-listening activities concentrate on more detailed comprehension and apply what you have learned to other communicative purposes.

- Communication: This section will provide you with knowledge and practice of basic strategies to accelerate your ability to communicate in Japanese.
- **Kanji**: Chapters 4 through 12 introduce a total of 127 **kanji** (Chinese characters). The section begins with useful information such as the composition of individual characters, word formation, and how to use Japanese dictionaries. The presentation of each character includes stroke order to help you master correct penmanship when writing in Japanese and to prepare you for the reading section.
- Reading: Each reading passage begins with a reading strategy, and includes pre- and post-reading activities designed to help you become a successful reader of Japanese. From Chapter 2, the text is written in all three scripts: **hiragana**, **katakana**, and **kanji**. **Hiragana** subscripts (**furigana**) are provided for **katakana** through Chapter 3, and for unfamiliar **kanji** and readings throughout the textbook. The readings include a small number of unknown words to help you develop strategies for understanding authentic texts.
- Integration: Integrated practice wraps up every chapter using discussion, interviewing, and role-play activities that interweave all the skills you've learned in the current and previous chapters.

STUDENT COMPONENTS

- Student Text: Your Student Text contains all the information and activities you need for in-class use. It is divided into two parts comprising twelve chapters plus a special chapter following Chapter 2 that introduces **katakana**. Each regular chapter contains vocabulary presentations and activities, a thematic dialogue and practice, grammar presentations and activities, cultural information, reading selections, writing practice, and ample communicative practice. Valuable reference sections at the back of the book include verb charts, a **kanji** list, and Japanese-English and English-Japanese glossaries.
- Text Audio Program: The Text Audio Program contains recordings of all the listening activities in the text as well as all active chapter vocabulary. The audio activity clips are also available on the Premium Website and iLrn™ Heinle Learning Center, and the vocabulary pronunciations can be found in the flashcards on iLrn. These audio materials are designed to maximize your exposure to the sounds of natural spoken Japanese and to help you practice pronunciation.
- Student Activities Manual (SAM): The Student Activities Manual (SAM) includes out-of-class practice of the material presented in the Student Text. Each chapter of the SAM includes a workbook section, which focuses on written vocabulary, grammar, **kanji** and writing practice, and a lab section, which focuses on pronunciation and listening comprehension, including Dict-a-Conversation dictation activities.
- SAM Audio Program: The SAM Audio Program corresponds to the audio portion of the SAM and reinforces your pronunciation and listening skills. The audio is available on the Premium Website and iLrn.
- Video Program: The two-tiered Nakama video program includes a storyline video, in which the experiences of Japanese-American exchange student Alice Ueda, featured in the chapter dialogues, are brought to life, and a series of cultural segments that depict everyday situations tied to the theme of each

chapter. You will be able to view the video in class on the Premium Website or iLrn.

- iLrn™ Heinle Learning Center: The new iLrn includes an audio- and video-enhanced eBook, interactive textbook activities, the complete Text and SAM Audio Programs, the complete Video Program, an online Student Activities Manual with audio, a diagnostic study tool to help you prepare for exams, and much more. A wealth of interactive exercises and games give you further practice with chapter topics. Vocabulary and grammar quizzes, audio flashcards for vocabulary, and kanji and pronunciation review help you monitor and assess your progress.
- Premium Website: With the Premium Website, you have access to the complete Text Audio Program, the complete SAM Audio Program, and the complete Video Program.

ACKNOWLEDGMENTS

The authors and publisher thank the following people for their recommendations regarding the content of *Nakama 1*. Their comments and suggestions were invaluable during the development of this publication.

Noriko Akatsuka
Carolyn Allemand
Laurie Arizumi
Mahua Bhattacharya
Akiko Brennan
Julie Bruch
Neta Cahill
Aloysius Chang
Maggie Childs
Takashi Ebira
Janet Fair
Miku Fukasaku
Len Grzanka
Masako Hamada
Hiroko Harada
Janet Ikeda
Mieko Ishibashi
Satoru Ishikawa
Noriko Iwasaki
Kimberly Jones
Sarachie Karasawa
Hiroko Kataoka
Yukio Kataoka
Yuko Kawabe
Michiya Kawai
Chisato Kitagawa
Lisa Kobuke
Chiyo Konishi
Junko Kumamoto-Healey
Yukari Kunisue
Yasumi Kuriya
John Mertz
Masahiko Minami
Akira Miura
Shigeru Miyagawa
Seigo Nakao
Hiroshi Nara
Machiko Netsu
Catherine Oshida
Yoko Pusavat
Yoshiko Saito-Abbott
Haruko Sakakibara
Kitty Shek
Ritsuko Shigeyama
Satoru Shinagawa
Zenryu Shirakawa
Shizuka Tatsuzawa
Miyo Uchida
Alexander Vovin
Paul Warnick
Yasuko Ito Watt
Kikuko Yamashita

The authors and publisher also thank the following people for field-testing *Nakama 1*. Their comments contributed greatly to the accuracy of this publication.

Nobuko Chikamatsu
Fusae Ekida
Junko Hino
Satoru Ishikawa
Yoshiko Jo
Sayuri Kubota
Yasumi Kuriya
Izumi Matsuda
Junko Mori
Fumiko Nazikian
Mayumi Oka
Amy Snyder Ohta
Mayumi Steinmetz
Keiko Yamaguchi

The authors are also grateful to the following people at Cengage Learning for their valuable assistance during the development of this project: Beth Kramer, Nicole Morinon, Gregory Madan, Ben Rivera, Morgan Gallo, Patrick Brand, Linda Jurras, and Lianne Ames.

They are especially grateful to Takuya Akaida and Richard Lutz for copyediting, to Satoru Ishikawa and Bill Weaver for proofreading, and to Michael Kelsey of Inari Information Services, Inc. Thanks go to Satoru Ishikawa for his work on the Student Activities Manual, Laurie Arizumi for her work on the web search activities, and Satoru Shinagawa for his work on the self-tests, tutorial quizzes, iLrn correlations, and PowerPoints.

Chapter 1

だいいっか

© Chanclos/Shutterstock.com

The Japanese Sound System and Hiragana

I. Introduction

II. Hiragana あ～そ
Useful Expressions: Forms of address; introducing yourself

III. Hiragana た～ほ
Useful Expressions: Daily greetings

IV. Hiragana ま～ん
Useful Expressions: Taking leave of friends and instructors

V. Hiragana が～ぽ: Voiced consonants
Useful Expressions: Thanking, apologizing, and getting attention

VI. Hiragana ああ～わあ: Long vowels
Useful Expressions: Understanding your instructor's requests

VII. Hiragana Small っ: Double consonants
Useful Expressions: Confirming information and making requests

VIII. Hiragana きゃ～ぴょ: Glides
Useful Expressions: Asking for Japanese words and English equivalents

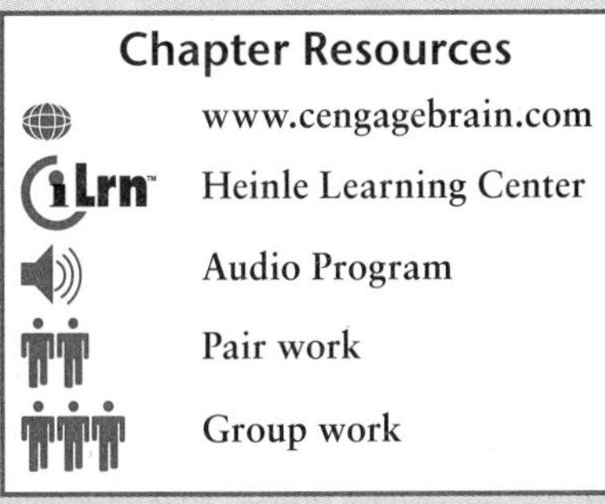
Chapter Resources

www.cengagebrain.com
Heinle Learning Center
Audio Program
Pair work
Group work

I. Introduction

Japanese is usually written with a combination of three types of script: **hiragana**, **katakana**, and **kanji** (Chinese characters). Individually, **hiragana** and **katakana** represent sounds, and **kanji** represent words. **Hiragana** are used for function words (words such as *in*, *at*, and *on*), for inflectional endings (indicating sound changes used to express tense, negation, and the like), and for some content words. **Katakana** are used for words borrowed from other languages, for example, **keeki** (cake); for onomatopoeic words expressing sounds, such as **wanwan** (the Japanese word for a dog's bark, equivalent to *bow-wow*); and for some scientific terms, such as the names of animals and plants in biology textbooks. **Kanji** are characters of Chinese origin; each **kanji** represents a morpheme or a word and is used for content words, such as nouns, verbs, and adjectives.

Hiragana

Like the individual letters in the English alphabet, **hiragana** represent sounds, but each **hiragana** character represents a vowel or a combination of a consonant and a vowel, such as **a**, **sa**, **ki**, **tsu**, **me**, and **yo**. **Hiragana** evolved through the simplification of Chinese characters during the Heian period (794–1185).

Having no writing system of their own, the Japanese began importing Chinese characters (**hanzi**) to write their own language in the late fourth or early fifth century. They employed two adaptation strategies while doing so. One was based on meaning and the other was based on sound. The meaning-based strategy involved using an individual **kanji** to write a Japanese word that was synonymous with the Chinese word the **kanji** represented. For example, the Japanese word for "wave" was expressed using the Chinese character with the same meaning, 波. Its pronunciation in Chinese, *puâ*, was replaced with the pronunciation of the corresponding Japanese word, **nami**.

The sound-based strategy, by contrast, used Chinese characters to represent Japanese sounds rather than meanings. For instance, the character 波 in this context was used to represent the syllable *ha* because of its close resemblance to the sound *puâ* in Middle Chinese. (The character is currently pronounced [ha], but was pronounced [pa] in classical Japanese, similar to the Middle Chinese [puâ].) In this usage, the meaning of the character 波 was completely ignored. This was a cumbersome system, however, because Japanese words usually contain several syllables and Chinese characters represent only one syllable each. In order to overcome this problem, Chinese characters were gradually simplified until they reached the forms used in present-day **hiragana**. These simplified characters appear in many literary works written by women, including the famous *Tale of Genji*, and for this reason **hiragana** was once called **onna de** (*women's hand*).

Hiragana as written today comprise 46 characters (Figure 1). Two diacritical marks in the shapes of two dots ゛ or a small circle ゜ are used to show voiced consonants (Figure 2). The basic syllabary can also be used to represent *glides*, which are combinations of characters that represent more complex sounds (Figure 3).

Look at Figure 1 and pronounce each character by repeating it after your instructor and/or the accompanying audio. This chart should be read from top to bottom and right to left. Japanese may be written vertically in this manner or horizontally, from left to right, as in English.

Figure 1

n	w	r	y	m	h	n	t	s	k		
ん	わ	ら	や	ま	は	な	た	さ	か	あ	a
		り		み	ひ	に	ち	し	き	い	i
		る	ゆ	む	ふ	ぬ	つ	す	く	う	u
		れ		め	へ	ね	て	せ	け	え	e
	を	ろ	よ	も	ほ	の	と	そ	こ	お	o

Figure 2

p	b	d	z	g	
ぱ	ば	だ	ざ	が	a
ぴ	び	ぢ	じ	ぎ	i
ぷ	ぶ	づ	ず	ぐ	u
ぺ	べ	で	ぜ	げ	e
ぽ	ぼ	ど	ぞ	ご	o

Figure 3

p	b	d (j)	j (z)	g	r	m	h	n	ch (t)	sh (s)	k	
ぴゃ	びゃ	ぢゃ	じゃ	ぎゃ	りゃ	みゃ	ひゃ	にゃ	ちゃ	しゃ	きゃ	ya
ぴゅ	びゅ	ぢゅ	じゅ	ぎゅ	りゅ	みゅ	ひゅ	にゅ	ちゅ	しゅ	きゅ	yu
ぴょ	びょ	ぢょ	じょ	ぎょ	りょ	みょ	ひょ	にょ	ちょ	しょ	きょ	yo

II. Hiragana あ～そ

In this section, you will learn fifteen **hiragana** and their pronunciations. The following charts show both printed and handwritten styles.

Note that some lines that are connected in the printed style are not connected in handwriting. For example, the vertical diagonal curved lines in the printed forms of き[ki] and さ[sa] are connected, but they are not connected in handwriting (き and さ). Also, the character そ[so] is written as a single stroke in the printed style, but as two strokes in handwriting (そ), where the diagonal line at the top is not connected with the rest of the character.

Printed style

s	k		
さ	か	あ	a
し	き	い	i
す	く	う	u
せ	け	え	e
そ	こ	お	o

Handwritten style

s	k		
さ	か	あ	a
し	き	い	i
す	く	う	u
せ	け	え	e
そ	こ	お	o

Learning hiragana

The mnemonic pictures and keys below have been provided to help you memorize the **hiragana** characters. Remember that the mnemonic pictures are rough, rather than precise representations of the shapes or the sounds of the characters.

a	あ	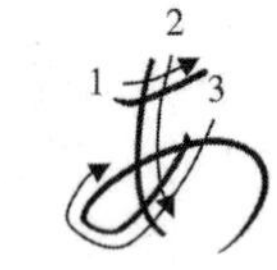 あ (strokes 1, 2, 3)	あ is similar to [ah] but is shorter.	 *Ah!* Ann is good at ice-skating.
i	い	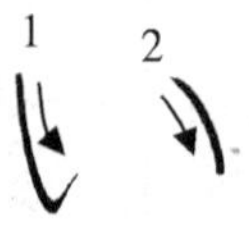 い (strokes 1, 2)	い is similar to the vowel sound in *ear* but is shorter.	 I have big *ears*.
u	う	 う (strokes 1, 2)	う is similar to the vowel sound in [ooh] but is shorter and the lips are not as rounded.	 *Ooh!* This is heavy.
e	え	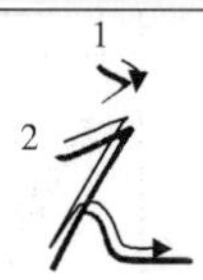 え (strokes 1, 2)	え is similar to the first vowel sound in *exercise* but the mouth is not opened as widely.	 I need *exercise*.

o	お	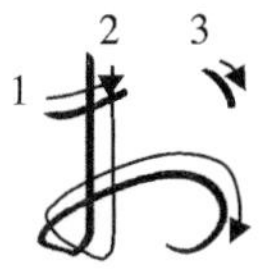 お	お is similar to the vowel sound [o] in *on* as the British pronounce it, but the lips are slightly more rounded.	 The ball will land *on* the green.
ka	か	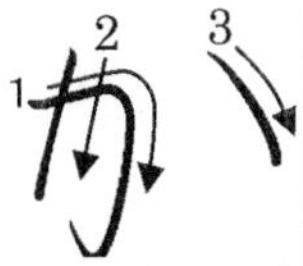 か	か is a combination of [k] and [a]. The Japanese [k] sound is less forceful than the English sound.	 *Karate* kick.
ki	き	 き	き is similar to *key* but the vowel sound is shorter.	 This is *a key*.
ku	く	 く	く is similar to the first syllable of *cuckoo* but the lips are not as rounded.	 This is a *cuckoo*.
ke	け	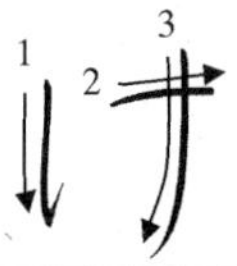 け	け is similar to the sound [ca] in *cane*, but without the [y] sound.	 A man with a *cane*.
ko	こ	 こ	こ is similar to the sound [co] in *coin* without the [y] sound.	 A ten yen *coin* is worth about a dime.
sa	さ	 さ	さ is a combination of [s] and [a]. The Japanese [s] sound is not as strong as the English [s] sound because less air is forced out between the teeth.	 Don't drink too much *sake*.
shi	し	 し	し is similar to *she* but is shorter and the lips are spread wider. Japanese does not have the sound [si] as in *sea*.	 This is how *she* wears her hair.
su	す	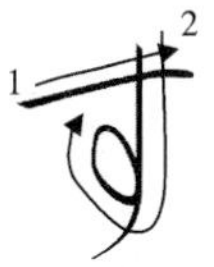 す	す is a combination of [s] and [u].	 *Swimming* is fun in the summer.
se	せ	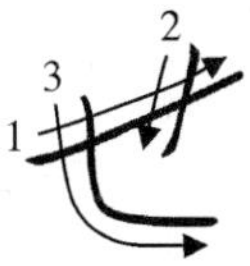 せ	せ is similar to the sound of [*se*] in *señor*.	 Hello, *Señor* García.
so	そ	 そ	そ is similar to *so* but is shorter.	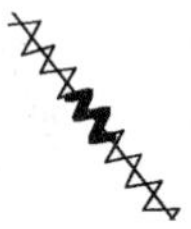 This character zigzags *so* much.

Reading hiragana

Read the following words, paying attention to intonation and devoiced sounds. Characters with a bar over them (for example, いけ) should be pronounced with a higher pitch than those without a bar. The [i] and [u] in き, く, し, す, ち, つ, ひ, and ふ may be devoiced between two voiceless consonants or at the end of a word. Characters with a small circle under them (き) contain a devoiced [i] or [u].

え	picture	いけ	pond
おかし	confectionery	いす	chair
き	tree	きく	chrysanthemum
かお	face	さけ	sake
あし	leg	えき	station
せかい	world	そこ	bottom
あさ	morning	しお	salt
あかい	red	あかい かさ	red umbrella
あおい	blue	あおい いす	blue chair

Useful Expressions

1. Forms of address

The Japanese always use a title to address people other than family members. Young people, however, sometimes refer to their close friends by name only, without using titles.

se n se e せんせい	se n se e 〜せんせい	sa n 〜さん
professor, teacher	Professor/Dr. 〜	Mr./Mrs./Miss/Ms. 〜

Example: t a n a k a s e n s e e たなかせんせい — Professor Tanaka; y a m a d a s a n やまださん — Mr./Mrs./Miss/Ms. Yamada

NOTES

- The せい in せんせい (sensee) is pronounced by stretching the [e]. You will learn more about long vowels in a later section.
- It is customary to address an instructor simply as せんせい .

- The literal meaning of せんせい is "born ahead," which by extension means "honorable master." For this reason, it is used to refer to other people but never to oneself. Further, it can be used to address people in professions other than teaching, especially when the person in question has recognized expertise or performs a mentoring function. Patients refer to their medical doctors as せんせい. But even for this function, せんせい should never be used in reference to oneself.
- Japanese people usually address each other using last names and titles, even when they have known each other for a long time. First names are used primarily among family members and close friends.
- ～さん is a generic term, but you should not use it when referring to yourself or to someone who should be addressed with a title such as せんせい.

2. Introducing yourself

ha ji me ma shi te　　de su　do o zo　yo ro shi ku

はじめまして。　～ です。どうぞ よろしく。

How do you do? I am ～ . Pleased to meet you.

(The English translation here is not a literal equivalent of the Japanese.)

Example: A: はじめまして。(hajimemashite) やまだ (yamada) です。(desu) どうぞ (doozo) よろしく。(yoroshiku)

B: はじめまして。(hajimemashite) すみす (sumisu) です。(desu) どうぞ (doozo) よろしく。(yoroshiku)

Mr. Smith　　Mr. Yamada

Notes

- The little circle at the end of each sentence is the equivalent of a period in written Japanese.
- You cannot use a title or さん when speaking of yourself.

はなして みましょう Conversation Practice

1. Today is the first day of Japanese class. Introduce yourself to your classmates. Listen to your classmates as they introduce themselves, and try to remember their names.
2. Did you greet your classmates with a bow? If you didn't, greet them again, and bow. If you don't know how to bow properly, ask your instructor to show you.

III. Hiragana た〜ほ

In this section, you will learn fifteen more **hiragana** and their pronunciations. Note that the right side of な [na] and the horizontal line in ふ [fu] consist of a single connected line in the printed style, but become two strokes in the handwritten style.

Printed style

h	n	t	
は	な	た	a
ひ	に	ち	i
ふ	ぬ	つ	u
へ	ね	て	e
ほ	の	と	o

Handwritten style

h	n	t	
は	な	た	a
ひ	に	ち	i
ふ	ぬ	つ	u
へ	ね	て	e
ほ	の	と	o

Learning hiragana

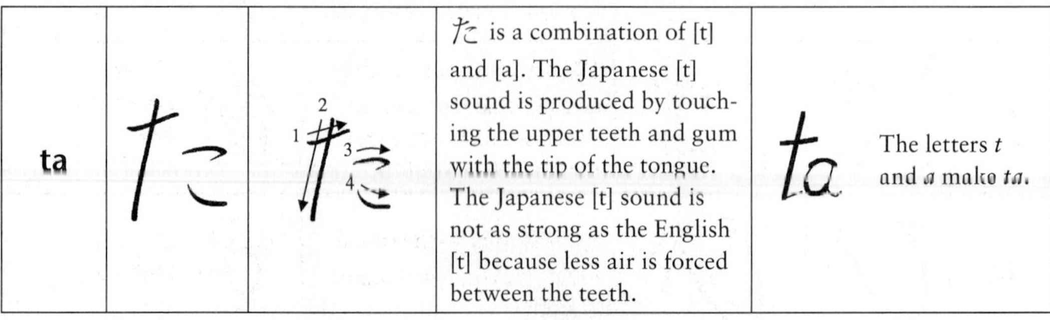

ta	た	た	た is a combination of [t] and [a]. The Japanese [t] sound is produced by touching the upper teeth and gum with the tip of the tongue. The Japanese [t] sound is not as strong as the English [t] because less air is forced between the teeth.	ta The letters *t* and *a* make *ta*.

chi	ち	 ち	ち The sound is [chi] as in *cheer*. Japanese does not have the sound [ti] as in *tea*.	 Being a *cheerleader* isn't easy.
tsu	つ	 つ	つ is similar to the sound [t's] in *cat's*.	 A *cat's* tail.
te	て	 て	て is similar to the first syllable of *table*, but without the [y] sound.	 Fruit on a *table*.
to	と	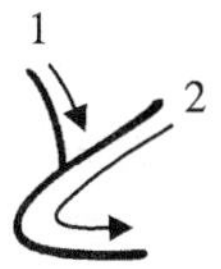 と	と is similar to the sound of *toe* but the [t] is softer.	 I've got a thorn in my *toe*.
na	な	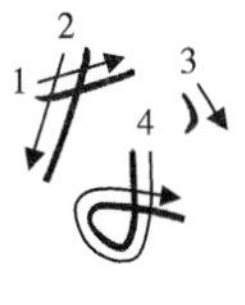 な	な is similar to the sound of [na] in *nod*, but the vowel sound is more like [a] as in *ah*.	 This person is *nodding* off to sleep.
ni	に	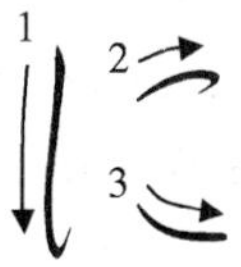 に	に is similar to the sound of *knee*, but the vowel sound is shorter.	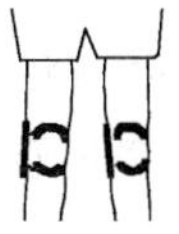 Look at my *knees*.
nu	ぬ	 ぬ	ぬ is similar to the first syllable of *noodle*, but the vowel sound is shorter.	 *Noodles* and chopsticks.
ne	ね	 ね	ね is similar to the sound of [*ne*] in *net*.	 I caught a fish in my *net*.
no	の	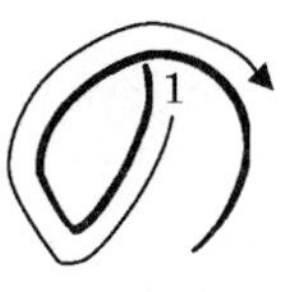 の	の is similar to the sound of the English *no*, but the vowel sound is shorter and the lips are not as rounded.	 See the *no* smoking sign.
ha	は	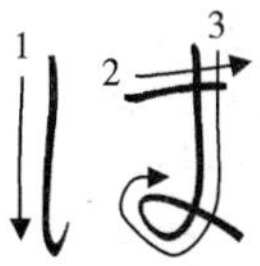 は	は is a combination of [h] and [a]. The Japanese [h] sound is much softer than the English equivalent.	 I bought a *house*.
hi	ひ	 ひ	ひ is similar to the sound of *he*, but the vowel sound is shorter.	 This is Mr. Hill. *He* is strong.

fu	ふ	ふ (stroke order 1–4)	ふ is a combination of [f] and [u]. The initial consonant [f] is produced by bringing the lips together as if blowing out a candle.	Mt. *Fuji* is beautiful.
he	へ	へ (stroke order 1)	へ is similar to the sound of *head*, without the final [d] sound.	I have a *headache.*
ho	ほ	ほ (stroke order 1–4)	ほ is similar to the initial part of *home*, without the [u] sound.	A house isn't a *home* without TV.

Reading hiragana

Read the following words, paying attention to intonation and devoiced sounds.

て	hand	にく	meat
つき	moon	ひと	person
おなか	stomach	ねこ	cat
はな	nose	いぬ	dog
くち	mouth	ふえ	flute
たき	waterfall	ほし	star
たな	shelf	うち	house
たかい	high, expensive	たかい にく	expensive meat
ひくい	low, flat	ひくい こえ	low voice

Useful Expressions

Daily greetings

Greeting people properly is important in all cultures. In Japanese, the phrases used when greeting people vary according to the time of day.

In the morning:

o ha yo o go za i ma su
おはよう ございます。

Good morning. / Hello. (formal speech)

o ha yo o
おはよう。

Good morning. / Hello. (casual speech)

o h a y o o
Examples: Student A: おはよう。

o h a y o o
Student B: おはよう。

o h a y o o g o z a i m a s u
Student: おはよう ございます。

o h a y o o
Teacher: おはよう。

o h a y o o g o z a i m a s u
Acquaintance A: おはよう ございます。

o h a y o o g o z a i m a s u
Acquaintance B: おはよう ございます。

In the afternoon:

ko n ni chi wa
こんにちは。

Good afternoon./ Hello.

k o n ni chi wa
Example: A: こんにちは。

k o n ni chi wa
B: こんにちは。

In the evening:

ko n ba n wa
こんばんは。

Good evening./Hello.

k o n ba n wa
Example: A: こんばんは。

k o n ba n wa
B: こんばんは。

Notes

- The よう in おはよう ございます [**ohayoo gozaimasu**] is pronounced by stretching the [o]. You will learn more about long vowels in a later section.
- In general, these phrases are used in both casual and formal situations. The expression おはよう ございます [**ohayoo gozaimasu**], however, has a less formal version, おはよう [**ohayoo**], which may be used with friends or family members. It is considered rude if used with superiors or in formal situations.
- If you see the same person more than once on the same day, using these phrases each time you meet would sound rather silly. In such cases, you should just bow slightly or talk about something else.
- The は in こんにちは [**konnichi wa**] and こんばんは [**konban wa**]

is pronounced [wa] rather than [ha].

- こんにちは [**konnichi wa**] and こんばんは [**konban wa**] are not used among family members.

はなして みましょう Conversation Practice

1. It is morning. You meet an elderly neighbor on the street. Greet him/her.
2. Imagine that class is about to begin in the morning. Greet your instructor and classmates, nodding slightly rather than bowing.
3. Greet a friend in the morning. Greet your instructor in the afternoon. Greet a friend in the evening.
4. Walk around the classroom. Greet five classmates, taking care to use the appropriate prhases as your instructor announces that it is morning, afternoon, or evening. Don't forget to bow slightly.

IV. Hiragana ま〜ん

In this section, you will learn the remaining **hiragana**. Notice that the right side of む [mu] consists of a single connected line in the printed style but has two strokes in the handwritten style む [mu]. Similarly, while ら [ra] and り [ri] are written in the printed style in a single stroke with all lines connected, in the handwritten style they are written in two strokes.

Printed style

n	w	r	y	m	
ん	わ	ら	や	ま	a
		り		み	i
		る	ゆ	む	u
		れ		め	e
	を	ろ	よ	も	o

Handwritten style

n	w	r	y	m	
ん	わ	ら	や	ま	a
		り		み	i
		る	ゆ	む	u
		れ		め	e
	を	ろ	よ	も	o

Learning hiragana

ma	ま	ま	ま is a combination of [m] and [a]. The Japanese [m] sound is like the [m] in *mom*, but is less forceful.	ま	*Mom*! I can't sit any longer.
mi	み	み	み is similar to the sound of *me*, but the vowel sound is shorter.	み	Who is twenty-one? *Me!*
mu	む	む	む is similar to the sound of *moo*, but the vowel sound is shorter.		Cows *moo*.
me	め	め	め is similar to the first syllable of *medal*.		An Olympic gold *medal*.
mo	も	も	も is similar to the sound of [mo] in *more*.	も	Catch *more* fish with a hook.
ya	や	や	や is a combination of the [y] and [a] sounds. The sounds [yi] and [ye] do not exist in Japanese.	や	A *yacht*.

yu	ゆ	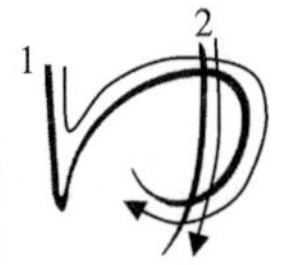	ゆ is similar to the first syllable of *ukulele*.		Can you play the *ukulele*?
yo	よ		よ is similar to the first syllable of *yo-yo*, but the vowel sound is shorter.		*Yo-yos* were once very popular.
ra	ら		ら The [r] sound in Japanese differs slightly from both the English [l] and [r]. To an English speaker's ears, its pronunciation lies somewhere between [r], [l], and [d]. It is produced by flicking the tip of the tongue against the gum behind the upper set of teeth. It is much lighter than the English [l].		A *rabbit*.
ri	り	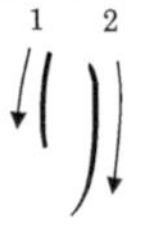	り is similar to the first syllable of *ribbon*. The position of the tongue is the same as in ら.		A *ribbon*.
ru	る		る is similar to the sound of *loop* without the [p] sound, but the vowel sound is shorter. The position of the tongue is the same as in ら.		A *loop* at the end.
re	れ		れ is similar to the sound of *let's* without the [t's]. The position of the tongue is the same as in ら.		*Let's* dance.
ro	ろ		ろ is similar to the sound *rope* without the [p] sound, but the vowel sound is shorter. The position of the tongue is the same as in ら.		A cowboy with his *rope*.
wa	わ	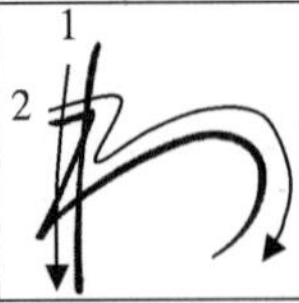	わ is similar to the English *wah*, but the lips are not as rounded or pointed.		*Wah!*
wo	を	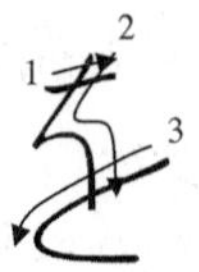	を is pronounced like お.		*Oh!* I can ride a unicycle.
n	ん		ん The pronunciation of ん changes according to the sound it precedes. It is [n] before [t], [s], [d], [z], [dz], [n], and [r], and [m] before [m], [n], [b]. It is a somewhat more nasal sound [ng], when it comes before [k] or [g], or at the end of a word.		The *end*.

Reading hiragana

Read the following words, paying attention to intonation and devoiced sounds.

あたま	head	はれ	clear (weather)
みみ	ear	とり	bird
め	eye	むすめ	daughter
ひる	afternoon	かわ	river
よる	night	やま	mountain
あめ	rain	からし	mustard
ゆき	snow	くすり	medicine
くも	cloud	うま	horse
しろい	white	しろい　とり	white bird
くろい	black	くろい　め	black eyes

Useful Expressions

Taking leave of friends and instructors

The phrase for good-bye differs according to the person you are addressing.

To instructors or social superiors:

shi tsu ree　shi ma su

しつれい　します。

Good-bye.

Example: Student: (se n se e　shi tsu r e e　shimasu) せんせい、しつれい　します。

Instructor: (j a　s a yo na ra) じゃ、さよなら。

Notes

- The literal translation of しつれい　します is *I am about to commit a rudeness* or *I am about to disturb you.*
- You should bow or nod slightly when you say good-bye.
- しつれい　します can also be used as a polite greeting (similar to "excuse me") when you enter the office of a professor or social superior.

To friends:

j a a ma ta
じゃあ、また。

See you later. (literally, *well then, again*)

Example: Student A: じゃあ、また。 (j a a m a ta)
Student B: じゃあ、また。 (j a a m a ta)

NOTE

- The 、mark represents a comma in Japanese. Unlike English commas, Japanese commas always slant to the lower right.

To someone you do not expect to see for an extended period of time:

sa yo o na ra / sa yo na ra
さようなら。/ さよなら。

Good-bye.

Example: Friend A: さよなら。 (s a yo na ra)
Friend B: さようなら。 (s a yo o na ra)

NOTE

- さようなら **[sayoonara]** or さよなら **[sayonara]** is usually used when you do not expect to see the person for an extended period of time, although these phrases, especially the more colloquial さよなら **[sayonara]** can be used more generally as well.

はなして みましょう Conversation Practice

1. Imagine that class is over. Say good-bye to your instructor and five classmates.
2. You are leaving your professor's office. Say good-bye to him/her.
3. Your friend is moving to a different city. Say good-bye to him/her.

V. Hiragana が〜ぽ: Voiced consonants

The consonants [k], [s], [t], [h] are voiceless, and they have voiced counterparts. The difference between voiceless and voiced consonants is the presence or absence of vibration. For instance, pronounce [k] and [g] one after another. The position of the tongue and the shape of the lips are identical for both sounds. In both cases you touch the back of your mouth with your tongue, then you quickly release the tongue to let the air flow. The only difference between the two is that your vocal chords vibrate when you pronounce [g], but not when you pronounce [k]. Feel the difference by putting your hand on your throat when you pronounce [k] and [g]. A voiced consonant is indicated by two dots (゛) and an unvoiced consonant by a small circle (゜) to the upper right corner of the character. For example, the voiced consonant [b] in ば has its voiceless counterpart [p] in ぱ.

					h		t	s	k	
ん	わ	ら	や	ま	は	な	た	さ	か	あ
		り		み	ひ	に	ち	し	き	い
		る	ゆ	む	ふ	ぬ	つ	す	く	う
		れ		め	へ	ね	て	せ	け	え
	を	ろ	よ	も	ほ	の	と	そ	こ	お

New hiragana

Printed style

p	b	d	z	g (ng)	
ぱ	ば	だ	ざ	が	a
ぴ	び	ぢ	じ	ぎ	i
ぷ	ぶ	づ	ず	ぐ	u
ぺ	べ	で	ぜ	げ	e
ぽ	ぼ	ど	ぞ	ご	o

Handwritten style

p	b	d	z	g (ng)	
ぱ	ば	だ	ざ	が	a
ぴ	び	ぢ	じ	ぎ	i
ぷ	ぶ	づ	ず	ぐ	u
ぺ	べ	で	ぜ	げ	e
ぽ	ぼ	ど	ぞ	ご	o

Note that [g] is sometimes represented as [ng] to reflect the softness of the sound.

Reading hiragana

Read the following words, paying attention to the voiced and voiceless consonants.

ひげ	beard	にほんご	Japanese language
ゆび	finger	かばん	bag
うで	arm	ちず	map
のど	throat	かぎ	key
ひざ	knee	かぜ	wind
からだ	body	えんぴつ	pencil
でんわ	telephone	てんぷら	tempura
ながい	long	ながい　うで	long arm
みじかい	short	みじかい　ゆび	short finger

Useful Expressions

Thanking, apologizing, and getting attention

Expressions of courtesy are important in every culture. Here are some of the basic ones in Japanese.

a ri ga to o go za i ma su
ありがとう　ございます。
Thank you.

do o i ta shi ma shi te
どういたしまして。
You are welcome.

su mi ma se n
すみません。
I am sorry, excuse me.

a no o su mi ma se n
（あのう、）すみません。
(Um,) Excuse me.

NOTE

- ございます, as in おはよう　ございます **[ohayoo gozaimasu]** and ありがとう　ございます **[arigatoo gozaimasu]** is a polite expression. The more informal おはよう **[ohayoo]** and ありがとう **[arigatoo]** are used in casual speech, among peers, but not with older people or with those of a higher social status.

はなして みましょう Conversation Practice

1. What would you say to your instructor if you forgot your homework?
2. Your instructor is talking to someone. You need to speak to him/her. How would you interrupt the conversation?
3. Your classmates are standing in front of the door. You want to leave the room. What would you say to them?
4. The student sitting next to you picks up the pencil you just dropped. What would you say to him/her?

VI. Hiragana ああ〜わあ : Long vowels

When the same vowel appears twice consecutively in a word, the two are pronounced as a continuous sound rather than as two separate vowels. This is called a long vowel.

In general, long vowels are written by adding あ to **hiragana** containing the vowel [a], い to **hiragana** containing the vowel [i] or [e], and う to **hiragana** containing the vowel [u] or [o]. Note that when い is added after the vowel [e] it is pronounced as [e]. (See the following chart.) Similarly, when う is added after the [o] sound, it is pronounced as [o]. There are some exceptions in which え and お are added instead of い and う, respectively, but you don't need to worry about them for now. You can learn them as they come up in new vocabulary.

	w	r	y	m	h	n	t	s	k		
ん	わあ	らあ	やあ	まあ	はあ	なあ	たあ	さあ	かあ	ああ	aa
		りい		みい	ひい	にい	ちい	しい	きい	いい	ii
		るう	ゆう	むう	ふう	ぬう	つう	すう	くう	うう	uu
		れい		めい	へい	ねえ ねい	てい	せい	けい	ええ えい	ee
	を	ろう	よう	もう	ほう	のう	とお とう	そう	こお こう	おお おう	oo

Reading hiragana

Read the following words, paying attention to long vowels.

せんせい	teacher	がくせい	student
ふうせん	balloon	さとう	sugar
おうさま	king	こうこう	high school
ていねい	polite	とけい	clock, watch
おにいさん	elder brother	いもうと	younger sister
おとうと	younger brother	おとうさん	father
おかあさん	mother	おばあさん	grandmother
おじいさん	grandfather		
ちいさい	small	ちいさい　とけい	small clock, watch

Here are some common exceptions that use え or お for long vowels.

ええ	yes	おねえさん	elder sister
とおり	street	こおり	ice
おおきい	big, large	おおきい　とおり	big street

Useful Expressions

Understanding your instructor's requests

Here are a few common expressions your instructor will use in class. When you hear words you don't understand, try to guess what the teacher is saying from the context or situation or by observing gestures.

きいて　ください。	Please listen.
みて　ください。	Please look.
かいて　ください。	Please write.
よんで　ください。	Please read.
いって　ください。	Please say it/repeat after me.
もう　いちど　いって　ください。	Please say it again.
おおきい　こえで　いって　ください。	Please speak loudly.

はなして　みましょう　Conversation Practice

1. Listen to your instructor's requests and try to determine what he/she wants you to do.
2. Working in pairs, take turns asking each other to perform various actions, using phrases you know.

VII. Hiragana Small っ: Double consonants

A small **tsu** っ indicates that the consonant that immediately follows it is preceded by a glottal stop and held for an additional syllable. This is called a double consonant. Double consonants often involve the glottis in speech, but may not necessarily require a full glottal stop. When written in a romanized form, they are indicated by a doubled consonant.

Horizontal writing

Printed	Handwritten
っか	っか
っき	っき
っく	っく
っけ	っけ
っこ	っこ

Vertical writing

Printed	Handwritten
っか	っか
っき	っき
っく	っく
っけ	っけ
っこ	っこ

Reading hiragana

Read the following words, paying attention to double consonants.

にっき	diary	ざっし	magazine
がっき	musical instrument	せっけん	soap
がっこう	school	はっぱ	leaf
きっぷ	ticket	こっき	national flag
きって	stamp	さっか	writer
ねっとう	boiling water	しっぽ	tail
りっぱな	fine, magnificent	りっぱな がっこう	fine school

Useful Expressions

Confirming information and making requests

わかりましたか。 *Do you understand (it)?*

はい、わかりました。 *Yes, I understand (it).*

いいえ、わかりません。 *No, I don't understand (it).*

If you have trouble understanding your teacher because he/she speaks too softly or too fast for you, you can make requests using the following phrases.

To hear something repeated:

もう いちど おねがいします。

Please say it again. (literally, *Once more, please.*)

Example: Student : せんせい、すみません。もう いちど おねがいします。

Excuse me, Professor, could you say that again?

Teacher: あ、すみません。じゃ、もう いちど いいます。

Oh, sorry. Okay, I'll say it again.

To hear something spoken more loudly:

おおきい こえで おねがいします。

Please speak loudly. (literally, *Loud voice, please.*)

Example: Student: あのう、すみません。おおきい こえで おねがいします。

Excuse me, Professor, could you say that again a bit louder?

Teacher: はい、わかりました。

Okay.

To hear something spoken more slowly:

もう すこし ゆっくり おねがいします。

Please say it slowly. (literally, *A bit more slowly, please.*)

Example: Student: すみません、もう すこし ゆっくり おねがいします。

Excuse me, could you say that once more, a bit more slowly?

Teacher: はい、わかりました。

Okay.

Notes

- These phrases can be used with (あのう、) すみません, which makes your request sound more polite.
- おねがいします is more polite than ～てください (as in いってください), because the latter is a command form. It is more appropriate to use おねがいします with a social superior such as your instructor.

はなして みましょう Conversation Practice

1. Your instructor says something and checks your comprehension. Respond to him/her.
2. Your instructor says something you don't understand completely because it was spoken too fast, too softly, etc. Make the appropriate request so that you can understand what was said.

VIII. Hiragana きゃ〜ぴょ： Glides

Sounds containing a consonant and [y], such as [kya], [kyu], or [kyo], are called glides (semi-vowels). Glides are written with a **hiragana** containing the sound [i] followed by a small や, ゆ, or よ.

ぱ	ば	だ	ざ	が	ん	わ	ら	や	ま	は	な	た	さ	か	
ぴ	び	ぢ	じ	ぎ			り		み	ひ	に	ち	し	き	[i]
ぷ	ぶ	づ	ず	ぐ			る	ゆ	む	ふ	ぬ	つ	す	く	
ぺ	べ	で	ぜ	げ			れ		め	へ	ね	て	せ	け	
ぽ	ぼ	ど	ぞ	ご		を	ろ	よ	も	ほ	の	と	そ	こ	

pya	bya	dya (ja)	ja (zya)	gya			rya		mya	hya	nya	cha (tya)	sha (sya)	kya
ぴゃ	びゃ	ぢゃ	じゃ	ぎゃ			りゃ		みゃ	ひゃ	にゃ	ちゃ	しゃ	きゃ
pyu	byu	dyu (ju)	ju (zyu)	gyu			ryu		myu	hyu	nyu	chu (tyu)	shu (syu)	kyu
ぴゅ	びゅ	ぢゅ	じゅ	ぎゅ			りゅ		みゅ	ひゅ	にゅ	ちゅ	しゅ	きゅ
pyo	byo	dyo (jo)	jo (zyo)	gyo			ryo		myo	hyo	nyo	cho (tyo)	sho (syo)	kyo
ぴょ	びょ	ぢょ	じょ	ぎょ			りょ		みょ	ひょ	にょ	ちょ	しょ	きょ

There are some variations in romanization; be careful because some, for example "dya" or "syo," represent computer inputs rather than pronunciation!

Horizontal writing

Printed style

きゃ
しゅ
ちょ

Handwritten style

きゃ
しゅ
ちょ

Vertical writing

Printed style

きゃ しゅ ちょ

Handwritten style

きゃ しゅ ちょ

Reading hiragana

Read the following words, paying attention to glides.

こうちゃ	black tea	きんじょ	neighborhood
でんしゃ	train	ひゃく	one hundred
いしゃ	doctor	さんびゃく	three hundred
しゃしん	photo	りょこう	trip

A glide can be combined with a double consonant.

しゅっぱつ	departure	ちょっかく	right angle
しゃっくり	hiccup	しょっき	tableware

Add あ or う to form a long vowel within a glide.

きょう	today	びょうき	sickness
きゅうり	cucumber	みょうじ	last name
にんぎょう	doll	しょうがつ	New Year's Day
りょう	dormitory	ぎゅうにゅう	milk

Useful Expressions

Asking for Japanese words and English equivalents

1. Asking for a Japanese word
   Look at the objects in your classroom. Is there anything you do not know the name of in Japanese?

If the object is close to you:

これは にほんごで なんと いいますか。
What do you call this in Japanese?

Example: Smith: これは にほんごで なんと いいますか。

What do you call this in Japanese?

Yamada: 「ほん」と／って いいます。

You call it **hon.**

Smith

Yamada

Notes

- To answer, say ～と／って いいます.
- The marks「」are the Japanese equivalent of quotation marks.

If the object is close to the other person and at a distance from you:

それは にほんごで なんと いいますか。

What do you call that in Japanese?

Example: Smith: それは にほんごで なんと いいますか。

What do you call that in Japanese?

Yamada: 「いす」と／って いいます。

You call it **isu.**

If the object is at a distance from both you and your interlocutor:

あれは にほんごで なんと いいますか。
What do you call that (over there) in Japanese?

Example: Smith: あれは にほんごで なんと いいますか。
What do you call that (over there) in Japanese?

Yamada: 「でんわ」と／って いいます。
You call it **denwa.**

Smith **Yamada**

Note that これ, それ, and あれ refer only to objects, and never to people.

If you want to know the Japanese word for an object that is out of sight, for something intangible, or for any English word:

〜は にほんごで なんと いいますか。
How do you say 〜 *in Japanese?*

Example: Smith: せんせい、「love」は にほんごで なんと いいますか。
Professor, how do you say "love" in Japanese?

Teacher: 「あい」と／って いいます。
You say **ai.**

2. Asking for the meaning of a Japanese word or phrase

   Do you know what がくせい means? How about だいがく and せんこう ? If you don't understand a Japanese word or expression, ask your instructor or a classmate:

   〜って なんですか。

What does 〜 *mean?*

Example: Student: せんせい、「すいか」って なんですか。

Professor, what does **suika** *mean?* (literally, *What is* **suika***?*).

Teacher: 「Watermelon」です。

It means watermelon.

To give the answer, say 〜です。

はなして みましょう Conversation Practice

1. Point at things that you are wearing and ask your instructor how to say them in Japanese.
2. Your instructor is in front of the class and you are sitting at a distance from him/her. What objects are near him/her? Ask your instructor what these objects are called in Japanese.
3. If the classroom has a window, ask your instructor the Japanese word for something you can see outside.
4. Ask your instructor the meanings of the following words: だいがく, せんこう, がくせい, つくえ, こくばん, まど, くるま.

たんご

Vocabulary

Nouns

せんせい　Teacher

Suffixes

～さん　Mr./Mrs./Miss/Ms. ～
～せんせい　Professor ～

Expressions

(あのう、) すみません。 (Um,) Excuse me.
ありがとう　ございます。 Thank you.
あれは　にほんごで　なんと　いいますか。 How do you say that (over there) in Japanese?
いいえ、わかりません。 No, I don't understand (it).
いって　ください。 Please say it. / Repeat after me.
おおきい　こえで　いってください。 Please speak loudly. (instructor request)
おおきい　こえで　おねがいします。 Please speak loudly. (student request)
おはよう。 Good morning. / Hello. (casual)
おはよう　ございます。 Good morning. / Hello. (formal)
かいて　ください。 Please write.
きいて　ください。 Please listen.
これは　にほんごで　なんと　いいますか。 How do you say this in Japanese?
こんにちは。 Good afternoon. / Hello.
こんばんは。 Good evening. / Hello.
さようなら。／さよなら。 Good-bye.
しつれい　します。 Good-bye. / Excuse me.
じゃあ、また。 See you later. (literally, Well then, again.)
すみません。 I am sorry. / Excuse me.
それは　にほんごで　なんと　いいますか。 How do you say that in Japanese?
～って　なんですか。 What does ～ mean?
～と　いいます。／～って　いいます。 You say ～. You call it ～.
どういたしまして。 You are welcome.
はい、わかりました。 Yes, I understand it.

はじめまして。 ～です。 どうぞ よろしく。 How do you do? I am ～.
Pleased to meet you.
～は にほんごで なんと いいますか。 How do you say ～ in Japanese?
みて ください。 Please look at it.
もう いちど いってください。 Please say it again. (instructor request)
もう いちど おねがいします。 Please say it again. (student request)
もう すこし ゆっくり おねがいします。 Please say it slowly.
よんで ください。 Please read.
わかりましたか。 Do you understand (it)?

Chapter 2

だいにか

© Sven Hagolani/Corbis

あいさつと　じこしょうかい

Greetings and Introductions

Objectives	Meeting people for the first time, introducing people, identifying people, telling time
Vocabulary	Countries, nationalities, languages, year in school and academic status, majors, time expressions
Dialogue	はじめまして *How do you do?*
Japanese Culture	First or last name, bowing or shaking hands, business cards
Grammar	I. Identifying someone or something, using ～は　～です II. Asking はい／いいえ questions, using ～は　～ですか III. Indicating relationships between nouns with の IV. Asking for personal information, using question words V. Using も to list and describe similarities
Listening	Listening for key words
Communication	Using あいづち (attentive feedback) 1; classroom manners
Reading	Using format as a clue

Chapter Resources

- www.cengagebrain.com
-  Heinle Learning Center
-  Audio Program
-  Pair work
-  Group work

たんご
Vocabulary

Nouns

アジアけんきゅう (あじあ)	アジア研究	Asian studies
アメリカ (あめりか)		America, the United States
イギリス (いぎりす)		England
いちねんせい	一年生	freshman, first-year student (The suffix せい may be dropped.)
いま	今	now
えいご	英語	English
オーストラリア (お すとらりあ)		Australia
がくせい	学生	student
カナダ (かなだ)		Canada
かんこく	韓国	South Korea
けいえいがく	経営学	management, business administration
こうがく	工学	engineering
こうこう	高校	high school
ごご	午後	p.m., afternoon
ごぜん	午前	a.m., morning
こちら		this person, this way
さんねんせい	三年生	junior, third-year student (The suffix せい may be dropped.)
スペイン (すぺいん)		Spain
せんこう	専攻	major
だいがく	大学	college, university
だいがくいんせい	大学院生	graduate student
だいがくせい	大学生	college student

たいわん	台湾	Taiwan
ちゅうごく	中国	China
なまえ	名前	name
にねんせい	二年生	sophomore, second-year student (The suffix せい may be dropped.)
にほん	日本	Japan
ビジネス びじねす		business
フランス ふらんす		France
ぶんがく	文学	literature
メキシコ めきしこ		Mexico
よねんせい	四年生	senior, fourth-year student (The suffix せい may be dropped.)
らいねん	来年	next year
りゅうがくせい	留学生	international student
れきし	歴史	history

Pronouns

ぼく	僕	I (normally used by males)
わたし	私	I (used by both males and females)

Copula Verb

です		(to) be

Time Expressions

いちじ	一時	one o'clock
にじ	二時	two o'clock
さんじ	三時	three o'clock
よじ	四時	four o'clock
ごじ	五時	five o'clock
ろくじ	六時	six o'clock
しちじ	七時	seven o'clock
はちじ	八時	eight o'clock

くじ	九時	nine o'clock
じゅうじ	十時	ten o'clock
じゅういちじ	十一時	eleven o'clock
じゅうにじ	十二時	twelve o'clock
はん	半	half past いちじはん 1:30

Question words

どこ		where
どちら		where (more polite than どこ), which way
なに／なん	何	what

Particles

か		question marker
の		noun modifier marker (of), ('s)
は		topic marker
も		similarity marker (also, too)

Prefix

お～	御～	polite prefix おなまえ polite form of なまえ (name)

Suffixes

～ご	～語	language
		にほんご Japanese language
～じ	～時	～ o'clock
～じん	～人	-nationality アメリカ(あめりか)じん American
～せい	～生	-student
		だいがくせい college student
		いちねんせい freshman
～ねん	～年	year いちねん first year

Interjections

あのう	uh, well . . .
いいえ	no, don't mention it, you're welcome
はい／ええ	yes

Expressions

いいえ、そうじゃありません／そうじゃないです	No, that's not so
ええ／はい、そうです	Yes, that's so
～から　きました	came from ～ [casual]
こちらこそ	It is I who should be saying that. Thank you. Same here.
そうですか	Is that so? I see.
～って　いいます	colloquial version of ～と　いいます
どうも　ありがとう　ございます	Thank you very much.
どこから　きましたか	Where are you from?
どちらから　いらっしゃいましたか	Where are you from? (A polite version of どこから　きましたか)

たんごの　れんしゅう　Vocabulary Practice

A. くに　Countries

Starting with this chapter, loan words (foreign words used in Japanese) will be written in **katakana**. They will have subscripts in hiragana, except for the symbol ー, which indicates a long vowel. For example: コーヒー (こ ひ) (*coffee*) is pronounced with an elongated [ko] and an elongated [hi].

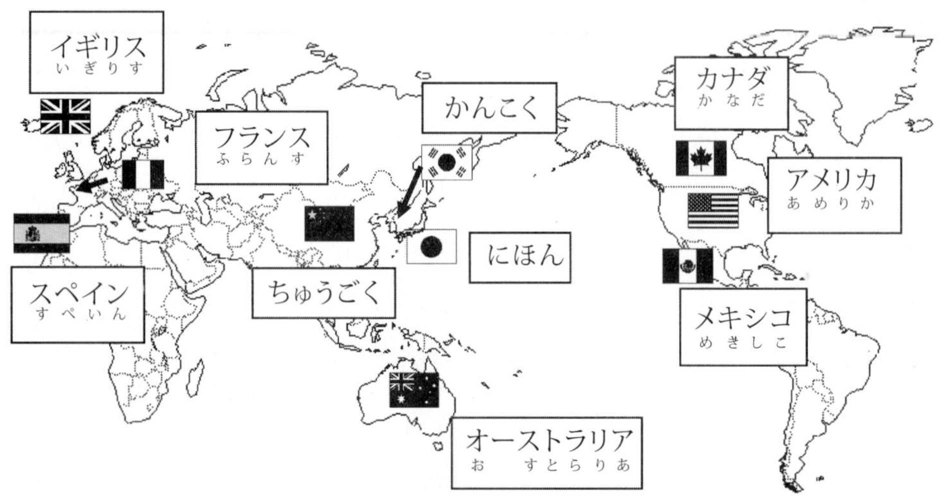

B. こくせきと　こくご　Nationalities and languages

Activity 1

In Japanese, identify the countries indicated on the map below, the nationality of the people from each country, and the principal language(s) spoken there.

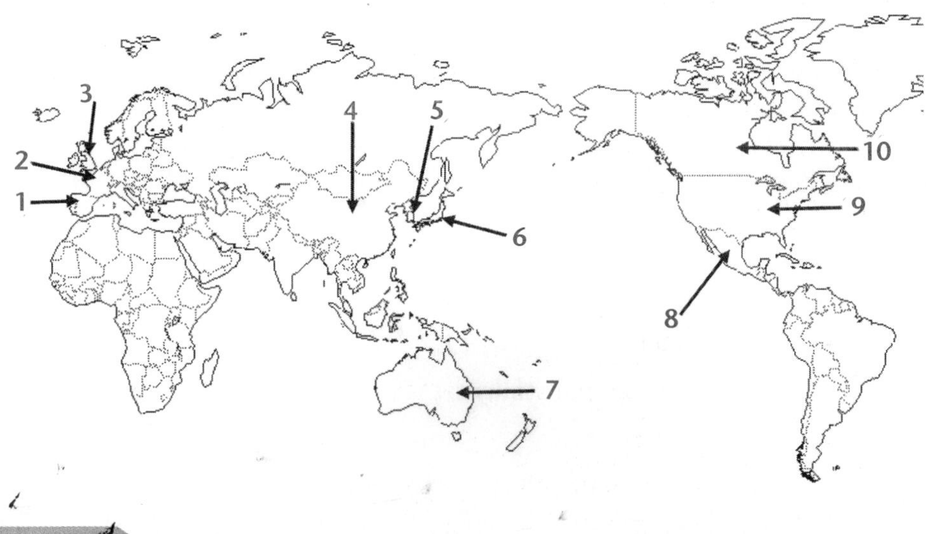

Activity 2

In Japanese, identify the countries represented by the flags below, the nationality of people from each country, and the principal language(s) spoken there.

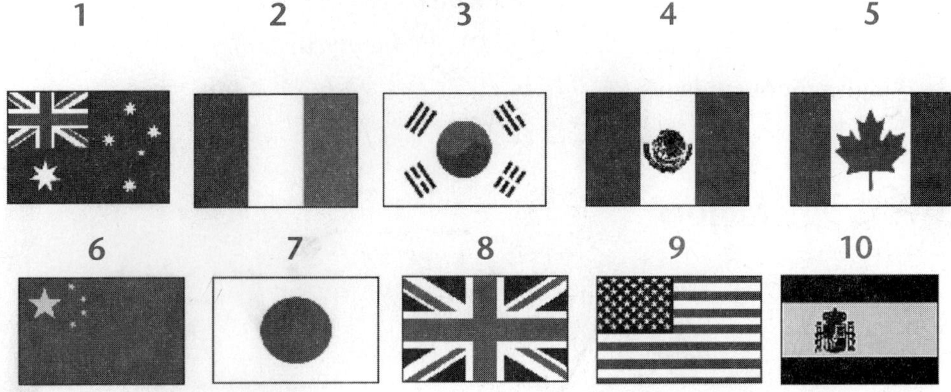

Activity 3

Identify or guess the language of each of the following greeting phrases.

1. Good morning.
2. Bonjour.
3. Buenos días.
4. Ni hao?／Zao chen hao.
5. An nyong haseyo.
6. おはよう(ございます)。

C. ～ねんせい Year in school and academic status

1	2	3	4	G
いちねんせい	にねんせい	さんねんせい	よねんせい	だいがくいんせい
freshman	sophomore	junior	senior	graduate student

がくせい	student
りゅうがくせい	international student
だいがく	college
こうこう	high school

Activity 4

Write your answers to the following questions in **hiragana**.

1. いま、なんねんせいですか。 (*Which year are you in now?*)
2. らいねん　なんねんせいですか。(*Which year will you be in next year?*)
3. "high school student" は　にほんごで　なんと　いいますか。
4. "graduate student" は　にほんごで　なんと　いいますか。

D. せんこう Majors

アジア(あじあ)けんきゅう	Asian studies
けいえいがく	management
こうがく	engineering
ぶんがく	literature
ビジネス(びじねす)	business
れきし	history

Activity 5

Answer the following questions in Japanese.

1. Which of these disciplines are you interested in?
2. Which of these disciplines is the most difficult to learn, in your opinion?
3. Which of these disciplines is the easiest to learn, in your opinion?
4. Do you know how to say your major in Japanese? If not, ask your instructor and write it down.

Supplementary Vocabulary: Academic majors

いがく	医学	medicine (medical science)
おんがく	音楽	music
かがく	化学	chemistry
きょういくがく	教育学	education
けいざいがく	経済学	economics
けんちくがく	建築学	architecture
こくさいかんけい	国際関係	international relations
コンピュータこうがく (こんぴゅ た)	コンピュータ工学	computer engineering
しゃかいがく	社会学	sociology
じょうほうかがく	情報科学	information science
じょうほうこうがく	情報工学	information technology
しんりがく	心理学	psychology
じんるいがく	人類学	anthropology
すうがく	数学	mathematics
せいぶつがく	生物学	biology
せいじがく	政治学	political science
びじゅつ	美術	fine arts
ぶつりがく	物理学	physics

E. じかん Time expressions

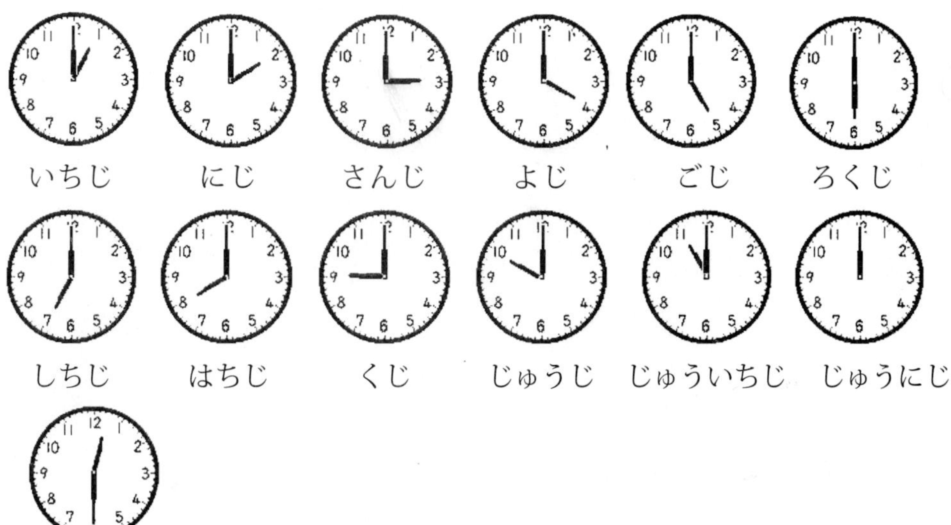

じゅうにじはん

You can probably guess how to say the numbers "1" through "12" from the time expressions and academic years presented above. For a complete explanation of Japanese numbers, see Chapter 3, vocabulary practice D (pp. 91–93).

Activity 6

State the time on the following clocks using time + です (*it's* ～).

Example: Q: いま　なんじですか。

What time is it now?

A: いちじです。

ダイアローグ(だいあろぐ)
Dialogue

はじめに Warm-up

Answer the following questions in English:

1. When you meet a Japanese person for the first time, how do you introduce yourself? Do you shake hands?
2. Suppose you have just been introduced to your host family in Japan. What kinds of things would you talk about?

リー(り)　　アリス(ありす)　うえだ

はじめまして *How do you do?*

Alice Ueda, a Japanese-American student, is attending an orientation session at the International Student Center at Joto University in Tokyo. A student sitting next to Ueda speaks to her.

リー(り)： あのう、すみません。いま　なんじですか。
うえだ： いちじですよ。
リー(り)： いちじですか。どうも　ありがとう　ございます。
うえだ： いいえ。
リー(り)： あのう。
うえだ： はい。
リー(り)： おなまえは　なんですか。ぼく、リー(り)って　いいます。

どうぞ　よろしく。

うえだ：　こちらこそ　どうぞ　よろしく。わたしの　なまえは　アリス（ありす）　うえだです。

リー（り）：　ああ、そうですか。ぼくは　たいわんから　きました。うえださんは？

うえだ：　シカゴ（しかご）です。わたしは　ウエストサイド（うえすとさいど）だいがくの　さんねんせいです。

リー（り）：　そうですか。ぼくも　さんねんせいです。せんこうは　なんですか。

うえだ：　ぶんがくです。リー（り）さんは？

リー（り）：　ぼくは　れきしです。

An International Student Center staff member and a Japanese man approach them.

りゅうがくせいセンター（せんた）の　ひと (*International Student Center staff member*)：　うえださんですか。

うえだ：　ええ、そうです。

りゅうがくせいセンター（せんた）の　ひと：　すずきさん、こちらは　うえださんです。うえださん、こちらは　ホストファミリー（ほすとふぁみり）の　すずきさんです。

うえだ：　はじめまして。アリス（ありす）です。どうぞ　よろしく。

すずき：　すずきです。こちらこそ、よろしく。

Dialogue Phrase Notes

- The particle よ (*I tell you*) in いちじですよ indicates the speaker's assertion and mild emphasis that he/she is providing information known to him/her but not to the listener.
- どうも can have many meanings. In the dialogue どうも means *very much*, so どうも　ありがとう　ございます (*thank you very much*) expresses a deeper appreciation than ありがとう　ございます (*thank you*).
- いいえ means *no*, but in the above dialogue, it means *don't mention it* or *you are welcome*, as in いいえ、どういたしまして. This usage of いいえ is common in Japanese conversation.

- あのう is a hesitation marker. It expresses the speaker's reluctance to bother the person to whom he/she is speaking. This hesitation shows the speaker's respect and consideration for the person he/she is approaching. It can appear by itself as in the dialogue, or with other phrases such as あのう、すみません as in Chapter 1.
- ～と／って　いいます (*[something/someone] is called* ～) was introduced in Chapter 1. This phrase can be used in self-introductions, as in the dialogue.
- ああ、そうですか (*oh, I see*) and そうですか (*I see / is that so?*) are used by the speaker to acknowledge that he/she has understood what has been said. ああ may also be used as a shorter way to convey the same meaning.

ダイアローグ(だいあろぐ)の　あとで　Comprehension

Complete the chart with information about Alice and Li.

	くに／まち Country/city	～ ねんせい Year in school	せんこう Major
うえだ			
リー(り)			

にほんの　ぶんか
Japanese Culture

First name or last name?

When you meet a Japanese adult for the first time, use your last name when introducing yourself. It is not customary to use a Japanese adult's first name, especially when the person is older or higher in social status. However, it is not uncommon to find close friends calling each other by their first names. Since many Japanese are aware that Westerners often use first names, a foreign student may be addressed by his/her first name, followed by さん, as in クリスさん. In family settings, older family members address younger ones by their first names, though younger family members do not use the first names of older members. Instead, they use kinship terms such as mother, father, older brother, and older sister. When a foreign student stays with a Japanese host family, the parents will call the student either by his/her first name only, or will use the first name with さん. The host sisters or brothers will most likely use first name + さん. In general, senior members are referred to by kinship terms and junior members by their first name plus さん (unisex), くん (for a young boy) or ちゃん (for small children). When in doubt, ask the members of the host family how they want to be addressed. Japanese use さん even with neighbors and friends they have known for years. People in certain occupations are adressed by their titles. Common titles include せんせい(teacher, professor), おいしゃさん (doctor), うんてんしゅさん (driver), おまわりさん (policeman). しゃちょう or しゃちょうさん (president of a company).

Bowing? Shaking hands?

The Japanese bow to one another as a greeting or parting gesture, as a way of expressing humility, respect or apology, and as an alternative to waving or saying "Hi." To be on the safe side, always bow when meeting a Japanese adult

for the first time. Bow with your feet together, bending about fifteen degrees from your waist. Drop your eyes as you bow. You may bow more deeply and more than once if you wish to show greater respect. Japanese people often bow every time they meet someone, even if they have already seen that person several times that day. Shaking hands is not customary in Japan, but if someone extends his or her hand, then respond accordingly. Do not squeeze the person's hand too firmly.

名刺 (business cards)
めいし

Who uses めいし? When and how do people exchange めいし?

In Japan, exchanging business cards is an important part of the ritual of meeting people for the first time. Professionals always have business cards, as do many graduate students. Undergraduate students usually do not have them since they are not yet considered to be full-fledged members of adult society. When a person expected to have a card does not have one on hand, he/she usually apologizes for his/her oversight by saying あいにく　めいしをきらせて しまい、　もうしわけ　ありません (*I am sorry for not having any name cards*).

Both parties need to stand up to exchange name cards even when they have been sitting. A person given a name card takes it with both hands. All parties involved give their affiliation and name and say よろしく　おねがい　いたします (*I'm looking forward to continuing our good relationship*). It is important to read the card carefully in order to identify the person's title or position and the name of the organization to which he/she belongs. Such information is considered essential in socializing with the proper degree of formality or politeness.

ぶんぽう
Grammar

I. Identifying someone or something, using ～は　～です

The sentences X は Y です (*X is Y*) and X は Y じゃありません／じゃないです (*X isn't Y*) are used to identify or characterize a person or thing. Japanese uses particles in addition to nouns, verbs, adjectives, etc. Particles most often consist of one character (sometimes two), and they are placed immediately after a noun or at the end of a sentence. Particles that appear after nouns assign a grammatical function to the noun they follow. Those that appear at the end of a sentence indicate the function of the preceding sentence or the speaker's attitudes or emotions. は, which is pronounced *wa*, indicates that the preceding noun X is the topic of the sentence.

Affirmative

Topic		Comment	
Noun	Particle (Topic)	Noun	Copula Verb
たなかさん	は	さんねんせい	です。

Mr./Ms. Tanaka is a junior.

Negative

Topic		Comment	
Noun	Particle (Topic)	Noun	Copula Verb
すずきさん	は	りゅうがくせい	じゃありません。 じゃないです。

Mr./Ms. Suzuki is not an international student.

In the above example sentences, the topic X は represents information already known to both the speaker and the listener. Y です is a comment about the topic. That is, Y represents information concerning the topic X. For example, in the sentence たなかさんは　さんねんせいです。(*Mr./Ms. Tanaka is a junior.*), たなかさん is what the speaker wants to talk about, or the topic, and さんねんせい is what the speaker wants to say about the topic.

わたしは　いちねんせいです。でも、たなかさんは
いちねんせいじゃありません。
I am a freshman, but Ms./Mr. Tanaka is not (a freshman).

ロペス(ろぺす)さんは　メキシコ(めきしこ) じんです。がくせいです。

Mr./Ms. Lopez is Mexican. He/She is a student.

モネ(もね)さんは　だいがくいんせいです。でも、リ(り)ーさんは
だいがくいんせいじゃありません。

Mr./Ms. Monet is a graduate student, but Mr./Ms. Li is not.

Notes

- The topic X は can be omitted if the speaker thinks the listener can identify what it is from the context. For example, わたしは is omitted in greetings such as はじめまして　～です。どうぞよろしく, because it is obvious that the speaker is talking about himself/herself.
- です and じゃありません／じゃないです do not change form according to the number of persons or things being discussed, nor according to the voice (first person, second person, or third person) of the subject. Compare the following Japanese and English sentences.

  わたしは　だいがくせい<u>です</u>。
  I <u>am</u> a college student.

  うえださんは　だいがくせい<u>です</u>。
  Ms. Ueda <u>is</u> a college student.

  わたしたちは　だいがくせい<u>です</u>。
  We <u>are</u> college students.

- じゃないです is more colloquial than じゃありません.
- While the English verb *to be* sometimes indicates location, such as *Tokyo is in Japan*, です and じゃありません／じゃないです do not.

はなして　みましょう Conversation Practice

Activity 1

Imagine that the following people live in your dormitory. Work with a partner and tell him/her about each person.

Example: たなかさんは　<u>にほんじん</u>です。
<u>だいがくいんせい</u>です。
せんこうは　<u>かんこくご</u>です。

Name	Nationality	Year in school	Major
たなか	にほんじん	だいがくいんせい	かんこくご
リー (り)	ちゅうごくじん	だいがくいんせい	アジアけんきゅう (あじあ)
ブラウン (ぶらうん)	オーストラリアじん (おすとらりあ)	よねんせい	ビジネス (びじねす)
スミス (すみす)	アメリカじん (あめりか)	さんねんせい	こうがく
キム (きむ)	かんこくじん	にねんせい	フランスご (ふらんす)
モネ (もね)	カナダじん (かなだ)	いちねんせい	ぶんがく

Activity 2

Complete the following chart by circling the appropriate words and by writing in your major (and nationality, if necessary) in Japanese. If you don't have a major yet, write せんこうは　まだ　わかりません (*I don't know my major yet*).

Your name	
Status	だいがくせい　だいがくいんせい
Major	
Year in school	いちねんせい　にねんせい　さんねんせい よねんせい　だいがくいんせい
Nationality	アメリカじん (あめりか)　ちゅうごくじん　かんこくじん __________________じん

Activity 3

Introduce yourself to your partner and describe yourself using the words in Activity 2, and the X は Y です pattern. If you don't have a major yet, say せんこうは　まだ　わかりません (*I don't know my major yet*).

Example: はじめまして。 (your name) です。どうぞ　よろしく。

(わたしは) (college student/graduate student) です。
(year) せいです。

せんこうは _______ です。わたしは (nationality) じんです。

Now listen to your partner's self-introduction and complete the following chart.

Partner's name	
Status	
Major	
Year in school	
Nationality	

Activity 4

Introduce a partner and yourself to another classmate.

Example: わたしは________です。__________じんです。
__________せいです。

せんこうは____________です。

こちらは__________さんです。

______さんは__________じゃありません／じゃないです。

__________です。

II. Asking はい／いいえ questions, using ～は　～ですか

It is very easy to formulate questions in Japanese. All you have to do is add the particle か to the end of the sentence.

Asking the listener's identity

Question		
	Copula Verb	Particle
すずきさん	です	か。

Are you Mr./Ms. Suzuki?

Answer		
		Copula Verb
はい／ええ、	そう	です。

Yes, I am.

Asking about people and things

Question	
	Particle
キム(きむ)さんは　かんこくじんです	か。

Is Mr./Ms. Kim Korean? /Are you Korean, Mr./Ms. Kim?

Affirmative Answer		
		Copula Verb
はい／ええ、	そう	です。

Yes, he/she is. / Yes, I am.

(literally, *Yes, it is so.*)

Affirmative Answer		
		Copula Verb
はい／ええ、	かんこくじん	です。

Yes, he/she is Korean. / Yes, I am Korean.

Negative Answer		
		Copula Verb
いいえ、	そう	じゃありません。 じゃないです。

No, he/she isn't. (literally, *No, it isn't so.)*

Negative Answer		
		Copula Verb
いいえ、	イギリス(いぎりす)じん	です。

No, he/she is British. / No, I am British.

おおき：うえださんですか。 *Are you Ms. Ueda?*

うえだ：はい、そうです。 *Yes, I am.*

おおき：うえださんは　にほんじんですか。 *Are you Japanese, Ms. Ueda?*

うえだ：いいえ、アメリカ(あめりか)じんです。 *No, I'm American.*

Notes

- The Japanese pronoun あなた, although it is equivalent to *you*, is not used as commonly as its English counterpart. It is more common to use the name of the person being addressed. Thus, アリス(ありす)さんは　がくせいですか can mean either *Are you a student, Alice?* or *Is Alice a student?* depending on whether you are talking to Alice or someone else.
- はい／ええ、そうです is an affirmative answer to questions, and means *Yes, I am / you are / it is / he/she is / they are / we are.* いいえ、そうじゃありません／いいえ、そうじゃないです is a negative answer, and it means *No, I'm not / you aren't / it isn't / he/she isn't / they aren't / we aren't.*

はなして　みましょう　Conversation Practice

Activity 1

Answer the following questions, using ええ、そうです or いいえ、そうじゃありません／いいえ、そうじゃないです.

Example: がくせいですか。　　ええ、そうです。

1. がっこうは　ウエストサイド(うえすとさいど)だいがくですか。
2. いちねんせいですか。
3. せんこうは　にほんごですか。
4. アメリカ(あめりか)じんですか。
5. りゅうがくせいですか。
6. せんせいは　にほんじんですか。

Activity 2

Find out how many of your classmates are in the same year of school as you by asking ～さんは　～ですか . Also, find out how many have the same major as you.

Example: A: たなかさんは　いちねんせいですか。

B: ええ、そうです。／いいえ、そうじゃありません／いいえ、そうじゃないです。

A: そうですか。せんこうは　にほんごですか。

B: ええ、そうです。／いいえ、そうじゃありません／いいえ、そうじゃないです。

Activity 3

Work with a partner. Choose an identity from the chart below, but don't tell your partner. Your partner will try to guess who you are by asking questions using ～は　～ですか. Answer with ええ、そうです or いいえ、そうじゃありません／いいえ、そうじゃないです.

Examples: A: にほんじんですか。
B: いいえ、そうじゃありません。

A: アメリカ(あめりか)じんですか。
B: ええ、そうです。

A: せんこうは　えいごですか。
B: ええ、そうです。

A: スミス(すみす)さんですか。
B: ええ、そうです。

Name	Nationality	Year in school	Major
スミス(すみす)	アメリカ(あめりか) じん	さんねんせい	えいご
ブラウン(ぶらうん)	アメリカ(あめりか)じん	いちねんせい	アジア(あじあ)けんきゅう
ロペス(ろぺす)	アメリカ(あめりか)じん	にねんせい	ぶんがく
ジョンソン(じょんそん)	アメリカ(あめりか)じん	だいがくいんせい	ビジネス(びじねす)
ハート(はと)	アメリカ(あめりか)じん	よねんせい	スペインご(すぺいん)
たなか	にほんじん	いちねんせい	スペインご(すぺいん)
やまだ	にほんじん	だいがくいんせい	けいえいがく
さとう	にほんじん	にねんせい	こうがく
もり	にほんじん	よねんせい	ぶんがく
すずき	にほんじん	さんねんせい	アジア(あじあ)けんきゅう

III. Indicating relationships between nouns with の

The particle の allows the first noun in a phrase to modify the second noun. Because の can convey a variety of relationships between two nouns, such as possession, group membership, or location, the particle's meaning depends on the context.

とうきょうだいがくの	リー(り)さん	Mr./Ms. Li from Tokyo University
とうきょうだいがくの	がくせい	student at Tokyo University
わたしの	せんこう	my major
れきしの	せんこう	history major
わたしの	せんせい	my teacher
せんせいの	ほん	teacher's book; book written by the teacher
メキシコ(めきしこ)の	うち	house in Mexico
にほんの	ほん	book about Japan; book from Japan
にほんごの	ほん	book written in Japanese; book about Japanese
とうきょうの	おかださん	Mr./Ms.Okada who lives in Tokyo; Mr./Ms. Okada who is from Tokyo

すずき：はじめまして。すずきです。
How do you do? I'm Suzuki.

きむら：はじめまして。りゅうがくせいセンター(せんた)の　きむらです。
How do you do? I'm Kimura of the International Student Center.
うえださん、こちらは　うえださんの　ホストファミリー(ほすとふぁみり)の　すずきさんです。
Ms. Ueda, this is Mr. Suzuki from your host family.

うえだ：はじめまして。アリス(ありす)　うえだです。どうぞ　よろしく。
How do you do? I'm Alice Ueda. Pleased to meet you.

すずき：こちらこそ。よろしく。
Same here.

たなか：ロペス(ろぺす)さんの　せんこうは　ビジネス(びじねす)ですか。
Is your major business, Mr./Ms. Lopez?

ロペス(ろぺす)：いいえ。わたしは　こうがくの　せんこうです。
No. I'm an engineering major.

Notes

- Possessive pronouns in English consist of one word, as in *my*, but the equivalent forms of Japanese consist of a pronoun followed by の, as in わたし/ぼく+ の. Also, the semantic relationship between the modifier and the word being modified is not always clear in this structure. The relationship depends on context and the meanings of the two nouns. For example, in the phrase たなかせんせいの ほん, Professor Tanaka may be the author or the owner of the book.
- The appositive relationship can also be expressed with の . The following example is translated into English as *Mr. Suzuki from my host family*. In contrast, すずきさんの ホストファミリー (ほすとふぁみり) is interpreted as *Mr. Suzuki's host family*.

ホストファミリー (ほすとふぁみり) の　すずきさん	*Mr. Suzuki, who is in (my) host family*
すずきさんの　ホストファミリー (ほすとふぁみり)	*Mr. Suzuki's host family*

はなして みましょう　Conversation Practice

Activity 1

Pretend that you are the moderator of a panel discussion on environmental protection. Introduce the following experts using noun の noun.

Example:　（やまだ）

こちらは　シカゴ (しかご) だいがくの　やまだせんせいです。

Activity 2

You meet a student from another school. Introduce yourself in terms of your school by using Noun の Noun.

Example: はじめまして。(わたしは)__________だいがくの
__________です。

Activity 3

Complete the following dialogue, using the information from the chart below.

Example: A: たなかさんの　せんこうは　えいごですか。

B: いいえ、そうじゃありません。かんこくごです。

Name	School	Major
たなか	とうきょうだいがく	かんこくご
リー (り)	にほんだいがく	アジア (あじあ) けんきゅう
ケリー (けり)	UCLA	ビジネス (びじねす)
スミス (すみす)	ハワイ (はわい) だいがく	こうがく
キム (きむ)	ヨンセイ (よんせい) だいがく	ぶんがく

1. A: __________の　せんこうは　アジア (あじあ) けんきゅうですか。

   B: ええ、そうです。

2. A: ケリー (けり) さんは　アジア (あじあ) けんきゅうの__________ですか。

   B: いいえ、ビジネス (びじねす) の　がくせいです。

3. A: スミス (すみす) さんの__________は　ハワイ (はわい) だいがくですか。

   B: ええ、そうです。

4. A: キム (きむ) さんは__________の　せんこうですか。

   B: ええ、そうです。

Activity 4

Use Noun のNoun to tell a classmate your friend's name, school, and major.

Example: __________さんは　わたしの　ともだち (*friend*) です。

__________さんの　だいがくは__________だいがくです。

せんこうは__________です。

IV. Asking for personal information, using question words

In Japanese, you don't have to change the word order of a sentence to form an information question. All you have to do is to use a question word, such as なん (*what*) or どこ (*where*), for things you want to ask about.

Asking about names and things, using なん

Question		
	Question Word	
おなまえは	なん	ですか。

Answer
アリス(ありす)です。

What is your name? *I am Alice.*

Question		
	Question Word + Suffix	
キム(きむ)さんは	なんねんせい	ですか。

Answer
さんねんせいです。

What year are you in, Mr./Ms. Kim? *I am a junior.*

Question		
	Question Word + Suffix	
いま	なんじ	ですか。

Answer
さんじです。

What time is it now? *It's 3 o'clock.*

もり： すみません。いま なんじですか。
Excuse me. What time is it?

すずき： よじはんですよ。
It's 4:30.

もり： そうですか。どうも。
Oh, is it? Thanks.

すずき： いいえ。
You're welcome.

To specify a.m. and p.m., add ごぜん (a.m.) or ごご (p.m.) in front of the time expression.

とうきょうは いま ごぜん じゅうじです。
In Tokyo it is 10 a.m. now.

ニューヨーク(にゅよく)は ごご ろくじはんです。
It is 6:30 p.m. in New York.

Using どこ and どちら to ask about places

Question		
Question word (place)	Particle	
どこ	から	きましたか。

Where are you from?
(literally, *Where did you come from?*)

Answer		
Noun (place)	Particle	
にほん	から	きました。

I'm from Japan.
(literally, *I came from Japan.*)

やまだ：ソフィー（そふぃ）さんは　どこから　きましたか。
Sophie, where are you from?

ソフィー（そふぃ）：カナダ（かなだ）から　きました。
I'm from Canada.

やまだ：そうですか。なんねんせいですか。
I see. What year are you in?

ソフィー（そふぃ）：いちねんせいです。やまださんは？
First year. How about you, Mr./Ms. Yamada?

やまだ：わたしは　にねんせいです。
I am a sophomore.

Notes

- In Japanese, a question word cannot be used as a topic or come before the particle は. It is a part of the です half of the sentence, and replaces the word that is in question. For example:

  やまだ：たなかさんは　なんねんせいですか。
  What year are you in, Mr./Ms. Tanaka?

  たなか：わたしは　いちねんせいです。
  I'm a freshman.

- どこから　きましたか。 is a way of asking about someone's hometown, home state, or native country. から is a particle that means *from*. きました is the past tense form of the verb きます (*come*). In formal situations use the more polite どちらから　いらっしゃいましたか (*where are you from*). When answering this more formal question, however, you should always use きました, and not いらっしゃいました.

- To find out the name of someone's school, use どこ. For example, やまださんの　だいがくは　どこですか。asks for the name of a school, and not the location of the school.

  A: やまださんの　だいがくは　どこですか。
  Where do you go to school, Mr./Ms. Yamada?

  B: とうきょうだいがくです。
  I go to the University of Tokyo.

  Do not use なんですか to ask for the name of a school:

  ~~やまださんの　だいがくは　なんですか。~~

はなして みましょう　Conversation Practice

Activity 1

Begin a dialogue by asking a question that corresponds to each of the following answers.

Example: スミス(すみす)です。
<u>あのう、おなまえは　なんですか。</u>

1. メキシコ(めきしこ)から　きました。
2. アジア(あじあ)けんきゅうです。
3. リー(り)です。
4. さんねんせいです。
5. フランス(ふらんす)ごです。
6. よじです。
7. だいがくいんせいです。
8. じょうとうだいがくです。

Activity 2

Ask your classmates about their majors and hometowns. Is there anyone who is majoring in the same subject as you?

Example:
A: ＿＿＿＿＿さんの　せんこうは　なんですか。
B: ＿＿＿＿＿です。～さんは？
A: わたしの　せんこうは＿＿＿＿＿です。
B: ああ、そうですか。

Activity 3

Ask your classmates and your instructor about their majors and hometowns. Find out who comes from the most distant place.

Example: A: ＿＿＿＿さんは　どこから　きましたか／
＿＿＿＿せんせいは　どちらから　いらっしゃいましたか。

B: ＿＿＿＿ から　きました。～さんは？

A: ＿＿＿＿ から　きました。

B: ああ、そうですか。

Activity 4

Work with a partner. Look at the map of world and ask each other what time it is in various cities.

Example: とうきょう (Tokyo)

A: とうきょうは　いま　なんじですか。

B: ごぜん　じゅういちじですよ。

A: そうですか。

1. ニューヨーク (New York)
   にゅ　よ　く
2. ホノルル (Honolulu)
   ほのるる
3. シドニー (Sydney)
   しどに
4. モスクワ (Moscow)
   もすくわ
5. バンクーバー (Vancouver)
   ばんく　ば
6. ロンドン (London)
   ろんどん
7. バンコク (Bangkok)
   ばんこく
8. デリー (Delhi)
   でり
9. カイロ (Cairo)
   かいろ

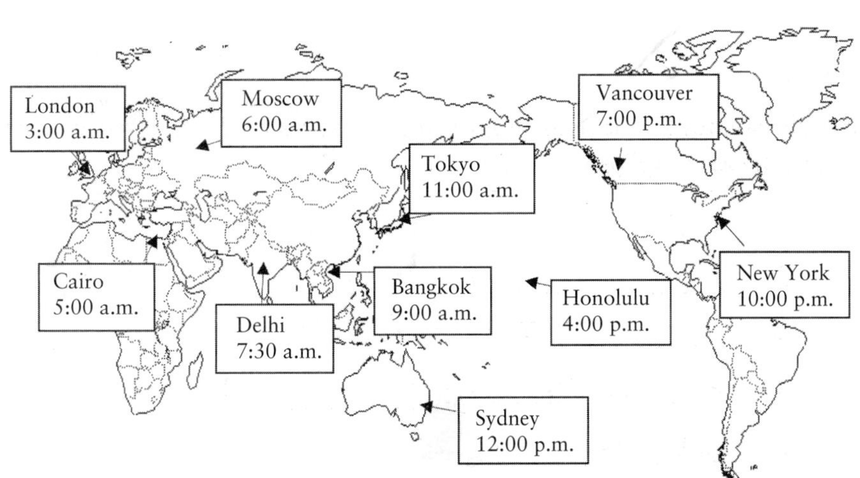

Activity 5

Work with a partner. You are traveling through a number of cities in the United States. Ask your partner what time it is in the city you are in now. The reference time indicates the current time in the last city you visited. Your partner will have to compute the time for the city you are asking about based on the reference time.

Example: Reference time: 7:30 a.m. EST
City you are in now: Chicago

A: あのう、すみません。いま　なんじですか。

B: ろくじはんですよ。

A: ああ、そうですか。どうも　ありがとうございます。

B: いいえ。

1. 7:30 p.m. EST, Denver
2. 9:00 a.m. CST, Seattle
3. 8:30 p.m. CST, New York
4. 2:30 p.m. MST, Anchorage
5. 1:00 p.m. MST, Atlanta
6. 11:30 p.m. PST, Salt Lake City
7. 1:30 a.m. PST, Honolulu
8. 11:00 p.m. PST, Boston

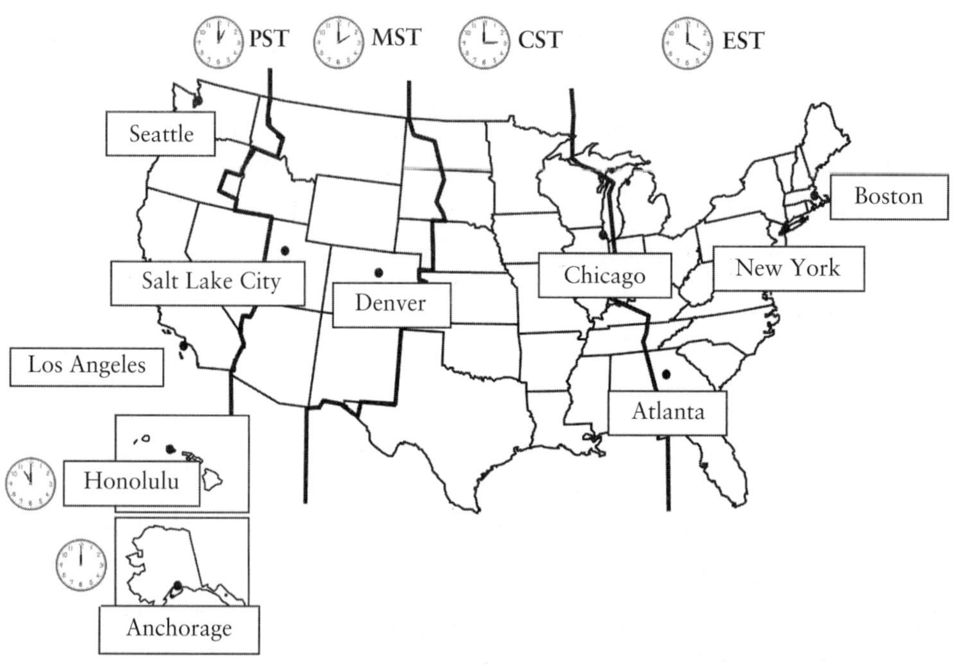

V. Using も to list and describe similarities

The particle も means *also* or *too*, and it is used to show the similarity between what has been just said and what you are saying.

Sentence 1		
	Particle	
わたしの　こうこう	は	ミルズ(みるず)　ハイスクール(はいすくーる)です。

My high school is Mills High School.

Sentence 2		
Noun Phrase	Particle	
トムさん(とむ)の　こうこう	も	ミルズ(みるず)　ハイスクール(はいすくーる)です。

Tom's high school is also Mills High School.

うえだ：キムさん(きむ)は　にほんごの　がくせいですか。
Are you a Japanese major, Mr./Ms. Kim? (literally, *are you a student of Japanese?*)

キム(きむ)：ええ、そうですよ。うえださんは？
Yes, I am. How about you, Ms. Ueda?

うえだ：わたしも　にほんごの　せんこうですよ。
I am a Japanese major, too.

キム(きむ)：ああ、そうですか。
Oh, is that so?

やまだ：すずきさんは　どこから　きましたか。
Ms. Suzuki, where are you from?

すずき：とうきょうから　きました。
I'm from Tokyo.

やまだ：そうですか。ぼくも　とうきょうから　きました。
Is that so? I'm from Tokyo, too.

すずき：ああ、そうですか。とうきょうの　どこですか。
Oh, really. Where in Tokyo?

やまだ：あさくさです。
Asakusa.

はなして みましょう Conversation Practice

Activity 1

Work with a partner. The following is a list of new students at the International Student Center. Introduce one of the students to your partner, and your partner will then introduce you to a student who shares the trait you have just described in the first introduction. Take turns making the introductions.

Example 1: A: こちらは キム(きむ)さんです。キム(きむ)さんは フランス(ふらんす)ごの がくせいです。

B: こちらは ロペス(ろぺす)さんです。ロペス(ろぺす) さんも フランス(ふらんす)ごの せんこうです。

Example 2: A: こちらは ワット(わっと)さんです。ワット(わっと)さんは イギリス(いぎりす)から きました。

B: こちらは モリス(もりす)さんです。モリス(もりす)さんも イギリス(いぎりす)じんですよ。

Name	Country /Nationality	Year in school	Major
キム(きむ)	かんこく	いちねんせい	フランス(ふらんす)ご
イー(い)	かんこく	だいがくいんせい	ぶんがく
リー(り)	ちゅうごく	よねんせい	こうがく
チョー(ちょ)	ちゅうごく	にねんせい	かんこくご
ブラウン(ぶらうん)	オーストラリア(おすとらりあ)	さんねんせい	れきし
スミス(すみす)	オーストラリア(おすとらりあ)	にねんせい	かんこくご
ロペス(ろぺす)	メキシコ(めきしこ)	よねんせい	フランス(ふらんす)ご
ガルシア(がるしあ)	メキシコ(めきしこ)	だいがくいんせい	こうがく
ワット(わっと)	イギリス(いぎりす)	いちねんせい	れきし
モリス(もりす)	イギリス(いぎりす)	さんねんせい	ぶんがく

Activity 2

Work with the class. Find a person who went to the same high school you attended.

Example: A: わたしの　こうこうは　セントラル(せんとらる)　ハイスクール(はいすくーる)です。

～さんの　こうこうは　どこですか。

B: わたしの　こうこうも　セントラル(せんとらる)　ハイスクール(はいすくーる)です。

or わたしの　こうこうは　ミルズ(みるず)　ハイスクール(はいすくーる)です。

Activity 3

Work with a partner. Ask your partner the time in the cities on the list.

Example 1: ペキン(ぺきん) (Beijing)　ホンコン(ほんこん) (Hong Kong)

A: ペキン(ぺきん)は　いま　なんじですか。

B: じゅういちじですよ。

A: そうですか。じゃあ、ホンコン(ほんこん)は　いま
なんじですか。

B: ホンコン(ほんこん)も　じゅういちじですよ。

Example 2: ペキン(ぺきん) (Beijing)　バンコク(ばんこく) (Bangkok)

A: ペキン(ぺきん)は　いま　なんじですか。

B: じゅういちじですよ。

A: そうですか。じゃあ、バンコク(ばんこく)は　いま
なんじですか。

B: バンコク(ばんこく)は　じゅうじですよ。

1.	シドニー (Sydney) しどに	グアム (Guam) ぐあむ
2.	とうきょう	タイペイ (Taipei) たいぺい
3.	ペキン (Beijing) ぺきん	タイペイ たいぺい
4.	タイペイ たいぺい	ホンコン (Hong Kong) ほんこん
5.	ソウル (Seoul) そうる	とうきょう
6.	ホンコン ほんこん	バンコク (Bangkok) ばんこく

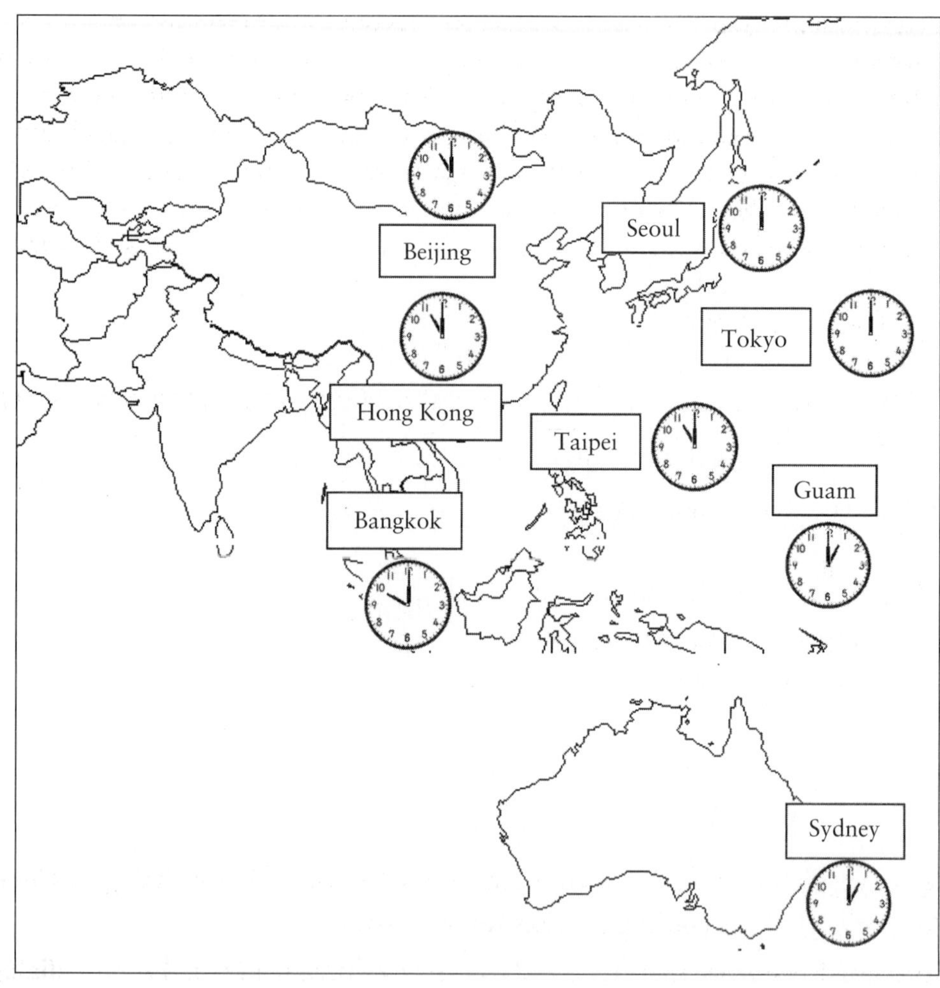

きく　れんしゅう
Listening

じょうずな　ききかた　Listening Strategy

Listening for key words

Listening comprehension passages for this section contain some unknown expressions and words so that you can develop skills to deal with real-life situations in which you may not understand every word. You may be surprised to find that natural speech is very redundant and that it is really not important to understand every single word. Try to focus on key words without worrying too much about the rest. For example, when someone is introduced to you, the most important word to understand is the person's name. Don't worry about the rest; just relax and listen.

きく　まえに　Warm-up

Listen to the dialogue and write the names of the two people who are being introduced.

ことばの　リスト(りすと)　Vocabulary

むすめ　(speaker's) daughter
ちち　(speaker's) father
はは　(speaker's) mother

すずきさんの　むすめさん　Mr. Suzuki's daughter

Read the statements below, then listen for the key words in the dialogue. Circle はい or いいえ, according to what you understood.

Situation: Remember that Alice and Mr. Suzuki already met in the main dialogue on page 42. Mr. Suzuki's daughter is standing next to him. He introduces her to Alice.

1. The name of Mr. Suzuki's daughter is Michiko.　はい　いいえ
2. Mr. Suzuki's daughter is a sophomore at Joto University.　はい　いいえ
3. Mr. Suzuki's daughter is majoring in economics.　はい　いいえ
4. Alice's father is Japanese.　はい　いいえ

ききじょうず　はなしじょうず
Communication

Communication Strategy

Using あいづち　(attentive feedback) 1

Being a good listener is one of the most important factors in communicating effectively in any language, but the strategies for being a good listener differ considerably between languages. For example, the Japanese tend to avoid frequent or prolonged eye contact, because they do not think that making eye contact indicates a person's interest in the conversation. A Japanese person will tend to feel intimidated or uneasy after prolonged eye contact, so it's a good idea to look away from time to time. Instead of eye contact, Japanese speakers use various other forms of feedback when they are listening. For example, they nod occasionally to show attentiveness. For this reason, Japanese students often nod in the classroom. Another common type of feedback is the frequent use of ええ or はい, which both mean *yes*. These expressions do not necessarily indicate agreement. They simply mean that the person is listening to you. If the listener remains silent, even if he/she is looking at the speaker, the speaker may consider the listener to be impolite, cold, or even uninterested. In Japanese, feedback given to confirm attentive listening is called あいづち.

Classroom Manners

It is considered inappropriate to eat or drink in the classroom in Japan. Equally inappropriate is putting one's feet or legs up on a chair or desk. Japanese instructors who are not used to such behavior may think these acts show a lack of seriousness or boredom on the part of the student.

れんしゅう Practice

A. Listen to your instructor talk about himself/herself. Sit up straight and nod occasionally to indicate interest while listening.

B. Work with a partner. Tell him/her about a friend. While listening, your partner should nod or say ええ or はい between sentences. Avoid prolonged eye contact.

よむ　れんしゅう
Reading

じょうずな　よみかた　Reading Strategy

Using format as a clue

めいし are generally written in **kanji** and **katakana**, and for a beginning student of Japanese, it may seem impossible to make any sense of them. Nevertheless, it is possible to identify a few facts if you know what to look for, and this is a very important first step in improving your reading skills.

The information provided on めいし typically includes name, position or title, the relevant employer or organization, address, phone and fax numbers, e-mail address, and web address. The information tends to follow a certain format. For example, the name appears in the center, and the organization and title will be next to or above the name.

よむ まえに　Pre-reading

1. Look at the horizontally formatted card and circle the telephone number and the name of the organization.
2. Look at the other card. Although it is written vertically, the basic format is the same as that of the first card. The second card is read from right to left. Circle the name of the card owner and the address.

インターネット　ジャパン　Inc.

代表取締役
クリシュナ・カーン

1234 Main Street Suite #100, Portland, OR 87654
TEL: (123) 456-7890　FAX: (123)456-7891

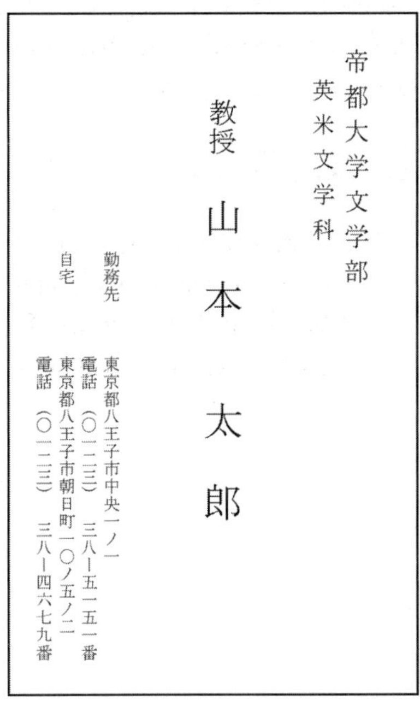

帝都大学文学部
英米文学科
教授
山本太郎
勤務先　東京都八王子市中央一ノ一
電話（〇一二三）三八ー五一五一番
自宅　東京都八王子市朝日町一〇ノ五ノ一
電話（〇一二三）三八ー四六七九番

れんしゅう Practice

ともだち　ぼしゅう　Looking for a friend

Japanese is usually written in **hiragana, katakana,** and **kanji** as appropriate. Printed Japanese is unlike English in that there are usually no spaces between words. The text in the reading sections of this book utilizes all three scripts rather than being limited to **hiragana** and **katakana,** so that you can become familiar with normal written Japanese.

The following are short introductory messages placed on a web page for people who are looking for pen pals. Read the messages and answer the following questions.

ことばの　リスト Vocabulary
りすと

ネイティブ　native (speaker)
ねいてぃぶ
〜を　さがしています　to be looking for 〜

Message 1

はじめまして！ 私は東京大学の学生です。なまえはけいこ
わたし　とうきょうだいがく　がくせい
です。専攻は英語です。今、一年生です。英語のネイティブの友達を
せんこう　えいご　いま　いちねんせい　えいご　ねいてぃぶ　ともだち
さがしています。どうぞよろしく。

Message 2

はじめまして。僕はたかしです。千葉大学の三年生です。専攻は
ぼく　ちばだいがく　さんねんせい　せんこう
アジアとアメリカの歴史です。どうぞよろしく。
あじあ　あめりか　れきし

Message 3

はじめまして。私はヤン・リーと言います。中国から来ました。京都
わたし　やん　り　い　ちゅうごく　き　きょうと
大学のりゅうがくせいです。日本文学の専攻です。二年生です。友達
だいがく　にほんぶんがく　せんこう　にねんせい　ともだち
をさがしています。よろしく。

Message 4

はじめまして。僕はリチャードです。オーストラリアのシドニーから
ぼく　りちゃど　おすとらりあ　しどに
来ました。今、大阪大学の四年生です。ビジネスの専攻です。よろしく。
き　いま　おおさかだいがく　よねんせい　びじねす　せんこう

よんだ　あとで　Comprehension

1. Complete the following with information about the four people who posted the messages above. Don't worry about writing **kanji** or **katakana**.

Message 1

Name ______________________

School ______________________

Year in school ______________________

Major ______________________

Hometown/country
(if mentioned) ______________________

Message 2

Name ______________________

School ______________________

Year in school ______________________

Major ______________________

Hometown/country
(if mentioned) ______________________

Message 3

Name ______________________

School ______________________

Year in school ______________________

Major ______________________

Hometown/country
(if mentioned) ______________________

Message 4

Name ______________________

School ______________________

Year in school ______________________

Major ______________________

Hometown/country
(if mentioned) ______________________

2. Are there any similarities between you and any of the four people? If there are, describe them.

Example:　わたしは　いちねんせいです。　けいこさんも
いちねんせいです。

3. Select one person from the list and write a message to him/her to introduce yourself. If you have yet to decide on a major, write せんこうは　まだ　わかりません, meaning "I don't know my major yet."

そうごう　れんしゅう
Integration

インタビュー Interview
いんたびゅ

1. Ask your classmates about their name, major, year in school, hometown, high school, and country of origin. Write the phrase you will use to greet them, and then make a list of questions to ask. Next, ask the questions, speaking with as many people as you can. Fill in the blanks with the information you gather.

   Greeting phrase: ______________________________

   Questions:

   なまえ (name) ______________________________

   〜ねんせい (year in school) ______________________________

   せんこう (major) ______________________________

   〜から　きました (hometown/country) ______________________________

   こうこう (high school) ______________________________

2. Based on the answers you get, introduce one of your classmates to another classmate. Write down what is said by each person during the conversation.

   __________ : ______________________________

   __________ : ______________________________

   __________ : ______________________________

   __________ : ______________________________

こちらは__________さんです。

__________は　__________から　きました。

__________だいがくの__________ねんせいです。

せんこうは　__________です。　どうぞよろしく。

ロールプレイ Role Play
ろ る ぷ れ い

1. Approach and introduce yourself to the person who is sitting next to you, using the following dialogue as a model.

You： あのう。

Partner：はい。

You： おなまえは　なんですか。　わたし／ぼく、
______________って　いいます。どうぞ　よろしく。

Partner：こちらこそ。どうぞ　よろしく。わたし／ぼくの
なまえは______________です。

You： ああ、そうですか。わたし／ぼくは______________から
きました。
______________さんは？

Partner：______________です。　わたし／ぼくは
______________だいがくの______________せい
です。

You： そうですか。　わたし／ぼくも______________せい
です。せんこうは　なんですか。

Partner：______________です。

You： そうですか。

2. Suppose that you are at an airport to pick up a Japanese person named Yamada whom you have never met. Approach someone and ask if he/she is the person you are looking for using the following dialogue as a starter. Then introduce yourself.

You： あのう、すみませんが。

Partner： はい。

You： やまださんですか。

3. Suppose you have found a Japanese student on campus. Naturally, you want to practice Japanese with him/her. Introduce yourself and strike up a conversation.

II. Katakana ア〜ソ

Study the first fifteen **katakana**. Using the mnemonic devices in the right-hand column, practice reading each character. Then practice writing them in your Student Activities Manual, following the correct stroke order.

a	ア	ア	ア		I'd like an *ice*-cream cone.
i	イ	イ	イ		I need an *easel* to draw.
u	ウ	ウ	ウ		It's a *wick* of a candle.
e	エ	エ	エ		An *egg* is on an egg stand.
o	オ	オ	オ		*Oh*, what an odd way to walk.
ka	カ	カ	カ		*Karate* kick.
ki	キ	キ	キ		This is a *key*.
ku	ク	ク	ク		A baby is sleeping in a *cradle*.
ke	ケ	ケ	ケ		This is a *crooked* K.
ko	コ	コ	コ		This letter has two *corners*.
sa	サ	サ	サ		This is a *saddle* on a horse.

shi	シ	シ	シ		*She* (the cat) is sleeping.
su	ス	ス	ス		Here is a *swing set.*
se	セ	セ	セ		Say, isn't that *Señor* García?
so	ソ	ソ	ソ		I'm *sewing* with a needle.

れんしゅう Practice

Read the following words in katakana and guess what they mean.

1. キス **2.** ケーキ **3.** サーカス **4.** ケース **5.** アイス
6. コース **7.** エース **8.** オアシス **9.** シーソー

III. Katakana タ(た)〜ホ(ほ)

Study the following カタカナ(かたかな). Using the mnemonic devices in the right-hand column, practice reading each character. Then practice writing them in your Student Activities Manual, following the correct stroke order.

ta	タ	タ	タ		A crooked *tie.*
chi	チ	チ	チ		A *chick* is trying to fly.
tsu	ツ	ツ	ツ		A cat *gets* up on her feet.
te	テ	テ	テ		The cat's *tail* is wagging to the left.
to	ト	ト	ト		An Indian *toma-hawk.*

na	ナ	ナ	ナ		A *knife*.
ni	ニ	ニ	ニ		A *neat* tennis court.
nu	ヌ	ヌ	ヌ		*Noodles* are difficult to eat with chopsticks.
ne	ネ	ネ	ネ		A *necker-chief* is around my neck.
no	ノ	ノ	ノ		Someone's *nose*.
ha	ハ	ハ	ハ		A *hat*.
hi	ヒ	ヒ	ヒ		A *heel*.
fu	フ	フ	フ		A child's *hood*.
he	ヘ	ヘ	ヘ		I have a bad *head-ache*.
ho	ホ	ホ	ホ		Two hands *hold* a cross.

れんしゅう Practice

Read the following words in katakana and try to guess what they mean. Remember that the small ッ indicates a double consonant.

1. カタカナ **2.** ネット **3.** セーター **4.** カヌー **5.** ノート

6. エチケット **7.** テキスト **8.** カッター **9.** ホット **10.** ニット **11.** テスト

IV. Katakana マ〜ン (まん)

Study the following カタカナ. Using the mnemonic devices in the right-hand column, practice reading each character. Then practice writing them in your Student Activities Manual, following the correct stroke order.

ma	マ	マ	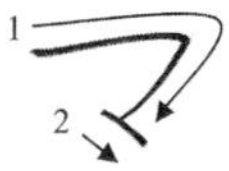 マ		A giant *mush-room.*
mi	ミ	ミ	 ミ		Who's three? *Me!*
mu	ム	ム	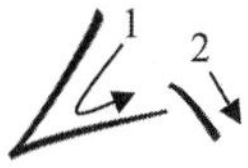 ム		The *moon* is sleep-ing.
me	メ	メ	 メ		The knife is *melting.*
mo	モ	モ	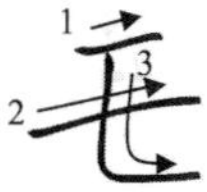 モ		A *monster* appears in Tokyo.
ya	ヤ	ヤ	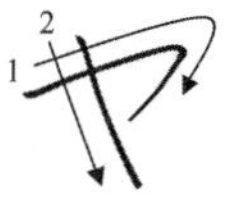 ヤ		A *yacht* in the ocean.
yu	ユ	ユ	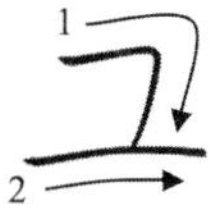 ユ		It's a *U-boat*!
yo	ヨ	ヨ	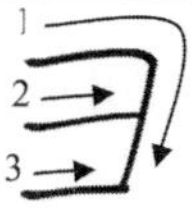 ヨ	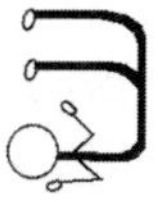	*Yoga* is fun.
ra	ラ	ラ	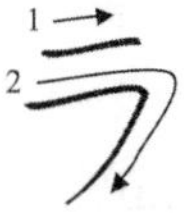 ラ		A *rabbit* with long ears.
ri	リ	リ	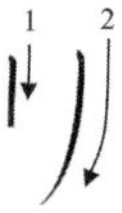 リ		This *rib-bon* has long tails.
ru	ル	ル	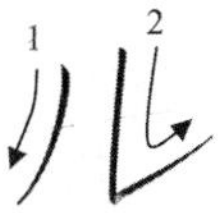 ル		A tree with deep *roots.*

re	レ	レ	レ		*Let's* write a capital L.
ro	ロ	ロ	ロ		A *loaf* of bread.
wa	ワ	ワ	ワ		A *wine* glass.
n	ン	ン	ン		A needle is sharp at the *end*.

れんしゅう Practice

Read the following words in katakana and try to guess what they mean.

1. ワシントン
2. ユタ
3. アイオワ
4. オハイオ
5. ノースカロライナ
6. アメリカ
7. イタリア
8. ロシア
9. テキサス
10. オクラホマ
11. ミネソタ
12. アーカンソー
13. サウスカロライナ
14. メキシコ
15. スイス
16. インドネシア
17. モンタナ
18. ミシシッピー
19. イリノイ
20. テネシー
21. メイン
22. オーストラリア
23. フランス

V. Transcribing katakana

A. Rules that apply to transcribing both hiragana and katakana

1. The diacritic marker [゛] indicates a voiced sound, as in ガ [ga] or ギ [gi]. A small circle [゜] indicates the [p] sound as in パ [pa].
2. Small ャュョ are used to form sounds such as キャ [kya], シュ [shu], and ミョ [myo].
3. A small ッ indicates a double consonant, as in ホットドッグ *hot dog*.

B. Conventions used in transcribing English words into katakana

1. The English sounds -er, -or, and -ar are heard as [aa] in Japanese. A dash represents the long vowels.

   カーター　Carter
   ハート　heart

When **katakana** is written vertically, the long vowel marker (ー) is also written vertically.

ハート
サッカー
リーダー

2. The English [v] is heard in Japanese as [b]. Accordingly, [va], [vi], [vu], [ve] and [vo] become [ba], [bi], [bu], [be] and [bo] in Japanese.

   カバー　cover
   バイオリン　violin

3. The English [l] and [r] are both heard as an [r] in Japanese.

   ライト　right or light
   リーダー　reader or leader
   ロビー　lobby or Robby

4. The English [th] as in *think* and *third* is heard as [s] and the [th] as in *that* or *mother* is heard as [z].

   サンクスギビング　Thanksgiving
   マザーグース　Mother Goose
   サードベース　third base
   バスルーム　bathroom

5. If an English word ends in [k], [g], [m], [f], [v], [l], [s], [z], [th], [p], or [b], the vowel [u] is added in Japanese. The vowel [u] is also added when these sounds are followed immediately by consonants in English.

   ミルク　milk
   リング　ring
   ホテル　hotel
   ミス　Miss
   ジャズ　jazz

6. If an English word contains [t] or [d], the vowel [o] is added in Japanese.

   コスト　cost
   スピード　speed
   ラスト　last
   ベッド　bed

7. The English vowel sounds in *bus* and *cut* or *bath* or *gas* are both heard as [a] in Japanese.

   バス　bus or bath
   カット　cut
   バット　bat
   ガス　gas

8. To approximate as much as possible the pronunciation of people's names and other borrowed sounds, the following combinations are commonly used. Note that these combinations are never used in **hiragana**.

ウィ [wi]	ウィンストン	Winston	ウィスコンシン	Wisconsin
ウェ [we]	ウェイン	Wayne	ハイウェイ	highway
ウォ [wo]	ウォルター	Walter	ウォッカ	vodka
シェ [she]	シェリル	Sheryl	シェーバー	shaver
ジェ [je]	ジェーン	Jane	ジェスチャー	gesture
チェ [che]	チェイス	Chase	チェロ	cello
ティ [ti]	カーティス	Curtis	アイスティー	iced tea
ディ [di]	ディーン	Dean	ディズニーランド	Disneyland
デュ [dju]	デューク	Duke	デュエット	duet
ファ [fa]	ジェニファー	Jennifer	ファッション	fashion
フィ [fi]	マーフィー	Murphy	フィンランド	Finland
フェ [fe]	フェイ	Fay	フェンシング	fencing
フォ [fo]	フォード	Ford	フォーク	fork

Try writing your name in katakana. Use the above conventions if your name contains any of the sounds listed.

れんしゅう Practice

A. The following words appeared in Chapter 1. Read them and write their meanings in English.

1. アジアけんきゅう ______________________
2. アメリカ ______________________
3. イギリス ______________________
4. オーストラリア ______________________
5. カナダ ______________________
6. スペイン ______________________
7. フランス ______________________
8. メキシコ ______________________

B. Guess what the following words are in English.

1. Food and drinks

1. ハンバーガー 2. ステーキ 3. ホットドッグ 4. カレー
5. スパゲティ 6. サンドイッチ 7. サラダ 8. トマト
9. レタス 10. オレンジ 11. レモン 12. フルーツ
13. バター 14. チーズ 15. ケーキ 16. アイスクリーム
17. チョコレート 18. クッキー 19. ジュース 20. ミルク
21. ポテトチップス 22. ビール 23. コーラ 24. ワイン

2. Sports

1. フットボール 2. バスケットボール 3. テニス 4. サッカー
5. ジョギング 6. スキー 7. スケート 8. バレーボール
9. ラケットボール 10. ゴルフ 11. サーフィン

3. Music

1. ピアノ 2. バイオリン 3. ギター 4. オーケストラ
5. トランペット 6. ジャズ 7. ロック 8. クラシック

4. Household items

1. キッチン 2. リビングルーム 3. ランプ 4. オーブン
5. トースター 6. ラジオ 7. レコード 8. ビデオ
9. カメラ 10. カレンダー

5. Countries

1. ブラジル 2. イギリス 3. ドイツ 4. オランダ
5. イタリア 6. スイス 7. イスラエル 8. ロシア
9. オーストラリア 10. インド 11. タイ 12. ベトナム
13. サウジアラビア

6. Cities

1. ニューヨーク 2. ボストン 3. シカゴ 4. ロサンゼルス
5. サンフランシスコ 6. トロント 7. モントリオール 8. ロンドン
9. パリ 10. ベルリン 11. モスクワ 12. カイロ
13. シドニー 14. バンコク 15. ホンコン

Chapter 3

だいさんか

まいにちの　せいかつ

Daily Routines

Objectives Describing daily routines

Vocabulary Daily activities, numbers, minutes, relative time, days of the week

Japanese Culture The academic year in Japan, college classes, college housing, financial aid

Dialogue じゅぎょうが　あります。 *I have a class.*

Grammar

I. Talking about routines, future actions, or events using the polite present form of verbs and the particles に, へ, を, or で

II. Presenting objects or events using ～が ありまず

III. Telling time using the particle に

IV. Using adverbs to express frequency of actions

V. Expressing past actions and events using the polite past form of verbs

Listening Listening for general ideas

Communication Using あいづち (attentive feedback) 2

Reading Scanning

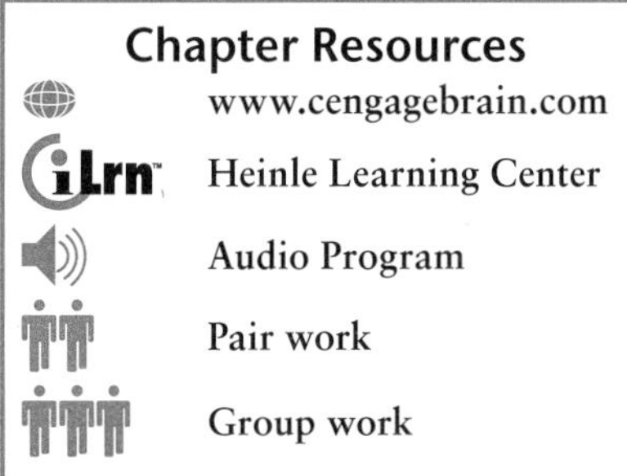

たんご
Vocabulary

Nouns

あさ	朝	morning
あさごはん	朝御飯	breakfast
あさって	明後日	the day after tomorrow
あした	明日	tomorrow
うち	家	home
えいが	映画	movie
おととい	一昨日	the day before yesterday
おふろ	お風呂	bath
がっこう	学校	school
かようび	火曜日	Tuesday
きのう	昨日	yesterday
きょう	今日	today
きんようび	金曜日	Friday
クラス (くらす)		class
げつようび	月曜日	Monday
コーヒー (こ ひ)		coffee
ごはん	御飯	meal, cooked rice
こんしゅう	今週	this week
こんばん	今晩	tonight
シャワー (しゃわ)		shower
しゅうまつ	週末	weekend
じゅぎょう	授業	class, course
しゅくだい	宿題	homework
すいようび	水曜日	Wednesday

せいかつ	生活	life, living
せんしゅう	先週	last week
つぎ	次	next
テレビ (てれび)		television, TV
でんわばんごう	電話番号	telephone number
としょかん	図書館	library
どようび	土曜日	Saturday
にちようび	日曜日	Sunday
ばん	晩	night, evening
ばんごはん	晩御飯	supper, dinner
ひる	昼	afternoon
ひるごはん	昼御飯	lunch
べんきょう	勉強	study
ほん	本	book
まいあさ	毎朝	every morning
まいしゅう	毎週	every week
まいにち	毎日	every day
まいばん	毎晩	every night
もくようび	木曜日	Thursday

う -verbs

あります		(something inanimate) exists; (to) be held, (to) have; the dictionary form is ある .
いきます	行きます	(to) go; the dictionary form is いく .
かえります	帰ります	(to) return, (to) go home; the dictionary form is かえる .
のみます	飲みます	(to) drink; the dictionary form is のむ .
はいります	入ります	(to) take (a bath), (to) enter; the dictionary form is はいる. おふろに　はいります take a bath
よみます	読みます	(to) read; the dictionary form is よむ .

る-verbs

あびます	浴びます	(to) take (a shower); the dictionary form is あびる. シャワーを　あびます take a shower
おきます	起きます	(to) get up, (to) wake up; the dictionary form is おきる.
たべます	食べます	(to) eat; the dictionary form is たべる.
ねます	寝ます	(to) go to bed; the dictionary form is ねる.
みます	見ます	(to) see, (to) watch; the dictionary form is みる.

Irregular verbs

きます	来ます	(to) come; the dictionary form is くる.
します		(to) do; the dictionary form is する.
べんきょうします	勉強します	(to) study; the dictionary form is べんきょうする.

Question word

いつ		when

Numbers

ゼロ		zero
れい	零	zero
いち	一	one
に	二	two
さん	三	three
よん、し	四	four
ご	五	five
ろく	六	six
なな、しち	七	seven
はち	八	eight
きゅう、く	九	nine
じゅう	十	ten

Counter

～ふん	～分	～ minute(s), (for) ～ minute(s)

Adverbs

あまり		not very often (used with negative verb forms)
いつも		always
ぜんぜん	全然	not at all (used with negative verb forms)
たいてい		usually
ときどき	時々	sometimes
よく		often, well

Particles

で		at, in, on, etc. (location of action or event) としょかんで べんきょうします
に		at, on, in (point in time) １０じに ねます
に		to (goal, activity) クラス(くらす)に いきます
へ		to (direction) がっこうへ いきます
を		direct object marker ほんを よみます

Prefixes

こん～	今～	this こんしゅう、こんばん
まい～	毎～	every まいしゅう、まいあさ、まいばん、まいにち

Suffixes

～ごろ	～頃	about ～ (used only with time expressions)
～ようび	～曜日	day (of the week)

たんごの　れんしゅう　Vocabulary Practice

A. まいにちの　せいかつ　Daily activities

おきます

(to) wake up

ねます

(to) go to bed

あさごはんを たべます

(to) eat breakfast

ひるごはんを たべます

(to) eat lunch

うちで ばんごはんを たべます

(to) eat dinner at home

べんきょうします／べんきょうを します

(to) study

としょかんで べんきょうします

(to) study at the library

しゅくだいを します

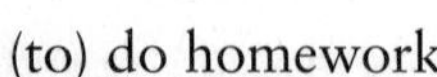

(to) do homework

ほんを よみます

(to) read a book

コーヒーを
こ ひ
のみます

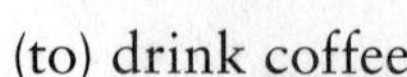

(to) drink coffee

テレビを
てれび
みます

(to) watch TV

えいがを みます

(to) watch a movie

シャワーを　あびます
しゃわ

(to) take a shower

おふろに はいります

(to) take a bath

じゅぎょうが ありますThere is / I have a class.

がっこうに／がっこうへ いきます
(to) go to school

クラス(くらす)に／クラス(くらす)へ きます
(to) come to the classroom

うちに／うちへ かえります
(to) go home

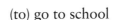

Activity 1

Say what activities you do in the morning, in the afternoon, and at night.

Example: あさ じゅぎょうが あります。 (*I have class in the morning.*)

1. あさ (*morning*)
2. ひる (*afternoon*)
3. ばん (*night*)

Activity 2

Work with a partner. Put the activities you have just described in chronological order and tell your partner what your day is like.

B. Relative time expressions

Japanese has a set of words that indicate points in time with respect to the current time. Their English equivalents are words such as *today*, *tomorrow*, and *yesterday*. These words are categorized as relative time expressions because the day we call "yesterday" today will not be "yesterday" tomorrow. On the other hand, time expressions that are fixed, such as *1977*, *three o'clock*, or *Friday*, are classified as absolute time expressions. Some relative time expressions follow.

いつ	when	きのう	yesterday
あさ	morning	おととい	the day before yesterday
ひる	afternoon	まいにち	every day
ばん	night	まいしゅう	every week
こんばん	tonight	まいあさ	every morning
しゅうまつ	weekend	こんしゅう	this week
きょう	today	まいばん	every night
あした	tomorrow	せんしゅう	last week
あさって	the day after tomorrow		

Activity 3

Answer the following questions.

1. いま、あさですか。ひるですか。ばんですか。
2. 「まいあさ」、「まいにち」、「まいばん」の「まい」って　なんですか。
3. 「まいしゅう」、「こんしゅう」、「せんしゅう」、「しゅうまつ」の「しゅう」って　なんですか。
4. 「こんばん」、「こんしゅう」の「こん」って　なんですか。

Activity 4

For each activity shown on pages 88–89, create a sentence using the time expressions that apply to your own daily routine. If you want to use きのう (*yesterday*) or せんしゅう (*last week*), change the verb form to ～ました instead of ～ます, as in みました (*watched*) instead of みます (*watch*).

Example: コーヒーを　のみます (to) drink coffee

あさ、コーヒーを　のみます。(*I drink coffee in the morning.*)

せんしゅう、えいがを　みました。(*I watched a movie last week.*)

C. ～ようび　Days of the week

Note that each day of the week ends with ようび.

Which day of the week?	なんようび
Sunday	にちようび
Monday	げつようび
Tuesday	かようび
Wednesday	すいようび
Thursday	もくようび
Friday	きんようび
Saturday	どようび

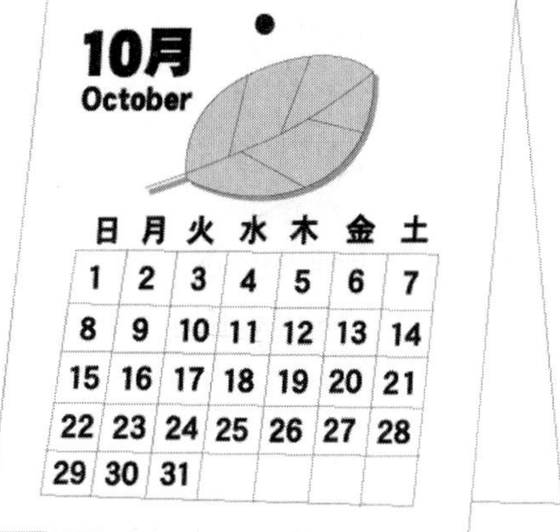

Activity 5

Look at the calendar and give the day of the week for the following dates.

1. 10/16
2. 10/26
3. 10/31
4. 10/1
5. 10/21
6. 10/4
7. 10/27
8. 10/8
9. 10/5
10. 10/7
11. 10/17
12. 10/25

Activity 6

Answer the following questions in Japanese.

1. きょうは　なんようびですか。
2. あしたは　なんようびですか。
3. あさっては　なんようびですか。
4. きのうは　なんようびでしたか。(でした = *was*)
5. おとといは　なんようびでしたか。(でした = *was*)
6. つぎ (*next*) の　にほんごの　クラス(くらす)は　なんようびですか。

D. すうじ　Numbers

Read the following numbers aloud.

0	ゼロ(ぜろ)、れい	7	なな、しち	20	にじゅう
1	いち	8	はち	30	さんじゅう
2	に	9	きゅう、く	40	よんじゅう
3	さん	10	じゅう	70	ななじゅう、しちじゅう
4	よん、し	11	じゅういち	90	きゅうじゅう
5	ご	12	じゅうに	99	きゅうじゅうきゅう、きゅうじゅうく
6	ろく	13	じゅうさん		

NOTES

- Numbers between 11 and 19 are formed by using the number ten followed by the appropriate single digit.

  11 = 10 + 1 じゅういち＝じゅう＋いち
  12 = 10 + 2 じゅうに＝じゅう＋に
  13 = 10 + 3 じゅうさん＝じゅう＋さん

- The numbers 20, 30, 40, 50, 60, 70, 80, and 90 are formed by using the appropriate single digit followed by 10.

  20 = 2 × 10 にじゅう＝に×じゅう
  30 = 3 × 10 さんじゅう＝さん×じゅう
  40 = 4 × 10 よんじゅう＝よん×じゅう

- Numbers like 23 and 35 are formed by combining the tens digit and the ones digit.

  23 = 2 × 10 + 3 にじゅうさん ＝ に×じゅう＋さん
  35 = 3 × 10 + 5 さんじゅうご ＝ さん×じゅう＋ご

- The numbers 4, 7, and 9 have two possible pronunciations. The number 40 is usually pronounced よんじゅう. The number 70 can be pronounced either ななじゅう or しちじゅう, and the number 90 is always pronounced きゅうじゅう.

Activity 7

Say the following telephone numbers (でんわばんごう) in Japanese. Use の to indicate a dash.

Example: 123-4567 いちにさんの　よんごろくなな

1. 356-2891
2. 245-6689
3. 8217-0370
4. 03-3986-5772
5. 06-4463-5998
6. 0895-23-5005
7. 090-7244-1456
8. 080-4647-4176

Activity 8

Take turns asking classmates their telephone numbers (でんわばんごう).

Example: A: あのう、でんわばんごうは　なんばんですか。
B: いちにさんの　よんごろくななです。
A: そうですか。どうも　ありがとう。

Activity 9

Read the following numbers aloud.

1. 2	6. 11	11. 75
2. 5	7. 17	12. 94
3. 6	8. 20	13. 81
4. 8	9. 49	14. 62
5. 10	10. 53	15. 99

Activity 10

Work in groups of three. One person writes five numbers in Arabic numerals on five separate slips of paper. As he or she shows the numbers, the other two members of the group compete to be the first to call out each number correctly.

E. ～ふん Minute(s)

Note: * indicates a sound change.

1	* いっぷん	8	* はっぷん／はちふん
2	にふん	9	きゅうふん
3	* さんぷん	10	* じゅっぷん／じっぷん
4	* よんふん／よんぷん	11	* じゅういっぷん
5	ごふん	12	じゅうにふん
6	* ろっぷん	20	* にじゅっぷん／にじっぷん
7	しちふん／ななふん	21	* にじゅういっぷん

* なんぷん *how many minutes?*

Activity 11

Say the following times in Japanese.

1. 4:10	5. 12:30	9. 4:17 p.m.	13. 6:55 a.m.
2. 2:25	6. 6:40	10. 9:18 a.m.	14. 9:03 p.m.
3. 7:37	7. 8:09	11. 7:11 p.m.	15. 3:53 p.m.
4. 1:44	8. 1:56	12. 9:02 a.m.	16. 8:30 a.m.

ダイアローグ
だいあろぐ

Dialogue

はじめに Warm-up

Answer the following questions in Japanese.

1. まいにち　じゅぎょうが　ありますか。
2. なんじに　じゅぎょうが　ありますか。
3. たいてい　どこで　ひるごはんを　たべますか。
4. たいてい　なんじごろ　うちに　かえりますか。
5. きのう　なんじごろ　うちに　かえりましたか。
6. せんしゅうの　しゅうまつ　なにを　しましたか。

じゅぎょうが　あります。 *I have a class.*

It is 9:45 a.m. Ueda is eating a sandwich in front of the foreign language building. Li passes by.

うえだ：　あ、リー(り)さん、おはよう。

リー(り)：　ああ、うえださん。おはよう。いま、あさごはんですか。

うえだ：　ええ、きょうは　はちじに　じゅぎょうが　ありました。

リー(り)：　そうですか。たいへんですね。

うえだ：　ええ。で、リー(り)さんは？

リー(り)：　ぼくは　としょかんへ　いきます。あさは　たいてい　としょかんで　しゅくだいを　します。

うえだ： そうですか。クラス（くらす）は？

リー（り）： いちじはんに　にほんごの　じゅぎょうが　あります。
うえださんは？

うえだ： じゅうじに　れきしの　クラス（くらす）が　あります。

リー（り）： そうですか。

Dialogue Phrase Notes

- In the dialogue, the topic particle は follows the time expressions きょう and あさ. In Japanese, a topic does not necessarily have to be the subject of sentence, but it does introduce the item about which the speaker wishes to comment. In the dialogue above, Ueda wants to say something about "today," and Li wants to say the same thing about "mornings." For further discussion of topic particles, refer to the supplementary notes titled "More about the topic particle は" on p. 116 of this chapter.
- たいへんですね means *that's hard*, in which たいへん means *tough, hard, serious*. ね is an affective particle that commonly appears in conversation to express shared feelings or assumptions. In the dialogue, ね expresses Li's sympathy toward Ueda.
- The で in the phrase で、リー（り）さんは？ is often used in conversation. It can be interpreted as *well then*, *so*, or *by the way*. It is not used in written Japanese.

ダイアローグ（だいあろぐ）の　あとで　Comprehension

A. Read each statement below. Then circle はい if the statement is true and いいえ if it is false.

1. はい　いいえ　リー（り）さんは きょうの　ごご としょかんで べんきょうします。

2. はい　いいえ　うえださんは　ごご じゅぎょうが ありま す。

3. はい　いいえ　うえださんは　きょうの　あさ　じゅぎょうが ありました。

B. Answer the following questions in Japanese.

1. うえださんは なんじごろ あさごはんを たべましたか。

2. にほんごの じゅぎょうは なんじに ありますか。

3. じゅうじに なにが ありますか。

にほんの　ぶんか
Japanese Culture

The academic year in Japan

Japanese colleges and universities usually begin the academic year in April. Summer vacation starts at the end of July. The fall semester, or session, runs from September or October through January or February. Winter break is usually short, from the end of December through the beginning of January.

© Yukiko Takada

College classes

As there are few graduate teaching assistants, professors do most of the teaching. Undergraduates usually spend four years at college. The usual class period in Japanese colleges is 90 or 100 minutes long. Class size varies from large lectures to small seminars. Many classes meet once a week for a semester, and the number of assignments, tests, and quizzes is much smaller than in US colleges. Major exams are usually held once, at the end of the semester, and students may work on group projects. According to a survey conducted by the Benesse Educational Research and Development Center (2012), most students in Japan attend over ninety percent of their classes, but do not study much outside of class. Only about half of college students study for more than one hour a week outside of class.

Courtesy of Kazumi and Yukiko Hatasa

College housing

The majority of Japanese colleges are commuter schools, and few have dormitories. Those dormitories that do exist are rarely found on campus. Most Japanese college students live at home or in

© Yukiko Takada

apartments. The average commute is about an hour, but commutes may be as long as two hours in large cities.

Financial aid

Many parents pay for their children's college education in Japan. Although there are scholarships available from various sources, student loans do not exist. According to the same report by Benesse, about 50 percent of students participate in extracurricular activities, called サークル (さくる), once or twice a week. Over 60 percent of students have part-time jobs known as アルバイト／バイト (あるばいと／ばいと) (from the German "arbeiten," meaning *work*). Common jobs for students include clerk positions at convenience stores or supermarkets, かていきょうし (private tutoring for junior and senior high school students), and waitstaff.

ぶんぽう
Grammar

I. Talking about routines, future actions, or events using the polite present form of verbs and the particles に , へ , を , or で

Chapter 2 (see p. 46) introduced the copula verb です and the topic particle は. This chapter deals with regular verbs and four additional particles.

A. Polite present form of verbs

Unlike English, all Japanese verbs have a polite form and a plain form. The polite form is used with acquaintances, people of different age groups, strangers in public places, on TV and radio broadcasts, and in letters. The plain form is used among family members, young children, close friends of the same age, and in newspapers and magazine articles. In this book, you will first learn the basics of Japanese verbs using the polite form.

Verb tenses

Japanese verbs have only two tenses: past and non-past. The non-past tense indicates both present and future actions or states.

Question			
		Verb	
がっこう	に	いきます	か。

Do you go to school? / Are you going to school?

Answer	
	Verb
いいえ、	いきません。

No, I don't. / No, I'm not.

In the above example, いきます can indicate either the habitual action of going to school or future action. The meaning must be understood from the context.

Verb classes

There are three classes of Japanese verbs: う-verbs, る-verbs, and irregular verbs. Japanese has only two irregular verbs: きます and します. (します can be combined with certain nouns to produce irregular compound verbs, as noted below.) These verb classes will become more useful as you learn different forms of inflection in Chapter 7 (see pp. 267–268).

	Polite affirmative form	Polite negative form	Verb class
to go	いきます	いきません	う -verb
to go home	かえります	かえりません	う -verb
to read	よみます	よみません	う -verb
to get up	おきます	おきません	る -verb
to go to bed	ねます	ねません	る -verb
to eat	たべます	たべません	る -verb
to come	きます	きません	Irregular
to do	します	しません	Irregular
to study	べんきょうします	べんきょうしません	Irregular

Note that べんきょうします is considered an irregular verb because it is a compound verb consisting of べんきょう and します. You will learn more compound verbs (noun +します) in later chapters.

B. Direct object particle, を

The particle を marks a direct object. The direct object receives the action of the verb. For example, in the sentence "John buys a car," *car* is the direct object. In English, the direct object is understood by its location (it generally appears immediately after the verb), but in Japanese it is followed by を, as in the following examples. The particle を was once pronounced *wo*, but is now pronounced *o*.

Topic	Direct object		Verb (action)
	Noun	Particle	
わたしは	ひるごはん	を	たべます。

I eat lunch. / I will eat lunch.

スミス(すみす)： しゅうまつ、よく　なにを　しますか。
What do you often do on weekends?

たなか： テレビ(てれび)を　みます。
I watch TV.

スミス(すみす)： そうですか。わたしも　よく　テレビ(てれび)を　みます。
Is that so? I often watch TV, too.

Notes

- べんきょうします consists of the noun べんきょう, which means *study*, and the verb します. Thus, it can be paraphrased as べんきょうを　します, which literally means *do the study*. In the latter sentence, use の to indicate what is being studied.

  にほんごを　べんきょうします。
  I study Japanese.

  にほんごの　べんきょうを　します。
  I study Japanese. (literally, *I do the study of Japanese.*)

- を may be omitted when the meaning can easily be inferred from the context of the conversation. However, it is not easy to determine exactly when to delete を. In this textbook you will sometimes see instances in which particles have been omitted.

C. Destination or goal particles に and へ

The particle に indicates a goal, a destination, or a point of arrival or contact. It is similar to the English prepositions *to*, *into*, or *onto*. The particle へ indicates a direction toward which something or someone moves. When used as a particle, the pronuciation of へ is exactly the same as that of え [e]. When used in other contexts, it is pronounced a little like the English word *hay*. Like を, the particles に and へ may be omitted when the meaning can be inferred easily from the context.

Destination/Goal		Verb
Place noun	Particle	
うち	に／へ	かえります。

I go home. / I will go home. / I am going home.

スミス（すみす）：　どこに　いきますか。　*Where are you going?*
たなか：　がっこうへ　いきます。　*I am going to school.*

へ can replace に in verbs of motion such as いきます, きます, and かえります, but these particles are not interchangeable with other types of verbs.

がっこうに／へ　いきます。
I go to school. / I will go to school.

だいがくに／へ　きます。
I come to the university. / I will come to the university.

おふろに　はいります。
I take a bath. / I will take a bath.

かばん (*bag*) に　ほんを　いれます (*put*)。
I put a book in the bag. / I will put a book in the bag.

D. Place of action and event, で

The particle で indicates the place at which an action or event takes place. It is translated as *in*, *at*, or *on* in English.

Place of action		Verb phrase (action)
Noun	Particle	
としょかん	で	えいがを　みます。

I see a movie at the library. / I am going to see a movie at the library.

スミス（すみす）：どこで　べんきょうしますか。
Where do you (will you) study?

たなか：としょかんで　します。
I study (will study) at the library.

はなして　みましょう　Conversation Practice

Activity 1

Complete each sentence using the appropriate particles.

Example: しゅくだい　／　します
しゅくだいを　します。

1. ほん　／　よみます
2. おふろ　／　はいります
3. うち　／　ねます
4. テレビ（てれび）　／　みます
5. クラス（くらす）　／　きます
6. としょかん　／　いきます
7. シャワー（しゃわ）　／　あびます
8. がっこう　／　ひるごはん　／　たべます
9. うち　／　かえります

Activity 2

Answer the following questions.

Example: よく　としょかんに　いきますか。
ええ、いきます。 or いいえ、いきません。

1. あさごはんを　たべますか。
2. まいあさ　コーヒー（こひ）を　のみますか。
3. よく　テレビ（てれび）を　みますか。
4. よく　えいがに　いきますか。
5. こんばん　としょかんで　べんきょうしますか。

Activity 3

Work with a partner. In the column headed わたし below, write はい if you are thinking of doing the stated activity today, and いいえ if you are not. Then ask your partner whether he/she is planning to do these activities. Start your questions with the phrase あとで (*later*). Switch roles after you reach the bottom of the list.

Example: A: あとで、ほんを　よみますか。
B: ええ、よみます。 or いいえ、よみません。

	わたし	パートナー (ぱ と な)
	はい／いいえ	はい／いいえ
ほん／よみます		
ほかの *(another)* じゅぎょう／いきます		
おふろ／はいります		
シャワー (しゃわ)／あびます		
えいが／みます		
にほんごの　しゅくだい／します		
テレビ (てれび)／みます		
ごはん／たべます		
うち／かえります		

II. Presenting objects or events using ～が　あります

The phrase X が　あります means *there is* X. This phrase is used to describe an object, event, or activity. Depending on the context, ～が　あります can also be used to express possession.

ほんが　あります。
There is a book. / I have a book.

えいがが　あります。
There is a movie.

しゅくだいが　あります。
There is homework. / I have homework.

スミス（すみす）：しゅうまつ　なにを　しますか。
What are you going to do this weekend?

たなか：がっこうに　いきます。
I am going to school.

スミス（すみす）：え、どうしてですか。
Really, why?

たなか：としょかんで　にほんの　えいがが　あります。
There is a Japanese movie (playing) at the library.

スミス（すみす）：あ、そうですか。
Oh, I see.

Notes

- Use the particle で to describe where an event will take place, as in the dialogue above.

  としょかんで　えいがが　あります。
  There is a movie at the library.

- When ～が　あります expresses possession, use ～は to indicate the possessor.

  ぼくは　じゅぎょうが　あります。
  I have a class.

  やまださんは　テレビ（てれび）が　ありません。
  Mr./Ms. Yamada does not have a TV.

はなして みましょう Conversation Practice

Activity 1

Work with a partner. You have the following event listing for Tokyo Disney Resort. Tell your friend about various shows and locations.

Example: ワールド・バザールで ドローイング・クラスが あります。
わるど ばざる どろいんぐ くらす

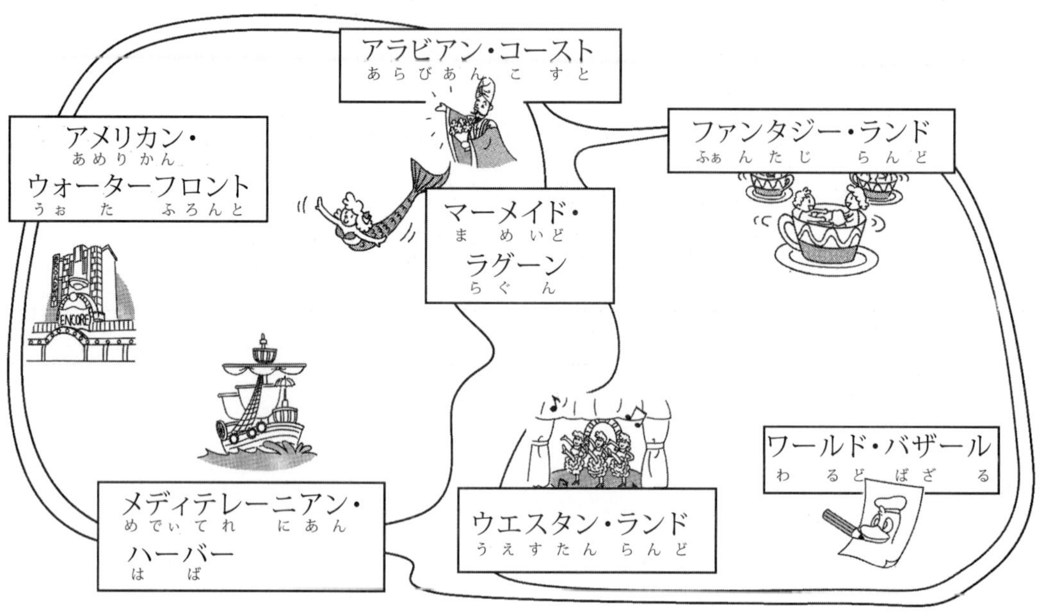

Tokyo Disney Resort Theme Park	Special Events
ワールド・バザール わ る ど ば ざ る	ドローイング・クラス ど ろ い ん ぐ く ら す
ファンタジー・ランド ふ ぁ ん た じ ら ん ど	アリスのティーパーティ あ り す て ぃ ぱ て ぃ
ウエスタン・ランド う え す た ん ら ん ど	フロンティア・レビュー ふ ろ ん て ぃ あ れ び ゅ
アメリカン・ウォーターフロント あ め り か ん う ぉ た ふ ろ ん と	ミュージカル「アンコール」 み ゅ じ か る あ ん こ る
メディテレーニアン・ハーバー め で ぃ て れ に あ ん は ば	ウォーター・カーニバル う ぉ た か に ば る
マーメイド・ラグーン ま め い ど ら ぐ ん	ミュージカル「アンダー・ザ・シー」 み ゅ じ か る あ ん だ ざ し
アラビアン・コースト あ ら び あ ん こ す と	マジック・ショー ま じ っ く し ょ

Activity 2

Work with the class. Ask at least three classmates if they have a class after Japanese class, and if they do, find out what and where it is. Then fill in the chart with the classmate's name, class and location.

Example: A: このあと (*after this class*) じゅぎょうが ありますか。

B: ええ、ぶんがくの じゅぎょうが あります。

A: そうですか。どこで ありますか。

B: スミス・ホール (すみす ほる) (*Smith Hall*) で あります。

or

A: このあと (*after this class*) じゅぎょうが ありますか。

B: いいえ、ありません。～さんは？

A: わたしは えいごの じゅぎょうが あります。

なまえ	じゅぎょう	ばしょ (location)

III. Telling time using the particle に

The particle に with a time expression indicates a specific point in time. This use of に corresponds to the English prepositions *at*, *in*, or *on*. It may be used to express clock times, days of the week, months, or years. For example:

ごじ<u>に</u> <u>at</u> 5 o'clock　　げつようび<u>に</u> <u>on</u> Monday
ごがつ<u>に</u> <u>in</u> May　　１９９６ねん<u>に</u> <u>in</u> 1996

The particle に is never used with the words きょう, いま, あさ, ばん, いつ, まい〜 (every 〜), こん〜 (this 〜), らい〜 (next 〜).

Point in time		
Time	Particle	
ろくじはん	に	おきます。

スミス(すみす)：　うえださんは　きょう　きますか。
Is Ms. Ueda coming today?

たなか：　ええ、ごじごろ（に）　きますよ。
Yes, she is coming around 5 o'clock.

スミス(すみす)：　リー(り)さんも　きますか。
Is Mr. Li coming, too?

たなか：　いいえ、リー(り)さんは　どようびに　きます。
No, he is coming on Saturday.

たなか：　すみません。いま　なんじですか。
Excuse me. What time is it now?

スミス(すみす)：　じゅうじ　よんじゅうさんぷんです。
It's 10:43.

たなか：　どうも　ありがとう。
Thank you very much.

スミス(すみす)：　いいえ。
Not at all.

NOTES

- For the pronunciation of numbers and number + ふん, refer to vocabulary sections D and E, pp. 91–93.
- The pronunciation of some numbers may change depending on the counters being used. For example:

  よん → よじ よんふん
  いち → いちじ いっぷん

- We have seen the use of はん meaning "half past the hour." Another way to say this is the more literal さんじゅっぷん. For example: さんじさんじゅっぷん／さんじはん = 3:30.
- When two or more time expressions are used together, list them from the largest to the smallest unit (for example, day and time), and connect them with の. A few words like まいにち do not take の. For example:

  どようびの　さんじに　きます。
  I am coming at 3 o'clock on Saturday.
  まいにち　はちじに　おきます。
  I wake up at 8 o'clock every day.

- Use ～ごろ or ごろ（に） to express an approximate time. For example:

  たなか：きょう　なんじごろ（に）　かえりますか。
  About what time are you going to go home today?
  スミス（すみす）：よじごろ　かえります。
  I will go home around 4 o'clock.

はなして みましょう Conversation Practice

Activity 1

Work with a partner. A Japanese film festival is going on all week at the student union. Look at the following schedule and ask each other what time the various screenings begin.

Example: A: となりの トトロ(ととろ)は いつ ありますか。
B: げつようびの ごぜん じゅういちじに あります。

Movie titles	Date and Time
となりの トトロ(ととろ)	Monday 11:00 a.m. Wednesday 5:35 p.m. Friday 8:30 p.m.
おくりびと *(Departures)*	Tuesday 10:50 a.m. Thursday 12:05 p.m. Saturday 3:15 p.m.
フラガール(ふらがある)	Wednesday 10:00 a.m. Friday 10:55 a.m. Sunday 7:45 p.m.
ゴジラ(ごじら)	Monday 9:40 p.m. Thursday 10:20 a.m. Saturday 12:00 p.m.
マジックアワー(まじっくあわあ)	Tuesday 4:25 p.m. Friday 6:08 p.m. Sunday 10:25 a.m.
こくはく *(Confessions)*	Wednesday 9:10 p.m. Thursday 12:00 p.m. Saturday 9:30 a.m.
手紙(てがみ) *(Letter)*	Monday 2:33 p.m. Tuesday 11:10 a.m. Sunday 11:44 a.m.

Activity 2

Combine the following phrases to form complete sentences. Use whatever particles are necessary.

Example: ごじ／かえります
<u>ごじに かえります。</u>

1. まいあさ／コーヒー(こひ)／のみます
2. あした／ばん／とうきょう／いきます
3. げつようび／じゅういちじごろ／かえります

4. らいしゅう／どようび／えいが／みます
5. まいにち／しちじごろ／おふろ／はいります
6. いま／クラス(くらす)／あります

Activity 3

Work with your classmates. Following the model in Box ① of the chart below, fill in all the blanks with the appropriate particles. Use an X to indicate that no particle is required. Then ask your classmates はい／いいえ questions based on the statements in the chart. If someone answers はい, write his or her name in the box. Try to fill an entire row or column with different names.

Example: A: スミス(すみす)さんは　まいにち　ほんを　よみますか。
B: はい、よみます。

Write スミス(すみす) in Box ①.

①________さん まいにち_X_ ほん_を_ よみます。	②________さん がっこう____ しゅくだい____ します。	③________さん きょう____ コーヒー(こひ)____ のみます。	④________さん まいしゅう____ げつようび____ としょかん___ いきます。
⑤________さん もくようび____ じゅぎょう____ あります。	⑥________さん としょかん____ べんきょう____ します。	⑦________さん こんばん____ しゅくだい____ します。	⑧________さん うち____ ひるごはん____ たべます。
⑨________さん あさはちじごろ ____ ごはん____ たべます。	⑩________さん じゅうにじはん ____ じゅぎょう____ あります。	⑪________さん まいあさ____ テレビ(てれび)____ みます。	⑫________さん にちようび____ がっこう____ きます。
⑬________さん まいばん____ おふろ____ はいります。	⑭________さん さんじごろ____ うち____ かえります。	⑮________さん こんばん____ はちじ____ テレビ(てれび)____ みます。	⑯________さん まいあさ____ しちじ____ シャワー(しゃわ)____ あびます。

Activity 4

Ask a partner about his or her class schedule for the week to complete the following chart. Then switch roles.

Example: A: げつようびは　じゅぎょうが　ありますか。
B: ええ、ありますよ。
A: そうですか。　いつですか。
B: ごぜんはちじに　にほんごの　じゅぎょうが　あります。
そして、くじに　ぶんがくの　じゅぎょうが　あります。

～ようび	じゅぎょう
げつようび	8 a.m.- にほんご　9 a.m.- ぶんがく
かようび	
すいようび	
もくようび	
きんようび	
どようび	

IV. Using adverbs to express frequency of actions

Japanese has a variety of adverbs that express how often one does something, as shown in the following illustration.

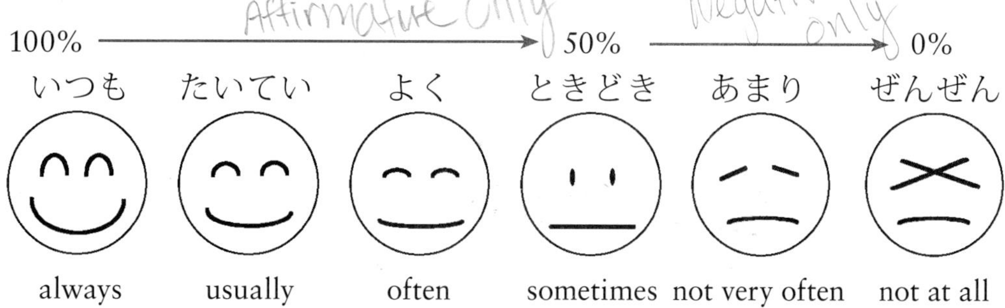

Sentences containing いつも, たいてい, よく or ときどき end with an affirmative verb form.

> わたしは　いつも　あさ　コーヒー(こーひー)を　のみます。
> *I always drink coffee in the morning.*
>
> わたしは　たいてい　じゅういちじに　ねます。
> *I usually go to bed at eleven o'clock.*
>
> わたしは　よく　としょかんに　いきます。
> *I often go to the library.*
>
> わたしは　ときどき　じゅうじごろ　おきます。
> *I sometimes get up about 10:00.*

The adverbs あまり and ぜんぜん must always be used with the negative form of the verb.

> わたしは　あまり　ほんを　よみません。
> *I don't read books very much.*
>
> わたしは　ぜんぜん　あさごはんを　たべません。
> *I don't eat breakfast at all.*

スミス(すみす)：いつも　あさごはんを　たべますか。
Do you always eat breakfast?

たなか：いいえ、ぜんぜん　たべません。
No, I never eat it.
スミス(すみす)さんは？
How about you, Mr. Smith?

スミス(すみす)：わたしは　たいてい　たべますよ。
I usually do.

たなか：そうですか。
I see.

V. Expressing past actions and events using the polite past form of verbs

Forming the polite past form of a verb is quite easy. All you need to do is to use ました instead of ます for an affirmative sentence, and ませんでした instead of ません for a negative sentence.

Question	
	Verb (past)
あさごはんを	たべましたか。

Did you eat breakfast?

Answer	
	Verb (past)
いいえ、	たべませんでした。

No, I didn't.

スミス（すみす）： きのう　しゅくだいが　ありましたか。
Was there an assignment yesterday?

たなか： いいえ、ありませんでしたよ。
No, there wasn't.

スミス（すみす）： そうですか。どうも。
I see. Thank you.

	Polite affirmative form		Polite negative form		Verb class
	present	past	present	past	
	～ます	～ました	～ません	～ませんでした	
to go	いきます	いきました	いきません	いきませんでした	う -verb
to eat	たべます	たべました	たべません	たべませんでした	る -verb
to come	きます	きました	きません	きませんでした	Irregular
to do	します	しました	しません	しませんでした	Irregular

はなして みましょう　Conversation Practice

Activity 1

The chart below lists everything Mr. Smith did yesterday. Looking at the chart, describe each of his activities.

Example: スミス（すみす）さんは　しちじに　おきました。

7:00 a.m.	Wake up	1:30 p.m.	English class
7:10 a.m.	Shower	2:30 p.m.	Study at the library
8:00 a.m.	Breakfast	4:30 p.m.	Go home
8:45 a.m.	Go to school	6:00 p.m.	Dinner
9:00 a.m.	Japanese class	7:30 p.m.	Watch TV
10:00 a.m.	Literature class	9:00 p.m.	Do homework
12:00 p.m.	Lunch at school	12:00 a.m.	Go to bed

Activity 2

Answer the following questions, based on Mr. Smith's chart in Activity 1.

Example: A: スミス(すみす)さんは　きのう　はちじに　おきましたか。
B: いいえ、おきませんでした。

1. スミス(すみす)さんは　きのう　おふろに　はいりましたか。
2. スミス(すみす)さんは　きのう　がっこうで　ひるごはんを　たべましたか。
3. スミス(すみす)さんは　きのう　れきしの　じゅぎょうが　ありましたか。
4. スミス(すみす)さんは　きのうのばん　シャワー(しゃわ)を　あびましたか。
5. スミス(すみす)さんは　きのう　としょかんへ　いきましたか。
6. スミス(すみす)さんは　うちで　しゅくだいを　しましたか。
7. スミス(すみす)さんは　じゅういちじごろ　ねましたか。

Activity 3

Work with a partner. Fill in the table below with as much detail as possible describing what you did yesterday. Your partner will ask you questions to figure out what you did. Compare the two tables when you are done.

Example: A: きのう　なんじに　おきましたか。
B: はちじごろ　おきました。～さんは？
A: わたしは　しちじに　おきました。
B: そうですか。あさごはんは　たべましたか。
A: いいえ、たべませんでした。でも *(but)* 、コーヒー(こひ)を のみました。

わたし		パートナー(ぱとな)	
6 a.m.		6 a.m.	
8 a.m.		8 a.m.	
9 a.m.		9 a.m.	
10 a.m.		10 a.m.	
11 a.m.		11 a.m.	
12 p.m.		12 p.m.	
1 p.m.		1 p.m.	
2 p.m.		2 p.m.	
3 p.m.		3 p.m.	
4 p.m.		4 p.m.	
5 p.m.		5 p.m.	
6 p.m.		6 p.m.	
7 p.m.		7 p.m.	
9 p.m.		9 p.m.	
11 p.m.		11 p.m.	

そうごう　れんしゅう
Integration

すずきさんの　まいにち

Form groups of three people. There should be three types of groups: A, B, and C. Your instructor will tell you which group you are in. Listen to the interview with Suzuki-san and take notes on the schedule sheet below. Discuss the interview with your partners and make sure that your information is correct. Then form a different group of three. All of the members in this group should come from different groups, one from Group A, another from Group B, and the third from Group C. Exchange information with the others to discover if there are discrepancies in your information.

～ようび	なにを　しますか。
にちようび	
げつようび	
かようび	
すいようび	
もくようび	
きんようび	
どようび	

ロールプレイ（ろ　るぷれい）　Role Play

Imagine that you are talking to a Japanese friend. Explain to him or her how a typical American college student might spend a week.

Chapter 4

第四課

© Kenneth Hamm/Photo Japan

にほんの　まち

Japanese Cities

Objectives	Asking about places and indicating location
Vocabulary	Buildings, landmarks, adjectives
Dialogue	このへんに　ぎんこうが　ありますか。 *Is there a bank around here?*
Japanese Culture	Geography and demographics of Japan
Grammar	I. Referring to things using これ, それ, あれ, どれ
	II. Asking for and giving locations using ～は　～に　あります／います and ここ, そこ, あそこ
	III. Describing people and things using adjectives + noun, and polite present forms of adjectives
	IV. Describing people, things, and their locations using ～に　～が　あります／います
	V. Using ね and よ
Listening	Using redundancy in speech
Communication	Getting someone's attention (1)
Kanji	Introduction to **kanji** 大　学　校　先　生
Reading	Using script types as clues to word boundaries

Chapter Resources

www.cengagebrain.com

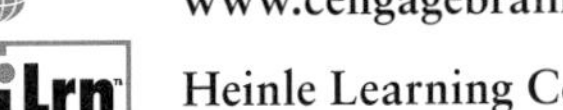

Heinle Learning Center

Audio Program

Pair work

Group work

単語 (たんご)
Vocabulary

Nouns

アパート		apartment
えき	駅	station
えんぴつ	鉛筆	pencil
かばん	鞄	luggage, bag
カフェ		coffee shop, café (recent term)
きっさてん	喫茶店	coffee shop (traditional term)
きょうかしょ	教科書	textbook
ぎんこう	銀行	bank
けしゴム	消しゴム	eraser
こうえん	公園	park
こうばん	交番	police box
このへん	この辺	this area
コンビニ		convenience store
じしょ	辞書	dictionary
スーパー		supermarket
たてもの	建物	building, structure
テスト		test
デパート		department store
ノート		notebook
ビル		building
びょういん	病院	hospital
ペン		pen
ボールペン		ballpoint pen

ほんや	本屋	bookstore
まち	町	town
ゆうびんきょく	郵便局	post office
りょう	寮	dormitory
レストラン		restaurant

る -verb

います		(to) be, (to) exist (used for animate beings); the dictionary form is いる.

Demonstrative words

あそこ		over there, that place (far away from both speaker and listener)
あれ		that, that object over there
ここ		here, this place
これ		this object, this
そこ		there, that place (close to the listener or slightly removed from both speaker and listener)
それ		that object, that (close to the listener or slightly removed from both speaker and listener)

い -adjectives

あおい	青い	blue
あかい	赤い	red
あたらしい	新しい	new
いい		good
おおきい	大きい	big
きいろい	黄色い	yellow
くろい	黒い	black
しろい	白い	white
たかい	高い	tall, high
ちいさい	小さい	small

ちゃいろい	茶色い	brown
ふるい	古い	old

な-adjectives

きれい(な)		clean, pretty, neat
ゆうめい(な)	有名(な)	famous
りっぱ(な)	立派(な)	fine, splendid, nice

Question words

だれ		who
どれ		which one
どんな		what kind of

Adverbs

どうも		very どうも ありがとう Thank you very much どうも すみません I'm very sorry
とても		very (always used with an affirmative form)

Suffix

～や	～屋	store (ほんや bookstore)

単語の練習 Vocabulary Practice
たんご れんしゅう

A. まち Towns

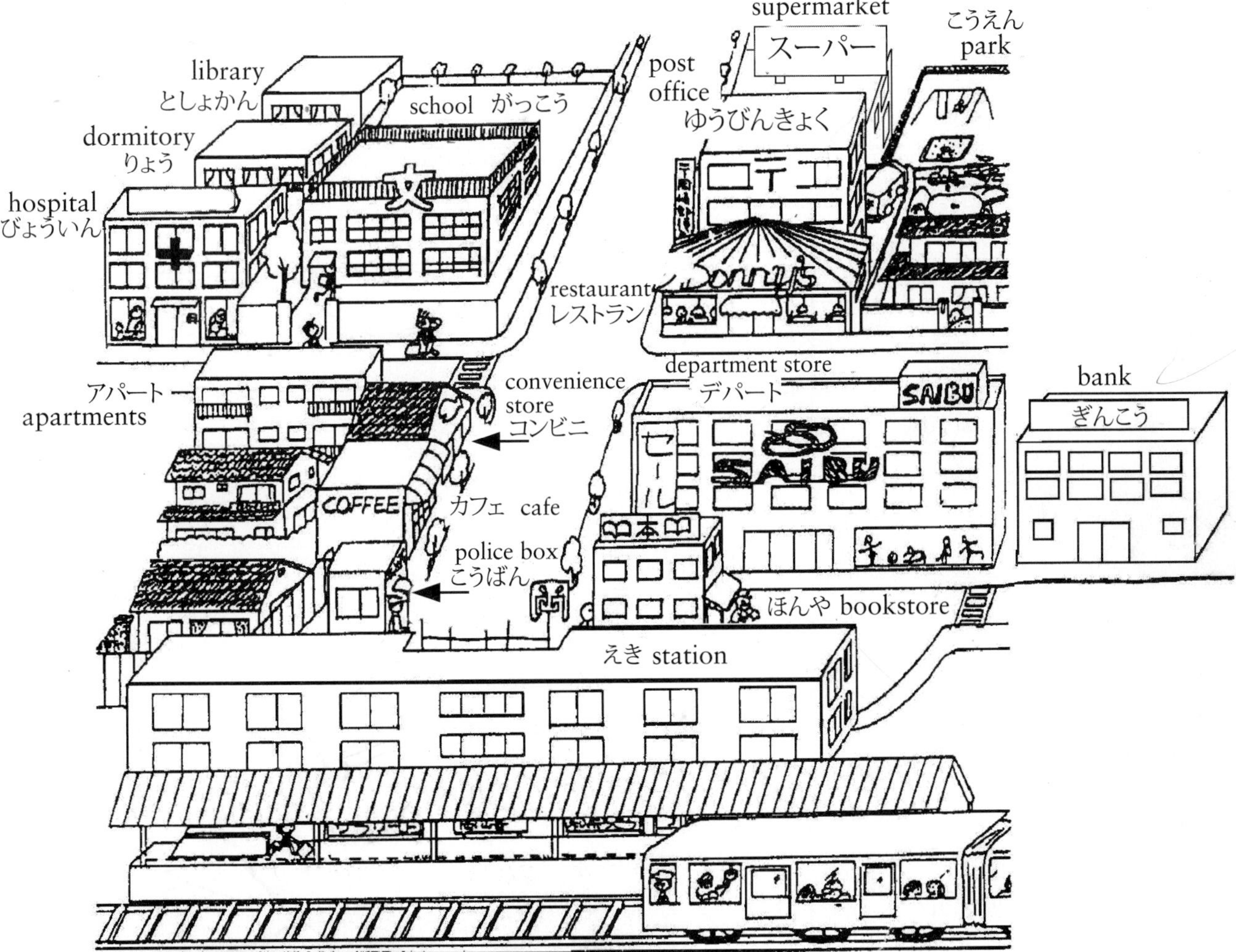

Activity 1

Complete the chart with the Japanese word for each symbol.

Location	Map Symbol	Japanese
station		
bank	¥	
post office	〒	
supermarket	S	
school	文 ⊗	
hospital		
restaurant		
coffee shop		
police box	X	
department store	D	
convenience store		

Activity 2

Answer these questions in Japanese.

1. よく　カフェに　いきますか。
2. よく　コンビニに　いきますか。
3. なんじごろ　うちに　かえりますか。
4. ～さんは　うちに　すんでいますか。アパートに　すんでいますか。りょうに　すんでいますか。(すんでいます *to live*)
5. せんしゅう　スーパーに　いきましたか。
6. しゅうまつは　ときどき　デパートに　いきますか。
7. よく　どこで　べんきょうしますか。
8. レストランで　よく　なにを　たべますか。

B. Adjectives

あたらしい	new	あおい	blue
大(おお)きい	big	あかい	red
たかい	tall, high	きいろい	yellow
ちいさい	small	くろい	black
ふるい	old	しろい	white
きれい(な)	clean, pretty, neat	ちゃいろい	brown
ゆうめい(な)	famous		
りっぱ(な)	fine, splendid, nice		

Activity 3

Write an antonym for each of the following words. Follow the example.

Example: きたない (*dirty*) ⇔ きれい

大(おお)きい	
あたらしい	
しろい	
あかい	
むめいの (*unknown*)	

Activity 4

Create as many sentences as you can using 〜は [adjective] です and the adjectives in the above list.

Example: わたしの 学校(がっこう)は 大(おお)きいです。

C. School supplies

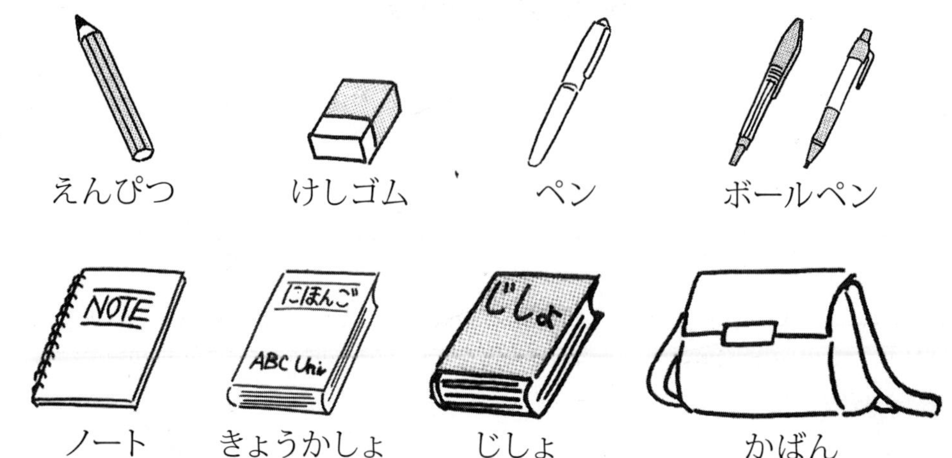

Activity 5

Create sentences describing the color(s) and/or size for each of the items above that you own.

Example: わたしの　かばんは　ちゃいろいです。

じしょは　しろいです。

ダイアローグ
Dialogue

はじめに　Warm-up

The Shibuya/Harajuku District is a popular hangout for young Japanese people. Look at the map of Shibuya and Harajuku below and try to identify some of the landmarks in the area.

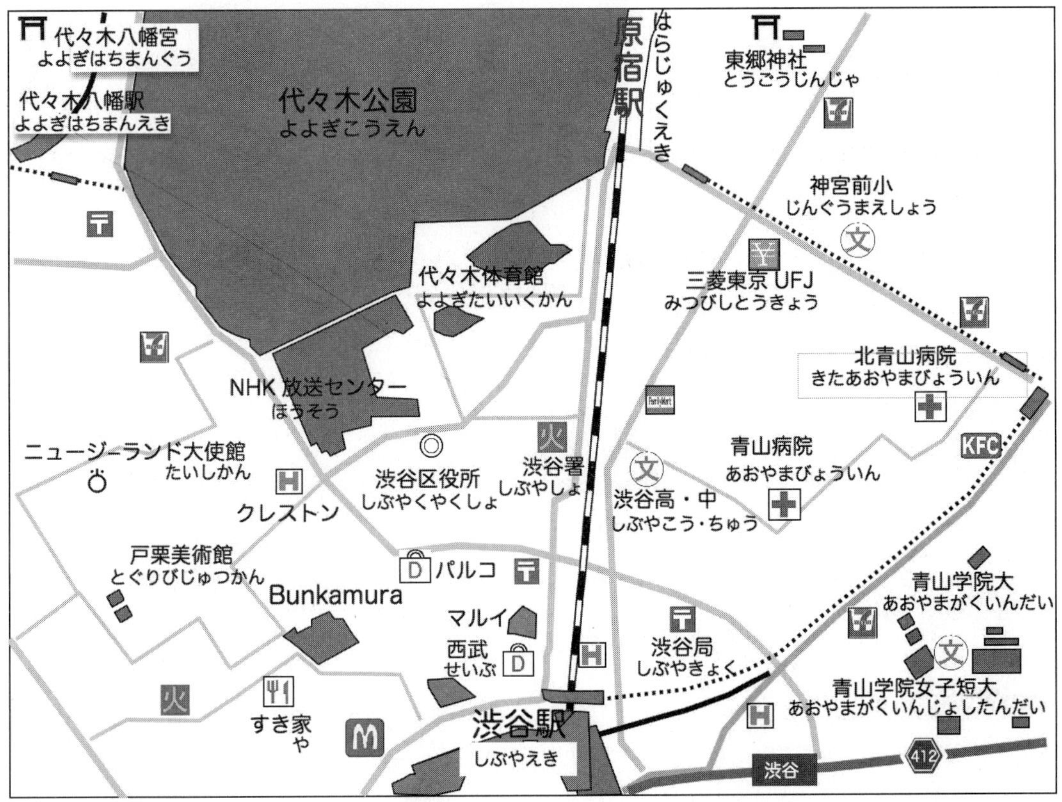

Shibuya and Harajuku

このへんに　ぎんこうが　ありますか。*Is there a bank around here?*

Ueda is meeting a friend in Shibuya. She has just gotten off the train, and realizes that she needs to withdraw some cash. She approaches a passerby (つうこうにん) in front of Shibuya Station (しぶやえき).

うえだ：　あのう、すみませんが。
つうこうにんA：　はい。
うえだ：　このへんに　ぎんこうが　ありますか。
つうこうにんA：　ええ、ありますよ。あそこに　たかい　ビルが　ありますね。
うえだ：　ええ。
つうこうにんA：　あれですよ。
うえだ：　あ、そうですか。どうも　ありがとう　ございます。
つうこうにんA：　いいえ。

In the building:

うえだ：　あのう、すみません。
つうこうにんB：　はい。
うえだ：　ぎんこうは　どこに　ありますか。
つうこうにんB：　あ、ぎんこうは　それですよ。
うえだ：　ああ、どうも。
つうこうにんB：　いいえ。

At the entrance of the bank:

うえだ：あのう、すみませんが、ATM は　どこですか。

こういん (*clerk*)：そこに　ございます。

うえだ：ああ、どうも。

Dialogue Phrase Notes

- When someone thanks you, it is common to say いいえ. In this case, いいえ means *Don't mention it*, or *You're welcome.*
- Like English, Japanese uses a variety of expressions, such as あ (*Ah / Oh*), ああ (*Oh / OK*), へえ〜(*Hmm / Oh*) to indicate understanding or surprise.
- どうも is an abbreviation of phrases such as どうも　ありがとう and どうも　すみません. It is very common to use only どうも in conversation.
- ございます is the polite form of あります. In this dialogue, the bank clerk uses it when speaking with Ueda.

ダイアローグの　後(あと)で　Comprehension

Answer the following questions in Japanese.

1. うえださんは　どこに　いきますか。
2. それは　しぶやえきに　ありますか。
3. どんな　たてものですか。

スミス： あれは　だれの　ノートですか。
Whose notebook is that over there?

たなか： あれですか。キムさんの　ノートです。
That one over there? It's Ms. Kim's.

スミス： そうですか。
Is that so?

Notes

- これ, それ, あれ, and どれ are pronouns and cannot be followed by another noun.
- It is rude to refer to people using これ, それ, あれ, or どれ, because they refer to things. However, you can use them to refer to a person in a picture because a picture is not considered a person.
- Actual distances that these words indicate vary depending on context. それ would imply much greater distance when it is used to point out a building than when it is used to point to an item in a room. In the picture below, これ refers to the building in front of the speaker and the listener, あれ refers to the house far away from them, and それ refers to the one that is somewhat away from them but not quite far enough for them to call it あれ.
- だれ means *who*, but it also means *whose* if followed by the particle の.

だれが　きますか。	*Who is coming?*
これは　だれの　ほんですか。	*Whose book is this?*

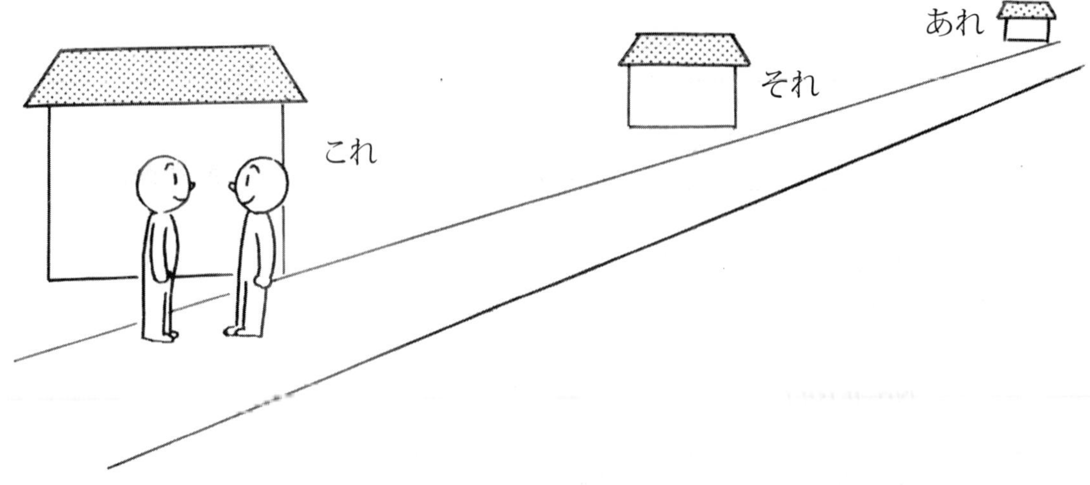

話(はな)してみましょう Conversation Practice

Activity 1

Look at the following drawing of a room. Smith is asking Kimura the Japanese words for various objects in the room. Complete the following conversations using これ, それ, and あれ.

Example: スミス： これは　にほんごで　なんと　いいますか。
きむら： けしゴムと　いいます。

1. スミス： __________は　にほんごで　なんと　いいますか。
   きむら： けしゴムと　いいます。
2. スミス： __________は　にほんごで　なんと　いいますか。
   きむら： じしょと　いいます。
3. スミス： __________は　にほんごで　なんと　いいますか。
   きむら： えんぴつと　いいます。
4. スミス： __________は　にほんごで　なんと　いいますか。
   きむら： ノートと　いいます。
5. スミス： __________は　にほんごで　なんと　いいますか。
   きむら： かばんと　いいます。

Activity 2

Work with a partner. Look at the following drawing. Pretend you are person A, and your partner is person B. Erasers, pencils, books, and dictionaries are scattered around the room. First, let your partner decide who among the following people owns each item and mark it on the drawing.

たなか先生(せんせい)　きむらさん　アリスさん　キムさん　スミスさん　リンさん

Then ask who owns each item and write it under the owner's name. After you finish, have your partner check your answers.

Example: A: これ／それ／あれは　だれの　ほんですか。

B: <u>きむらさんの　ほん</u>です。

Activity 3

Work with a partner. Looking at the map below, ask a classmate to locate certain buildings using これ, それ, and あれ. Assume that both of you are standing in front of the police box.

Example: A: これ／それ／あれは　____________ですか。

B: はい、そうです。 or いいえ、そうじゃありません。

Activity 4

Work with a partner. Look at the following town maps. Imagine that your partner is a new student and you are showing him/her the campus. First, decide where you and your partner are among the locations numbered 1 through 4. Then, describe the buildings around you, using これ, それ, あれ, and どれ.

Example: A: これ／それ／あれは____________です。
B: そうですか。じゃあ、これ／それ／あれは　なんですか。
A: __________です。

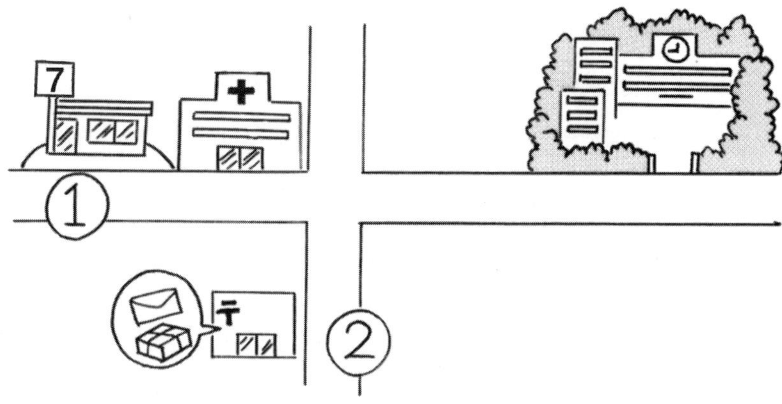

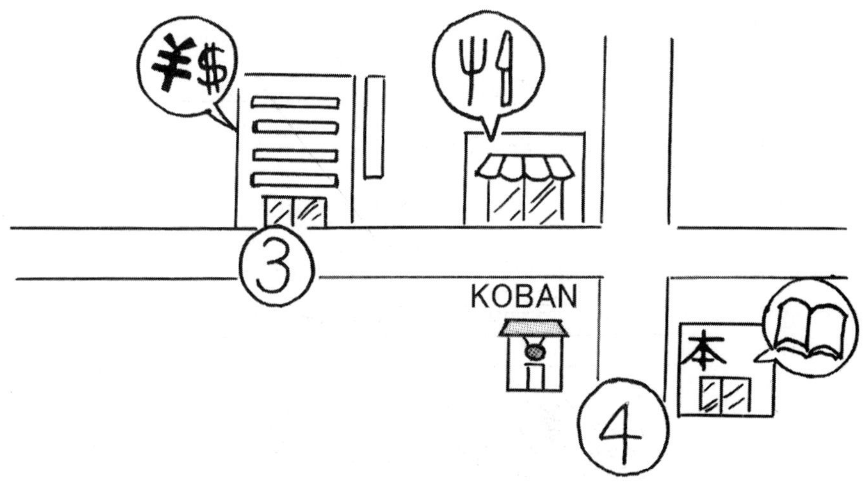

II. Asking for and giving locations using ～は　～に　あります／います and ここ, そこ, あそこ

A. ここ、そこ、あそこ、どこ

The words これ, それ, あれ, and どれ refer to objects. When these words are used to point out a building, the speaker is viewing the building as an object rather than as a location. However, buildings and facilities are also considered places or locations. When referring to a location, you need to use ここ, そこ, あそこ, or どこ instead.

ここ means *here* or *this place*, and refers to the area close to the speaker.

そこ means *there* or *that place,* and refers to an area close to the listener but away from the speaker, or between them, or some distance from both of them.

あそこ means *that place over there*, and refers to an area far away from both the speaker and the listener.

どこ means *where.*

B. ～は　～に　あります

In Chapter 3 (p. 103), you learned that the verb あります (*there is X*) is used to describe the existence of an object or event. It is commonly used to ask or identify the location of objects such as pens, books, and buildings. To ask about location, use ～は　どこに　ありますか. Here に is a particle that indicates the location of an object.

じしょは　どこに　ありますか。　*Where is the dictionary?*

りょうは　どこに　ありますか。　*Where is the dormitory?*

The answer to these questions might be: Location に　あります.

ここに　あります　*It's here.*

あそこに　あります。　*It's over there.*

The word あります is never used to indicate the location of animate objects such as people, pets, and other animals, because it is used only for lifeless objects. Use います to talk about the location of living beings.

キム：まもるさんは　どこに　いますか。　*Where is Mamoru?*

スー：ここに　います。　*He is here.*

スミス：あのう、すみませんが、ゆうびんきょくは　どこに　ありますか。
Um, excuse me, but where is the post office?

たなか：そこに　あります。
It's there.

スミス：あ、そうですか。どうも。
I see. Thanks.

(The teacher is taking attendance, but he doesn't see Ms. Kim.)

先生(せんせい)：　キムさんは　どこに　いますか。
Where is Ms. Kim?

ブラウン：　いま　としょかんに　います。
She is in the library now.

先生(せんせい)：　あ、そうですか。じゅぎょうに　きますか。
I see. Is she coming to class?

ブラウン：　さあ、よくわかりません。
Well, I am not sure.

Notes

- Location に　あります／います can be abbreviated as Location です.

なかがわ：　スミスさんの　りょうは　<u>どこですか</u>。
Where is Mr. Smith's dormitory?
スミス：　<u>あそこです</u>。
Over there.

先生(せんせい)：　キムさんは　どこに　いますか。
Where is Ms. Kim?
ジョンソン：　としょかんです。
In the library.

- You cannot use the particle で in this structure because で indicates a location at which an event or activity takes place. When you are merely asking or indicating the location of a building or object, no activity is implied.

スミス：　どこ<u>で</u>　えいがが　ありますか。
Where is the movie?
なかがわ：　あそこ<u>で</u>　あります。
It will be over there.

キム：　こうえんは　どこ<u>に</u>　ありますか。
Where is the park?
やまだ：　あそこ<u>に</u>　あります。
It's over there.

話(はな)してみましょう Conversation Practice

Activity 1

Work with a partner. Look at the drawing of a room. One person asks questions about the location of objects and people, 〜は　どこに　あります／いますか, and the other person responds using ここ／そこ／あそこ and 〜に　あります／います or 〜です. Follow the model.

Example: A: <u>ノート</u>は　どこに　ありますか。

B: <u>ここに　あります。／ここです。</u>

1. けしゴム
2. やまださん
3. にほんごの　じしょ
4. スミスさん
5. ボールペン
6. きょうかしょ

Activity 2

Look at the following drawing of a street. Your partner will ask you where the following buildings are. Answer his/her questions based on the picture.

Example: A: あのう、としょかんは　どこに　ありますか。
B: そこに　あります。
A: ああ、そこですね。どうも。

1. こうえん
2. こうばん
3. ゆうびんきょく
4. ほんや
5. としょかん

III. Describing people and things using adjectives + noun, and polite present forms of adjectives

There are two types of adjectives in Japanese. Both of them modify nouns directly and can be used at the end of sentences to describe a noun. One is called an い -adjective because it ends in い before a noun, as in 大(おお)きい　うち (*big house*) and ちいさい　うち (*small house*). The other type is called a な -adjective, because the adjective takes な before a noun as in りっぱな　うち (*fine house*) and きれいな　うち (*pretty house*).

A. Describing people and things using adjective + noun

りょうは　ふるい　たてものです。
The dormitory is in an old building.

えきビルは　ゆうめいな　たてものです。
The station building is a famous building.

The formation of adjective + noun is the following. Note that the dictionary form is the form in which dictionaries list adjectives and verbs.

い -adjectives

Dictionary form　大(おお)きい
大(おお)きい ＋ うち → 大(おお)きい　うち

な -adjectives

Dictionary form:　きれい
きれいな ＋ うち → きれいな　うち

やまなか：あれは　わたしの　うちです。
That one over there is my house.

スミス：へえ、大(おお)きい　うちですね。
Wow, it's a large house, isn't it?

ジョンソン：ゆうびんきょくは　どこに　ありますか。
Where is the post office?

ほんだ：ゆうびんきょくですか。あそこです。
The post office? Over there.

ジョンソン：ああ、りっぱな　たてものですね。
I see, it's a nice building.

B. Describing and commenting on places and objects using adjectives (polite affirmative and negative forms), and とても and あまり.

Polite affirmative form

わたしの　かばんは　あかいです。
My bag is red.

おがわさんの　りょうは　とても　ちいさいです。
Mr. Ogawa's dorm is very small.

びょういんは　とても　きれいです。
The hospital is very clean.

Polite negative form

わたしの　かばんは　くろくありません。
My bag is not black.

わたしの　かばんは　くろくないです。
My bag is not black.

びょういんは　あまり　大(おお)きくありません。
The hospital is not very big.

びょういんは　あまり　大(おお)きくないです。
The hospital is not very big.

すずきさんの　りょうは　あまり　りっぱじゃありません。
Mr. Suzuki's dorm is not very nice.

すずきさんの　りょうは　あまり　りっぱじゃないです。
Mr. Suzuki's dorm is not very nice.

The following charts show the formation of polite forms and adjective + noun for い- and な-adjectives.

い -adjectives

Dictionary form	Polite affirmative form	Polite negative form	Adjective + noun
大(おお)きい (*large*)	大(おお)きいです	大(おお)きくありません 大(おお)きくないです	大(おお)きいうち
いい * (*good*)	いいです	よくありません よくないです	いいうち

* the い -adjective いい, meaning *good*, has an irregular negative form.

な-adjectives

Dictionary form	Polite affirmative form	Polite negative form	Adjective + noun
ゆうめい (*famous*)	ゆうめいです	ゆうめいじゃありません ゆうめいじゃないです	ゆうめいな うち

ジョンソン：ほんださんの　うちは　どれですか。
Which one is your house, Mr. Honda?

ほんだ：それです。
It's that one.

ジョンソン：ああ、とても　きれいな　うちですね。
Wow, it's a very nice house, isn't it.

ほんだ：ありがとう。でも、　あまり　大(おお)きくありませんよ。／大(おお)きくないですよ。
Thank you, but it is not very big.

Notes

- The alternative negative form, ～ないです, is considered colloquial and only used in spoken language.
- Note that the negative form of a な-adjective is the same as that of a noun + です.

  Negative of noun + です　大学生(だいがくせい)じゃありません。

  Negative of な -adjective　きれいじゃありません。

  りょうは　とても　きれいです。
  The dormitory is very nice/clean.
  りょうは　あまり　きれいじゃありません。
  The domitory is not very nice /clean.

- The adverbs とても and あまり are often used with adjectives, and both may be translated as *very* in English. とても occurs with an affirmative form, and あまり occurs with a negative form. The combination of あまり　～ません／ないです means *not very.*
- Use どんな (*what kind of* ～) to ask about characteristics of people and objects.

  イー：どんな　たてものですか。
  What kind of building is it?
  ホン：くろい　たてものです。
  It is a black building

話(はな)してみましょう Conversation Practice

Activity 1

Describe buildings, objects, and people using the boxed adjectives and the phrases listed below.

Example: わたしの　りょう／たてもの

<u>わたしの　りょうは　ふるい　たてものです。</u>

大(おお)きい	ちいさい	あたらしい	ふるい	たかい	
あかい	あおい	しろい	くろい	きいろい	いい
きれい	りっぱ	ゆうめい	ちゃいろい		

1. わたしの　大学(だいがく)／大学(だいがく)
2. わたしの　うち／たてもの
3. わたしの　かばん／かばん
4. にほんごの　先生(せんせい)／ひと (*person*)
5. びょういん／たてもの
6. 先生(せんせい)の　ペン／ペン

Activity 2

Work with a partner. Ask your classmates what kinds of place they prefer for doing one of the following activities:

Example: うちを　かいます。(*to buy*)

A: どんな　うちが　いいですか。

B: ふるい　うちが　いいですね。

1. 大学院(だいがくいん)に　はいります。
2. カフェで　べんきょうします。
3. びょういんに　いきます。
4. りょうに　すみます (*to live in*)。
5. レストランで　ごはんを　たべます。

Activity 3

Look at the chart describing various buildings, and answer the following questions, paying attention to はい, いいえ, とても and あまり.

Examples: A: ゆうびんきょくは　大(おお)きいですか。
B: いいえ、大(おお)きくありません。
or いいえ、大(おお)きくないです。
A: ぎんこうは　大(おお)きいですか。
B: はい、とても　大(おお)きいです。

	ゆうびんきょく	ぎんこう	スーパー	びょういん
大(おお)きい	いいえ	とても	あまり	はい
あたらしい	とても	いいえ	はい	あまり
いい	あまり	いいえ	とても	とても
きれい	はい	いいえ	はい	はい
ゆうめい	いいえ	あまり	いいえ	はい
りっぱ	あまり	とても	いいえ	はい

1. スーパーは　いいですか。
2. ゆうびんきょくは　あたらしいですか。
3. びょういんは　きれいですか。
4. びょういんは　あたらしいですか。
5. ゆうびんきょくは　いいですか。
6. ぎんこうは　りっぱですか。
7. ぎんこうは　ゆうめいですか。

Activity 4

Work with a partner. Using the adjectives you have just learned, tell your partner about your home and belongings. Then ask your partner whether his/her place and belongings also share these characteristics. Follow the model.

Example: A: わたしの　アパートは　あたらしいです。
～さんの　アパートも　あたらしいですか。
B: ええ、とても　あたらしいです。／
いいえ、あまり　あたらしくありません。

IV. Describing people, things, and their locations using 〜に　〜が　あります／います

The phrase 〜に　〜が　あります／います *means there is a person/object in a certain location*. It uses the same verbs and location particle に as 〜は　〜に　あります／います, but their usage is different. Whereas 〜は　〜に　あります/います is used to ask for or tell the location of something or someone, 〜に　〜が　あります／います is used to describe a scene in which someone or something exists in a given location or to ask what is in that location.

あ、ここに	ねこが	います。	*Oh, there is a cat right here.*
ほら、あそこに	すずきさんが	います。	*Look! There's Mr. Suzuki, over there.*
大学(だいがく)に	ほんやが	あります。	*There is a bookstore in the university.*
えきに	ゆうびんきょくが	あります。	*There is a post office in the station.*

ブラウン：そこに　ほんが　ありますか。
Is there a book there (near you)?

おがわ：ええ、ありますよ。ブラウンさんの　ほんですか。
Yes, there is. It that yours?

ブラウン：ええ、そうです。ありがとう。
Yes, it is. Thank you.

たなか：このへんに　なにが　ありますか。
What is in this area?

スミス：とても　ゆうめいな　こうえんが あります。
There is a very famous park.

うえだ：すみません、このへんに　スーパーが　ありますか。
Excuse me. Is there a supermarket around here?

つうこうにん (*passerby*)：ええ、ありますよ。
Yes, there is.

うえだ：そうですか。どこに　ありますか。
I see. Where is it?

つうこうにん (*passerby*)：あそこですよ。
It is over there.

Notes

- The location may be marked by には instead of just に, if the location is the topic of a sentence.

  Example: にほんには　ふじさんが　あります。
  As for Japan, Mt. Fuji is there.

- ～に　～が　あります cannot be replaced with ～は　～です.

話(はな)してみましょう Conversation Practice

Activity 1

The box below represents a room. You are at location A. Decide where to place the objects listed in the chart and fill in blanks 2 through 8 accordingly. Then, assuming you are talking with a person at location B, complete the chart with the location number and correct location noun (ここ, そこ or あそこ). Finally, create sentences describing the location of each object, following the example.

Example: ここに　くろい　ペンが　あります。

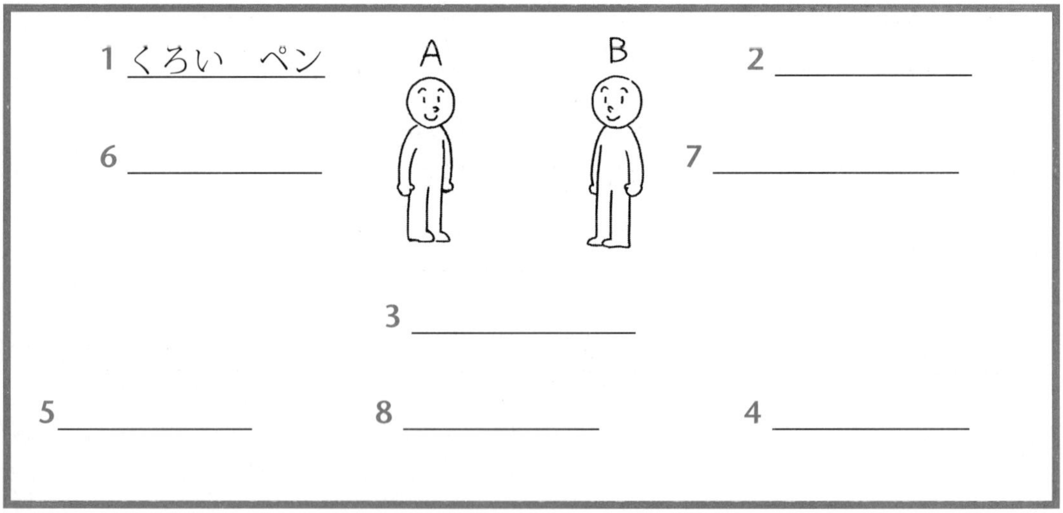

1 くろい　ペン　　A　　B　　2 ______

6 ______　　7 ______

3 ______

5 ______　　8 ______　　4 ______

Location 1–8	ここ／そこ／あそこ	Object
1	ここ	くろい　ペン
		あかい　ボールペン
		ふるい　かばん
		しろい　かばん
		きいろい　ノート
		ちゃいろい　えんぴつ
		ふるい　じしょ
		きれいな　きょうかしょ

Activity 2

Work with a partner. Ask your partner where the objects in Activity 1 are located on his/her map for the same exercise, and write in the name of the objects in the correct location below. Use the location number to specify the exact location.

Example: A: 1に　なにが　ありますか。
B: くろい　ペンが　あります。

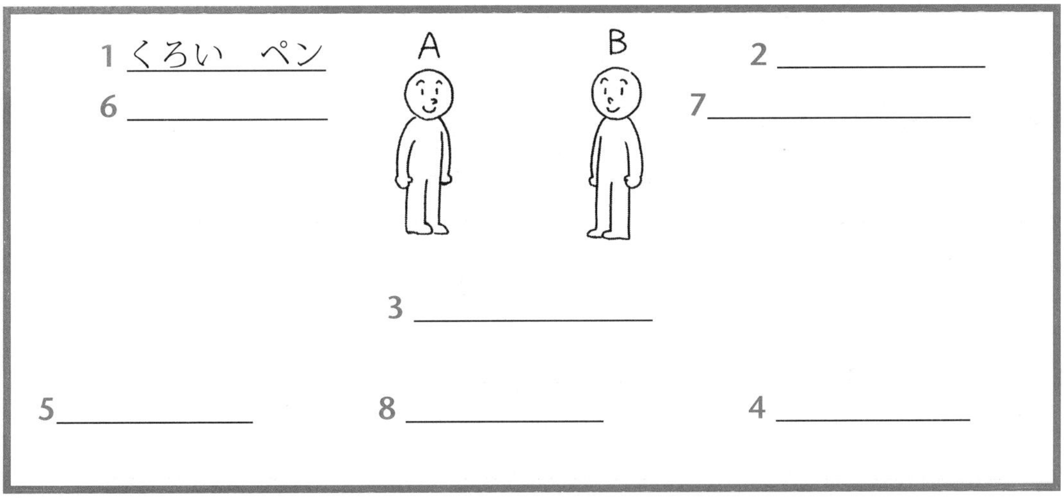

1 くろい　ペン　A　B　2 ________
6 ________　7 ________
3 ________
5 ________　8 ________　4 ________

Activity 3

Work with a new partner. Ask your partner about buildings in his/her neighborhood. Then write a description of the neighborhood using adjectives you have just learned.

Example: A: このへんに　どんな　たてものが　ありますか。

B: ぎんこうが　あります。

A: どんな　たてものですか。

B: たかい　たてものです。 でも (*but*)、あまり きれいじゃありません。

Activity 4

Work in a group of four. One person will think of a famous city or country. Try to guess the name of the city or country by asking who lives there or what landmarks are found there. Use そこ to refer to the target city or country.

Examples: A: そこに　なにが　ありますか。

B: ビッグベン (*Big Ben*) が　あります。

A: ロンドンですか。

B: はい、そうです。

V. Using ね and よ

Japanese employs a variety of sentence final particles to indicate the speaker's assumptions, intentions, and other subtle nuances. Two of the most common particles used in conversation are ね and よ.

A. The particle ね

The particle ね can be translated as 〜*isn't it?/right?/correct?* in English. It indicates that the speaker thinks the listener shares the same information, opinions, or feelings. ね is used when the speaker is seeking the listener's agreement, or confirming a fact, or to create a sense of togetherness between them. For example, in the following exchange, Li is confirming that a **kanji** quiz is scheduled for that day.

リー： きょう　かんじの　テストが　ありますね。
We have a kanji test today, right?

キム： ええ。
Yes.

In the following sentence, Li thinks that Yoyogi Park is pretty and assumes Kim thinks the same. He is seeking her agreement.

リー： 代々木公園(よよぎこうえん)は　きれいですね。
Yoyogi Park is pretty, isn't it?

キム： ええ、ほんとうに　きれいですね。
Yes, it is indeed pretty.

In the following example, John does not necessarily assume that Yamashita shares the same opinion about the park. Instead, he invites Yamashita to share his opinion by using ね. The speaker uses ね in this way to create a sense of togetherness or familiarity with the listener.

やました： こうえんは　あそこです。
The park is over there.

ジョン： ああ、りっぱな　こうえんですね。
Wow, it is a nice park, isn't it?

B. The particle よ

The particle よ can be translated as *I tell you* or *you know* in English. よ indicates the speaker's assumption that the listener does not share the speaker's opinion or information. Therefore, it is used when the speaker wishes to emphasize to the listener that he/she is imparting completely new information, and can sound authoritative. When overused or used improperly, よ sounds pushy and overly aggressive.

リー： 先生(せんせい)、あした　テストが　ありますか。
Are we going to have a test tomorrow?

先生(せんせい)： いいえ。テストは　あさってですよ。
No, it will be the day after tomorrow.

ブラウン： このへんに　ぎんこうが　ありますか。
Is there a bank around here?

つうこうにん (*passerby*)： ええ、そこに　ありますよ。
Yes, there it is.

ブラウン： あ、あかい　たてものですね。
Ah, the red building, right?

つうこうにん (*passerby*)： ええ、そうです。
Yes, it is.

話(はな)してみましょう　Conversation Practice

Activity 1

Complete the following conversations by choosing ね or よ.

Example: A: あのう、このへんに　コンビニが　ありますか。
B: ええ、　あります (ね／(よ))。あそこです。
A: あ、あれです ((ね)／よ)。どうも　ありがとう　ございます。

1. A: すみません、いま　なんじですか。
   B: 3じはんです (ね／よ)。
   A: そうですか。どうも　ありがとう。
2. A: きょう　なんじに　かえりますか。
   B: 6じごろ　かえります。
   A: 6じごろです (ね／よ)。じゃあ、6じはんに　いきます。
3. A: あの、これは　スミスさんの　じしょですか。
   B: いいえ、それは、うえださんの　じしょです (ね／よ)。
   A: あ、そうですか。どうも。
4. A: あの、先生(せんせい)、テストは　あしたです (ね／よ)。
   B: ええ、そうです。

5. A: あの、先生(せんせい)、らいしゅうの　かようびは　やすみ (*a day off*) です（ね／よ）。
   B: いいえ、かようびは　じゅぎょうが　あります。やすみは　すいようびです（ね／よ）。
6: A: すみません。ゆうびんきょくは　どこですか。
   B: あそこに　たかい　ビルが　あります（ね／よ）。
   A: ええ。
   B: ゆうびんきょくは　あそこに　あります。
   A: ああ、そうですか。どうも。
   B: いいえ。

Activity 2

Work with a partner. The following conversations sound slightly unnatural because they are missing the particle ね or よ. Revise the conversation using ね or よ where appropriate.

Example: A: あのう、すみませんが、やまだびょういんは　どこですか。
B: やまだびょういんですか。あそこです。
A: あ、あれです<u>ね</u>。どうも　ありがとう　ございます。
B: いいえ。

1. A: あのう、このへんに　びょういんが　ありますか。
   B: いいえ、ありません。びょういんは　とおい (*far away*) です。
   A: そうですか。どうも。
2. A: そこに　しろい　たてものが　あります。
   B: ええ。
   A: それは　なんですか。
   B: それは　ほんやです。
3. A: これは　なんですか。
   B: なっとうです。
   A: え、なっとう？　なっとうって　なんですか。
   B: Fermented soy beans です。
4. A: あれは　デパートですか。
   B: いいえ、スーパーです。
   A: とても　りっぱな　スーパーです。
   B: そうです。

聞く　練習
き　れんしゅう
Listening

上手な　聞き方　Listening Strategy
じょうず　き　かた

Using redundancy in speech

In Chapters 2 and 3 (see p. 65 and p. 117), you learned that it is not necessary to understand every single word in order to understand a conversation, and that it is important to pick up only a few key words. In face-to-face conversations, there are many clues to what a person is saying, such as facial expressions, gestures, and intonation. Context and general knowledge will also help you guess words you may have missed.

学生街　Campus Town
がくせいがい

聞く　前に　Warm-up
き　まえ

Listen to the following conversations. They take place on a busy street that runs near Joto University. Since there is a lot of background noise, some of the words in the conversations cannot be heard. Try to guess the missing words and write them down.

1. ____
2. ____
3. ____

聞いた　後で　Comprehension
き　あと

Based on the conversations you have just heard, complete the following sentences with the correct building names.

1. しろい　たてものは____________です。
2. ____________は　ほんやの　ちかくに　あります。
3. その　ちゃいろい　たてものは____________です。

聞き上手　話し上手
き　じょうず　はな　じょうず
Communication

Communication Strategy

Getting someone's attention (1)

In Chapter 1 (p. 18), you learned the phrase, あのう、すみません (*Excuse me*) as a way of getting someone's attention. In this chapter, you will learn more about すみません along with other phrases commonly used in this context.

In current Japanese, すみません has three separate functions: to apologize, to get someone's attention, or to thank. すみません is probably the phrase most commonly used to get someone's attention. It is often preceded by あのう (*ah . . .*) or ちょっと (*well . . .*) and followed by が (*but*), as in あのう　すみませんが, ちょっと　すみませんが, and あのう　ちょっと　すみませんが.

あのう by itself may also be used to get someone's attention. For example, if someone wants to initiate a conversation at a meeting or a party, the person can say あのう and wait for the listener to respond. あのう is also used as a conversation filler when one cannot think of the right word. If you want to ask someone a personal question, first say しつれいですが or あのう　しつれいですが (literally, *I am being rude, but . . .*). For instance, あのう　しつれいですが、にほんの　かたですか is a polite way of asking someone whether he/she is Japanese.

Finally, along with あのう or すみません，おねがいします (literally, *I am requesting*) may also be used to get the attention of someone who provides a service, such as a store clerk.

練習 Practice
れんしゅう

A. Listen to three dialogues and identify the phrase used to approach the listener in each dialogue.

B. You are looking for a certain building or facility, and your classmates are all strangers. Ask for its location politely using the appropriate expressions.

漢字 (かんじ)
Kanji

漢字 (かんじ) Introduction to kanji

In addition to **hiragana** and **katakana**, the Japanese writing system makes extensive use of **kanji**, which are characters borrowed from Chinese. When the Japanese adopted **kanji**, they also adopted the Chinese way of reading them. At the same time, the Japanese gave the Chinese characters Japanese readings for existing Japanese words. Consequently, a **kanji** character usually has two or sometimes more readings. The Chinese reading of a **kanji** is called the **on** reading, and the Japanese reading is called the **kun** reading. For example, the **on** reading for the **kanji** 大 (*big*) is だい as in 大学 (だいがく). Its **kun** reading is おお as in 大 (おお) きい. Chinese words incorporated into Japanese are usually given **on** readings, as in 大学 (だいがく), 学生 (がくせい) and 先生 (せんせい).

A **kanji** can be used only for its specific meaning. Thus, even if 五 (*five*) is read ご, one may not use it to replace the **hiragana** ご in おはようございます or あさごはん.

Kanji originated as pictographs and some of the characters still retain their pictorial qualities. For example, 川 (*river*) developed from the picture 巛, 大 (*big*) from 大 (a man extending arms and legs), and 生 (*life*) from 㞢 (picture of a plant sprouting). The exact number of existing **kanji** has never been clear, but it is estimated to be more than 40,000. Approximately 3,000 **kanji** are commonly used in Japan. The Japanese Ministry of Education has designated 2,136 for use in publications such as newspapers and magazines.

Learning **kanji** can be a laborious process. However, once a certain number of **kanji** have been learned, it becomes easier because **kanji** can be grouped on the basis of their components. In dictionaries, **kanji** are classified according to 214 basic component shapes, or radicals, each of which has a unique meaning. The following **kanji**, which share the common radical 言, all have something to do with language: 訳 (*translation*), 話 (*talk*), 語 (*language*), and 読 (*reading*).

A **kanji** is written according to a fixed stroke order. The general rule is to write from top to bottom, and left to right. Also, a horizontal line is usually drawn before a vertical one.

In Japanese, **kanji** are used mostly for nouns and the stems of verbs, adjectives, and adverbs. Grammatical markers, such as particles and inflectional endings, are not written in **kanji**. For example, in the following sentence, the nouns わたし and さかな are written with the **kanji** 私 and 魚, and the verb stem た of たべます is written with the **kanji** 食. The particles は and を as well as the verb ending べます are written in **hiragana**.

私は魚を食べます。(わたしは　さかなを　たべます。*I eat fish.*)

Note the following format for the **kanji** charts used in this book The charts will contain the typeset version of the character, a handwritten version, and stroke order. The **on** readings are in **katakana** and the **kun** readings are in **hiragana**.

学	学	to study, learn まな(ぶ)　ガク・ガッ　学校 (がっこう)　大学 (だいがく)	丶	丷	丷丶	𭕄	⺍冖	⺍冖乛	学	学		

How to write kanji: Stroke order

Stroke order is very important not only in writing but also in reading, especially when reading handwritten **kanji**. In the handwritten style, lines are often connected and some strokes are simplified. The following are the basic rules for writing **kanji**.

1. Write from left to right.
2. Write from top to bottom.
3. Write 冂 as shown.
4. When enclosing a square, write the bottom line last.

It is also important to distinguish the following three types of strokes:

stop 生

release 大

hook 学

大 大 big, large
おお(きい)　ダイ　大学生(だいがくせい)　大きいビル(おお)

学 学 to study, learn
まな(ぶ)　ガク・ガッ　学校(がっこう)　大学(だいがく)

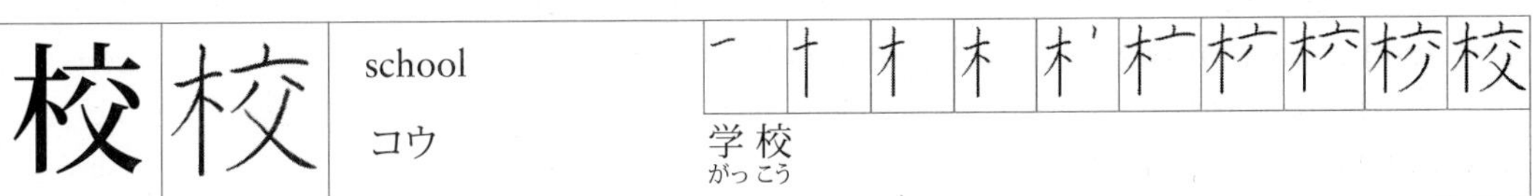

校 校 school
コウ　学校(がっこう)

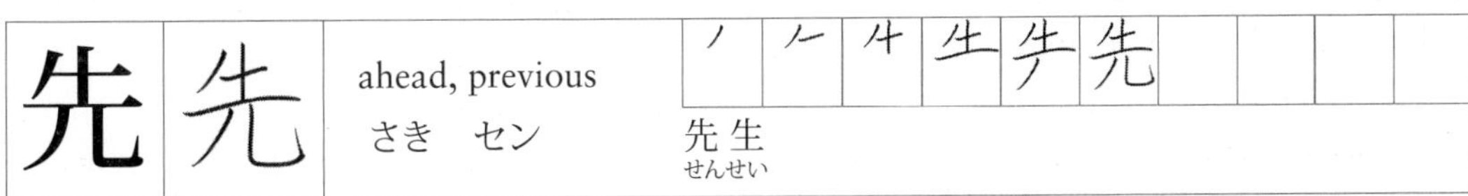

先 先 ahead, previous
さき　セン　先生(せんせい)

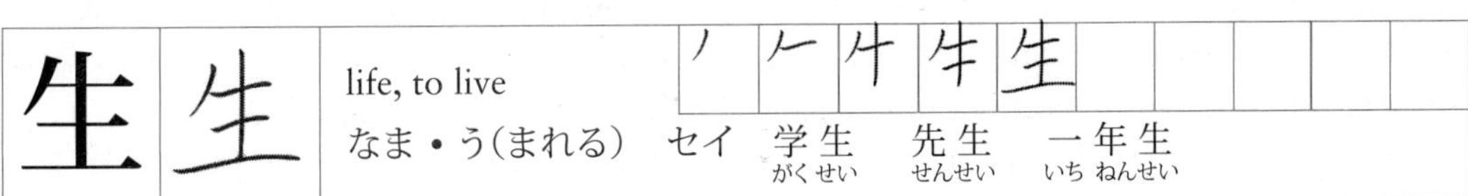

生 生 life, to live
なま・う(まれる)　セイ　学生(がくせい)　先生(せんせい)　一年生(いちねんせい)

練習(れんしゅう) Practice

Read the following sentences.

1. スミスさんはニューヨーク大学の学生です。
2. あの大きいたてものは学校です。
3. 学生：「やまだ先生、おはようございます。」
   先生：「あっ、きむらさん、おはよう。」

読む 練習
よ れんしゅう
Reading

上手な 読み方 Reading Strategy
じょうず よ かた

Using script types as clues to word boundaries

Unlike English, in Japanese, words are not separated by spaces. However, there are certain ways of identifying word and phrase boundaries. For example, **katakana** and **kanji** are almost always used for content words such as nouns, verbs, and adjectives. If a series of **katakana** appears within a sentence, it usually indicates a word or name. **Hiragana** is always used for particles like は, が, の and に and for the endings of verbs and adjectives. Other content words are written in **hiragana** as well. When several **hiragana** appear in the middle of a sentence, you should read them carefully because they may contain more than one word.

練習 Practice
れんしゅう

Read the following sentences and try to identify word boundaries using script types as a clue. In this exercise, each noun should be grouped with its particle as one word. Then insert a slash between the words. Don't worry about understanding the meaning of the sentences completely, and don't be overwhelmed at the sight of **kanji** you don't know the readings for.

私はアメリカのウエストサイド大学の三年生です。
専攻は歴史とフランス語です。でも、日本語も勉強しています。

城東（じょうとう）大学 Joto University

Scan the following reading and circle the words you don't know. Then read the passage and try to guess from context what the unknown words mean.

城東（じょうとう）大学は東京（とうきょう）にあります。学生は三万人（さんまんにん）ぐらいいますが、教授（きょうじゅ）は千人（せんにん）ぐらいです。とても古（ふる）い大学です。キャンパスはあまり大きくありませんが、きれいな建物（たてもの）がたくさんあります。公園（こうえん）もあります。それから、大学の図書館（としょかん）はとても有名（ゆうめい）です。城東（じょうとう）大学には経済学部（けいざいがくぶ）と文学部（ぶんがくぶ）と商学部（しょうがくぶ）と法学部（ほうがくぶ）があります。留（りゅう）学生センターもあります。アメリカとオーストラリアからたくさん留（りゅう）学生が来（き）ます。

読（よ）んだ 後（あと）で Comprehension

Answer these questions in Japanese.

1. 城東（じょうとう）大学は　どこに　ありますか。
2. 城東（じょうとう）大学は　あたらしい　大学ですか。
3. 城東（じょうとう）大学の　キャンパスは　どんな　キャンパスですか。
4. 城東（じょうとう）大学には　ゆうめいな　たてものが　ありますか。
5. 城東（じょうとう）大学には　どんな　学生が　たくさん　いますか。

総合練習
そうごうれんしゅう
Integration

学校しょうかい School introductions

Form groups of three or four. Have each person create one or two sentences about your school such as its location, size, things you see on campus, famous buildings, etc. Then work together to write a brief paragraph describing your school to students in Japan who are interested in studying abroad.

ロールプレイ Role Play

With a partner, act out each of the following scenarios, then switch roles.

1. You want to go to a hospital. You see a white building in the distance as you pass a police box. Ask the police officer if it is a hospital.
2. You are looking for a bank. Approach a passerby and ask if there is a bank in the neighborhood.
3. You have invited a Japanese friend to your neighborhood. Show your friend around your house.

Chapter 5

第五課(だいごか)

日本(にほん)の うち

Japanese Homes

Objectives Asking about places; stating location and distance

Vocabulary Campus facilities, objects in the room and classroom, nature, more adjectives

Dialogue リーさんの アパート Mr. Li's apartment

Japanese Culture Japanese houses

Grammar

I. Referring to people, places, and things using この, その, あの, どの

II. Using location nouns: 中(なか), そと, となり, よこ, ちかく, うしろ, まえ, 上(うえ), 下(した), みぎ, ひだり

III. Referring to things mentioned immediately before, using noun/adjective + の (pronoun)

IV. Expressing distance and duration using the particles から, まで, and で and the suffix ～ぐらい／くらい

V. More about the topic marker は and the similarity marker も (double particles and は vs. が)

Listening Distinguishing sounds in words and phrases

Communication Getting someone's attention (2)

Kanji **Kanji** derived from pictures and symbols (1)
山 川 田 人 上 中 下 小 日 本

Reading Using visual clues

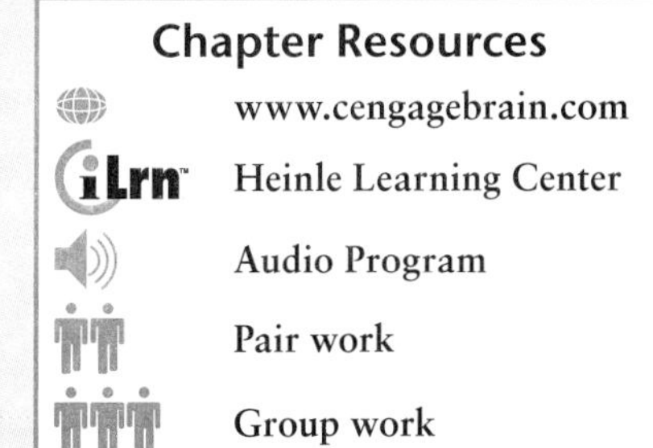

単語（たんご）
Vocabulary

Location nouns

うえ	上	on, above, over
うしろ	後ろ	behind, in back of
した	下	under, beneath
そと	外	outside
ちかく	近く	near, in the vicinity of
となり	隣	next to
なか	中	in, inside
ひだり	左	to the left, left side
まえ	前	in front of, in the front
みぎ	右	to the right
よこ	横	next to, at the side of

Nouns

いす	椅子	chair
いぬ	犬	dog
え	絵	picture
おしいれ	押し入れ	Japanese-style closet, storage space
がくしょく	学食	school cafeteria (a shortened form of 学生しょくどう)
がくせいかいかん	学生会館	student union
かわ	川	river
き	木	tree
きょうしつ	教室	classroom
くるま	車	car
けいたい（でんわ）	携帯（電話）	cell phone (cf. スマホ smart phone)
こくばん	黒板	chalkboard
コンピュータ		computer

じてんしゃ	自転車	bicycle
しゃしん	写真	photograph
ソファ		sofa
たいいくかん	体育館	gym
たんす	箪笥	chest, drawers
つくえ	机	desk
テーブル		table
でんわ	電話	telephone
ドア		door
トイレ		toilet, restroom
とけい	時計	clock, watch
ところ	所	place
ねこ	猫	cat
バス		bus
ビデオ		video
ひと	人	person
ふとん	布団	futon
ベッド		bed
へや	部屋	room
ほんだな	本棚	bookshelf
まど	窓	window
もの	物	thing (tangible)
やま	山	mountain
ルーム		room, コンピュータ・ルーム computer room, computer lab

う -verb

かかります	to take (time), it costs; the dictionary form is かかる.

Demonstrative words

あの	that [+ noun] over there
この	this [+ noun]
その	that [+ noun]
どの	which [+ noun]?

い -adjectives

あかるい	明るい	bright
くらい	暗い	dark
せまい	狭い	cramped, narrow
はやい	速い	fast, quick
ひろい	広い	spacious, wide

な -adjective

しずか (な)	静か (な)	quiet

Particles

から		from
で		by means of, by, with
まで		until, to

Suffixes

～ぐらい／くらい		about ～ (duration or quantity)
～じかん		～ hours

Conjunction

でも		but

Expressions

あがってください	上がって下さい	Please come in.
あるいて	歩いて	on foot
いらっしゃい		Welcome! Come in.
おじゃまします	お邪魔します	Thank you. (literally, *I will intrude on you.*) (said before going inside someone's house or apartment)
ごめんください	御免下さい	Excuse me, anyone home?

Question word

どのぐらい／どのくらい		how long, how much, how many

単語(たんご)の練習(れんしゅう) Vocabulary Practice

A. キャンパス College campus

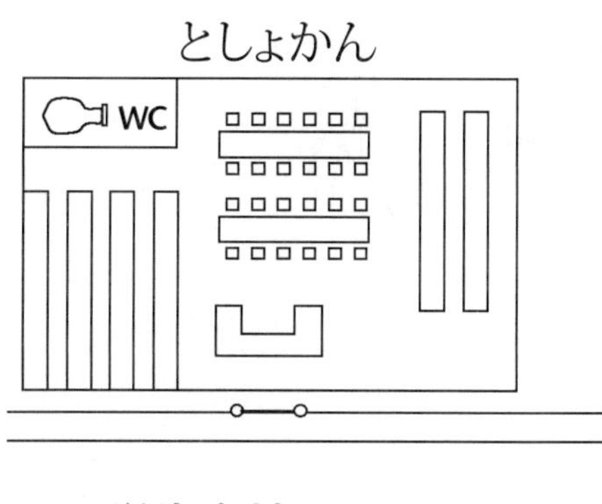

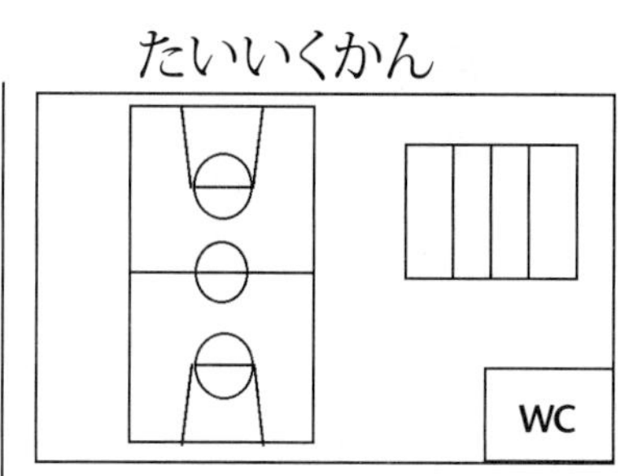

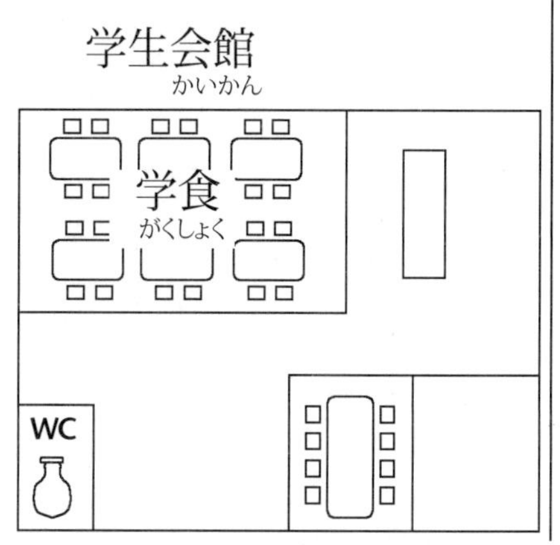

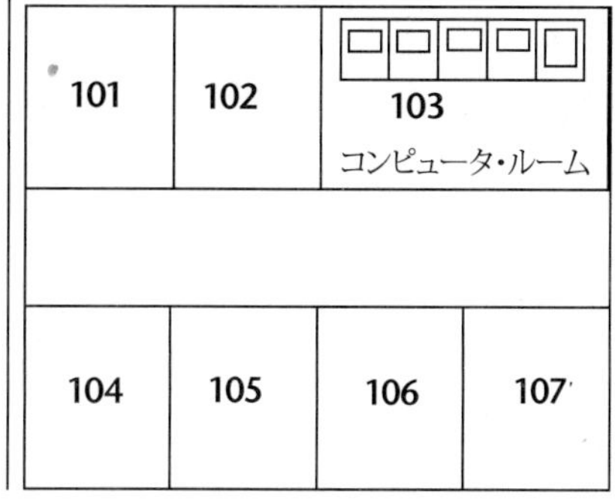

学食(がくしょく)	school cafeteria	たいいくかん	gym
学生会館(かいかん)	student union	トイレ	restroom
きょうしつ	classroom	メディアセンター	media center
コンピュータ・ルーム	computer lab		

Activity 1

しつもんに　こたえて下(くだ)さい。 Answer these questions in Japanese.

1. コンピュータ・ルームで　なにを　べんきょうしますか。
2. コンピュータ・ルームは　どこに　ありますか。
3. 学生会館(かいかん)に　どんなものが　ありますか。
4. たいいくかんは　どこに　ありますか。
5. 学生会館(かいかん)に　学食(がくしょく)が　ありますか。
6. よく　学食(がくしょく)で　べんきょうしますか。
7. 学生会館(かいかん)に　きょうしつが　ありますか。
8. トイレは　どこに　ありますか。

B. へやと きょうしつ Rooms and classrooms

ドア	door
まど	window
おしいれ	Japanese-style closet
いぬ	dog
ねこ	cat
つくえ	desk
とけい	clock, watch
え	picture
しゃしん	photograph
こくばん	chalkboard
ベッド	bed
ふとん	futon
たんす	chest, drawers
ビデオ	video
コンピュータ	computer
でんわ	telephone
けいたい(でんわ)	cell phone
いす	chair
ソファ	sofa
テーブル	table
本棚(ほんだな)	bookshelf

Activity 2

Look at the pictures on page 170 and name all the objects you see.

Example: ドアが　あります。

Activity 3

しつもんに　こたえて下(くだ)さい。Answer these questions in Japanese.

1. きょうしつに　どんな　ものが　ありますか。
2. ～さんの　へやに　どんな　ものが　ありますか。
3. としょかんに　どんな　ものが　ありますか。
4. メディアセンターに　どんな　ものが　ありますか。

C. しぜん　Nature

山(やま)　*mountain*

き　*tree*

川(かわ)　*river*

Courtesy of Kazumi and Yukiko Hatasa

Activity 4

しつもんに　こたえて下(くだ)さい。Answer these questions in Japanese.

1. このへんに　山(やま)が　ありますか。
2. このへんに　川(かわ)が　ありますか。
3. 大学の　キャンパスに　川(かわ)が　ありますか。山(やま)が　ありますか。
4. キャンパスに　大きい　きが　ありますか。どこに　ありますか。

D. のりもの Transportation

くるま
car

じてんしゃ
bicycle

バス
bus

Activity 5

In small groups, guess who owns a car or a bicycle and write the number in the YOUR GUESS column. Then ask each person in your group whether he/she has a car or a bicycle, and write the correct total in the ANSWER (こたえ) column.

Example: A: ～さんは　くるまが　ありますか。
B: ええ、あります。～さんも　くるまが　ありますか。
or いいえ、ありません。～さんは　くるまが　ありますか。
A: ええ、あります。
or いいえ、ありません。
B: そうですか。

	YOUR GUESS	ANSWER (こたえ)
くるま		
じてんしゃ		

E. Describing buildings and rooms

あかるい	bright	せまい	cramped, narrow
くらい	dark	ひろい	spacious, wide
しずか (な)	quiet		

Activity 6

Work with the entire class. Ask each other what kinds of rooms your classmates have.

Example: A: ～さんの　アパートは　どんな　アパートですか。
B: あまり　ひろくありません。でも、あかるいです。

ダイアローグ
Dialogue

はじめに　Warm-up

しつもんに　こたえて下(くだ)さい。 Answer these questions in Japanese.

1. 今(いま)　どんな　ところに　すんでいますか。(*to live*) アパートですか。りょうですか。うちですか。
2. 〜さんのへやは　どんな　へやですか。
3. 〜さんのへやに　どんな　ものが　ありますか。

リーさんの　アパート　*Mr. Li's apartment*

Ueda pays a visit to Li's apartment.

上田(うえだ)：　ごめん下(くだ)さい。

リー：　あ、上田(うえだ)さん。いらっしゃい。どうぞ　上(あ)がって下(くだ)さい。

上田(うえだ)：　おじゃまします。

上田(うえだ)：　わあ、とても　あかるいですね。

リー：　ええ。この　アパートは　たかい　ところに　ありますから。

上田(うえだ)：　あそこに　りっぱな　たてものが　ありますね。あれは大学ですか。

リー： ええ、あれは　じょうとう大学の　たいいくかんですよ。

上田（うえだ）： え、じゃあ、たいいくかんの　となりの　ちゃいろい　ビルは なんですか。

リー： あれは　としょかんです。そして、その　まえのが　学生会館（かいかん）です。

上田（うえだ）： そうですか。ここから　大学まで　どのくらい　かかりますか。

リー： バスで　にじゅっぷんぐらい　かかります。
でも、ぼくは　たいてい　じてんしゃで　いきますよ。

上田（うえだ）： そうですか。じてんしゃでは　どのくらい　かかりますか。

リー： じゅうごふんぐらいです。

上田（うえだ）： へえ、はやいですね。

Dialogue Phrase Notes

- ごめん下（くだ）さい means *Is anyone home?* It is used when you have arrived at the entrance of someone's residence and need to get his or her attention.
- いらっしゃい means *welcome.* 上（あ）がって下（くだ）さい means *please enter.* Both are common expressions to invite someone inside.
- おじゃまします means *thank you* and is used when you enter someone's house or room.
- Sentence + から means *It's because* ～.

  この　アパートは　たかい　ところに　ありますから。
  It's because this apartment is high up (on a hill).
- へえ means, *Is that so?* or *Really?* へえ indicates the speaker's mild surprise about what has just been said. はやい means *fast.* Ueda expresses her surprise about how fast Li can get to school by saying へえ、はやいですね (*Really, that fast?*).

ダイアローグの後(あと)で　Comprehension

Answer the following questions in Japanese.

1. リーさんの　アパートは　どんな　ところですか。
2. リーさんの　アパートから　大学まで　じてんしゃで　どのくらい　かかりますか。
3. たいいくかんは　どんな　たてものですか。
4. としょかんは　どこに　ありますか。

日本(にほん)の文化(ぶんか)
Japanese Culture

Japanese houses

Traditional Japanese houses are found in many parts of Japan, especially in rural areas. They are made of wood, and rooms are separated by sliding doors, ふすま, or by paper screens, しょうじ. Flooring consists of straw mats called たたみ. The room may have an area (とこのま) where flower arrangements, wall scrolls, or other decorations are placed. A traditional Japanese room also contains a large closet, called おしいれ, to store ふとん (*Japanese bedding*). ふとん are spread on たたみ mats at bedtime, then folded and put away in the morning so that the room can be used for other purposes. The futon sofa is an American invention.

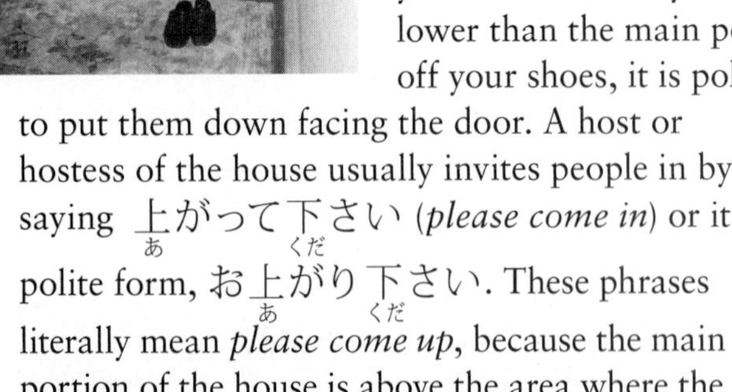

Although modern Western-style houses are popular nowadays, some elements of traditional houses have been incorporated into these as well. For example, a contemporary house often contains a traditional Japanese-style room.

Both traditional and contemporary houses have a mudroom, or げんかん , inside the entrance, where you must take off your shoes. Typically, this area is lower than the main portion of the house. After taking off your shoes, it is polite to put them down facing the door. A host or hostess of the house usually invites people in by saying 上(あ)がって下(くだ)さい (*please come in*) or its polite form, お上(あ)がり下(くだ)さい. These phrases literally mean *please come up*, because the main portion of the house is above the area where the shoes are left.

Most contemporary rooms have wood floors. Carpet is not a popular choice because the high level of humidity in summer poses a potential hazard for bacteria and germs. The door to a room, whether Japanese or Western style, is almost always closed. A closed door doesn't necessarily mean *don't disturb*, so knock to find out if anyone is in the room. Still, don't be surprised if a Japanese person comes into your room without knocking. This happens often among family members.

Japanese bathrooms

Courtesy of Kazumi and Yukiko Hatasa

Most Japanese people prefer to take a bath every night, instead of taking a shower in the morning. The Japanese bathroom, or おふろ, is a room only for bathing. The toilet is in a separate room. The bathroom has a tiled area for washing and rinsing prior to entering the tub. The water is usually very hot (about 110°F/41–42°C). Cold water may be added from the faucet if it is too hot, but overdoing it means that the water won't be warm for the rest of the family, who will use the same hot water. When finished, instead of draining the tub, the cover is replaced to retain the heat. Although Japanese-style toilets are still used in Japan, western-style toilets are now more common in private homes, and often come equipped with a cleansing device called a Washlet® (ウォシュレット). These operate similarly to bidets, but offer a range of high-tech features. Most models have seat-warming controls, and some even have sensors to raise and lower the toilet lid automatically.

A pair of slippers is usually placed inside the restroom. Be careful not to walk out with these slippers on! The door to a restroom, public or private, should be kept closed at all times. Always knock on the door to see if the room is occupied, and do not forget to close the door afterward.

Public restrooms are often marked W.C. (water closet) or with the Japanese term お手(て)洗(あら)い / 御(お)手(て)洗(あら)い (literally, *handwashing*). The sign for the men's room is usually indicated by a male icon or the character for man (男(おとこ)). A female icon or the character for woman (女(おんな)) indicates the women's room. In some women's restrooms, an electronic device called 音姫(おとひめ) ® conveniently provides the white noise of running water or air. While it's sometimes necessary to press a button, most 音姫(おとひめ) ® are sensor-activated.

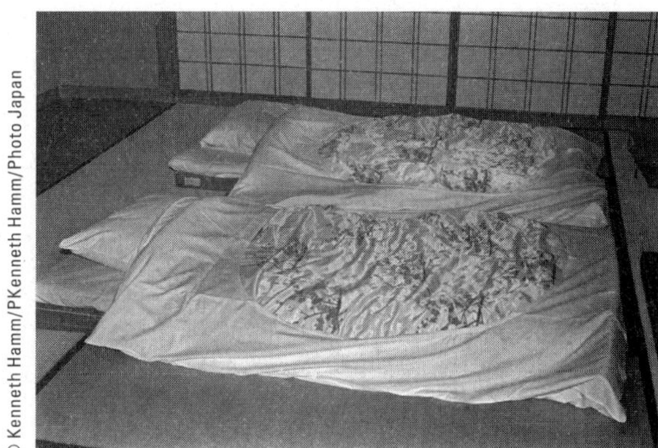

© Kenneth Hamm/PKenneth Hamm/Photo Japan

文法
ぶんぽう
Grammar

I. Referring to people, places, and things using この, その, あの, どの

The words この, その, あの, どの constitute another series of demonstrative words that indicate the location of an object in relation to the speaker and listener, but they are adjectives that must modify nouns and cannot be used by themselves. In contrast, これ, それ, あれ, どれ and ここ, そこ, あそこ, どこ are nouns that must be used alone.

この + **Noun**	this [Noun] (close to the speaker)
その + **Noun**	that [Noun] (away from the speaker and close to the listener, or somewhat away from both the speaker or the listener.)
あの + **Noun**	that [Noun] over there (far away from both the speaker and the listener.)

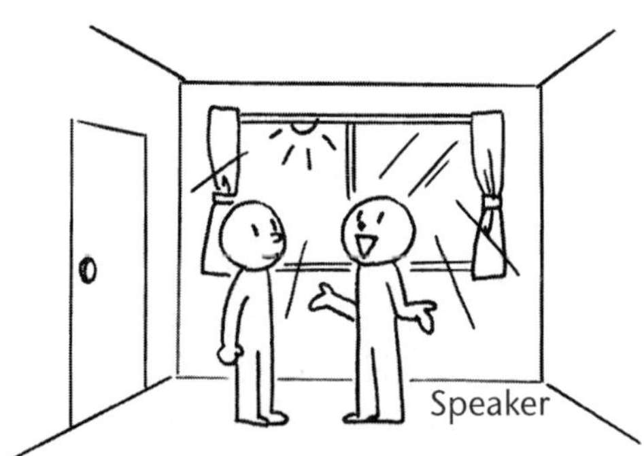

	Noun		
この	へや	は	あかるいですね。

This room is bright, isn't it?

	Noun		
その	人（ひと）	は	田中（たなか）さんですか。

Is that person Mr./Ms. Tanaka?

	Demonstrative Adjective	Noun	
すずきさんの　うちは	どの	たてもの	ですか。

Which building is your house, Ms. Suzuki?

	Noun	
あの	うち	です。

It's that house over there.

山中(やまなか)：本田(ほんだ)さんの　うちは　どの　うちですか。
Which house is your house, Mr. Honda?

本田(ほんだ)：それです。
It's that one.

山中(やまなか)：りっぱな　うちですね。
Oh, it's splendid, isn't it!

本田(ほんだ)：いいえ。
Not at all.

Notes

- これ, それ, あれ, どれ are not used to refer to people unless you are discussing people in a photo or drawing, but この, その, あの, どの can be used to refer to people without being impolite, such as この人(ひと), その人(ひと), あの人(ひと), どの人(ひと).
- A more polite way to refer to people is to say このかた, そのかた, あのかた, どのかた instead of この人(ひと), その人(ひと), あの人(ひと), どの人(ひと). Use かた to refer to someone you don't know well, whom you want to treat politely.
- その can be used to refer to something previously mentioned.

  山中(やまなか)：上田(うえだ)さんは　ウエストサイド大学の　学生です。
  Ms. Ueda is a student at Westside University.

  チョイ：<u>その</u>　人(ひと)は　日本人(にほんじん)ですか。
  Is she (literally, *that person) Japanese?*

話(はな)してみましょう Conversation Practice

Activity 1

Look at the drawing of the bedroom. Imagine that 上田(うえだ)さん is standing on the left side of the room (A), and you are at location B. You are making comments about the room to 上田(うえだ)さん. Change the following sentences into your comments addressed to 上田(うえだ)さん, using この, その, あの, どの.

Example: いい　ベッドですね → その　ベッドは　いいですね。

1. ひろい　へやですね。
2. 大きい　きですね。
3. あたらしい　つくえですね。
4. りっぱな　テレビですね。
5. ふるい　とけいですね。
6. 大きい　いぬですね。

Activity 2

Work with a partner. Look at the drawing of the living room. You are sitting on the sofa (location A) and your partner is at location B. Your partner will name some items. Create statements about each item using この, その, あの.

Example: Your partner: ソファ

You: <u>この</u> ソファは きれいですね。

II. Using location nouns: 中(なか), そと, となり, よこ, ちかく, うしろ, まえ, 上(うえ), 下(した), みぎ, ひだり

Location nouns such as まえ (*front*) and うしろ (*back*) are used to describe the location of an object relative to another object, such as *X is in front of* Y and *Z is behind* Y.

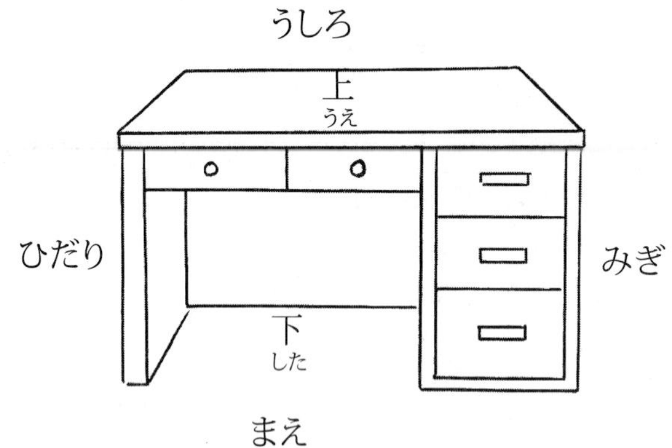

ちかく

つくえの	まえ	in front of	the desk
つくえの	うしろ	behind	the desk
つくえの	上(うえ)	on/above	the desk
つくえの	下(した)	below/under	the desk
つくえの	みぎ	to the right of	the desk
つくえの	ひだり	to the left of	the desk
つくえの	ちかく	close to	the desk

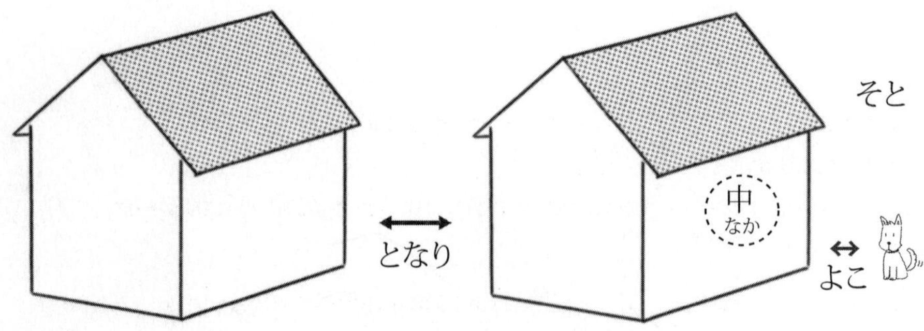

うちの	中(なか)	inside	the house
うちの	そと	outside	the house
うちの	となり	next to	the house
うちの	よこ	next to/adjacent to	the house

Both となり and よこ mean *next to*. Use となり if two things next to each other are of the same type, such as two houses or two desks. Use よこ if two things belong to different categories such as a dog next to a house.

わたしは　こくばんの　まえに／へ　いきました。
I went to the chalkboard. (literally, *I went to the front of the chalkboard*)

ドアの　まえまで　きました。
I came to the door. (literally, *I came as far as the front of the door*)

チョイ：どこで　ひるごはんを　たべますか。
Where do you eat lunch?

高田(たかだ)：わたしは　よく　その　きの　下(した)で　たべます。
I usually eat it under that tree.

ブラウン：山田(やまだ)さんは　どこですか。
Where is Mr. Yamada?

大川(おおかわ)：たいいくかんの　ちかくで　みましたよ。
I saw him near the gym.

中山(なかやま)：そこに　いぬが　いますか。
Is there a dog there?

ジョンソン：ええ、つくえの　下(した)に　いますよ。
Yes, it is under the desk.

アリソン：学食(がくしょく)は　どこですか。
Where is the school cafeteria?

山本(やまもと)：学生会館(かいかん)の　中(なか)です。
It's inside the student union.

Notes

- Expression with location nouns can be used with any place particle, such as に, へ, で.
- Location nouns can be used with the Noun の Noun construction. For example:

うちの　うしろの　山(やま)	*the mountain behind my house*
うちの　まえの　川(かわ)	*the river in front of my house*
となりの　うち	*the house next door*
となりの　人(ひと)	*a person next to me, my next-door neighbor*
上(うえ)の　アパート	*the apartment above my floor*

話(はな)してみましょう Conversation Practice

Activity 1

Look at the drawing of a classroom. Answer the following questions, using location nouns and ～は ～に ありります／います.

Example: こくばんは どこに ありますか。／こくばんは どこですか。
先生の うしろに あります。／先生の うしろです。

1. コンピュータは どこに ありますか。
2. いぬは どこに いますか。
3. 先生の かばんは どこに ありますか。
4. ノートは どこに ありますか。
5. まどは どこに ありますか。
6. テレビは どこに ありますか。
7. えんぴつは どこに ありますか。
8. けしゴムは どこに ありますか。
9. けいたい（でんわ）は どこに ありますか。

Activity 2

Look at the drawing of the room. Some objects are missing and their locations are indicated with numbers. Ask your partner what is in each location, then write in the names of the objects in the appropriate locations. Your partner will answer the questions using the drawing on page 180.

Example: A: つくえの　上(うえ)に　なにが　ありますか。
B: かばんが　あります。

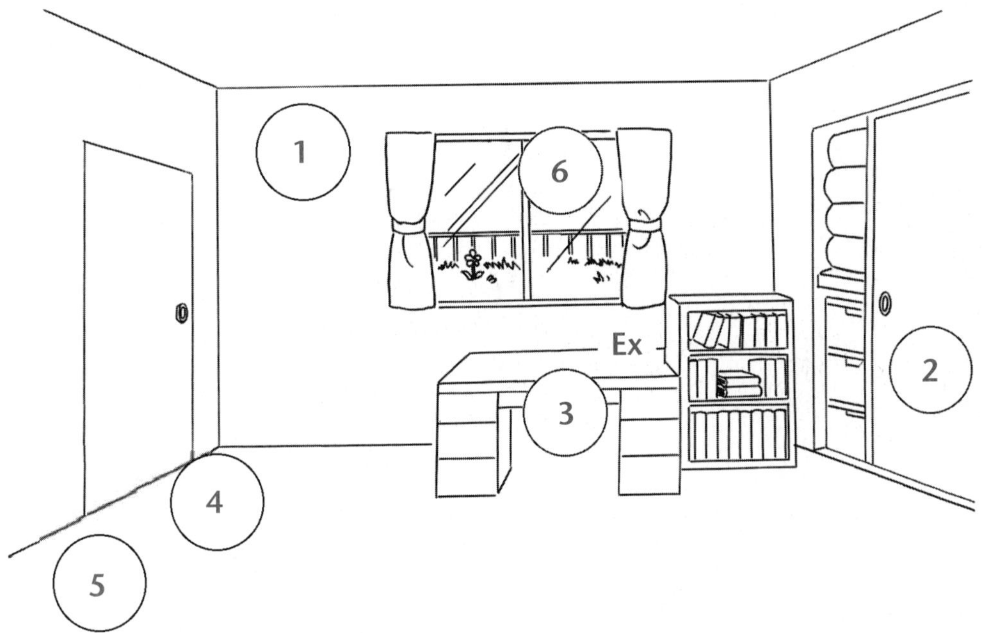

Activity 3

Work with a partner. Have your partner draw the following objects in the picture. As you ask your partner about their locations, write the items in your own copy of the house. When you are done, check your drawing with your partner's.

Example: A: 山(やま)は　どこに　ありますか。／山(やま)は　どこですか。
B: うちの　うしろに　あります。

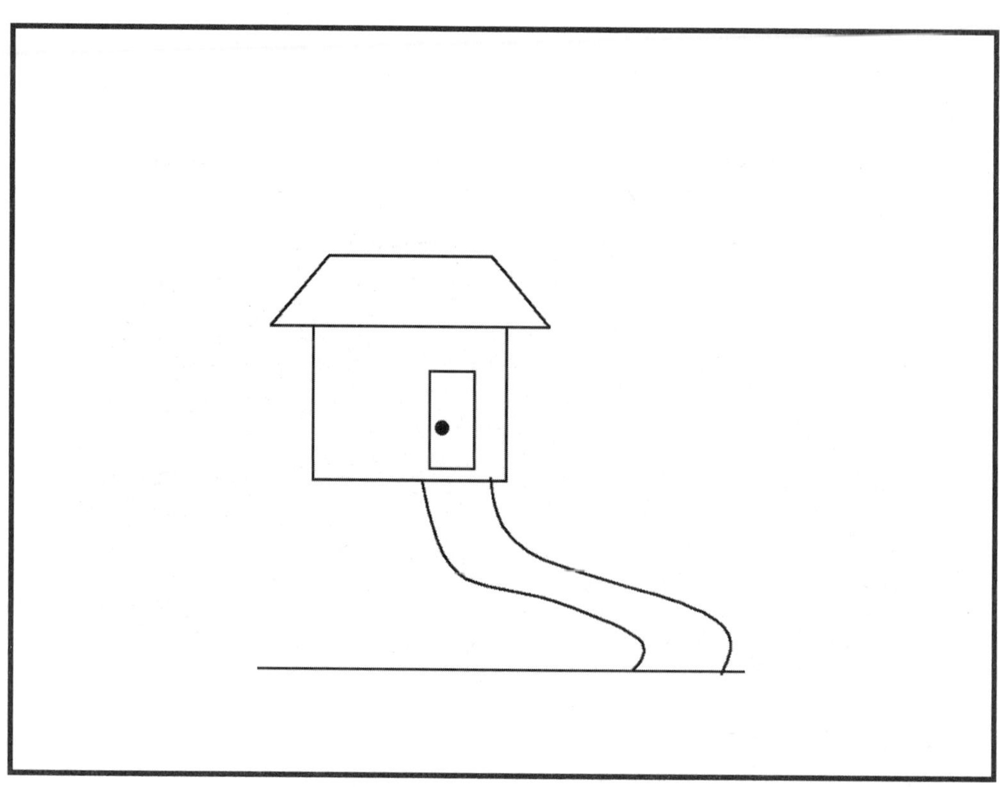

1. まど
2. ドア
3. 山(やま)
4. 川(かわ)
5. き
6. くるま
7. いぬ
8. ねこ
9. じてんしゃ

Activity 4

Look at the drawing of the campus. Your partner will ask you where the following buildings are. Answer his/her questions based on the picture.

Example: A: あのう、すみません。本やは　どこですか。

B: その　大きい　たてものの　うしろに　あります。

A: そうですか。どうも　ありがとう　ございます。

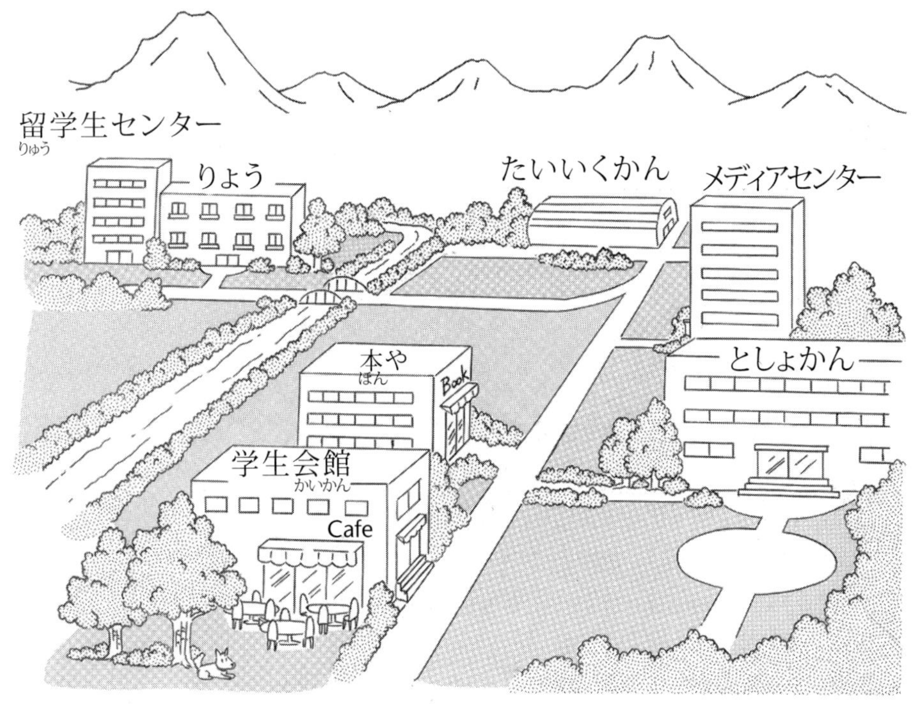

1. 留(りゅう)学生センター
2. たいいくかん
3. コンピュータ・ルーム
4. 学食(がくしょく)
5. としょかん

Activity 5

Ask a partner about the location of various buildings on your campus. Take notes, then check your partner's answers against a campus map.

Example: A: あのう、すみません。

コンピュータ・ルームは　どこに　ありますか。／
コンピュータ・ルームは　どこですか。

B: この　ビルの　中(なか)に　あります。／この　ビルの　中(なか)です。

A: あ、そうですか。どうも　ありがとう　ございます。

III. Referring to things mentioned immediately before, using noun/adjective + の (pronoun)

The pronoun の means *one* or *ones* in English, as in “red one” and “big one.” の usually refers for things and is rarely used for people. It must be directly preceded by an adjective or a noun.

い -adjective +	の	ちゃいろいの	*brown one*
な -adjective +	の	きれいなの	*pretty one*
Noun +	の	スミスさんの	*Mr. Smith’s*

イアン： この　りっぱな　かばんは　だれのですか。
Whose is this nice bag?

中本(なかもと)： その　大きいのですか。
That big one?

それは　田中(たなか)さんの　かばんですよ。
It’s Mr. Tanaka’s.

石川(いしかわ)： この　あかい　ソファは　きれいですね。
This red sofa is pretty.

中田(なかだ)： ええ、でも、あの　くろいのも　いいですよ。
Yes, but that black one over there is nice, too.

石川(いしかわ)： あの　大きいのですか。
Do you mean, that big one over there?

中田(なかだ)： ええ。
Yes.

石川(いしかわ)： ああ、あれも　いいですね。
Oh, that one is nice, too.

Note that the pronoun の cannot be used with the particle の or with この, その, あの or どの.

話してみましょう Conversation Practice

(話: はな)

Activity 1

Work with a partner. The following table shows items that four students own. Ask each other about who owns what, using の.

Example: A: あかい　けいたいは　だれのですか。
B: チンさんのです。
A: じゃあ、あおいのは？
B: あおいのは　キムさんの　けいたいです。

	山田さん (やまだ)	チンさん	ホセさん	キムさん
けいたい (でんわ)	brown	red	black	blue
じてんしゃ	nice	pretty	new	old
へや	spacious	cramped	bright	dark

Activity 2

Work with a partner. Using the same chart as Activity 1, comment on an item from the chart, then talk about your and your partner's belongings. Note that も is a similarity marker.

Example: A: 山田(やまだ)さんの　じてんしゃは　りっぱですね。
B: いいですね。わたしのは　あまりきれいじゃありません。
A: そうですか。わたしのも　ふるいですよ。

IV. Expressing distance and duration using the particles から, まで and で and the suffix ～ぐらい／くらい

The particles から (*from*) and まで (*until, to*) express starting and end points in time and space. The particle で specifies a tool or means such as transportation, craft tools, and kitchen utensils. The suffix ぐらい／くらい (*about, approximately*) indicates approximate distance, duration of time, or amount. These expressions are often used to talk about how long someone does something or how long it takes to get from one place to another. Note that くらい and ぐらい are interchangeable.

A. ～から (*from*),　～まで (*until, to*)

アパートから　学生会館(かいかん)まで　いきました。　*I went from the apartment to the student union.*

ここから　あの川(かわ)まで　１０ぷん　かかります。　*It will take ten minutes from here to that river.*

月曜日(げつようび)から　金曜日(きんようび)まで　じゅぎょうが　あります。　*I have a class from Monday through Friday.*

５じから　６じまで　やすみです。　*I have a break from 5 o'clock to 6 o'clock.*

B. で (*by means of, by, with*)

なんで　きましたか。　*How* (literally, *by what means*) *did you come?*

バスで　かえります。　*I go home by bus.*

テレビで　みました。　*I saw it on TV.*

えんぴつで　かきます。　*I write with a pencil.*

Note that the particle で cannot be used to express *on foot*. Use あるいて instead.

あるいて　いきます。　*I go on foot. / I walk.*

C. ～ぐらい／くらい (*about, approximately*)

８じかんぐらい／くらい　ねました。　*I slept about eight hours.*

どのぐらい／くらい　かかりますか。　*How long does it take?*

３０ぷんぐらい／くらい　かかります。　*It will take about 30 minutes.*

山本(やまもと)：　ここから　小川(おがわ)さんの　うちまで　どのぐらい　かかりますか。
How long does it take from here to your house, Mr. Ogawa?

小川(おがわ)：　じてんしゃで　５ふんぐらい　かかります。
It's about five minutes by bicycle.

山本(やまもと)：　そうですか。はやいですね。
I see. That's fast.

NOTES

- 〜じ as in いちじ, にじ means *o'clock*. To indicate duration, use 〜じかん.

  いちじかん (*for one hour*) にじかん (*for two hours*) にじかんはん (*for two and a half hours*)
- 〜ふん can be used to indicate both a specific time, as in いちじじゅっぷん (*1:10*), and duration, as in じゅっぷん (*for ten minutes*).
- Omit ぐらい／くらい if you want to talk about a precise duration of time:

  大学から　えきまで　バスで　２３ぷん　かかります。
  It takes 23 minutes by bus from the university to the station.

  たいいくかんまで　あるいて　５ふん　かかります。
  It takes five minutes to get to the gym on foot.

話(はな)してみましょう　Conversation Practice

Activity 1

State how long it takes to get to each destination in the chart below. Follow the model.

Example: うち　学校　じてんしゃ　about 5 minutes
うちから　学校まで　じてんしゃで　ごふんぐらい／くらい
かかります。

Starting point	Destination	Transportation	Time
うち	学校	じてんしゃ	5 minutes
ここ	としょかん	あるいて	about 10 minutes
としょかん	びょういん	くるま	15 minutes
ボストン	ニューヨーク	バス	4.5 hours
ボストン	ニューヨーク	くるま	about 4 hours

Activity 2

Working with a partner, ask how long it takes to get from location A to B and fill out the information.

Example: A: うちから　学校まで　あるいて　どのぐらい／くらい かかりますか。

B: 20 ぷんぐらい／くらい　かかります。

A: そうですか。

Location A	Location B	あるいて	じてんしゃ	バス	くるま
うち	学校				
としょかん	たいいくかん				
うち	びょういん				
このまち	となりのまち				

Activity 3

Ask your partner what he/she is planning to do after class today. Use 〜から〜まで as well as the time expressions and daily routine vocabulary that you have learned in earlier chapters.

Example: A: 今日(きょう)は　これから　なにを　しますか。

B: そうですね。３じから　４じまで　じゅぎょうが あります。そして (*and*)、５じごろ　かえります。

A: そうですか。

B: 〜さんは？

A: わたしは　うちに　かえります。

そして、ばんごはんまで　べんきょうします。

V. More about the topic marker は and the similarity marker も (double particles and は vs. が)

As explained in the supplementary note in Chapter 2, the particle は specifies the topic of a sentence. Because it is the part of a sentence about which the speaker wishes to make some statement, it usually appears at the beginning of the sentence. The particle は can be used to mark any type of noun as the topic of a sentence, including the subject or direct object, a location, or a time expression.

This section introduces more uses of は in relation to particles that have some related characteristics, such as the similarity marker も and the subject marker が.

A. Double particles with the topic marker は and the similarity marker も

Both は and も may replace を (direct object) or が (subject) but they must follow after other particles.

Subject	わたしは　学生です。 上田(うえだ)さんも　学生です。	I am a student. Ms. Ueda is a student, too.
Direct Object	コーヒーは　あさ　のみます。 ジュースも　あさ　のみます。	I drink coffee in the morning. I drink juice in the morning too.
Place of action で	としょかんでは　べんきょうしました。 ラボでも　べんきょうしました。	I studied in the library. I studied in the lab, too.
Place of existence に	いすの　下(した)には　ねこが　います。 いすの　上(うえ)にも　います。	There is a cat under the chair. There is one on the chair, too.
Starting point から	先生からは　でんわが　ありました。 ともだちからも　でんわが　ありました。	I got a phone call from the teacher. I got one from my friend, too.

Occasionally, some particles such as に (point in time) and に／へ (goal) may be deleted if they are easily understood from the context. For example, the time particle に is often deleted when the noun indicates a day of the week.

Time に	火曜日(かようび)（に）は　クラスが　あります。 木曜日(もくようび)（に）も　あります。	I have a class on Tuesday. I have one on Thursday, too.
Goal に／へ	びょういん（に／へ）は　明日(あした)　いきます。 ぎんこう（に／へ）も　いきます。	I will go to the hospital tomorrow. I will go to the bank, too.

ペギー： しゅうまつは　なにを　しましたか。
What did you do on the weekend?

下田(しもだ)： 山(やま)に／へ　いきました。
I went to the mountains.

ペギー： いいですね。山(やま)（に／へ）は　よく　いきますか。
That's nice. Do you go to the mountains often?

下田(しもだ)： ええ、らいしゅうの　土曜日(どようび)（に）も　いきます。
Yes, I am going there next Saturday, too.

アリソン： 大学までは　あるいて　どのぐらい　かかりますか。
How long does it take to get to school on foot?

川中(かわなか)： 1じかんぐらい　かかります。
It takes about an hour.

アリソン： え、そうなんですか。毎日(まいにち)　あるいて　きますか。
Is that so? Do you walk to school every day?

川中(かわなか)： いいえ、バスで　きます。
No, I come to school by bus.

Note: Relative time expressions such as 今日(きょう) and 明日(あした) do not take a particle. は and も follow the noun directly.

今日(きょう)は　びょういんに　いきます。　明日(あした)も　いきます。
I will go to the hospital today. I will go tomorrow as well.

B. は vs. が

The particle は cannot be used together with a question word, because は specifies the topic of a sentence, which is information already known to the speaker. On the other hand, it is possible to use は when there is a question word in the comment (the part of the sentence that follows the topic).

学生会館(かいかん)は　どこですか	*Where is the student union?*
山田(やまだ)さんは　どの人(ひと)ですか。	*Which person is Mr. Yamada?*
たいいくかんは　どこに　ありますか。	*Where is the gym?*
チョイさんは　どこへ　いきましたか。	*Where did Ms. Choi go?*

The particle が marks the grammatical subject of a sentence. Always use が when the subject is, or contains, a question word.

どの人(ひと)が	先生ですか。	*Which person is the teacher?*
そこに　なにが	ありますか。	*What is there?*
だれが	いきますか。	*Who will go?*

Also use が when information about a subject is important or situationally new to the listener and/or the speaker. This use of が generally occurs when the speaker introduces a situation or scene he/she has just noticed.

あ、あそこに　ねこが　いますよ。　*Look, there is a cat over there!*

あ、中本(なかもと)さんが　きました。　*Ah, Ms. Nakamoto has just arrived.*

Once a subject noun has been mentioned, は is often used when referring to the same subject in subsequent sentences. For example:

本田(ほんだ)：あそこに　いぬが　いますね。
There is a dog over there.

小川(おがわ)：ええ、あれは　わたしの　いぬです。
Yes, that's my dog.

Note: それ can also be used to refer to something mentioned previously. In this usage, それ means *it* in English. その～ and そこ can be used in the same way.

あそこに　かばんが　あります。
There is a bag over there.

それ／そのかばんは　田中(たなか)さんのです。
It is Mr./Ms. Tanaka's.

学生会館(かいかん)に　学食(がくしょく)が　あります。
There is a cafeteria in the student union.

そこは　とても　ひろいです。
It (that place) is very spacious.

話(はな)してみましょう Conversation Practice

Activity 1

First circle the question words, then complete the following sentences with が or は.

Example: (だれ) が 学生ですか。

1. リーさん________どの　人(ひと)ですか。
2. どれ________びょういんですか。
3. どの　コンピュータ________あたらしいですか。
4. 学食(がくしょく)________どこですか。
5. アリスさん________どんな　人(ひと)ですか。
6. だれ________いますか。
7. デパート________どこに　ありますか。
8. すずきさん________どちらから　きましたか。
9. あの　きれいな　たてもの________なんですか。

Activity 2

Create two sentences based on each sentence below. One should express a similarity with the first sentence; the other should contrast with the first sentence.

Example: あさごはんを　たべます。
ばんごはんも　たべます。でも、ひるごはんは　たべません。

1. バスは　じゅうじに　きました。
2. 留学生(りゅうがくせい)は　日本(にほん)から　きます。
3. バスで　大学に　いきます。
4. 昨日(きのう)　おふろに　はいりました。
5. 昨日(きのう)の　ばん　シャワーを　あびました。

Activity 3

Work with a partner. Ask your partner a question using the words supplied in column A. Your partner will answer the question using the words in column B to create a topic from the subject of the question (underlined in the example).

Example:

A	B
いつ／コーヒーを　のみます。	あさ

A: いつ　コーヒーを　のみますか。

B: コーヒーですか。コーヒーは　あさ　のみますね。

	A	B
1.	どこ／えいがを　みました。	学生会館（かいかん）
2.	なに／びょういんに　いきました。	くるま
3.	いつ／その　えいがを　みました。	昨日（きのう）
4.	どこ／いきました。	きっさてん
5.	なに／えきから　いきました。	バス
6.	だれ／きょうしつに　いました。	先生
7.	いつ／しゅくだいを　します。	しゅうまつ
8.	どんな　くるま／きました。	小（ちい）さい　くるま

Activity 4

Work with a partner. Choose two cities with which you're both familiar and write their names in the following chart. First discuss, then list, the aspects they share in common. Think of as many things as you can.

Example: とうきょう, シカゴ

A: とうきょうには　いい　レストランが　ありますよ。

B: そうですか。シカゴにも　たくさん　ありますよ。

A: そうですか。きれいな　カフェも　ありますか。

B: ええ、たくさん　ありますよ。

Similarity	City 1:__________	City 2:__________

Interrogative Expressions

You have learned a lot of question words. Here is a summary of Japanese interrogative expressions.

だれ	who	だれの　へやですか。 *Whose room is it?*
なに／なん	what	あさ　なにを　のみますか。 *What do you drink in the morning?*
		何年(なんねん)生ですか。 *What year are you in school?*
		いま　なんじですか。 *What time is it now?*
いつ	when	山田(やまだ)さんは　いつ　きますか。 *When will Mr. Yamada come?*
どこ	where	山田(やまだ)さんは　どこに　いますか。 *Where is Mr. Yamada?*
どの + noun	which	山田(やまだ)さんは　どの　人(ひと)ですか。 *Which person is Mr. Yamada?*
		山田(やまだ)さんの　りょうは　どの　たてものですか。 *Which building is Mr. Yamada's dormitory?*
どれ	which one	山田(やまだ)さんの　りょうは　どれですか。 *Which one is Mr. Yamada's dormitory?*
どんな + noun	what kind of	山田(やまだ)さんの　へやは　どんな　へやですか。 *What is your room like, Mr. Yamada?*

聞く 練習
き れんしゅう
Listening

上手な聞き方 Listening Strategy
じょうず き かた

Distinguishing sounds in words and phrases

Listening to conversations in Japanese can feel like reading long sentences without **kanji** or other clues to distinguish word boundaries. It takes practice to be able to distinguish words and phrases out of a succession of sounds. Listening for repeated words, familiar words, intonation, and pauses can help you to identify word boundaries. If you are listening to an announcement, anticipate what to expect and try to listen for important information.

ひっこしを てつだう **(Helping a friend move into a new apartment)**

Useful Expressions

おきます	to place
おいて下さい (くだ)	please place/put

聞く前に Warm-up
き まえ

When you're moving into a new place, what kinds of words do you expect to use? Circle the terms you are most likely to use.

き　　まえ　　ベッド　　山（やま）　　バス　　よこ　　テレビ

たいいくかん　　ぎんこう　　いす　　みぎ　　ひだり　　ちかく

Now listen to the conversation and write down words you hear repeatedly.

1. ______________________
2. ______________________
3. ______________________
4. ______________________
5. ______________________
6. ______________________

聞(き)いた後(あと)で　Comprehension

Listen to the conversation again. Then verify the layout of the apartment. Are all the objects in the room properly described?

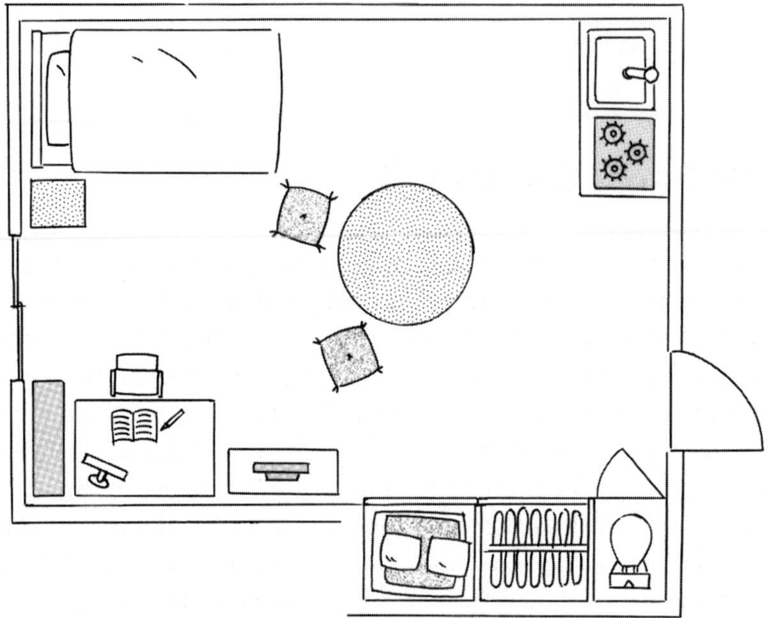

Describe each object in the room as thoroughly as you can, using different location nouns.

Now describe the place where you live in a few sentences.

聞き上手　話し上手

き　じょうず　はな　じょうず

Communication

Communication Strategy

Getting someone's attention (2)

Talking to someone in a language you are still learning can be a strain, especially if the person is a stranger. This is certainly true in Japan as well, where people tend to be less open with strangers. One explanation for this is that Japan was isolated from the Western world for over 250 years under the government's seclusion policy, from the seventeenth to the mid-nineteenth century. During that period Japan remained a relatively homogeneous nation. Moreover, under the feudal order, a strong sense of hierarchy was developed. The sense of hierarchy and distinction between in-group and out-group remains strong in modern Japan. In-group refers to one's family, people at one's place of work, classmates, etc. The Japanese are very aware of the difference in intimacy that should be maintained between those in the in-group and out-group, and act accordingly. Any non-Japanese by definition belongs to the out-group, and thus, along with the fear of not being able to communicate, a Japanese person might deliberately avoid contact with non-Japanese, even at the risk of appearing distant. This of course is a generalization, and there is a great deal of variation in individual behavior. It is important, however, to understand this background, and to use the appropriate phrases in approaching a stranger or someone you don't know well. The following is a summary of some useful expressions and other strategies you can employ.

Approaching people:

あのう（ちょっと）

すみませんが／しつれいですが。

あのう　すみませんが／しつれいですが。

ちょっと　すみませんが／しつれいですが。

あのう　ちょっと　すみませんが／しつれいですが。

おねがいします。　(used to get the attention of someone who provides services, such as a store clerk)

Thanking someone:

すみません。
（どうも）ありがとう　ございます。

Giving feedback as a listener:

Nodding
Avoiding prolonged eye contact
ええ／いいえ

練習 (れんしゅう) Practice

A. Imagine that you are in Japan and want to ask someone the time. Approach the person to get attention. Ask the time. Thank him/her. Try to act out the scene with a partner.

B. Imagine that you are at a party on a college campus and want to meet someone from Japan. There are many Asian students at the party, but you are not sure if they are Japanese. Approach someone and find out if he/she is Japanese. If the person is from Japan, introduce yourself.

漢字
かんじ
Kanji

Kanji derived from pictures and symbols (1)

Kanji derived from pictures

The number of **kanji** derived from pictures and symbols totals to only about 200, but these characters tend to represent basic or core meanings. Many of them also appear in more complex characters. Therefore, it is important to become familiar with their shapes and meanings.

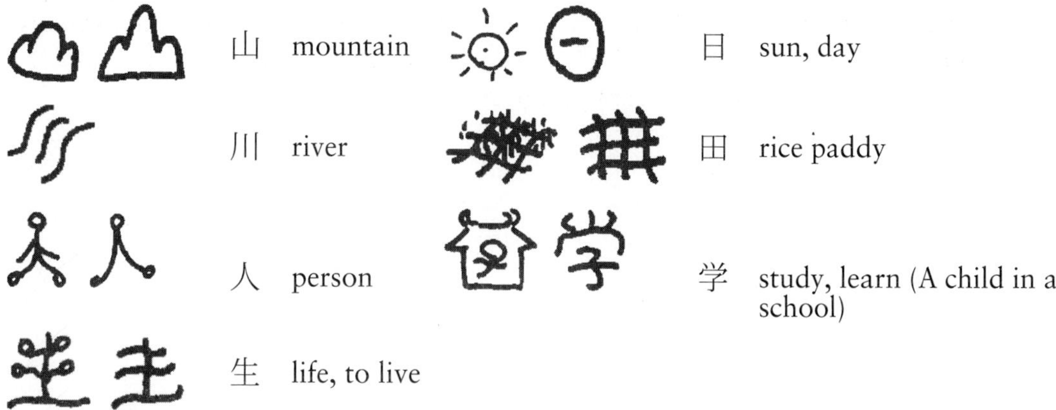

Some **kanji** that represent abstract ideas have been created from symbols.

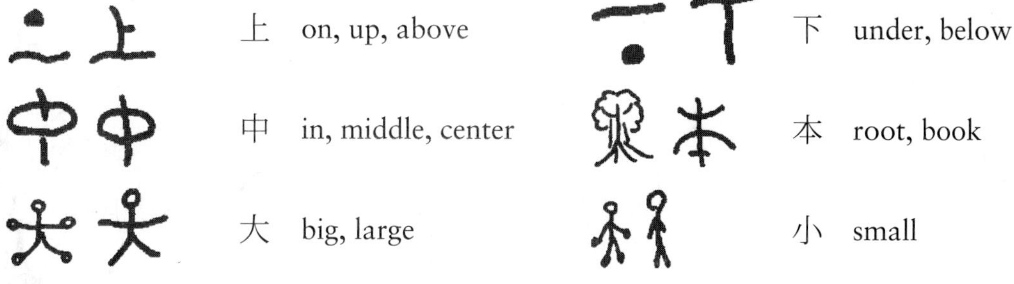

Kanji	Handwritten	Meaning / Readings	Stroke order	Examples
山	山	mountain やま　サン・ザン	丨 山 山	山川さん（やまかわ）　富士山（ふじさん）　山の上（やま うえ）
川	川	river かわ・がわ　セン	丿 川 川	小川さん（おがわ）　川中さん（かわなか）　ミシシッピ川（がわ）
田	田	rice paddy た・だ　デン	丨 冂 冂 田 田	上田さん（うえだ）　田中さん（たなか）
人	人	person ひと　ジン・ニン	丿 人	日本人（にほんじん）　あの人（ひと）
上	上	on, up, above うえ・かみ・あ(がる)　ジョウ	丨 卜 上	テーブルの上（うえ）　上がって下さい（あ くだ）
中	中	in, middle, center なか　チュウ	丨 冂 口 中	へやの中（なか）　中国（ちゅうごく）
下	下	under, below した・くだ(さい)　カ・ゲ	一 丅 下	まどの下（した）　いって下さい（くだ）
小	小	small ちい(さい)　ショウ	亅 小 小	小さいへや（ちい）
日	日	sun, day ひ・び　ニチ・ニ・ジツ・カ	丨 冂 日 日	日本（にほん）　昨日*（きのう）　今日*（きょう）　明日*（あした）
本	本	root, book もと　ホン・ボン・ポン	一 十 才 木 本	山田さんの本（やまだ ほん）　日本（にほん）

An asterisk (*) indicates an irregular reading.

よめるようになったかんじ (Kanji and compounds you can now read)

山　川　田中　日本人　上　下　中　小さい　日本　本　本棚(だな)　本屋(や)
学食(しょく)　毎日(まい)　中国(ごく)　今日(きょう)　明日(あした)　明後日(あさって)　昨日(きのう)　一昨日(おととい)　日曜日(よう)
上(あ)がって下(くだ)さい

日本人のなまえ (Japanese family names): 山川(やまかわ)　山下(やました)　山本(やまもと)　山田(やまだ)　上田(うえだ)
下田(しもだ)　高田(たかだ)　本田(ほんだ)　田中(たなか)　中田(なかだ)　中山(なかやま)　中本(なかもと)　山中(やまなか)　川中(かわなか)　中川(なかがわ)
小川(おがわ)　大川(おおかわ)　石川(いしかわ)

練習(れんしゅう) Practice

Read the following sentences.

1. 山田先生は日本大学の先生です。
2. 「上田」は日本語(ご)のなまえですが、上田さんはアメリカ人です。
3. きょうしつの中に小さいとけいがあります。
4. ふとんの下にねこがいます。
5. 日本にはきれいな山と川がたくさんあります。
6. なまえをかいて下さい。

読む 練習 Reading

上手な読み方 Reading Strategy

Using visual clues

Photos, illustrations, and graphs can often help you understand what you read. For example, it's much easier to understand a description of a room or a house while looking at a floor plan. Such visuals not only help create context, but they may also provide additional information not included in the text.

読む前に Pre-reading

Look at the picture of an office, and determine what kinds of information it conveys.

田中先生の研究室(けんきゅうしつ) Professor Tanaka's Office

Vocabulary

奥(おく) the inner part of a building, room, etc.
手前(てまえ) this side (side closer to the speaker)
鉢植(はちうえ) potted plant
たくさん many, a lot

田中先生の研究室(けんきゅうしつ)はとても広(ひろ)いです。部屋(へや)の右(みぎ)には大きい本棚(だな)があります。本棚(だな)には本がたくさんあります。本棚(だな)の横(よこ)には窓(まど)があります。窓(まど)は部屋(へや)の右(みぎ)にあります。窓(まど)の外(そと)には小さい鉢植(はちうえ)があります。そして、窓(まど)の近(ちか)くには先生の机(つくえ)があります。机(つくえ)の上には本がたくさんあります。机(つくえ)は部屋(へや)の左側(ひだりがわ)にあります。机(つくえ)の上にはコンピュータと電話(でんわ)があります。部屋(へや)の手前(てまえ)には小さいソファがあります。ソファの上にも本がたくさんあります。ソファの横(よこ)に小さい椅子(いす)があります。ソファの下にねこがいます。

読(よ)んだ後(あと)で Comprehension

Identify four discrepancies between the text and the drawing, and write them on the lines below.

1. ______________________
2. ______________________
3. ______________________
4. ______________________

総合練習
そうごうれんしゅう
Integration

アパートさがし Looking for an apartment

1. You are a Tokyo real estate agent. Bring to class or draw a floor plan of an apartment indicating the location of the door, windows, bedrooms, kitchen (キッチン), bathroom, and any other rooms. Then complete the information below.

Number of bedrooms____

Apartment location ____

Distance from campus____

Facilities near the apartment ____

2. Your instructor will divide the class into two groups. Half of the class will act as real estate agents, and the other half will try to rent an apartment. Prospective tenants should talk to as many agents as possible, take notes on each rental property, and decide which apartment to rent.

ロールプレイ Role Play

1. You are showing around a visitor from Japan who doesn't speak English. Tell the visitor about your campus as he/she asks you questions.
2. Your host family asks you what kind of place you live in. Describe your dorm or apartment.

Chapter 6

第六課 (だいろっか)

Courtesy of Kazumi and Yukiko Hatasa

休(やす)みの　日
Leisure Time

Objectives Describing routine and leisure activities

Vocabulary Routine activities (2), leisure activities, adjectives of emotion and condition

Dialogue 週末(しゅうまつ)は　どうでしたか。*How was your weekend?*

Japanese Culture College Life in Japan

Grammar
I. Using the particles と and に
II. Commenting about the past, using polite past adjectives and the copula verb です
III. Connecting verb and adjective phrases and sentences using the て-form of verbs; making requests using the て-form
IV. Connecting phrases, using the て-forms of verbs and adjectives
V. Extending an invitation using ませんか

Listening Making sense of missing pronouns

Communication Using そうですか and そうですね

Kanji **Kanji** derived from pictures and symbols (2)
今 私 月 火 水 木 金 土 曜 何 週 末 休

Reading Identifying missing nouns

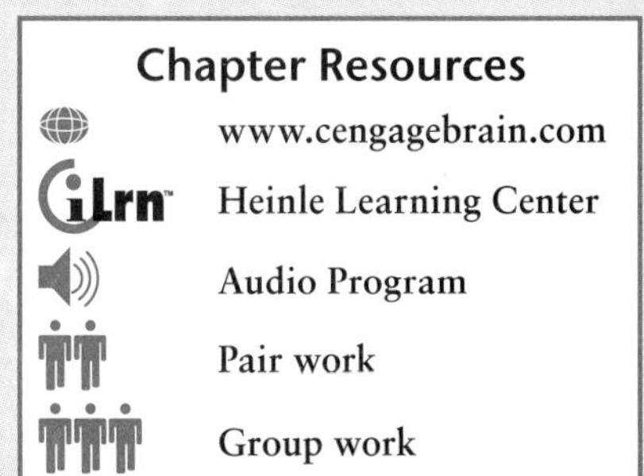

単語 (たんご)
Vocabulary

Nouns

アルバイト		part-time job, バイト can be used in casual conversation
うんどう	運動	exercises うんどう（を） します (to) exercise (を is commonly deleted)
おんがく	音楽	music
かいもの	買い物	shopping かいもの（を） します (to) go shopping
ゲーム		game
コンサート		concert
こんど	今度	next time
ざっし	雑誌	magazine
さんぽ	散歩	walk, stroll さんぽ (を) します (to) take a walk
しごと	仕事	job
しつもん	質問	question しつもん (を) します (to) ask a question
ジョギング		jogging
しんぶん	新聞	newspaper
せんたく	洗濯	laundry ～のせんたくを します or ～を せんたくします (to) wash / do laundry
そうじ	掃除	cleaning ～のそうじを します or ～を そうじします (to) clean up
てがみ	手紙	letter
テニス		tennis テニスを します (to) play tennis
ともだち	友達	friend
パーティ		party パーティを します (to) host a party
ピクニック		picnic

プール		pool
メール		e-mail
やすみ	休み	rest, absence, a day off
やすみのひ	休みの日	a day off, holiday
りょうしん	両親	parents
りょうり	料理	cooking, cuisine りょうり（を） します (to) fix a meal

う -verbs

あいます	会います	(to) meet; the dictionary form is あう.
あそびます	遊びます	(to) play; the dictionary form is あそぶ.
あるきます	歩きます	(to) walk, ～まで あるきます (to) walk (up) towards; the dictionary form is あるく.
いいます	言います	(to) say; the dictionary form is いう.
およぎます	泳ぎます	(to) swim; the dictionary form is およぐ.
かきます	書きます	(to) write; the dictionary form is かく.
ききます	聞きます / 聴きます	(to) ask（聞きます）, (to) listen to（聴きます）; the dictionary form is きく.
はなします	話します	(to) talk; the dictionary form is はなす.
まちます	待ちます	(to) wait; the dictionary form is まつ.
よびます	呼びます	(to) call (someone), (to) invite; the dictionary form is よぶ.

る -verbs

かけます		(to) make (a phone call); the dictionary for is かける. でんわを かけます
でかけます	出かけます	(to) go out; the dictionary form is でかける.

い -adjectives

いそがしい	忙しい	busy
うれしい	嬉しい	happy
おもしろい	面白い	interesting
かなしい	悲しい	sad
さびしい	寂しい	lonely
たのしい	楽しい	fun

つまらない		boring
むずかしい	難しい	difficult
やさしい	易しい、優しい	easy (易しい), kind (優しい)

な -adjectives

げんき (な)	元気 (な)	healthy, cheerful, lively (person)
ざんねん (な)	残念 (な)	sorry, regrettable
だいじょうぶ (な)	大丈夫 (な)	all right, no problem
たいへん (な)	大変 (な)	tough
にぎやか (な)	賑やか (な)	lively (place or event)
ひま (な)	暇 (な)	free, idle, unscheduled

Question Word

どう		how?

Adverbs

いっしょに	一緒に	together
ぜひ	是非	By all means. / I'd love to.
ゆっくり		slowly, ゆっくりします, (to) relax, (to) take it easy

Particles

と		with, together with (association)
と		and (exhaustive listing)
に		in order to, for (purpose)
に		to (goal, receiver)

Conjunction

そして		and

Expressions

ちょっと つごうが わるくて	ちょっと都合が悪くて	I'm a little busy. (*literally*, Sorry, it's a little inconvenient.)
ちょっと ようじが あって	ちょっと用事があって	Sorry, I have some errands/ business to attend to.

単語(たんご)の練習(れんしゅう) Vocabulary Practice

A. 毎週(まいしゅう)すること Household chores and other activities

りょうりを します
(to) fix a meal

せんたくを します
(to) do laundry

そうじを します
(to) clean /dust a room

アルバイトを します
(to) have a part-time job

しごとを します
(to) work

しんぶんを よみます
(to) read a newspaper

かいものを します
かいものに いきます

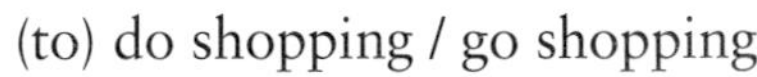

(to) do shopping / go shopping

メールを かきます
(to) write e-mail

先生に ききます
(to) ask the teacher

しつもんします
(to) ask a question

日本語(ご)で はなします
(to) talk in Japanese

でんわを
します／かけます
(to) make a phone call

Activity 1

Charades. Work in groups of three or four. Take turns performing an action from the list below while the rest of the group tries to guess the expression.

ごはんを　たべます
りょうりを　します
せんたくを　します
そうじを　します
シャワーを　あびます
おふろに　はいります
しゅくだいを　します
コーヒーを　のみます
アルバイトを　します
しんぶんを　よみます
かいものに　いきます
メールを　かきます
日本語で　はなします
テレビを　みます
ともだちに　でんわを　かけます
先生に　しつもんします

Activity 2

Work in pairs. Ask each other what things you do every day, sometimes, not very often, and never. List each of your partner's activities in the appropriate box.

Example: A: ～さんは　毎日　あさごはんを　たべますか。
B: いいえ、たべません。
A: そうですか。じゃあ、ひるごはんは　たべますか。

	パートナーの　こたえ (*Answers*)
毎日　します。	
ときどき　します。	
あまり　しません。	
ぜんぜん　しません。	

B. 休(やす)みの日に　すること　Things to do on a day off

おんがくを　ききます

(to) listen to music

コンサートに　いきます

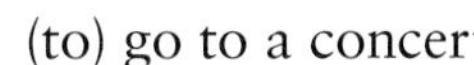

(to) go to a concert

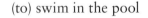

ピクニックに
いきます

(to) go on a picnic

うんどうします
(to) exercise

テニスを　します
(to) play tennis

ジョギングを　します
(to) go jogging

プールで　およぎます

(to) swim in the pool

でかけます

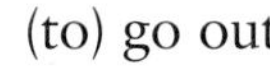

(to) go out

ともだちに／と
あいます

(to) meet a friend

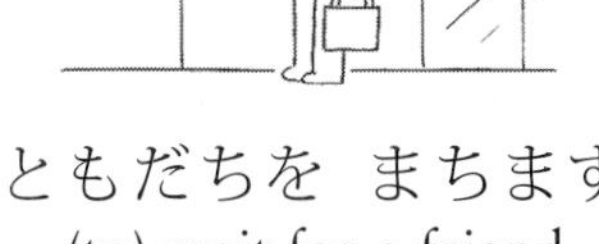

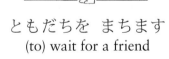

ともだちを　まちます
(to) wait for a friend

さんぽを　します
(to) take a walk

あそびます
(to) play/have fun

ゲームを　します
(to) play a game

うちで　ゆっくりします
(to) relax at home

てがみを　かきます
(to) write a letter

ざっしを よみます

(to) read a magazine

パーティを します

(to) have a party

ともだちを
うちに よびます

(to) invite / call a friend over

C. きもちや ようすを あらわす ことば Adjectives of emotion and condition

いそがしい	busy
うれしい	happy
おもしろい	interesting
かなしい	sad
ざんねん（な）	sorry, regrettable
ひま（な）	free, idle, unscheduled
大丈夫(な) (だいじょうぶ)	all right, no problem
つまらない	boring
やさしい	easy, kind
むずかしい	difficult
たのしい	fun
大変（な）(たいへん)	tough

VOCABULARY NOTES

- (お) げんきですか
  げんきですか and its polite version おげんきですか can be translated as *How are you?*, but this expression is not used in the same way as in English. げんきですか／おげんきですか is used when you have not seen someone you know for an extended period of time. In function, its sense is closer to *How have you been?* For daily greetings, use おはよう（ございます), こんにちは, こんばんは.
- ざんねん vs. すみません
  Both ざんねん and すみません may be translated as *sorry*, but their usage is very different. すみません is used for apologizing, but ざんねん merely expresses regret, disappointment, or sympathy (and may also function as an adjective). For example, if you are not able to finish your homework by the due date, you might say すみません to your teacher. The teacher might then reply ざんねんですね, to express his/her disappointment. すみません can also be used to approach someone (meaning *Excuse me. / Pardon me.*), or to express thanks. ざんねん cannot be substituted in these instances.

ダイアローグ
Dialogue

はじめに　Warm-up

しつもんに　こたえて下さい。Answer these questions in Japanese.

1. 週末(しゅうまつ)は　うちで　よく　何(なに)を　しますか。
2. 週末(しゅうまつ)は　よく　どこに　あそびに　いきますか。
3. 休(やす)みの日に　よく　でかけますか。どこへ　いきますか。
4. 休(やす)みの日に　よく　何(なに)を　しますか。

週末(しゅうまつ)は　どうでしたか。　*How was your weekend?*

Ueda and Li meet in class on Monday.

上田：　リーさん、おはようございます。

リー：　あ、上田さん、おはようございます。週末(しゅうまつ)は　どうでしたか。

上田：　とても　たのしかったです。

リー：　それは　よかったですね。

上田：　ええ、みちこさんと　しぶやに　かいものに　いって、

リー：　ええ、

上田：　コンサートへ　いきました。

リー： そうですか。いいですね。

上田： リーさんの 週末(しゅうまつ)は どうでしたか。

リー： 先週(せんしゅう)は しゅくだいが たくさん あって、週末(しゅうまつ)は ずっと うちで べんきょうしました。

上田： それは 大変(たいへん)でしたね。

リー： ええ。だから、いそがしくて、ぜんぜん おもしろくなかったです。

上田： じゃあ、来週(らいしゅう)の 週末(しゅうまつ)は どうですか。

リー： 来週(らいしゅう)は あまり いそがしくありません。

上田： じゃあ、うちに あそびに きませんか。

リー： えっ、いいんですか。

上田： ええ。土曜日(どようび)は どうですか。

リー： ええ、大丈夫(だいじょうぶ)です。

上田： じゃあ、くるとき、でんわしてくれませんか。

リー： わかりました。じゃあ、土曜日(どようび)に。

DIALOGUE PHRASE NOTES

- The それ in それは よかったですね in line 5 refers to Ueda's statement that she had fun. It does not refer to any physical object in the scene. Similarly, the それ in それは 大変(たいへん)でしたね in line 13 refers to Li's having studied all weekend.
- Li interjects ええ while Ueda is talking in line 7. This ええ is the あいづち you learned about in Chapters 2 and 3. In this case, he is signaling to Ueda that he is following her story and wants her to continue. Similarly, Ueda says ええ in line 20 after Li's utterance. あいづち are generally used at phrase boundaries, for example, immediately after the て-form of verbs as shown in this dialogue, or after the conjunction が.
- ずっと means *for a long time*. In this context, it suggests *all day long*.
- In addition to modifying verbs, ぜんぜん can be used with the negative form of an adjective, as in ぜんぜん おもしろくありません・なかったです (not at all interesting).
- えっ、いいんですか means *Are you sure?*
- あとで means *later*.
- In Japanese, あそびに きませんか is often used to invite a friend to get together or hang out, as in Ueda's invitation in line 18.
- くる とき means *when you come*.

ダイアローグの後(あと)で Comprehension

A. Read each statement and circle はい if the statement is true or いいえ if it is false.

1. はい いいえ リーさんは 日曜日(にちようび)に べんきょうしました。
2. はい いいえ リーさんは 土曜日(どようび)に でかけました。
3. はい いいえ リーさんは おもしろい えいがを みました。
4. はい いいえ 上田さんは キムさんと コンサートに いきました。
5. はい いいえ 上田さんは 先週(せんしゅう)の 週末(しゅうまつ)に かいものを しました。

B. しつもんに こたえて下さい。 Answer these questions.

1. 上田さんは 先週(せんしゅう) 何(なに)を しましたか。
2. リーさんは 週末(しゅうまつ) 何(なに)を しましたか。
3. リーさんは 来週(らいしゅう)の 週末(しゅうまつ) いそがしいですか。
4. リーさんは 来週(らいしゅう) 何(なに)を しますか。

文法(ぶんぽう) Grammar

I. Using the particles と and に

A. Particle と

The particle と has two separate usages that are conceptually related.

1. と, *with, together with*

The first usage indicates association between two items and is translated as *with* or *together with*. For example:

私(わたし)は	チョイさんと	べんきょうしました。	*I studied with Ms. Choi.*
リーさんは	田中さんと	えいがを　みました。	*Mr. Li watched a movie with Mr. Tanaka.*
私(わたし)は	ペギーさんと	でんわで　はなします。	*I talk with Peggy on the phone.*
中山さんは	ともだちと	かいものに　いきます。	*Mr. Nakayama goes shopping with a friend.*

2. と, *and*

The second usage is to connect two or more nouns.

スミスさんと	私(わたし)は	学生です。	*Mr. Smith and I are students.*
そうじと	せんたくを	しました。	*I did cleaning and laundry.*
しんぶんと	ざっしを	よみました。	*I read a newspaper and a magazine.*
金曜日(きんようび)と	土曜日(どようび)に	ここへ　きます。	*I will come here on Friday and Saturday.*
ナイフと	フォークで	たべます。	*(I) eat with a knife and a fork.*

All of the above examples show that the particle と connects nouns only. It cannot be used to connect two or more sentences, or verb or adjective phrases.
Use the て-form of verbs (see p. 230, Grammar III) or the conjunction そして to connect sentences and verb phrases.

そうじを して、 せんたくも しました。
I did the cleaning and the laundry.

そうじをしました。そして、せんたくも しました。
I cleaned the house. Then I did the laundry.

B. The particle に

So far, you have learned three functions of the particle に: に for time, as in 土曜日に (<u>on</u> *Saturday*) and いちじに (<u>at</u> *one o'clock*); に for goals/destinations, as in 学校に いきます (*go* <u>to</u> *school*) ; and に for the location of a person or object, as in うちに あります／います (*It/Someone is* <u>in</u> *my house*.) This chapter introduces two more usages of the particle に, but they are related to に used for goals.

1. に to (recipient, target, goal, destination)

に can indicate the recipient or the target person to which an action is directed.

	Noun	Particle	
私は	ともだち	に	てがみを かきます。

I write a letter to a friend. / I will write a letter to a friend.

ともだちに	でんわを かけます。	*I make a phone call to a friend.*
りょうしんに	メールを かきます。	*I write e-mail to my parents.*
先生に	ききます。	*I ask my teacher.*
先生に	しつもんします。	*I ask my teacher a question.*
先生に	はなします。	*I talk to/tell my teacher.*
ともだちに	あいます。	*I meet my friends.*

Notes

- に in this usage indicates the endpoint of an action, so it is conceptually related to the goal ～に／へ いきます／きます／かえります. However, unlike the above usage, ～に／へ いきます／きます／かえります cannot take a person as a goal.
- In some cases, the particle と association (with) is used instead of に with verbs like あいます and はなします. Although the English translation does not differentiate between に or と, the meaning is very different in Japanese. When に is used, the action is uni-directional, so 先生に はなします indicates that the speaker is telling something or speaking to the teacher, but not having a conversation. Conversely, と indicates bi-directional orientation, so 先生と はなします indicates that the speaker and the teacher collaboratively engage in conversation.

  先生に はなします *I speak to/tell something to the teacher.*
  先生と はなします *I converse with the teacher.*

  Similarly, ともだちに あいます is used when the speaker goes to the friend to talk or bumps into the friend on the street, but ともだちと あいます suggests that the speaker and the friend have made a prior arrangement to meet each other.

2. Purpose に いきます／きます／かえります／でかけます

に can also indicate the purpose for going somewhere. It is used with the verbs いきます, きます, かえります and でかけます. The purpose may be a noun indicating an activity such as かいもの and コンサート.

アリソンさんは かいものに でかけました。	*Alison went shopping.*
リーさんは コンサートに いきます。	*Mr. Li is going to a concert.*

When purpose is represented by a verbal expression such as テニスを します or ごはんを たべます に should be attached to the verb stem (the part of verb that comes before ます).

	Verb stem	Particle	Verb of movement
ごはんを	たべ	に	でかけます。

I'm going out to eat.

Note that いきます, きます, かえります and でかけます are commonly used with an expression of a desination such as としょかんに／へ いきます. When combined with the purpose, the sentence can have more than one に, such as としょかんに べんきょうしに いきます (*go to the library to study*).

うちに ねに かえります。	*I am going home to take a nap.*
上田さんに あいに きました。	*I came to see Ms. Ueda.*
上田さんに あいに ここに きました。	*I came here to see Ms. Ueda.*

キム： あ、どこへ いきますか。
Where are you going?

田中： たいいくかんに およぎに いきます。
I am going to the gym to swim.

キム： そうですか。
I see.

話(はな)してみましょう　Conversation Practice

Activity 1

The pictures below show what Mr. Suzuki did last week. Complete the following statements using the appropriate particles.

鈴木(すずき)さんは　ともだちに　でんわを　かけました。

Activity 2

Based on each situation, create a sentence stating a purpose, using a verb stem + に　いきます／きます／かえります.

Example: 昨日(きのう)　スーパーへ　いきました。そして、アルバイトを　しました。
昨日(きのう)　スーパーへ　アルバイトを　しに　いきました。

1. たいいくかんへ　いきました。そして、およぎました。
2. アパートに　かえります。そして、ゆっくり　します。
3. ここに　きました。そして、りょうりを　しました。
4. としょかんへ　いきました。そして、しんぶんを　よみました。
5. 先生の　けんきゅうしつ (*office*) に　いきます。そして、しつもんします。
6. このカフェに　よく　きます。そして、ともだちに　あいます。

Activity 3

Work in groups of three. One person chooses a place in the box below but does not tell anyone. The other two ask questions about the purpose of going there and try to figure out which place it is. The person who has chosen the place will answer はい or いいえ. Take turns.

としょかん	たいいくかん	学食(しょく)	きょうしつ	本屋(や)	こうえん
ぎんこう	ゆうびんきょく	カフェ	コンビニ	びょういん	こうばん
デパート	ともだちのうち	日本	中国(ごく)	かんこく	フランス
スペイン	オーストラリア	カナダ	メキシコ	アメリカ	イギリス

Example: B chooses としょかん

A: うんどうしに　いきますか。

B: いいえ。

C: 本を　よみに　いきますか

B: はい。

C: としょかんですか。

B: はい、そうです。

Activity 4

Based on the sentences you completed in Activity 1, narrate Mr. Suzuki's day. Try to use transition words like そして when you can. To make the story sound more natural, try to fill in some information such as when Mr. Suzuki went out and came back, and when Yumi visited him and went home.

II. Commenting about the past, using polite past adjectives and the copula verb です

In Chapter 4, adjectives were introduced to describe the physical characteristics of an object. Another common use of adjectives is to comment on objects and events in the present and the past. This chapter introduces the past tense forms of adjectives and the copula verb です. Like the present tense forms, the formation of past tense forms differs depending on the adjective type.

A. い -adjectives

The past affirmative form of い-adjectives is formed by replacing い with かったです. The past negative form is formed by replacing い with くありませんでした or くなかったです. いい becomes よかったです in the affirmative form and よくありませんでした or よくなかったです in the negative form.

Dictionary form	Polite affirmative forms		Polite negative forms	
	Present	Past	Present	Past
あかい *(red)*	あかいです *(It is red.)*	あか<u>かったです</u> *(It was red.)*	あかくありません あかくないです *(It is not red.)*	あか<u>くありませんでした</u> あか<u>くなかったです</u> *(It was not red.)*
いい *(good)*	いいです *(It is good.)*	よかったです *(It was good.)*	よくありません よくないです *(It is not good.)*	よく<u>ありませんでした</u> よく<u>なかったです</u> *(It was not good.)*

B. な -adjectives and the copula verb です

The ending of the な-adjectives and the copula verb are very similar. In both cases, you will change です to でした for the past affirmative form, じゃありません／じゃないです to じゃありませんでした／じゃなかったです for the past negative form.

Dictionary form	Polite affirmative forms		Polite negative forms	
	Present	Past	Present	Past
きれい *(pretty)*	きれいです *(It is pretty.)*	きれい<u>でした</u> *(It was pretty.)*	きれいじゃありません きれいじゃないです *(It is not pretty.)*	きれいじゃ<u>ありませんでした</u> きれいじゃ<u>なかったです</u> *(It was not pretty.)*
ゲーム *(game)*	ゲームです *(It is a game.)*	ゲーム<u>でした</u> *(It was a game.)*	ゲームじゃありません ゲームじゃないです *(It is not a game.)*	ゲームじゃ<u>ありませんでした</u> ゲームじゃ<u>なかったです</u> *(It was not a game.)*

スミス：週末(しゅうまつ)は　どうでしたか。
How was your weekend?

山下：とても　たのしかったです。
It was really fun.

スミス：そうですか。よかったですね。
I see. I'm glad to hear that. (literally, *that was good.*)

上田：パーティは　どうでしたか。
How was the party?

リー：とても　にぎやかでした。
It was very lively.

上田：山田先生と　はなしましたか。
Did you talk with Professor Yamada?

リー：いいえ、先生は　いませんでした。
No, he wasn't there.

上田：そうですか。ざんねんでしたね。
I see. That's too bad.

チョイ：今日(きょう)、いそがしいですか。
Are you busy today?

本田：ええ、テストが　あります。
Yes, I have a test.

チョイ：そうですか。大変(たいへん)ですね。
I see. That's tough!

話(はな)してみましょう　Conversation Practice

Activity 1

Work with a partner. One person plays the role of a new student, asking about local places and facilities. The other person should respond to the questions based on his/her experiences, using the past affirmative or negative form of adjectives.

Example:
A: このへんでは、どのカフェが　いいですか。
B: そうですね。スタバ (*Starbucks*) が　おいしかったですよ。
A: がくせいかいかんの　カフェは　どうですか。
B: う〜ん、あまり　おいしくなかったですよ。

1. どの　けいたい（でんわ）が　いいですか。
2. どの　えいごの　じしょが　いいですか。
3. デートを　します。どの　レストランが　いいですか。

4. しゅうまつに　あそびに　いきます。どこが　いいですか。
5. ジョギングを　します。どこが　いいですか。

Activity 2

Chat with a partner about events and occasions listed in the chart below. Discuss which ones were interesting, easy, difficult, etc., and complete the chart.

Examples: 1. A: 日本語(ご)の　テストは　どうでしたか。
B: とても　<u>やさしかったです</u>。
A: そうですか。<u>よかったですね</u>。

2. A: 日本語(ご)の　テストは　どうでしたか。
B: あまり　<u>よくなかったです。／</u>
とても　<u>むずかしかったです。</u>
A: そうですか。<u>ざんねんでしたね。／大変(たいへん)でしたね</u>。

	私(わたし)	パートナー
日本語(ご)の　テスト		
日本語(ご)の　じゅぎょう		
週末(しゅうまつ)		
パーティ		

Activity 3

With your partner, take turns asking about life in high school (高校生活(こうこうせいかつ)) and learning about each other's high school classes and teachers. Fill in the chart as you ask and answer questions.

Example: A: 高校生活(こうこうせいかつ)は　どうでしたか。
B: とても　たのしかったです。
A: そうですか。よかったですね。
B: ～さんの　高校生活(こうこうせいかつ)は　どうでしたか。
A: わたしの　高校生活(こうこうせいかつ)も　とても　よかったです。

	私(わたし)	パートナー
高校生活(こうこう せいかつ)		
じゅぎょう		
先生		

III. Connecting verb and adjective phrases and sentences using the て-form of verbs; making requests using the て-form

Chapter 1 introduced request forms such as きいて下さい and みて下さい, in which 下さい roughly means *please*. The forms きいて and みて are the て-forms of the verbs ききます and みます, respectively. Also, Chapter 5 introduced the phrase あるいて いきます, in which あるいて is the て-form of あるきます (*to walk*) and indicates how the speaker goes from one place to another. You may have also noticed headings such as はなして みましょう (*Let's try speaking*) and きいて みましょう (*Let's try listening*) in the chapters of this textbook. The form みましょう means *let's try*, and the preceding て-forms indicate what to try out. These are only a few uses of the て-form. As you continue to study Japanese, you will learn a variety of structures that use this form. This section explains the formation of the て-form of verbs and three request forms using the て-form and 下さい／下さいませんか／くれませんか.

A. Verb て-forms

The て-form of る-verbs and irregular verbs is easy to form. All you have to do is to replace ます with て.

Verb class		Polite affirmative form	て-form
る-verbs	to eat	たべます	たべて
	to watch	みます	みて
	to make (a phone call)	かけます	かけて
Irregular verbs	to come	きます	きて
	to do	します	して
	to study	べんきょうします	べんきょうして

The て-form of う-verbs is more complicated. There are five basic patterns and they are determined by the sound before ます, as shown in the chart below. The て-form of the verb いきます is いって though it is an う-verb. This is considered an exception.

Verb class		Polite affirmative form	て -form	Formation Patterns
う -verbs	to talk	はなします	はなして	し→して
	to listen	ききます	きいて	き→いて
	to swim	およぎます	およいで	ぎ→いで
	to say	いいます	いって	い、ち、り→って
	to wait	まちます	まって	
	to take (a bath), enter	はいります	はいって	
	to read	よみます	よんで	み、び、に→んで
	to call	よびます	よんで	
	to die	しにます	しんで	
	to go	いきます	いって	Exception

B. 〜て下さい／〜て下さいませんか／〜てくれませんか

〜て下さい, 〜て下さいませんか and 〜てくれませんか are all used to make a request. Each expression generally indicates a polite request, but 〜て下さい is the most forceful form among the three forms because it is a command form. While a social superior such as your teacher or someone much older than you may use 〜て下さい to ask you to do something, it would be rude for you to say 〜て下さい to your social superior. Instead, use 〜て下さいませんか, a more polite request form commonly used for a social superior. 〜てくれませんか is less formal than 〜て下さいませんか, so it can be used with someone of equal social status or similar age.

To a social inferior:

CDを　きいて下さい。　*Please listen to the CD.*
こくばんを　みて下さい。　*Please look at the chalkboard.*
本を　よんで下さい。　*Please read the book.*

To a social superior:

先生、かんじを かいて下さいませんか。
Could you write the kanji?

先生、もういちど いって下さいませんか。
Could you say it again?

先生、明日(あした)まで まって下さいませんか。
Could you wait until tomorrow?

To a peer:

上田さん、明日(あした) メールしてくれませんか。
Could you e-mail me tomorrow?

上田さん、としょかんへ いってくれませんか。
Could you go to the library?

上田さん、この てがみを よんでくれませんか。
Could you read this letter?

話(はな)してみましょう Conversation Practice

Activity 1

Your teacher gives you one of the following commands in Japanese. Act out the command.

Example: Your teacher says ここに きて下さい.
You walk toward the teacher.

1. Come here.
2. Go to the back of the room.
3. Read the textbook.
4. Look at the chalkboard.
5. Write your name in Japanese.
6. Speak Japanese to a classmate next to you.
7. Turn in your work. (しゅくだいを だします。)
8. Make a phone call.

Activity 2

Working with a partner, make the requests in Activity 1, using ～てくれませんか. Your partner will act out the requested behaviors. You can create your own requests if you like, using other known verbs.

Example: You say ここに きてくれませんか.
Your partner walks toward you.

Activity 3

Use the table below to make a request to the addressee. Pay attention to the relationship between you and your addressee and choose ～て下さい or ～て下さいませんか or ～てくれませんか.

Example: 先生　wants students to speak Japanese.

日本語(ご)で　はなして下さい。

	You	Your addressee	Request
Example	先生	学生	Speak Japanese
1	学生	学生	Invite/call Tanaka-san
2	学生	先生	Write e-mail to you
3	学生	先生	Read this letter
4	先生	学生	Turn in the homework
5	学生	学生	Clean up the room
6	いしゃ (*doctor*)	かんじゃ (*patient*)	Walk every day
7	いしゃ (*doctor*)	かんじゃ (*patient*)	Relax at home
8	大学院生(いんせい)	大学の先生	Meet me next week
9	学校１の先生 (*teacher at school 1*)	学校２の先生 (*teacher at school 2*)	Write a letter to school

Activity 4

Work with a partner. Create dialogues in which you make requests in each of the following situations, using ～て下さい, ～て下さいませんか, or ～てくれませんか.

Example: You are a teacher, and you are taking your students on a field trip tomorrow. So you want them to come to school at 7 a.m.

明日(あした)のあさ　7じに　学校へきて下さい。

1. You are sick and can't go to school. You want your roommate to call your teacher.
2. You want to use **kanji** to write your name. Ask your teacher to write your name in **kanji**.
3. You are a teacher. Your students performed very poorly on the test and you want them to study.
4. You have a visitor who is much younger than you. But you are busy with work so you want him/her to wait for you here.
5. Your neighbor comes to your house to discuss a neighborhood dispute with you. She/he is at the door. Invite him/her in.

IV. Connecting phrases, using the て -forms of verbs and adjectives

A. The て -form of verbs indicating "and"

Another basic usage of the て-form is to connect phrases. As was mentioned in Grammar I, A-2 (p. 222), the particle と cannot be used to connect two or more sentences or verb phrases. The て-form is used instead. Note that the て-form by itself does not express when the action takes place or has taken place. The timing of the action is determined by the phrase at the end of the sentence. For example, テレビをみて、ねます indicates that the speaker goes or will go to bed after watching TV, but テレビを みて、ねました indicates that he/she went to bed after watching TV.

しんぶんを よんで、学校に いきます — *I read the newspaper and go to school .*

おんがくを きいて、ねます。 — *I listen to music and go to bed.*

うちに かえって、ゆっくりしました。 — *I went home and relaxed.*

ともだちを よんで、ゲームを しました。 — *I called my friend and played a game.*

いぬの さんぽを して、でかけました。 — *I walked my dog and went out.*

アルバイトが あって、いそがしかったです。 — *I had to work part-time and/so I was busy.*

田中さんが いて、にぎやかでした。 — *Mr. Tanaka was there, and/so it was lively.*

Phrases connected by the て-form may indicate a chronological relationship or a cause-effect relationship, because the て-form loosely connects phrases without specifying how they should be related.

B. The て -form of adjectives indicating "and"

The て-form of adjectives and the copula verbs can connect phrases as well. The formation of the adjective て-form is relatively simple. い (です) is replaced by くて for い-adjectives, です is replaced by で for な-adjective and the copula verb. The て-form of いい is よくて.

い -adjectives	な -adjectives	Copula verb
たのしいです (*it is fun.*)	にぎやかです (*it is lively.*)	休(やす)みです (*It is a day off.*)
たのしくて (*it is fun, and*)	にぎやかで (*it is lively, and*)	休(やす)みで (*It is a day off, and*)

上田さんは　やさしくて、　きれいです。
Ms. Ueda is kind and pretty.

リーさんは　げんきで、おもしろいです。
Mr. Li is cheerful and interesting.

かんじは　むずかしくて、大変(たいへん)です。
Kanji is difficult and tough.

パーティは　にぎやかで、たのしかったです。
The party was lively and fun.

ひまで、　うちに　います。
I have nothing to do and stay at home.

しごとで、　フランスへ　いきます。
I am going to France for work.

さびしくて、　ともだちに　でんわしました。
I was lonely, and/so I called my friend.

話(はな)してみましょう Conversation Practice

Activity 1

The following illustrations show what Ms. Yamamoto did last Sunday. Describe her activities using the て-form of verbs.

Example: あさ　8じに　おきて、うんどうしました。

8:00 a.m.

8:30 a.m.

About 9:00 a.m.

9:30 a.m.

About 10:00 a.m.

11:00 a.m.

About 11:30 a.m.

12:00 p.m.

12:15 p.m.

12:30 p.m.

About 4:00 p.m.

6:00 p.m.

7:00 p.m.

8:00 p.m.

About 11:00 p.m.

Activity 2

Comment on the following things using the て-form of adjectives.

Example: えいごのじゅぎょう
えいごのじゅぎょうは　やさしくて、おもしろいです。

1. 日本語(ご)
2. そうじ
3. せんたく
4. アルバイト
5. おんがく
6. うんどう
7. コンピュータ・ゲーム

Activity 3

With a partner, discuss a movie, a TV program (テレビばんぐみ) you've seen, a concert you've attended, or some music you have listened to recently. Comment on the experiences using the て-form. Then complete the chart.

Example: A: さいきん (*recently*) どんな　えいがを　みましたか。
B: スパイダーマンを　みました。
A: どうでしたか。
B: とても　おもしろくて、よかったですよ。

Category	Type/Title	How was it?
えいが		
コンサート		
テレビばんぐみ		
おんがく		

V. Extending an invitation using ませんか

The negative question form of a verb 〜ませんか is often used to extend an invitation. It conveys the idea in English of *won't you* 〜, or *why don't we* 〜. 〜ませんか is often used with the phrase いっしょに (*together*) when the speaker wants to invite someone for an activity.

いっしょに　ジョギングを　しませんか。
Why don't we go jogging together?

今度(こんど)の　休(やす)みに　いっしょに　ピクニックに　いきませんか。
Why don't we go to a picnic on the next day off?

私(わたし)と　いっしょに　べんきょうしませんか。
Won't you study with me?

Notes

- Before extending an invitation, the speaker often checks the listener's availability, interest, or willingness. Because an overt rejection can often strain a relationship, Japanese people tend to avoid creating a situation in which a person may have to reject an offer or an invitation.

ジョンソン：　今度(こんど)の　休(やす)みは　いそがしいですか。
Are you busy during the next holiday?

木村(きむら)：　いいえ、いそがしくありません。
No, not really.

ジョンソン：　じゃあ、およぎに　いきませんか。
Then, why don't we go swimming?

山田：　テニスは　よく　しますか。
Do you play tennis often?

上田：　ええ、しますよ。
Yes, I do.

山田：　じゃあ、土曜日(どようび)に　テニスを　しませんか。
Well, why don't we play tennis on Saturday?

- Japanese people often avoid explicitly saying no to an invitation, in order not to hurt other people's feelings. When you cannot accept an invitation, it's customary to apologize for not being able to accept it, and then give a reason. If you don't want to give a specific reason, use the following phrases.

すみません、ちょっと　つごうが　わるくて。
Sorry, I'm a little busy. (literally, *Sorry, it's a little inconvenient.*)

すみません、ちょっと ようじが あって。
Sorry, I have some errands/business to attend to.

- Some common expressions for accepting an invitation are:

いいですね。	*That sounds great.*
ええ、ぜひ。	*Yes, I'd love to.* (literally, *Yes by all means.*)
ええ、いいですよ。	*Yes, that would be fine.*

話(はな)してみましょう Conversation Practice

Activity 1

Work with a partner. Look at the following drawings and extend an invitation to each activity. Your partner will accept your invitation by saying ええ、いいですよ, いいですね or ええ、ぜひ.

Example: A: ～さん、いっしょに かいものに いきませんか。
B: ええ、いいですよ。

Activity 2

Work with the class. In the chart below, write three activities that you want to do with someone on each day of this weekend. Invite at least one person for each activity. If someone invites you to do an activity, either accept using one of the phrases you've just learned, or decline the invitation politely if you're not interested.

Example: You have written えいがを　みる for 金曜日(きんようび).

A: 金曜日(きんようび)に　えいがを　みませんか。

B: ええ、いいですよ。

or すみません、ちょっと　つごうが　わるくて。

ちょっと　ようじが　あって。

～曜日(ようび)	すること (Activities to invite for)	なまえ (People who accepted)
金曜日(きんようび)		
土曜日(どようび)		
日曜日(にちようび)		

Activity 3

Invite a partner to do the following activities together. Before extending your invitation, ask about his/her availability and/or interest.

Example: A: 今週(こんしゅう)の　金曜日(きんようび)は　いそがしいですか。

B: いいえ、いそがしくないですよ。

A: じゃあ、いっしょに　パーティに　いきませんか。

B: いいですね。

1. いっしょに　かいものに　いきます。
2. いっしょに　おんがくを　ききます。
3. いっしょに　しゅくだいを　します。
4. いっしょに　えいがを　みます。
5. いっしょに　こうえんの　そうじを　します。

Supplementary Note

In Japanese, verbal expressions can be abbreviated using です when the meaning can be guessed from context. This use of です appears often in response to a wh-question.

田中： だれを よびましたか。
Who did you invite?
ペギー： 上田さんと アリソンさんです。
Ms. Ueda and Alison.

木村(きむら)： いつ かえりますか。
When will you come back?
リー： 来週(らいしゅう)の 火曜日(かようび)です。
Next Tuesday.

山中： だれと はなしましたか。
Who did you talk to?
チョイ： スミスさんです。
Mr. Smith.

In English, you can simply use nouns such as people's names without a verb, but in Japanese it sounds abrupt and can be rude to omit the verb, especially in formal conversations. In cases like this, です can be used instead of more specific verbal expressions.

This is true in the classroom, where the instructor asks many questions. You should try to respond to your teacher with the verb from the question or with です when it is appropriate to do so. (But be careful not to overuse です, because excessive repetition may be interpreted as a lack of interest in class!)

聞く練習 Listening

(きく れんしゅう)

上手な聞き方 Listening Strategy

(じょうず きき かた)

Making sense of missing pronouns

Just as in writing, pronouns are often omitted in a conversation when they can be inferred from the context. Imagine that two people are talking with each other. If one person asks a question without an overt subject pronoun, the missing subject is likely to be *you*. If that person then makes a statement without a subject, the subject is most likely to be the speaker himself/herself. As you become more proficient with the language, you will understand who is mentioned without having to listen for subject pronouns.

A. だれの はなし？ **Whose story is it?**

Listen to the following short dialogues. In each of the conversations, the subject in the man's speech is either *I* or *you*, but it's missing. Identify the missing subjects.

1. I you
2. I you
3. I you
4. I you
5. I you

B. 私の 生活 (わたし せいかつ)

Listen to the following conversations, then the statements about them. Circle はい if a statement is true, or いいえ if it is false.

1. a. はい いいえ
 b. はい いいえ
 c. はい いいえ
 d. はい いいえ
 e. はい いいえ
 f. はい いいえ
 g. はい いいえ
 h. はい いいえ

2. a. はい いいえ
 b. はい いいえ
 c. はい いいえ
 d. はい いいえ
 e. はい いいえ
 f. はい いいえ

聞(き)き上手(じょうず) 話(はな)し上手(じょうず)
Communication

Communication Strategy

Using そうですか and そうですね

The expressions そうですか and そうですね are used often in conversation. These expressions are instrumental in making a conversation go smoothly. However, it is sometimes difficult to know which one to use. There are two そうですか: one with a falling intonation and one with a rising intonation. そうですか with a falling intonation means "I see" (and *I didn't know that*). It is used when you have just received new information. It is often preceded by ああ. そうですか with a rising intonation means "Is that so?" It is used to question what you have just heard, and is commonly preceded by えっ (*What!?*).

そうですね is usually spoken with a falling intonation. It means "That's right" so it would not be appropriate to say そうですね when you have just heard something new. そうですね is often preceded by ええ or はい.

練習(れんしゅう) Practice

A. Listen to the six short conversations. After each one, put a check mark in the box that corresponds to the correct meaning of そうですか／そうですね in the context of the conversation.

	1	2	3	4	5	6
I see.						
Is that so?						
That's right.						

B. Working with a partner, read the sentences below one at a time, and choose one of these three phrases as your reply. More than one answer may be correct, as long as you know why you have chosen it.

ああ、そうですか。　えっ、そうですか。　ええ、そうですね。

1. 山田先生は いい 先生です。
2. 山田先生は れきしの 先生です。
3. ブラウンさんは 日本人の ともだちと でかけました。
4. このしゅくだいは むずかしかったですね。
5. 昨日(きのう)は いそがしかったですね。
6. 明日(あした) 日本に いきます。

漢字 (かんじ) Kanji

Kanji derived from pictures and symbols (2)

月	月 (moon)	火	火 (fire)
水	水 (water)	木	木 (tree)
金	金 (gold)	土	土 (earth)
末	末 (end; tree with a focal point at the top)		

Kanji	Meaning / Readings	Stroke order	Examples
今	now いま　コン	ノ 八 今 今	今(いま)、何時(なんじ)ですか。　今週(こんしゅう)　今日(きょう)*
私	I; private わたし・わたくし　シ	ノ 二 千 禾 禾 私 私	私(わたし)は日本人です。
月	moon, month つき　ゲツ・ガツ	ノ 刀 月 月	月曜日(げつようび)
火	fire ひ　カ	丶 丷 少 火	火曜日(かようび)
水	water みず　スイ	亅 刁 水 水	水曜日(すいようび)
木	tree き　モク	一 十 才 木	大きい木(き)　木曜日(もくようび)
金	gold, money, metal かね　キン	ノ 八 人 今 全 余 金	金曜日(きんようび)

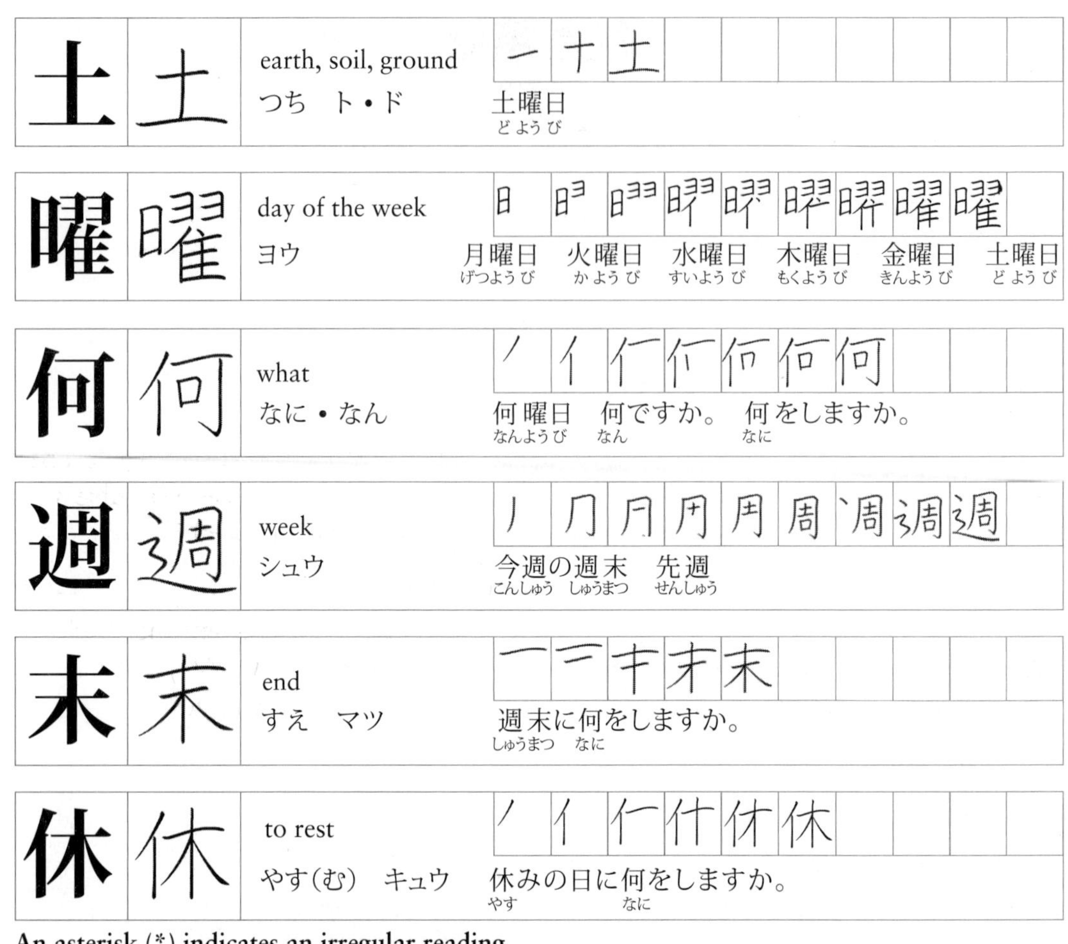

Kanji	Meaning / Readings	Examples
土	earth, soil, ground つち　ト・ド	土曜日(どようび)
曜	day of the week ヨウ	月曜日(げつようび)　火曜日(かようび)　水曜日(すいようび)　木曜日(もくようび)　金曜日(きんようび)　土曜日(どようび)
何	what なに・なん	何曜日(なんようび)　何(なん)ですか。　何(なに)をしますか。
週	week シュウ	今週(こんしゅう)の週末(しゅうまつ)　先週(せんしゅう)
末	end すえ　マツ	週末(しゅうまつ)に何(なに)をしますか。
休	to rest やす(む)　キュウ	休(やす)みの日に何(なに)をしますか。

An asterisk (*) indicates an irregular reading.

読(よ)めるようになった漢字(かんじ) (Kanji and compounds you can now read)

今　今日(きょう)　今日(こんにち)は　今晩(ばん)　今週　来(らい)週　先週　私　月曜日　火曜日　水曜日　木曜日　木　金曜日　土曜日　日曜日　何をしますか。　何ですか。何曜日　何時(じ)　週末　今度(こんど)　大変(たいへん)な　大丈夫(だいじょうぶ)です　毎(まい)週　休みの日

日本人の名前(なまえ)：木村(きむら)　鈴木(すずき)

練習(れんしゅう)　Practice

Read the following sentences.

1. 日曜日　月曜日　火曜日　水曜日　木曜日　金曜日　土曜日
2. 大川：「中田さんは今週の週末に何をしますか。」
   本田：「土曜日に山にいきます。」
3. 先週の月曜日は休みでした。
4. 上田：「本田さん、金曜日のばん、私のうちにあそびにきませんか。」
   本田：「いいですね。じゃあ7時(じ)ごろいきます。」
5. 中川：「今日のごご、何をしますか。」
   山中：「アルバイトがあります。」

読む練習
よ れんしゅう
Reading

上手な読み方 Reading Strategy
じょうず よ かた

Identifying missing nouns

In Japanese, it is not necessary to repeat nouns or pronouns in writing if they can be inferred from context. These omitted nouns are most likely to be either the subject or the topic, although they can be any other type of noun such as an object, place, or time. For example, in the sentences 私は 学生です。三年生(さんねん)です。, the topic of the second sentence, 私は is missing because it is mentioned in the first sentence and can be inferred. This type of deletion makes a paragraph more cohesive. As you become more proficient with the language, this will become second nature to you.

読む前に Pre-reading
よ まえ

A. Identify any missing nouns in the following sentences.

1. 先週の日曜日は はちじに おきました。そして、くじごろ でかけました。
2. キムさんは 昨日(きのう) しゅくだいを しませんでした。でも、今日 しました。
3. アリスさんに でんわを かけました。てがみも かきました。
4. パーティには 鈴木(すずき)さんを よびました。でも、田中さんは よびませんでした。

B. In Japanese, jot down five activities that you often do on weekends.

大川さんの週末

ことばの リスト (Vocabulary)

[Sentence +] から	Because [+ sentence]
汚(きたな)い	dirty
ですから	so
はやく	early

先週の土曜日に両親(りょうしん)が私に会(あ)いに来(き)ました。とてもうれしかったですが、忙(いそが)しくて大変(へん)でした。木曜日と金曜日にテストがあって時間(じかん)がなかったから、アパートはとても汚(きたな)かったです。ですから、土曜日の朝早(あさはや)く起(お)きて、掃除(そうじ)と洗濯(せんたく)をしました。それから、スーパーに買(か)い物(もの)に行(い)きました。

12時(じ)ごろに両親(りょうしん)が私のアパートに来(き)ました。少(すこ)し話(はなし)をして、アパートの近(ちか)くのショッピング・センターに行(い)って、昼(ひる)ご飯(はん)を食(た)べました。その後(あと)、買(か)い物(もの)をして、キャンパスに行(い)きました。図書館(としょかん)で上田さんに会(あ)いましたから、いっしょに図書館(としょかん)のカフェに行(い)って、コーヒーを飲(の)んで話(はなし)をしました。両親(りょうしん)は5時(じ)ごろ帰(かえ)りました。

読(よ)んだ後(あと)で Comprehension

A. しつもんに こたえて下さい。Answer these questions in Japanese.

1. 大川さんの 週末は どうでしたか。
2. 大川さんは 金曜日に 何を しましたか。
3. 大川さんは 土曜日の あさ 何を しましたか。
4. 大川さんは だれと 昼(ひる)ご飯(はん)を 食(た)べましたか。
5. どこで 食(た)べましたか。
6. 土曜日の ごご、キャンパスで 何を しましたか。

B. Identify any missing nouns for each sentence of the reading.

C. Write a letter to a friend in Japan describing your weekend activities.

総合練習 そうごうれんしゅう Integration

山田さんと　さとうさんの一日(いちにち)　A Day in the Lives of Ms. Yamada and Mr. Sato

The illustration below shows a typical day for two Japanese college students, Ms. Yamada and Mr. Sato. Ms. Yamada lives with her parents. Mr. Sato lives in an apartment because he is from another part of Japan. In groups of four or five, complete the following tasks.

1. Describe what each student does in a day.
2. Compare and contrast Ms. Yamada's and Mr. Sato's routines.
3. Discuss simlarities and differences between their daily routines and your own.

ロールプレイ Role Play

You are conducting a telephone survey of people's daily routines. With a partner, come up with five questions that you would like to ask. Then pretend to make a phone call. Politely ask to speak with someone (your partner). Once he/she comes to the phone, say すみません。アンケートちょうさなんですが、いいですか。(*Excuse me. I am doing a survey. May I . . . ?*) Ask the five questions and take notes. Once the call is complete, reverse roles with your partner. Compare notes with several people in the class to see if your routines share anything in common.

Chapter 7

第七課（だいななか）

Courtesy of Kazumi Hatasa

好きなものと　好きなこと

Favorite Things and Activities

Objectives Describing likes, dislikes, and preferences

Vocabulary Food, beverages, sports, music, leisure activities

Dialogue 上田さんと　リーさんのしゅみ *Ms. Ueda's and Mr. Li's Hobbies*

Japanese Culture Popular leisure activities and popular consumer goods in Japan

Grammar

I. Expressing likes or dislikes using 好き or きらい and the particle や

II. Forming noun phrases using の and plain present affirmative verbs (dictionary form)

III. Making contrasts using the particle は, and expressing *but* using が

IV. Making comparisons using 一番 and ～（の）方が　～より, and ～も～も and expressing lack of preference

V. Giving reasons using the plain form + ので

Listening Identifying conversation fillers

Communication Giving positive feedback with も; making contrasts with は

Kanji 時　間　分　半　毎　年　好　語　高　番　方　新　古　安　友

Reading Understanding word formation

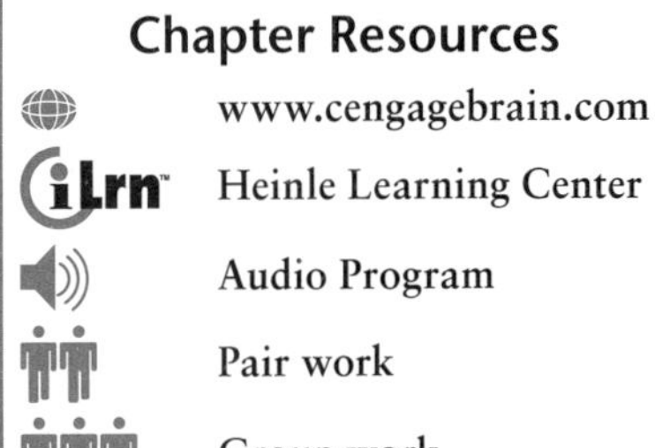

単語
たんご

Vocabulary

Nouns

うた	歌	song
おちゃ	お茶	tea, green tea
オレンジ		orange
カラオケ		Karaoke, sing-along
ぎゅうにゅう	牛乳	cow's milk
くだもの	果物	fruit
クラシック		classical music
ケーキ		cake
こうちゃ	紅茶	black tea
コーラ		cola
こと		thing (intangible)
ゴルフ		golf
さかな	魚	fish
さけ	酒	rice wine, alcoholic beverage (おさけ is also common)
ジャズ		jazz
ジュース		juice
しゅみ	趣味	hobby
しょくじ	食事	dining しょくじする to dine
スキー		skiing
スポーツ		sports
たいそう	体操	physical exercise, calisthenics
たべもの	食べ物	food
たまご	卵／玉子	egg
つり	釣り	fishing
トマト		tomato

ドライブ		driving (for pleasure)
にく	肉	meat
にんじん		carrot
のみもの	飲み物	beverage, drink
ハイキング		hiking
バスケットボール		basketball (abbreviated as バスケット or バスケ)
バナナ		banana
ヒップホップ		hip-hop music
ビール		beer
フットボール		(American) football (アメフト is also common)
ポップス		pop music
みず	水	water (おみず is also common)
ミルク		milk (for babies), creamer (for coffee etc.)
やきゅう	野球	baseball
やさい	野菜	vegetable
ラップ		rap music
りょこう	旅行	traveling りょこうする to travel
りんご		apple
レタス		lettuce
ロック		rock and roll
ワイン		wine

う -verbs

うたう	歌う	to sing
おわる	終わる	(for something) to end えいがが　おわる the movie ends
つくる	作る	to make
とる	撮る	to take (a photograph) しゃしんを　とる
はじまる	始まる	(for something) to begin じゅぎょうが　はじまる the class begins

い-adjectives

おいしい		delicious, good, tasty
たかい	高い	expensive (Chapter 4: high, tall)
やすい	安い	inexpensive

な-adjectives

きらい(な)	嫌い(な)	dislike, hate
すき(な)	好き(な)	like

Adverb

もっと		more

Particle

や		and (when listing examples) おちゃや　コーヒー tea, coffee, and so on

Prefix

だい	大	very much, 大すき like very much

Conjunctions

それから		and, in addition, then
たとえば	例えば	for example

Expressions

すきでもきらいでもありません	好きでも嫌いでもありません	I neither like nor dislike it.
～（は）ちょっと		~is a bit
～（は）どうですか		How about ～?

単語の練習 Vocabulary Practice

A. たべもの　Food

Name each item in the picture.

1. さかな　fish
2. にく　meat
3. たまご　egg
4. やさい　vegetable
5. くだもの　fruit
6. レタス　lettuce
7. にんじん　carrots
8. トマト　tomato
9. バナナ　banana
10. オレンジ　orange
11. りんご　apple
12. ケーキ　cake

Activity 1

しつもんに　日本語で　こたえて下さい。 Answer these questions in Japanese.

1. にくを　よく　たべますか。さかなは　どうですか。
2. スーパーで　よく　何を　かいますか。　(かいます *to buy*)
3. 何を　あまり　たべませんか。
4. 今　どんなものが　高いですか。

★ You can ask your instructor how to say other foods in Japanese as desired.

Supplementary Vocabulary: Food

えび	海老	shrimp
ぎゅうにく	牛肉	beef
とりにく	鳥肉	chicken
ぶたにく	豚肉	pork
キャベツ		cabbage
きゅうり		cucumber
たまねぎ	玉ねぎ	onion
なす		eggplant
ねぎ		green onion
ピーマン		green pepper
ほうれんそう	ほうれん草	spinach
いちご	苺	strawberry
ぶどう		grape
みかん		tangerine
メロン		melon

B. のみもの Beverages

Look at the pictures below and read each word in Japanese.

Notes

- お in おちゃ is a polite prefix for the noun ちゃ, but ちゃ is rarely used alone. Most people say おちゃ to refer either to green tea specifically, or to tea as a general category of beverages.
- お in おさけ is also a polite prefix for the noun さけ. Although people say both おさけ and さけ, the latter tends to sound more masculine. (お)さけ can mean either Japanese rice wine or alcoholic beverages in general.
- お水（みず） is commonly used for water, as it sounds softer and more polite.
- アイスコーヒー (*iced coffee*) is very common in Japan.

Activity 2

しつもんに　日本語で　こたえて下さい。Answer these questions in Japanese.

1. あなたのくに (*your country*) の人は　おさけを　のみますか。のみませんか。
2. どんなおさけを　のみますか。
3. よく　おちゃを　のみますか。のみませんか。
4. どんなおちゃを　のみますか。
5. どんなのみものを　よく　のみますか。どんなのみものは　あまり　のみませんか。
6. 学食には　どんなのみものが　ありますか。
7. スーパーには　どんなのみものが　ありますか。

C. スポーツ　Sports

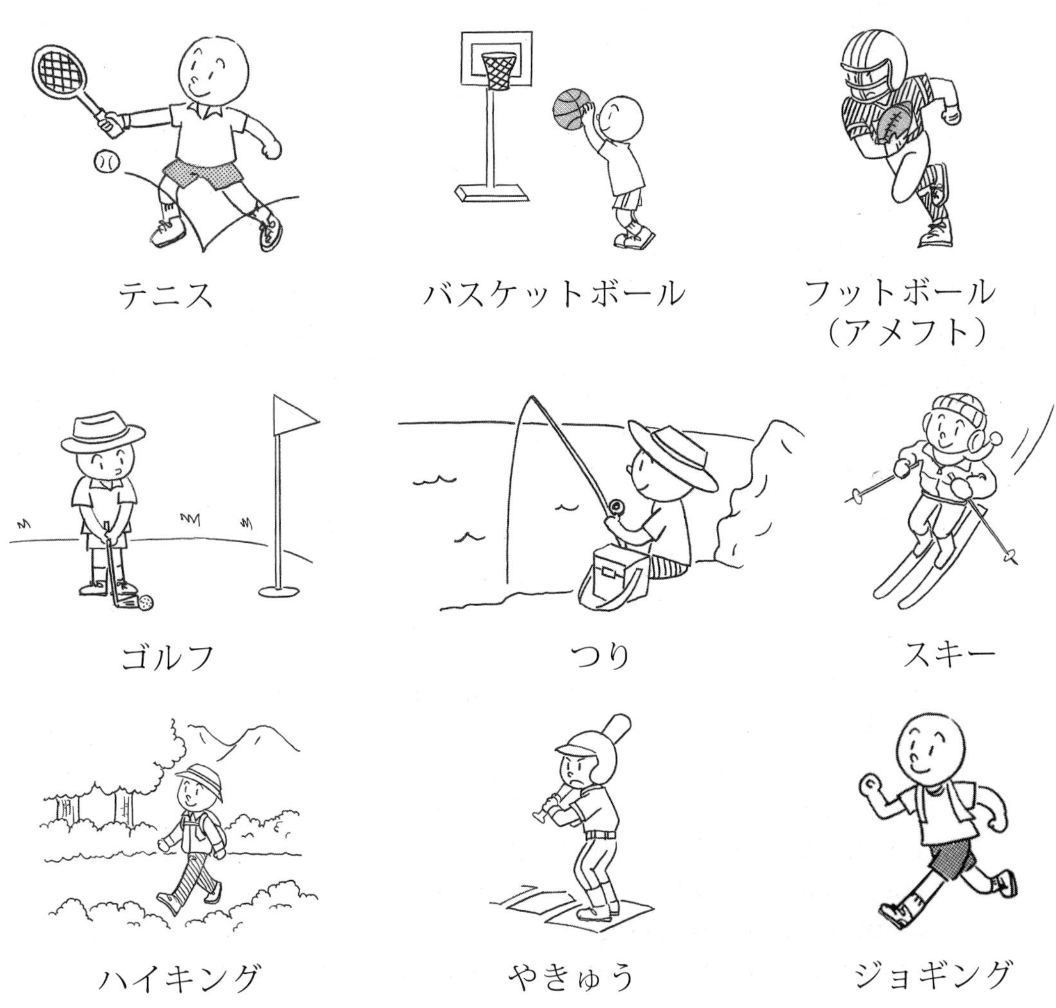

Activity 3

Match the Japanese words with their English equivalents in the above list.

_______1. たいそう	a. golf
_______2. バスケットボール	b. football
_______3. フットボール	c. jogging
_______4. ゴルフ	d. fishing
_______5. つり	e. hiking
_______6. スキー	f. skiing
_______7. ハイキング	g. physical exercise, calisthenics
_______8. やきゅう	h. basketball
_______9. ジョギング	i. baseball

Activity 4

しつもんに　日本語(ご)で　こたえて下さい。 Answer these questions in Japanese.

1. どのスポーツを　よく　しますか。
2. どのスポーツを　よく　みますか。
3. ～さんの友達(ともだち)は　どのスポーツを　よくみますか。

Supplementary Vocabulary: Sports

エアロビクス		aerobics
きんトレ	筋トレ	weight training
サッカー		soccer
じゅうどう	柔道	judo
すいえい	水泳	swimming
スケート		skating
スノーボード		snowboarding
ソフトボール		softball
バレーボール		volleyball
ボウリング		bowling

D. おんがく Music

クラシック
classical music

ジャズ
jazz

ロック
rock and roll

ポップス
pop music

ラップ、ヒップホップ
rap, hip-hop

Activity 5

Find the above words in the grid and circle them.

ク	ラ	シ	ラ	ク	ズ	ロ	ッ	プ
ジ	ク	ッ	ギ	タ	シ	ポ	ラ	ク
ポ	プ	ラ	ピ	ャ	ア	ッ	ジ	ズ
ッ	ズ	ッ	シ	ポ	ャ	プ	ポ	ロ
ノ	ノ	プ	ア	ッ	ズ	ス	ッ	ッ
シ	ラ	プ	ジ	ノ	ク	ラ	ク	ズ
ズ	ロ	ッ	ク	ス	ッ	ジ	ャ	ク
ク	ギ	シ	ッ	ク	ポ	ジ	ラ	プ
プ	ッ	ホ	プ	ッ	ヒ	ス	ズ	ク

E. レジャーと しゅみ Hobbies and leisure activities

Starting with this chapter, verbs are presented in dictionary form (plain present affirmative form).

りょこうする／
りょこうに いく
to travel

ドライブに いく／
ドライブを する
to go for a drive

うたを うたう
to sing songs

えを かく
to draw

りょうりを する／つくる
to cook

カラオケに　いく
to go sing karaoke

しゃしんを　とる
to take pictures

そとで　しょくじする
to dine out

Activity 6

Charades. Work in groups of three or four. Take turns acting out one of the activities listed above while the rest of the group tries to guess what it is in Japanese.

Activity 7

Say as many leisure activities as you can, using the following review expressions.

コンサート、おんがく、レストラン、かいもの、ビデオ、でんわ、テレビ、ゲーム、パーティ、およぐ（およぎます）、さんぽ、こうえん、あそぶ（あそびます）、メール、本

Supplementary Vocabulary: Hobbies and Leisure activities

いけばなを　する	生け花をする	(to) do **ikebana** (Japanese flower arrangement)
おどりに　いく	踊りに行く	(to) go dancing
ガーデニングを　たのしむ	ガーデニングを楽しむ	(to) enjoy gardening
ギターを　ひく	ギターを弾く	(to) play guitar
きってを　あつめる	切手を集める	(to) collect stamps
サイクリングに　いく	サイクリングに行く	(to) cycle, bike
せいじについて　はなす	政治について話す	(to) talk about politics
ピクニックに　いく	ピクニックに行く	(to) go on a picnic
ブログを　かく	ブログを書く	(to) write a blog
ペットと　あそぶ	ペットと遊ぶ	(to) play with a pet
ボランティアかつどうに　さんかする	ボランティア活動に参加する	(to) participate in a volunteer activity

ダイアローグ
Dialogue

はじめに Warm-up

しつもんに 日本語で こたえて下さい。Answer these questions in Japanese.

1. しゅみは　何ですか。
2. よく　スポーツを　しますか。
3. よく　スポーツばんぐみ (*program*) を　みますか。
4. どんなおんがくを　ききますか。

上田さんと リーさんのしゅみ *Ms. Ueda's and Mr. Li's Hobbies*

上田： リーさんのしゅみは　何ですか。

リー： そうですね。スポーツと　おんがくが　好きですね。

上田： そうですか。どんなスポーツが　好きですか。

リー： やきゅうや　バスケットボールが　好きですね。上田さんは？

上田： 私は　ジョギングが　一番　好きです。でも、バスケットも　好きですよ。

リー： そうですか。バスケットは　よく　しますか。

上田： いいえ、バスケットは　するより　みる方が　好きですね。リーさんは　どうですか。

リー：　バスケットは　みるのも　するのも　大好(だいす)きです。

上田：　そうですか。いいですね。

リー：　ところで、上田さんは　おんがくが　好(す)きですか。

上田：　ええ、好(す)きですよ。

リー：　そうですか。どんなおんがくが　好(す)きですか。

上田：　しずかなおんがくが　好(す)きなので、ジャズを　よく　ききます。

リー：　そうですか。ジャズは　ぼくも　大好(だいす)きですよ。

上田：　そうですか。じゃあ、クラシックは　どうですか。

リー：　ざんねんですが、クラシックは　あまり。クラシックより
ジャズやポップスの方(ほう)が　好(す)きですね。

Dialogue Phrase Notes

- ところで means *by the way.*
- When used before 好(す)き, 大(だい) does not mean *big*, but *very.*

ダイアローグの後(あと)で Comprehension

A. Circle はい if the following statement is true, and circle いいえ if it is false.

1. はい いいえ リーさんは やきゅうが 好(す)きです。
2. はい いいえ 上田さんと リーさんは バスケットボールが 好(す)きです。
3. はい いいえ 上田さんは バスケットボールを するのが 好(す)きです。
4. はい いいえ 上田さんは ジャズが 好(す)きです。
5. はい いいえ リーさんは クラシックの方(ほう)が ジャズより 好(す)きです。

B. Complete the following passage by filling in an appropriate word in each blank.

リーさんは よく ______________________________ します。

上田さんは____________が 好(す)きです。__________も 好(す)きです。

日本の文化(ぶんか)

Japanese Culture

Popular Leisure Activities

The 2011 white book (an official publication of the national government) indicates that the following are the most popular leisure activities in Japan:

Rank	Activity	# of participants
1	パソコン (*personal computer*) で　あそぶ*	78,080,000
2	ドライブを　する	63,100,000
3	こくないりょこう (*domestic travel*) を　する	61,660,000
4	そとで　しょくじ　する	60,640,000
5	えいがを　みる	51,710,000
6	どうぶつえん (*zoo*) や　びじゅつかん (*art museum*) や　はくぶつかん (*museum*) や　すいぞくかん (*aquarium*) や　しょくぶつえん (*botanical garden*) に　いく	48,120,000
7	おんがくを　きく	47,200,000
8	カラオケを　する	46,990,000
9	ビデオを　みる	45,660,000
10	たからくじを　かう (*buy lottery tickets*)	44,530,000
11	テレビゲームを　する	42,990,000
12	ゲームを　する (*play card or board games*)	39,710,000
13	ガーデニングを　する (*gardening*)	37,350,000
14	しらべものを　する (*looking things up*)	34,580,000
15	ピクニックや　ハイキングや　さんぽを　する	33,860,000

*(Note: This computer usage may not be "leisure activity" in a pure sense, as it includes time spent online and so may include email and other uses.)

Over eighty percent of the population participates in some kind of sport. Of these, 45% participate at least once a week, and about half of this number do so more than three times each week.

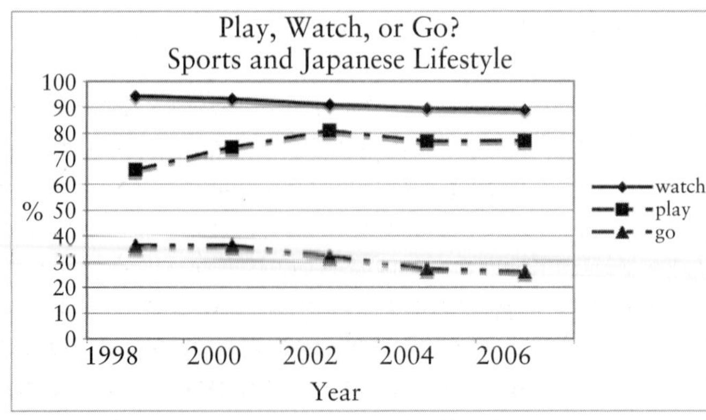

The three most popular athletic activities are walking, calisthenics, and jogging, followed by weight training, bowling, cycling and swimming. Although many people watch baseball and soccer, the number of people who participate in these team sports is smaller than for solo activities.

Traditional arts such as いけばな (*flower arrangement*), さどう (*tea ceremony*), and しょどう (*calligraphy*) ranked very low in number of participants.

Popular Consumer Goods

Smart phones (スマホ) and tablet PCs (タブレット) are very popular in Japan. You can watch TV on a smart phone or cell phone, or use it like a debit card to make retail purchases, in addition to more well-known functions like e-mail, taking photos, recording video, playing games, surfing the internet, and downloading and listening to music.

Another well-known obsession of the Japanese, particularly among women, is a love of "fast fashion" clothing (ファスト・ファッション) and luxury designer goods such as Gucci, Chanel, and Prada. Fast fashion clothing collections can be seen in UNICLO, H&M, Zara, Forever 21, and other clothing chains. They are based on the most recent fashion trends, and manufactured quickly and cheaply to allow mainstream consumers to take advantage of current styles at a low price. Fast fashion clothing became popular around 2000, and is seen as allowing people to enjoy fashion inexpensively. Japan's continuous economic depression since the early 1990s has made people more conservative in their spending habits. Even so, most major Japanese department stores have designer-goods sections. Even young people will often have one or more luxury items. Wherever you go in Japan, you can see women carrying designer handbags and wearing expensive accessories. This popularity has continued for more than three decades and does not seem to be affected by economic conditions.

Why do the Japanese love brand-name items so much? One explanation is that Japanese people traditionally place a high value on quality. After the Meiji Restoration (1868), many expensive foreign goods were imported from Europe, creating an association between quality and European luxury items. Today, brand names imply high quality, impeccable service, luxury, and status. Unlike fancy houses or even furniture, these items are still within reach of the average consumer. Owning them gives some people the satisfaction of possessing something valuable and unique. At the same time, many others consider a preoccupation with brand names to be shallow.

文法(ぶんぽう)
Grammar

I. Expressing likes or dislikes using 好(す)き or きらい and the particle や

In Japanese, 好(す)き (*like*) and きらい (*dislike*, *hate*) are used to express one's likes and dislikes. In English, *like*, *dislike*, and *hate* are verbs, but in Japanese 好(す)き and きらい are な - adjectives. Therefore, the negative form is じゃありません or じゃないです. The object of 好(す)き and きらい cannot be indicated by を because they are not verbs. Instead, use が to mark the object.

Topic (person, animal)		Noun (thing that s/he likes)	Particle	
私の友達(ともだち)	は	テニス	が	好(す)きです。

My friend likes tennis.

To list two or more items you like or dislike, use the particle と (and) as introduced in Chapter 5. However, と indicates that you like only the specific items you mentioned. For more items that you like or dislike, and for which you wish to show an example, use the particle や.

私は りんごと オレンジが 好(す)きです。
I like apples and oranges (but nothing else).

私は りんごや オレンジが 好(す)きです。
I like apples and oranges (and other food).

スミスさんは にんじんと たまごが きらいです。
Mr. Smith dislikes carrots and eggs.

スミスさんは にんじんや たまごが きらいです。
Mr. Smith dislikes carrots and eggs (and other things).

キム： はやしさんは どんなのみものが 好(す)きですか。
What kinds of drinks do you like, Ms. Hayashi?

はやし： そうですね。私は こうちゃや 日本のおちゃが 大好(だいす)きですね。
Well, I love black tea and Japanese tea (and so on).

キム： じゃあ、おさけは どうですか。
How about alcoholic beverages?

はやし： おさけは ちょっと。
Alcohol is a bit . . . (= I don't like alcoholic beverages very much.)

Notes

- 好(す)き and きらい can also be used before nouns. In this case, 好(す)き means *preferred* or *favorite* and きらい is the opposite.

  私の好(す)きな　くだものは　りんごです。
  A fruit I like is the apple.
  私のきらいな　くだものは　バナナです。
  A fruit that I don't like is the banana.

- You might want to avoid using きらい in an answer to a question because it has a strong negative connotation. You can use expressions such as ～は　ちょっと (～ *is a bit*) or あまり.
- In Chapters 2 through 5, ～は　どうですか meant *How is* ～*?* Another meaning of ～は　どうですか is *How about* ～ *?*

  大木(おおき)：私は　ワインが　好(す)きです。
  I like wine.
  水田(みずた)：じゃあ、ビールは　どうですか。
  Well, how about beer?
  大木(おおき)：ビールも　好(す)きですよ。
  I like beer, too.

- The prefix 大(だい) is commonly used with 好(す)き and きらい. 大好(だいす)き means *love* or *really like*, and 大(だい)きらい means *hate* or *really don't like*. 大好(だいす)き and 大(だい)きらい are more commonly used than とても　好(す)き or とても　きらい.
- If you don't like or dislike something, use 好(す)きでも　きらいでも　ありません or 好(す)きでも　きらいでも　ないです (*I neither like nor dislike it*).

話(はな)してみましょう　Conversation Practice

Activity 1

The following chart indicates what Mr. Yamada and Ms. Brown like and dislike. Express what they like or dislike, using 好(す)き, きらい. Use the particles と or や wherever appropriate.

Example:　山田さんは　りんごが　好(す)きです。

	山田さん		ブラウンさん	
	好き	きらい	好き	きらい
たべもの	apples	carrots and eggs	meat, fish, etc.	vegetables, fruit, etc.
のみもの	juice and coffee	milk	wine, beer, etc.	juice, black tea, etc.
スポーツ	golf, tennis, etc.	football	football	golf, jogging, etc.
おんがく	pop, jazz, etc.	classical music	rap and rock	classical music

Activity 2

Ask a partner what types of food, drinks, sports, and music he/she likes and dislikes. Your partner will give you examples using や.

Example: A: ～さんは　どんなたべものが　好きですか。
B: ケーキや　くだものが　好きです。
A: そうですか。

	私		パートナー	
	好き	きらい	好き	きらい
たべもの				
のみもの				
スポーツ				
おんがく				

Activity 3

Now work with the class. Ask your classmates what kinds of food, drinks, sports, and music they like and dislike. See if you can determine the most popular item in each category.

Example: A: ～さんは　どんなたべものが　好きですか。
B: ～が　好きです。
A: そうですか。じゃあ、きらいなたべものが　ありますか。
B: そうですね。～は　あまり　好きじゃありませんね。

	好き	きらい
たべもの		
のみもの		
スポーツ		
おんがく		

II. Forming noun phrases using の and plain present affirmative verbs (dictionary form)

The plain present affirmative form of a verb is also called the dictionary form because this is the form used for dictionary entries. This form also appears in time expressions, relative clauses, gerunds, and other structures. It is used in casual conversation, newspapers, expository writing, and other contexts. Learning when to use it appropriately can take some time.

In this section, you will learn to use the plain present affirmative form with の to convert verb phrases into noun phrases. This use of の is different from the pronoun の (one) and from the particle の in the structure Noun の Noun.

A. Plain present affirmative verbs (dictionary form)

The charts below show how to create the dictionary forms of verbs from their polite forms.

う -verbs

ます -form			Plain present affirmative (dictionary) form	
よみます (*read*)	yom + i + masu	→	yom + u	よむ
かきます (*write*)	kak + i + masu	→	kak + u	かく
あいます (*meet*)	a + i + masu	→	a + u	あう
はなします (*talk*)	hanash + i + masu	→	hanas + u	はなす
のみます (*drink*)	nom + i + masu	→	nom + u	のむ

る -verbs

ます -form			Plain present affirmative (dictionary) form	
たべます (*eat*)	tabe + masu	→	tabe + ru	たべる
ねます (*sleep*)	ne + masu	→	ne + ru	ねる
います (*be, exist*)	i + masu	→	i + ru	いる
おきます (*get up*)	oki + masu	→	oki + ru	おきる

Irregular verbs

ます -form			Plain present affirmative (dictionary) form	
します (*do*)	shi + masu	→	su + ru	する
きます (*come*)	ki + masu	→	ku + ru	くる

Once you know the plain affirmative form, it is relatively easy to identify the group to which it belongs (う-verb, る-verb, or irregular verb) by using the following three steps:

1. Remember that する and くる are the only irregular verbs.
2. If a dictionary form ends in -**Xiru** or -**Xeru** (X represents any consonant here), it is a る-verb. For example, since たべる ends in **beru** and おきる ends in **kiru**, they are る-verbs. However, つくる, おわる, and はじまる are not る-verbs, because they end in -**Kuru**, -**Waru**, and -**Maru**, and not -**Xiru** or -**Xeru**.
3. The rest are all う-verbs. There are some exceptions to this rule. Among them, the ones you have learned are かえる (*return*) and はいる (*enter*). These are う-verbs.

B. The plain present affirmative form + のが 好きです・きらいです (like/dislike doing ～)

The plain present affirmative form (dictionary form) + のが 好きです・きらいです is used to express one's likes or dislikes in terms of doing something. In English, the gerund (-ing) form of a verb and the infinitive (*to* + verb) may be used as nouns, as in examples such as *seeing is believing* or *to play a musical instrument is fun*. In a similar manner, Japanese adds の to the plain present affirmative form to create a noun phrase.

	Noun phrase				
		Verb (dictionary form)		Particle	
私は	本を	よむ	の	が	好きです。

I like reading books.

Here are some more examples.

私は えいがを みるのが 好きです。
I like watching movies.

えいがを みるのは おもしろいです。
Watching movies is fun.

スミス：田中さんは 何を するのが 好きですか。
What do you like to do, Ms. Tanaka?

田中：そうですね。私は インターネットで あそぶのが 好きですね。スミスさんは どうですか。
Let's see. I like to surf the Internet. How about you, Mr. Smith?

スミス：ぼくは クラシックおんがくを きくのが 好きです。
I like to listen to classical music.

話(はな)してみましょう Conversation Practice

Activity 1

Create questions using the following expressions and ～のが　好(す)きですか.

Example: てがみを　かきます
　　　　てがみを　かくのが　好(す)きですか。

1. 友達(ともだち)のしゃしんを　とります
2. そとで　しょくじを　します
3. ジョギングを　します
4. カラオケに　いきます
5. うたを　うたいます
6. ごはんを　つくります
7. えを　かきます
8. 日本語(ご)を　はなします
9. おふろに　はいります
10. およぎます

Activity 2

Work with a partner. Using the questions you created in Activity 1, ask your partner which activities he/she likes to do.

Example: たべます

A: たべるのが　好(す)きですか。

B: ええ、大好(だいす)きです。

or　いいえ、あまり　好(す)きじゃないです／好(す)きじゃありません。

Activity 3

Work with the class. First, decide what activities you like and dislike. Ask your classmates about what they do or don't like and find out who has tastes similar to your own.

Example:

A: どんなことを　するのが　好(す)きですか。

B: 私は　たいそうを　するのが　好(す)きです。～さんは　どうですか。

A: 私も　たいそうを　するのが　好(す)きです。／私は　うたを　うたうのが　好(す)きです。

A: どんなことを　するのは　あまり　好(す)きじゃありませんか。

B: 私は　およぐのは　あまり　好(す)きじゃないです。～さんは　どうですか。

A: 私も　およぐのは　好(す)きじゃありません。／私は　おさけを　のむのが　好(す)きじゃありません。

Activity 4

The following pictures illustrate activities that Kimura-san likes to do. Describe them using ～のが　好きです.

Example: 木村さんは　テニスを　するのが　好きです。

Activity 5

Ask a partner what he/she likes to do during school breaks.

Example: A: ～さんは　やすみの日に　何を　するのが　好きですか。
B: そうですね。ねるのが　好きですね。

III. Making contrasts using the particle は, and expressing *but* using が

A. Using は for contrast

Besides indicating a topic, は can indicate a contrast between two items. In both of the following sentences, the second は in the example puts りょうり and そうじ in contrast.

私は よく りょうりを します。でも、そうじは あまり しません。
I cook often but I don't do the cleaning very often.

キムさんは りょうりが 好(す)きです。でも、そうじは 好(す)きじゃ ありません。
Mr. Kim likes cooking but he does not like cleaning.

The particle は for contrast is often used in sentences ending with negative forms. Often, there is no explicit item of contrast in this case.

田中： 明日(あした)も きますか。 *Are you coming tomorrow?*

スミス： いいえ、明日(あした)は きません。 *No, I am not coming tomorrow.* (but I may come some other time).

The use of は for contrast may appear in more than one sentence or clause to make the contrast explicit. In the following example sentences, the topic of the first sentence is 私, so it is marked with the topic marker は. And although this first sentence does not end in a negative form, コーヒー also takes は, because it is in contrast with コーラ in the second sentence.

私は コーヒーは 好(す)きです。 でも、コーラは あまり 好(す)き じゃありません。
I like coffee. But I don't like cola very much.

は for contrast can be used with any type of noun as well. Like は for topic, and も for similarity, は replaces を (direct object) or が (subject), but it is usually added to another particle, as in the examples below. Some particles, such as に (point of time) and に／へ (goal) may be deleted if they can be easily understood from context.

よく としょかんで べんきょうします。でも、学生会館(かいかん)では しません。
I often study in the library. But, I don't (study) in the student union.

ここに ねこが います。 あそこには いません。
There is a cat here. It's not over there.

山田さんは 今日は きません。でも、土曜日 (に) は きます。
Mr. Yamada will not come today. But he will come on Saturday.

B. Expressing *but* using が

The particle が can be used to connect two sentences or clauses that oppose each other. が is attached at the end of the first sentence.

Clause	Particle (but)	Clause
こうちゃは　好きです	が、	おちゃは　あまり　好きじゃないです。

I like black tea but I don't like green tea very much.

Since が often connects two clauses in a contrasting or negative relationship, the contrast marker は is often used with が as well. For example:

ゴルフを　するのは　好きですが、みるのは　あまり　好きじゃありません。
I like playing golf but I don't like watching it.

あさは　ごはんを　たべませんでしたが、ひるは　たべました。
I did not eat breakfast but I did eat lunch.

そうじは　しましたが、せんたくは　しませんでした。
I did the cleaning but I didn't do laundry.

友達と　えいがは　みませんでしたが、テレビは　みましたよ。
I didn't watch a movie with my friends, but we did watch TV.

ゆうびんきょくには　いきませんでしたが、ぎんこうには　いきました。
I didn't go to the post office, but I did go to the bank.

Note

- が can also be used to open a conversation, or to introduce a topic of conversation. This is called a "weak but." It does not introduce a strong negative relation, and it is similar to the use of *but* in English as in: "Excuse me, but could you turn on the TV?"

  あのう　すみませんが、今　何時ですか。
  Excuse me, but what time is it?

  私のうちは　あれですが、田中さんのは　どれですか。
  My house is that one over there, but which one is Ms. Tanaka's?

話(はな)してみましょう Conversation Practice

Activity 1

Look at the drawings below and describe what Yamada-san likes, doesn't like very much, and positively dislikes. Use は to contrast his likes and dislikes.

Example: 山田さんは りんごが 好(す)きですが、トマトは あまり 好(す)きじゃありません。

Activity 2

Work with a partner. Referring to the items in the table below, ask questions to determine your partner's preferences. Try to use both particles も and は correctly in your follow-up questions.

Example: A: 〜さんは どんなたべものが 好(す)きですか。

B: レタスが 好(す)きです。

Follow-up questions:

A: そうですか。にんじんも 好(す)きですか。

B: いいえ、にんじんは あまり 好(す)きじゃありません。

A: じゃあ、トマトは どうですか。

B: はい、トマトは 好(す)きです。

Categories	Items
たべもの	トマト　にんじん　レタス　バナナ　オレンジ
どうぶつ	いぬ　ねこ　さかな　くま *(bear)*　とり *(bird)* さる *(monkey)*
のみもの	ビール　ワイン　コーラ　こうちゃ　コーヒー ぎゅうにゅう　ジュース　（お）水(みず)
スポーツ	たいそう　ハイキング　テニス　フットボール ゴルフ
おんがく	クラシック　ジャズ　ポップス　ロック　ラップ　ヒップホップ

Activity 3

For each statement below, create two sentences. One should express a similarity with the statement; the other should express a contrast.

Example: 私は　あさごはんを　たべます。
　　ばんごはんも　たべます。でも、ひるごはんは　たべません。

1. 私は　よく　テレビを　みます。
2. 月曜日に　アルバイトを　します。
3. 昨日(きのう)　山本さんに　メールを　かきました。
4. スミスさんは　先生に　しつもんしました。
5. 山本さんの友達(ともだち)は　週末　よく　おんがくを　ききます。
6. 毎日(まいにち)　りょうりを　します。

Activity 4

Describe what each person likes and does not like to do.

Example: 山田さんは　パーティに　いくのが　好(す)きですが、
　　パーティを　するのは　あまり　好(す)きじゃありません。

山田	パーティに　いきます	パーティを　します
小川	あそびます	べんきょうします
山本	そとで　しょくじを　します	うちで　たべます
大川	えいがを　みます	ゲームを　します
金田(かねだ)	コンサートに　いきます	うたを　うたいます
田中	しゃしんを　とります	えを　かきます

IV. Making comparisons using 一番(いちばん) and ～（の）方(ほう)が ～より, and ～も～も and expressing lack of preference

In English, preference can be expressed by changing the form of an adjective into a superlative (e.g., the best, the prettiest, the nicest, the most wonderful) or a comparative (e.g., better, prettier, nicer, more wonderful). Japanese has a similar set of expressions, but the adjective forms do not change. Instead, preference is expressed in other parts of the sentence. This chapter introduces the superlative with the adverb 一番(いちばん), the comparative with ～の方(ほう)が　～より, and lack of preference using ～も～も.

A. Superlatives using 一番(いちばん)

一番(いちばん) means *number one* or *first*, and it is used to form a superlative, such as the *nicest person*, *prettiest house*, *the best movie*, and *I like X the best*. 一番(いちばん) must be followed by an adjective or adverb. For example, *the best movie* should be expressed as 一番(いちばん)　いい　えいが. 一番(いちばん)　えいが is a common mistake made by native English speakers.

としょかんは　一番(いちばん)　大きい　たてものです。
The library is the biggest building.

このたまごが　一番(いちばん)　安(やす)いです。
These eggs are the cheapest.

ジャズが　一番(いちばん)　好(す)きです。
I like jazz the best.

山本さんが　一番(いちばん)　よく　べんきょうします。
Ms. Yamamoto studies the hardest.

私の一番(いちばん)　好(す)きな　たべものは　バナナです。
My favorite food is bananas.

To indicate the scope of a preference, use the phrase ～の中で.

スポーツの中で　何が　一番(いちばん)　おもしろいですか。
Which sport is the most interesting?

くだものの中で　何を　一番(いちばん)　よく　たべますか。
Which fruits do you eat most often?

のみものの中で　コーヒーが　一番(いちばん)　好(す)きです。
Coffee is the beverage I like best.

If the preceding noun is a place noun, 中 is omitted:

このクラスで 山田さんが 一番(いちばん) よく べんきょうします。

Mr. Yamada studies the hardest in this class.

富士山(ふじさん)は 日本で 一番(いちばん) 高(たか)い 山です。

Mt. Fuji is the highest mountain in Japan.

田中： このクラスで どの人が 一番(いちばん) よくべんきょうしますか。

Which person studies the most in this class?

石田(いしだ)： 山田さんが 一番(いちばん) よく べんきょうします。
／山田さんです。

Mr. Yamada studies the hardest. / It's Mr. Yamada.

スミス： たべものの中で 何が 一番(いちばん) 好(す)きですか。

Which type of food do you like best?

大田(おおた)： さかなが 一番(いちばん) 好(す)きです。

I like fish the best.

B. Comparatives using ～(の)方(ほう)が ～より

The expression ～(の)方(ほう)が ～より is used to compare two items. The item preceding ～(の)方(ほう)が is emphasized or preferred over the item that precedes ～より. These items can be either noun phrases or verb phrases ending in the dictionary form.

Noun (Preferred)	Particle	Noun	Particle	Noun (Less preferred)	Particle	
きょうと	の	方(ほう)	が	(とうきょう	より)	きれいです。

Kyoto is prettier than Tokyo.

とうきょうの方(ほう)が ニューヨークより 大きいです。

Tokyo is larger than New York.

このさかなの方(ほう)が にくより 安(やす)いです。

This fish is cheaper than meat.

りょうりは つくる方(ほう)が たべるより 好(す)きです。

I like cooking more than eating.

やきゅうは みるより する方(ほう)が たのしいです。

Playing baseball is more fun than watching it.

To ask someone's preference between two items, use 〜と〜と　どちらの方(ほう)が.

Noun (Choice A)	Particle	Noun (Choice B)	Particle	Question word	Particle	Noun	Particle	
とうきょう	と	きょうと	と	どちら	の	方(ほう)	が	きれいですか。

Which is prettier, Tokyo or Kyoto?

とうきょうと　ニューヨークと　どちらの方(ほう)が　大きいですか。
Which is larger, Tokyo or New York?

さかなと　にくと　どちらの方(ほう)が　安(やす)いですか。
Which is cheaper, fish or meat?

To ask about two actions, use the dictionary form + の. This の is the same one used in 〜のが　好(す)きです.

テニスを　みるのと　するのと　どちらの方(ほう)が　好(す)きですか。
Which do you like better, watching tennis or playing it?

ここに　いるのと　でかけるのと　どちらの方(ほう)が　いいですか。
Which is better, staying here or going out?

リー：大川さんと　山本さんと　どちらの方(ほう)が　よく　りょうりを　しますか。
Who cooks more often, Mr. Okawa or Ms. Yamamoto?

上田：山本さんの方(ほう)が　よく　りょうりを　します。
Ms. Yamamoto cooks more often.

リー：上田さんは　どうですか。
How about you, Ms. Ueda?

上田：そうですね。私は　りょうりを　するより　たべる方(ほう)が　いいですね。
Well, eating is better than cooking in my case.

When you want to compare the preference between two actions, use the dictionary form of verb + 方(ほう)が.

Notes

- If 〜より is obvious from the context, then it can be omitted, as in the above example conversation between Mr. Li and Ms. Ueda.
- The adverb もっと is used with adjectives or verbs, and it means *more* or *even more*.

もっと　たべませんか。 *Why don't you eat more?*

私のいぬは　もっと　大きいです。 *My dog is (even) bigger.*

C. Expressing lack of preference (comparisons of equality)

If you do not have a preference for one item over another, use ～も ～も. Items can be two noun phrases or two verb phases ending with の.

Noun A	Particle	Noun B	Particle	
とうきょう	も	きょうと	も	好(す)きです。

I like both Tokyo and Kyoto.

Noun A	Particle	Noun B	Particle	
とうきょう	も	きょうと	も	好(す)きじゃありません。／ 好(す)きじゃないです。

I don't like Tokyo or Kyoto.

田中：ペプシと　コカコーラと　どちらの方(ほう)が　おいしいですか。
Which is more delicious, Pepsi or Coca-Cola?

中山：ペプシも　コカコーラも　おいしいです。
Both Pepsi and Coca-Cola are delicious.

でも、私は　ペプシの方(ほう)が　好(す)きです。
But I like Pepsi better.

ペギー：うちで　たべるのと　そとで　しょくじするのと
どちらの方(ほう)が　好(す)きですか。
Which do you like better, eating at home or dining out?

あやか：そうですね。うちで　たべるのも　そとで
しょくじするのも　好(す)きですが、
Well, I like both eating at home and dining out.

たいてい　うちで　たべます。
But I usually eat at home.

NOTE

- ～も　～も can be used in either a positive or negative statement. A も B も+ affirmative statement means *both A and B*. A も B も + negative statement (or in a negative statement) means *neither A nor B*.

  やきゅうも　バスケットも　好(す)きです。
  I like both baseball and basketball.
  ロックも　ジャズも　好(す)きじゃありません。
  I don't like either rock or jazz very much.

話(はな)してみましょう Conversation Practice

Activity 1

Answer the questions.

Example: おんがくの中で　何が　一番(いちばん)　好(す)きですか。
ジャズが　一番(いちばん)　好(す)きです。

1. スポーツの中で　何が　一番(いちばん)　好(す)きですか。
2. たべものの中で　何が　一番(いちばん)　きらいですか。
3. のみものの中で　何を　一番(いちばん)　よく　のみますか。
4. どんなおんがくを　一番(いちばん)　よく　ききますか。
5. このクラスで　だれが　一番(いちばん)　よく　日本語(ご)を　はなしますか。

Activity 2

Ask a partner about places and things that have the most in some attribute, using the nouns and adjectives provided. Follow the example.

Example: アメリカ／川／大きい
A: アメリカでは　どの川が　一番(いちばん)　大きいですか。
B: ミシシッピ川(がわ)が　一番(いちばん)　大きいです。

1. アメリカ／まち／古(ふる)い
2. 日本／山／高(たか)い
3. せかい (*world*)／まち／きれい
4. キャンパス／たてもの／新(あたら)しい
5. アメリカ／しゅう (*state*)／小さい
6. アメリカ／たべもの／おいしい

Activity 3

First determine the order of the two items in parentheses using the adjectives provided. Then form a comparative sentence.

Examples: 好(す)き　(こうちゃ／コーヒー)
こうちゃの方(ほう)が　コーヒーより　好(す)きです。

むずかしい (日本語(ご)で　かく / はなす)
日本語(ご)で　かく方(ほう)が　はなすより　むずかしいです。

1. いい（いぬ／ねこ）
2. しずか（としょかん／カフェ）
3. いそがしい（先生／学生）
4. 好き（たべる／ねる）
5. 大きい（ニューヨーク／とうきょう）
6. むずかしい（日本語／スペイン語）
7. きらい（りょうりを する／そうじを する）
8. 大変（べんきょうする／しごとを する）

Activity 4

Work with a partner. Using the items in Activity 3, taking turns asking each other three comparative questions.

Example: 好き　（こうちゃ／コーヒー）

A: こうちゃと　コーヒーと　どちらの方が　好きですか。

B: コーヒーの方が　好きです。

A: 日本語で　かくのと　はなすのと　どちらの方が むずかしいですか。

B: かく方が　はなすより　むずかしいです。

Activity 5

Work with a partner. Ask your partner about at least two things he/she likes, and then ask him/her to rank them. If he/she likes both equally, write both words in Column 1.

Example: A: どんなくだものが　好きですか。

B: りんごや　オレンジが　好きです。

A: じゃあ、りんごと　オレンジと　どちらの方が　好きですか。

B: そうですね。オレンジの方が　好きです。

or りんごも　オレンジも　好きです。

Category	1	2
くだもの	オレンジ	りんご
のみもの		
スポーツ		
おんがく		

V. Giving reasons using the plain form + ので

The conjunction ので indicates a reason, and it is attached to the end of the clause that expresses the reason. If a sentence contains both a reason and result, the clause for the reason must come before the clause indicating the result. For example, in the sentence 来(らい)週から　テストが　はじまるので、今週は　よく　べんきょうします。(*I will study hard this week because exams begin next week.*), the reason is stated at the beginning of the sentence and it ends with ので ; the result is mentioned in the latter half of the sentence.

Clause (reason)	Particle (reason)	Clause (result)
いちごが　好(す)きな	ので、	よく　かいます。

I like strawberries, so I often buy some.

しごとが　もうすぐ　おわるので、ここで　まって下さい。
My job will be finished soon, so please wait here.

J-ポップが　好(す)きなので、よく　J-ポップのうたを　うたいます。
I like J-pop (Japanese pop music), so I often sing J-pop songs.

The ～ので construction is preceded by a clause ending with the plain form of a verb or adjective. The charts on the following pages show the plain affirmative and negative forms of verbs and adjectives. In these charts, *I*, *it*, *he*, and *she* are given as subjects in English, but these forms can also be used to indicate *you*, *we*, and *they*, depending on context.

Plain form + ので / noun or な-adjective + な + ので

な -adjectives

In the case of な-adjectives, the affirmative is expressed by using the stem + な + ので.

Dictionary form	Prenominal form	Plain negative form	～ので (because ～)	
			Affirmative (Plain)	Negative (Plain)
きれい *pretty*	きれいな (もの) *pretty (thing)*	きれい じゃない *not pretty*	きれいなので *because it is pretty*	きれいじゃないので *because it is not pretty*

Noun + です (copula verb)

Noun + な expresses the affirmative.

Dictionary form	Noun + な	Plain negative form	～ので (because ～)	
			Affirmative (Plain)	Negative (Plain)
日本人 *Japanese person*	日本人な *Japanese*	日本人じゃない *not Japanese*	日本人なので *because he/she is Japanese*	日本人じゃないので *because he/she is not Japanese*

い -adjectives

The plain affirmative form of an い-adjective is the same as its dictionary form. The plain negative form is created by deleting です from the polite version.

Dictionary form / Plain affirmative form	Plain negative form	～ので (because ～)	
		Affirmative (Plain)	Negative (Plain)
うれしい *happy, be happy*	うれしくない *not happy*	うれしいので *because he/she is happy*	うれしくないので *because he/she is not happy*

う -verbs

To form the negative of a う-verb, delete ます from the ます-form, change the vowel sound of the last letter [i] to [a], and add ない.

ます -form	Dictionary form / Plain affirmative form	Plain negative form	～ので (because ～)	
			Affirmative (Plain)	Negative (Plain)
よみます /yom/+/i/+/masu/ *read*	よむ /yom/+/u/ *read*	よまない /yom/+/a/+/nai/ *not read*	よむので *because he/she reads*	よまないので *because he/she does not read*
かきます /kak/+/i/+/masu/ *write*	かく /kak/+/u/ *write*	かかない /kak/+/a/+/nai/ *not write*	かくので *because he/she writes*	かかないので *because he/she does not write*
はなします /hanash/+/i/+ /masu/ *talk*	はなす /hanas/+/u/ *talk*	はなさない /hanas/ +/a/+ /nai/ *not talk*	はなすので *because he/she talks*	はなさない ので *because he/she does not talk*
おわります /owar/+/i/+/masu/ *end*	おわる /owar/+/u/ *end*	おわらない /owar/+/a/+/nai/ *not end*	おわるので *because it ends*	おわらない ので *because it does not end*

If there is no consonant before the [i] sound of the ます-form, as in あいます, change [i] to [wa] instead of [a]. The plain present negative form of あります is ない.

ます -form	Dictionary form/ Plain affirmative form	Plain negative form	～ので (because ～)	
			Affirmative (Plain)	Negative (Plain)
あいます /ai /+ /masu/ *meet*	あう *meet*	あわない /awa/ +/nai/ *not meet*	あうので *because he/she meets*	あわないので *because he/she does not meet*
あります /ari/+ /masu/ *be, exist**	ある *be, exist*	ない /nai/ *not be, exist*	あるので *because there is* ～	ないので *because there isn't* ～

*Remember that あります is used only for inanimate objects or events.

る -verbs

Change ます to ない to form the plain negative form.

ます -form	Dictionary form/ Plain affirmative form	Plain negative form	～ので (because ～)	
			Affirmative (Plain)	Negative (Plain)
たべます *eat*	たべる *eat*	たべない *not eat*	たべるので *because he/she eats*	たべないので *because he/she does not eat*
ねます *sleep*	ねる *sleep*	ねない *not sleep*	ねるので *because he/she sleeps*	ねないので *because he/she does not sleep*
います *be, exist**	いる *be, exist*	いない *not be, exist*	いるので *because there is* ～	いないので *because there isn't* ～

*Remember that います is used only for living beings such as people and animals.

Irregular verbs

ます -form	Dictionary form/ Plain affirmative form	Plain negative form	～ので (because ～)	
			Affirmative (Plain)	Negative (Plain)
します *do*	する *do*	しない *not do*	するので *because he/she does*	しないので *because he/she does not do*
きます *come*	くる *come*	こない *not come*	くるので *because he/she comes*	こないので *because he/she does not come*

話してみましょう Conversation Practice

Activity 1

Combine the following pairs of sentences using 〜ので. Make sure to start with the sentence that expresses a reason and follow it with ので.

Example: にくを たべます。さかなは きらいです。
さかなは きらいなので、にくを たべます。

1. 毎日 しごとを します。いそがしいです。
2. よく デパートに いきます。かいものが 好きです。
3. 七時に おきます。八時に じゅぎょうが はじまります。
4. トマトが たくさん あります。トマトで りょうりを します。
5. うちで ゆっくりします。今日は いそがしくありません。
6. 今日は じゅぎょうが ありません。ひるまで ねます。

Activity 2

Work with a partner. Ask your partner which of the following items he or she prefers and why.

Example: マクドナルド (*McDonald's*) ウェンディーズ (*Wendy's*)

A: マクドナルドと ウェンディーズと どちらの方が いいですか。

B: ウェンディーズの方が おいしいので、ウェンディーズの方が いいですね。

		私	パートナー
Example: マクドナルド	ウェンディーズ		ウェンディーズ おいしい
ターゲット	ウォルマート		
アメリカのくるま	日本のくるま		
タブレット (*tablet*)	ノートパソコン (*laptop*)		
アンドロイド (*Android*)	iPhone		

Activity 3

Work with a partner. Invite your partner to do an activity together. He/She will refuse the invitation and give a reason using ので.

Example: A: 来(らい)週の水曜日に　コンサートに　いきませんか。

B: ありがとうございます。でも、水曜日は、りょうしんがくるので。

A: あ、そうですか。ざんねんですね。

B: すみません。あの、また　今度(ど)　さそってくれませんか。(さそう *to invite*)

A: いいですよ。じゃあ、また、今度(ど)。

聞く練習（き　れんしゅう）
Listening

上手な聞き方（じょうず　き　かた） Listening Strategy

Identifying conversation fillers

In conversations in English, you hear many empty words and expressions such as *hmm*, *uh*, and *well*. Their approximate equivalents in Japanese are えーと, あのう, and そうですね. These words are referred to as conversation fillers. While the words themselves have little meaning, they are used to keep the conversation flowing when the person speaking is still thinking of what to say next.

練習（れんしゅう） Practice

Listen to the following statements and short conversations. Circle the fillers you hear.

1. あのう　えーと　そうですね
2. あのう　えーと　そうですね
3. あのう　えーと　そうですね
4. あのう　えーと　そうですね

日本人学生に　きく　Interviews with Japanese students

Listen to the interviews between a reporter for a student newspaper and four Japanese students who are visiting the college campus. Fill in the chart with their names and what each one likes to do.

	なまえ	好き（す）
Interview 1		
Interview 2		
Interview 3		
Interview 4		

聞き上手 話し上手
Communication

上手な話し方 Communication Strategy

Giving positive feedback with も; making contrasts with は

Like そうですか and そうですね, the particles も (similarity) and は (contrast) can be used to carry on a conversation more smoothly. If a person mentions something that you have in common, use も to give that person positive feedback.

中田：　大川さんは　どんなスポーツが　好きですか。
大川：　やきゅうが　好きですね。
中田：　ああ、そうですか。私も　やきゅうが　大好きですよ。

By establishing that you both like baseball, the conversation can now progress to subtopics, such as which teams you do like. In cases where you do not share common interests, you can use は to mark a contrast.

スミス：　高山さんは　どんなスポーツが　好きですか。
高山：　そうですね。やきゅうが　好きですね。
スミス：　ああ、そうですか。私は　テニスが　大好きです。

Be careful not to focus too much on your differences, however, since this may become disruptive or seem unfriendly. Instead, you might want to follow up with other questions to find something you do have in common.

上田：　リーさんは　どんなスポーツが　好きですか。
リー：　そうですね。やきゅうや　ゴルフが　好きですね。
上田：　そうですか。じゃあ、サッカーも　好きですか。
or　　　サッカーは　どうですか。
リー：　ええ、サッカーも　よく　みますよ。
or　　　そうですね、サッカーは　ちょっと。

Carrying on a conversation in any language is like playing catch. You must take turns speaking and listening while sustaining common topics. It is especially important to be aware of these strategies when trying to speak a second language. Being a good listener is key to participating successfully in a conversation.

練習 Practice

With a partner, choose a topic below, or come up with one of your own. Discuss your preferences, incorporating the communicative strategies you have learned.

1. leisure activities
2. music
3. sports
4. movies
5. food
6. books

漢字
かんじ
Kanji

History of the Japanese Writing System

Historically, Chinese characters have been classified into six categories, known as the 六書 (りくしょ). The first four categories are based on structural composition and the last two are based on usage. The distinction among them is not clear-cut, because some belong to more than one category and the definitions are not always clear.

象形文字 (しょうけいもじ) (pictographs) are based on pictures of objects they represent, as explained in Chapter 5. For example, 大 in Chapter 4, 人, 山, 川, 田 in chapter 5, and 月, 火, 水, 木, 金, 土, and 日 are all in this category. Some of them are very different from the original illustration, and it can often be hard to see a character's origin. The number of **kanji** in this category is only a few hundred.

指事文字 (しじもじ) (logograms or ideographs) originated from simple graphic representations of abstract concepts. The number of **kanji** in this category is extremely limited, as they are primarily used for direction, like 上 and 下, and numbers, like 一, 二, 三, 四, 八, 十, and 百. Others include 本 and 末.

会意文字 (かいいもじ) (compound ideographs or ideographs) use a combination of pictographs and logograms to repent an overall meaning. For example, the combination of 人 (*person*) and 木 (*tree*), becomes 休 (*to rest*), and the combination of 日 and 月 becomes 明 (*bright*). Other examples are 学 and 先.

形声文字 (けいせいもじ) (semantic-phonetic characters, phonetic-ideographic characters) are by far the largest **kanji** category, including such common kanji as 曜, 時, and 週. Their proportion of kanji varies depending on the total number of **kanji** considered, but it is usually estimated to be between 80 to 90 percent of characters. They usually consist of a phonetic component, which indicates **on**-reading of the **kanji**, and the semantic component, which indicates the categorical meaning of the **kanji**. For example, the left side of 語, 言 means *to say*, indicating 語 has something to do with speech or language. The right side 吾 provides the pronunciation /go/ for this **kanji**. The combination of the two indicates that 語 refers to language and is pronounced ご. Other semantically-related words such as 話 (/wa/ story, talking), 読 (/doku/ reading), 訳 (/yaku/ translation), and 説 (/setsu/ explanation) all include 言 but have different pronunciations.

転注文字 (てんちゅうもじ) (derivative characters) is not a well-defined category and thus is rather problematic. It refers to **kanji** where the meaning has changed dramatically from the original usage. For example, 楽 (*music, comfort, ease*) is thought by some to have begun as a picture of a drum, and by others to have represented bells on a plank of wood. The number of **kanji** in this category is extremely limited.

仮借文字 (かしゃもじ) (phonetic loan characters) are characters where pronunciation in Chinese, but not meaning, were imported into Japanese . For example, 来 was a pictograph that meant *wheat* in the ancient Chinese. When this **kanji** was imported, its pronunciation /rai/ was adopted but the meaning was not. Since one of the meanings of /rai/ is *to come* in Japanese, 来 is used to indicate the verb *to come* and has the **on**-reading /rai/. Other commonly-used characters in this category include 今, 五, 六, and 七, but the total number in this category is also very limited.

時	time, hour	とき　ジ	一時(いちじ)　二時半(にじはん)　五時間(ごじかん)べんきょうします。　その時(とき)　時計*(とけい)
間	interval, duration	あいだ　カン	時間(じかん)がありません。
分	to divide, to understand, minute	わ(ける)・わ(かる)　フン・ブン・プン	二十分(にじゅっぷん)　分(わ)かりました。
半	half	ハン	毎日六時半(まいにちろくじはん)におきます。
毎	every	マイ	毎週(まいしゅう)シカゴにいきます。　毎日(まいにち)　毎月(まいつき)
年	year	とし　ネン	三年生(さんねんせい)　毎年(まいとし)
好	to like	す(き)　コウ	テニスが好(す)きです。　大好(だいす)き
語	language, word	かた(る)　ゴ	日本語(にほんご)　フランス語(ご)ではなします。
高	high, expensive	たか(い)　コウ	古(ふる)い高校(こうこう)　高(たか)い山
番	number, order, turn	バン	やさいが一番好(いちばんす)きです。
方	direction, person (polite)	かた　ホウ	サッカーの方(ほう)がフットボールより好(す)きです。

新	新	new あたら(しい)　シン	新(あたら)しいレストラン　新聞(しんぶん)
古	古	old ふる(い)　コ	カラオケで古(ふる)いうたをうたいます。
安	安	inexpensive, cheap やす(い)　アン	今日はやさいが安(やす)いです。
友	友	friend とも　ユウ	友達(ともだち)とかいものにいくのが好(す)きです。

An asterisk (*) indicates an irregular reading.

読(よ)めるようになった漢字(かんじ) (**Kanji** and compounds you can now read)

一時　八(はち)時半　時々(ときどき)　時計(とけい)　三(さん)時間　二(に)週間　三十(さんじゅっ)分　分かりました

毎日　毎朝(あさ)　毎晩(ばん)　毎週　毎年　毎月　来(らい)年　好き　大好き　日本語

英(えい)語　中国語(ちゅうごく)　高い　高校　一(いち)番　新しい　新聞(しんぶん)　古い　安い　友達(だち)　水(みず)

日本人のなまえ：高山(たかやま)　大木(おおき)　大田(おおた)　金田(かねだ)　水田(みずた)　石田(いしだ)

練習(れんしゅう)　Practice

Read the following sentences written in **hiragana, katakana,** and **kanji.**

1. 私の友達(だち)は毎日５時半におきます。
2. 小川さんは古いきっさてんも新しいカフェも大好きです。
3. 大川さんは毎週テニスを二(に)時間します。
4. 本田：「安いワインと高いワインとどちらの方が好きですか。」
   金田：「安いワインや高いワインより、おいしいワインが一(いち)番好きです。」
5. スミスさんは日本の高校で一(いち)年間べんきょうしました。その時、日本語もべんきょうしました。
6. 山本：「今、何時ですか。」
   高田：「８時１５分です。」

読む練習 (よ れんしゅう)
Reading

上手な読み方 (じょうず よ かた) Reading Strategy

Understanding word formation

Many words are made up of one or more words as well as prefixes and suffixes. It is important to examine the components of a word to guess its meaning and increase your vocabulary. For example, the suffix 〜や indicates a *store* or *shop* in Japanese, and さかな means *fish*. So what does さかなや mean? How about にくや and くだものや?

読む前に (よ まえ) Pre-reading

Take apart the following words and give their meanings. Follow the example.

Example: 大学院生 (いんせい)

大学院 (いん) and 生, graduate school + student = graduate student

1. フランス人
2. しょくじする
3. そうじする
4. 大学生
5. 三年生
6. 毎日
7. のみもの
8. 大好き

本田さんのしゅみ

言葉のリスト (ことば)

時間がかかる	to take time
ベートーベン	Beethoven
モーツァルト	Mozart

私の趣味(しゅみ)はスポーツと音楽(おんがく)です。スポーツの中ではテニスが一番好きです。それから、たいそうとスキーも大好きです。でも、野球(やきゅう)やゴルフは時間がかかるので、あまり好きじゃないのです。バスケットボールは見(み)るのは好きですが、するのはあまり好きじゃありません。

音楽(おんがく)はにぎやかな音楽(おんがく)の方が好きなので、クラシックよりポップスやロックをよく聞(き)きます。クラシックには好きなのもありますが、きらいなのもあります。たとえば、モーツァルトはよく聞(き)きますが、ベートーベンはあまり好きじゃないので、聞(き)きません。

読(よ)んだ後(あと)で　Comprehension

A. しつもんに　日本語で　こたえて下さい。Answer these questions in Japanese.

1. 本田さんのしゅみは　何ですか。
2. 本田さんは　スキーと　バスケットと　どちらの方が　好きですか。
3. 本田さんは　どんなスポーツが　きらいですか。
4. 本田さんは　どんなおんがくを　よく　ききますか。
5. 本田さんは　だれのおんがくを　ききますか。

B. Underline the following transitional words in the text, and observe how they help indicate relationships between sentences.

それから　in addition, also, and
でも
たとえば　for example

C. Write a short paragraph about your hobbies. Describe at least two hobbies and provide details such as where, when, how often, and with whom you do them.

総合練習
そうごうれんしゅう
Integration

A. Work with a partner. You need to pick out a birthday present for your partner from a mail-order catalogue. In order to do so, you want to find out his/her hobbies, favorite things, and things that he/she wants. Ask your partner questions to come up with as many options as you can.

Example: A: ～さんのしゅみは 何ですか。

B: そうですね。私は しゃしんを とるのが 好きですね。

A: そうですか。しゃしんですか。いいですね。

ほかにも (*In addition*) しゅみが ありますか。

B: ええ、スポーツが 好きですよ。

A: どんなスポーツが 好きなんですか

B: ハイキングや ゴルフが 好きですね。

A: そうですか。たべものは どうですか。

B: たべものですか。ケーキや くだものが 好きですね。

B. Work with a new partner. Look at the items in a mail-order catalogue (pictured on the next page). Ask each other about each person's previous partner's hobbies and favorite things. Then discuss and decide on what to buy for the previous partner. Compare at least two items.

Example: A: ～さん (previous partner) は 何が 好きですか。

B: そうですね。しゃしんを とるのが 好きです。そして、ゴルフと ハイキングも 好きです。

A: たべものは どうですか。

B: ケーキや くだものが 好きです。

A: そうですか。じゃあ、誕生日(たんじょうび) (*birthday*) には どんなものが いいですか。

B: そうですね。このフォトフレーム (*photo frame*) は どうですか。

A: いいですね。でも、新しいデジカメも ありますよ。

B: そうですね、でも、フォトフレームの方が デジカメより安いので、フォトフレームの方が いいです。

A: じゃあ、このフォトフレームは どうですか。

一番安いですよ。

B: そうですね。いいですね。

D. Hurst/Alamy

ピクチャーカラー
フォトフレームS
定価 700 円

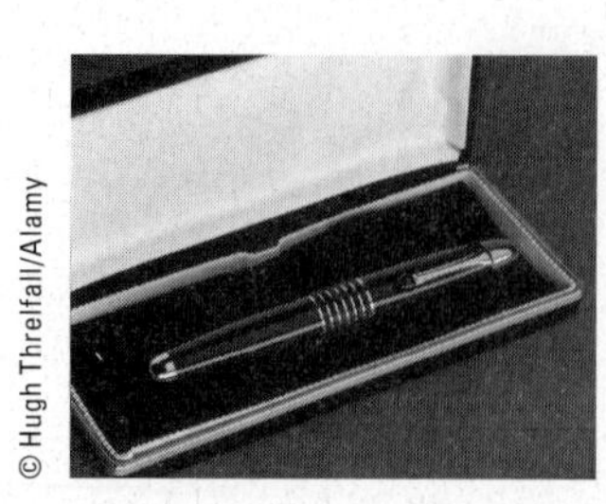
© Hugh Threlfall/Alamy

パーカー クラシック
GT ボールペン
定価 4,000 円

© Chiyacat/Shutterstock.com

ミラックス デジタル
カメラ
ウルトラミニ 1 千万画素
定価 25,000 円

© Hugh Threlfall/Alamy

マグカップ
定価 750 円

© Bloomimage/Collage/Corbis

おまかせフラワー
アレンジ
定価 4,000 円

© Lew Robertson/Flame/Corbis

トラベル キャリーケース
定価 3,000 円

ロールプレイ

1. Work with a partner. Using the dialogue as a model conversation, create a new conversation in which you ask your partner about his/her favorite things and hobbies.
2. You are at a party. Introduce yourself to someone and start a conversation. Find out whether he/she shares some of your interests.
3. You are planning a blind date for a friend. Find out what kind of person she/he likes.
4. You are looking for an apartment. Tell your real estate agent what kind of place you'd like. Mention your preferences for size, rooms, location, and other details that are important to you.

Chapter 8

第八課(だいはちか)

© Kenneth Hamm/Photo Japan

買い物(かいもの)
Shopping

Objectives Making requests, expressing quantities and numbers, talking about prices, shopping

Vocabulary Clothing, accessories and departments; numbers 100 and above, expressions related to merchandise, prices, and activities in a store

Dialogue デパートで *At a department store*

Japanese Culture Shopping, department stores, customer service, and methods of payment

Grammar

I. Requesting and giving explanations or additional information, and creating harmony and shared atmosphere using ～んです

II. Expressing desire using ほしい・ほしがっている and ～たい・～たがっている

III. Expressing quantities with numbers and the counters まい, 本, ひき, and さつ

IV. Expressing quantities using Japanese-origin numbers

V. Talking about prices using 円(えん); indicating floor levels with かい

Listening Recognizing the characteristics of speech

Communication Asking for paraphrases and repetition

Kanji Using **kanji** for numbers

一　二　三　四　五　六　七　八　九　十　百
千　万　円　店

Reading Scanning

Chapter Resources

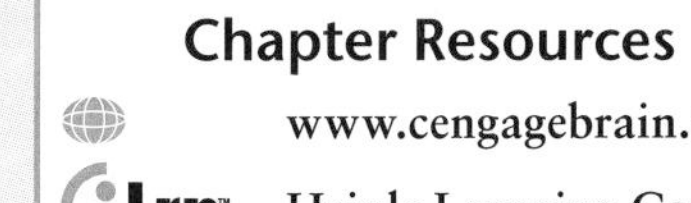

www.cengagebrain.com

Heinle Learning Center

Audio Program

Pair work

Group work

単語 (たん) Vocabulary

Nouns

アクセサリー		accessories
アクセサリーうりば	アクセサリー売り場	accessory department
イヤリング		earring
うでどけい	腕時計	wristwatch
うりば	売り場	department, section (of a store)
おきゃくさん	お客さん	customer, guest
かさ	傘	umbrella
くつ	靴	shoes
くつした	靴下	socks
コート		coat
CD/DVD うりば	CD/DVD 売り場	CD/DVD section
ジーンズ		jeans
ジャケット		jacket
シャツ		shirt
しょくひん	食品	food
しょくひんうりば	食品売り場	food department
しんしふく	紳士服	menswear
しんしふくうりば	紳士服売り場	menswear department
スーツ		suit
スカート		skirt
ストッキング		stockings, pantyhose
セーター		sweater
セール		sale
たんじょうび	誕生日	birthday
ちか	地下	basement　ちかいっかい　B1
Tシャツ		T-shirt

ドレス		formal dress
ネクタイ		tie
ネックレス		necklace
はこ	箱	box
パンツ		trousers, shorts
ハンドバッグ		handbag
ふく	服	clothing
ふじんふく	婦人服	woman's clothing
ふじんふくうりば	婦人服売り場	women's clothing section
ブラウス		blouse
ぶんぼうぐ	文房具	stationery
ぶんぼうぐうりば	文房具売り場	stationery section
ベルト		belt
ぼうし	帽子	hat, cap
みせ	店	store, shop
ゆびわ	指輪	ring
ワンピース		dress (worn on informal occasions)

う -verbs

かう	買う	to buy
とる	取る	to take 取る is a general equivalent for *to take*, but 撮る is for taking pictures or recording video.

る -verbs

いれる	入れる	to put　はこに　いれる to put in a box
みせる	見せる	to show

Adverbs

すこし	少し	a little, a few
たくさん		a lot, many, much
ちょっと		a little, a few (more casual than すこし)

もう		～ more, another ～
もう　すこし	もう少し	a little more
もう　ちょっと		a little more

Counters

～えん	～円	Yen, counter for Japanese currency
～かい	～階	counter for floors of a building
～さつ	～冊	counter for bound objects (e.g. books, magazines)
～つ		general counter (Japanese-origin number)
～ひき	～匹	counter for fish and small four-legged animals
～ほん	～本	counter for long, cylindrical objects (e.g. bottles, films, pens, pencils)
～まい	～枚	counter for thin objects (e.g. film, paper, plates, shirts)

Question words

いかが		how (polite form of どう)
いくつ		how many
いくら		how much (money)
どうして		why

Numbers

せん	千	thousand
ひゃく	百	hundred
まん	万	ten thousand (note that ten thousand is a unit in Japanese)

Expressions

いらっしゃいませ		Welcome
ぜんぶで	全部で	all together
～は　ありませんか		Do you have ～? Do you carry ～? (literally, *Isn't there ～?*)
やさしい　ことばで　いってください	やさしい言葉で言って下さい	Please say it in easier words
～を　ください	～を下さい	Please give me ～

単語の練習 Vocabulary Practice

A. ふくとアクセサリー Clothing and accessories

シャツ
shirt

T シャツ
T-shirt

セーター
sweater

ブラウス
blouse

ジャケット
jacket

ワンピース／ドレス
dress

コート
coat

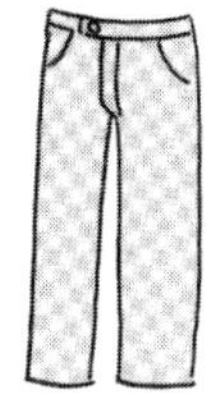
パンツ
pants

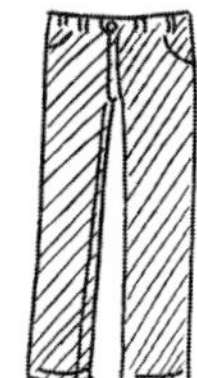
ジーンズ
jeans

スカート
skirt

スーツ
suit

ネクタイ
tie

ベルト
belt

靴下（くつした）
sock

ストッキング
stockings, pantyhose

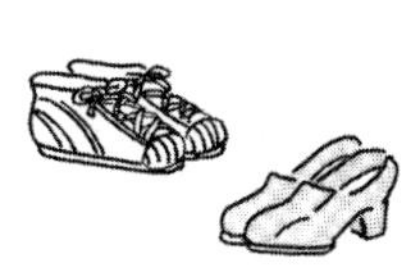
くつ
shoes

かばん
bag, luggage

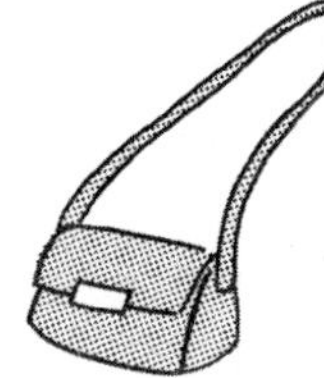
ハンドバッグ
handbag

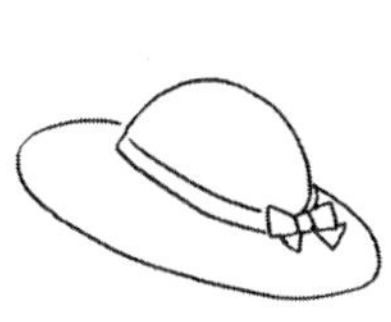
ぼうし
hat/cap

腕時計（うでどけい）
wristwatch

ネックレス
necklace

イヤリング
earrings

ゆびわ
ring

かさ
umbrella

Activity 1

Name the clothing that the following people are wearing.

Activity 2

Work with a partner. Name the clothing and accessories that your partner is wearing and list them.

Activity 3

しつもんに　日本語で　こたえて下さい。 Answer the questions in Japanese.

1. さいきん (*recently*) どんなふくを　かいましたか。
2. さいきん (*recently*) どんなアクセサリーを　かいましたか。
3. アクセサリーの中で　何が　一番好きですか。
4. ふくの中で　何が　一番好きですか。

Supplementary Vocabulary: clothing

あさ	麻	linen
ウール		wool
きもの	着物	kimono (traditional Japanese clothing)
コットン		cotton
サンダル		sandal(s)
したぎ	下着	underwear
シルク		silk
スカーフ		scarf
スニーカー		sneaker(s)
トレーナー／スウェット		sweat shirt, “sweats”
パーカー		hooded sweatshirt, “hoodie”
ブーツ		boot(s)
ブレスレット		bracelet

B. うりば Store Departments

アクセサリーうりば	accessory section
かばんうりば	luggage section
しょくひんうりば	food section
しんしふくうりば	menswear section
婦人服(ふじんふく)うりば	women's clothing section
ぶんぼうぐうりば	stationery section
CD ／ DVD うりば	CD/DVD section

Activity 4

Imagine where various sections of a large department store in your home country might be located in the building. Then jot down a few items that you would find in each section. See page 328 for useful vocabulary.

Example: A: 一(いっ)かいに　何が　ありますか。

B: アクセサリーうりばが　あります。

A: そうですか。アクセサリーうりばには　どんなものが ありますか。

B: ハンドバッグやネックレスが　あります。

Floor	うりば	Items
ろっかい (6F)		
ごかい (5F)		
よんかい (4F)		
さんがい (3F)		
にかい (2F)		
いっかい (1F)		

C. 100から上の数字(すうじ) Numbers above 100

100	ひゃく	1,000	せん	10,000	いちまん
200	にひゃく	2,000	にせん	20,000	にまん
300	さんびゃく	3,000	さんぜん	30,000	さんまん
400	よんひゃく	4,000	よんせん	40,000	よんまん
500	ごひゃく	5,000	ごせん	50,000	ごまん
600	ろっぴゃく	6,000	ろくせん	60,000	ろくまん
700	ななひゃく	7,000	ななせん	70,000	ななまん
800	はっぴゃく	8,000	はっせん	80,000	はちまん
900	きゅうひゃく	9,000	きゅうせん	90,000	きゅうまん

Notes

- ひゃく (*hundred*) and せん (*thousand*) change their pronunciation with some numbers in the same way as ふん (*minute*).
- Numbers like 346, 995, and 6,126 are formed by combining the thousands digit, hundreds digit, tens digit, and ones digit.

346	さんびゃくよんじゅうろく
995	きゅうひゃくきゅうじゅうご
6,126	ろくせんひゃくにじゅうろく

- For numbers 10,000 or larger, まん becomes a base unit.

10,000	いちまん
100,000	じゅうまん
1,000,000	ひゃくまん
20,000	にまん
200,000	にじゅうまん
2,000,000	にひゃくまん
35,000	さんまんごせん
350,000	さんじゅうごまん
3,500,000	さんびゃくごじゅうまん

Activity 5

Say the following numbers in Japanese.

Example: 100ひゃく

1. 200
2. 300
3. 400
4. 500
5. 600
6. 700
7. 800
8. 900
9. 1,000
10. 2,100
11. 3,333
12. 20,600
13. 88,666
14. 142,918
15. 153,000

Activity 6

Write the following mathematical problems in Japanese. The plus sign (+) is pronounced たす, and the minus sign (–) is pronounced ひく. The topic marker は is used for the equal sign (=).

Example: 100+200=300 ひゃく たす にひゃくは さんびゃくです。

1. 300 + 9,500 =
2. 660 – 40 =
3. 12,350 + 45 =
4. 3,900 + 700 =
5. 45,000 – 870 =
6. 3,210 + 28 =
7. 7,600 – 283 =

Activity 7

Work with a partner. Your partner will write a three-digit number on your back. Say the number.

Example: Your partner writes 100 on your back. You say: ひゃく.

Activity 8

Work in groups of three or four. Each member writes five-digit numbers on two different cards. Show one card to the other members of the group, and have them read it aloud as quickly as they can. Give the card to the winner.

Activity 9

Work in groups of three or four. One person writes a number between 100 and 90,000 on a sheet of paper. The rest of the group guesses the number using comparative expressions.

Example: A: そのすうじ (*number*) は 百(ひゃく)より 大きいですか。小さいですか。

B: 大きいです。

C: じゃあ、二百(にひゃく)より 大きいですか。小さいですか。

B: 小さいです。

D: 百五十(ひゃくごじゅう)より 大きいですか。小さいですか。

B: 大きいです。

D. 店(みせ)で つかう ことば Useful expressions in a store

～は ありませんか	Do you have ～ ?
～を 下さい	Please give me ～
～を とって下さい	Please get, pick up ～ (とる *to pick up*)
～を はこに いれて下さい	Please put ～ in a box (いれる *to put*)
～を みせて下さい	Please show me ～ (みせる *to show*)
セール	sale
Money/time します	It costs/takes ～ (する *to cost/to take*)

Activity 10

Work with a partner. Take turns asking questions or making requests using one of the expressions from the table. Your partner either acts out or responds to the question.

かさを とる	本を かばんに いれる	シャツを みせる
セールが ある	ジャケットを みせる	腕時計(うでどけい)を とる
10ドル (*dollars*) する	ネックレスを はこに いれる	靴下(くつした)を みせる

Activity 11

Work with a partner. Take turns playing the roles of customer and store clerk. Each of you should make at least two requests.

Example: あのコートを　とって下さい。
Your partner pretends to get a coat for you.

E. サイズ、りょう、ねだん Size, quantity, and price

たくさん	a lot
もっと　たくさん	more (quantity)
もっと　高い	more expensive
もっと　安い	less expensive
もっと　大きい	larger
もっと　小さい	smaller
すこし／ちょっと	a little, less (すこし and ちょっと are interchangeable.)
もう すこし／もう　ちょっと	a little more
もう すこし　大きい／もう　ちょっと　大きい	a little bigger
もう すこし　小さい／もう　ちょっと　小さい	a little smaller

Activity 12

Work with a partner. Complete the following conversation using the appropriate quantity and size expressions. There may be more than one possible answer.

Example: A: コーヒーを　のみますか。
B: ええ、大好きなので、<u>たくさん</u>　のみます。

1. A: このセーターは　いかがですか。
   B: 小さいですね。 __________のは　ありませんか。
2. A: このシャツは　いかがですか。
   B: すこし　高いですね。__________のは　ありませんか。
3. A: このくつは　いかがですか。
   B: ちょっと　大きいです。__________のを　みせて下さい。
4. A: このストッキングは　あまり　よく　ありませんね。
   B: じゃあ、__________ですが、こちらは　いかがですか。

ダイアローグ

はじめに　Warm-up

しつもんに日本語でこたえて下さい。Answer these questions in Japanese.

1. よく　デパートに　いきますか。
2. デパートで　何を　よく　かいますか。
3. あなたのくに (*your country*) のデパートには　どんなものが　ありますか。
4. よく　どんな店(みせ)に　かいものに　いきますか。

デパートで　*At a department store*

来週(らい)は　石田(いし)さんの誕生日(たんじょうび) (*birthday*) です。上田さんは　デパートに　いきました。

あんないがかり (*information assistant*)：　いらっしゃいませ。

上田：　すみません。しんしふくうりばは　どこに　ありますか。

あんないがかり：　しんしふくうりばは　三(さん)がいで　ございます。

上田：　そうですか。じゃあ、しょくひんうりばは　何がいですか。

あんないがかり：　地下一(ちかいっ)かいで　ございます。

上田さんは　しんしふくうりばにいきました。

店(みせ)の人 (*sales clerk*)：　いらっしゃいませ。
上田：　あのう、　そのネクタイを　みせて下さい。
店(みせ)の人：　これですか。　どうぞ。
上田：　いくらですか。
店(みせ)の人：　一万円(いちまんえん)です。
上田：　そうですか。もうすこし　安いのは　ありませんか。
店(みせ)の人：　じゃ、こちらは　いかがでしょうか。
上田：　これは　いくらですか。
店(みせ)の人：　四千円(よんせんえん)です。
上田：　いいですね。じゃあ、これ　下さい。
店(みせ)の人：　かしこまりました。では、　一万円(いちまんえん)　おあずかりします。
おくりものですか。
上田：　はい、そうです。

店(みせ)の人は　ネクタイを　はこに　いれました。

店(みせ)の人：　六千円(ろくせんえん)の　おかえしで　ございます。どうも
ありがとうございました。

上田さんは　しょくひんうりばに　います。

店(みせ)の人：　いらっしゃいませ。
上田：　あのう、このりんごのケーキを　三(みっ)つ　下さい。
それから　そのオレンジのケーキを　五(いつ)つ　下さい。
店(みせ)の人：　はい。りんごのケーキを　三(みっ)つと　オレンジのケーキ
五(いつ)つですね。ぜんぶで３，９５０円(えん)に　なります。

Dialogue Phrase Notes

- ～で　ございます is a polite form of ～です.
- ～に　なります is commonly used by store clerks instead of です.
- いかがでしょうか is a polite expression for どうですか.
- おあずかりします is a polite expression for あずかる, which means *to keep* or *to hold temporarily.*
- おくりもの means *present* or *gift.*
- おかえし is a polite expression for *change* (money returned).

ダイアローグの後(あと)で　Comprehension

A. Fill in the blanks with the appropriate words.

上田さんは____________________に　いきました。____________________で りんごのケーキと______________________を　かって、_______________で ________________をかいました。ぜんぶで______________________円(えん)でした。

B. Circle はい if a statement is true and いいえ if it is false.

1. はい　いいえ　　上田さんは　オレンジのケーキを　三(みっ)つ　かいました。
2. はい　いいえ　　しんしふくうりばは　三(さん)がいに　あります。
3. はい　いいえ　　上田さんは　一万円(いちまんえん)の　ネクタイを　かいました。
4. はい　いいえ　　しょくひんうりばは　地下(ちか)に　あります。

文法(ぶんぽう)
Grammar

I. Requesting and giving explanations or additional information, and creating harmony and shared atmosphere using ～んです

The structure ～んです is frequently used in conversation instead of ～ます. The use of ～んです helps to establish or maintain rapport with the listener. By using ～んです the speaker treats the addressee as a member of his/her own social group rather than as an outsider. On the other hand, ～ます merely conveys a fact as it is observed, so statements with ～ます sound more neutral or impersonal in tone. Japanese people often use ～んです to sound friendly and show concern for each other, as a way to be polite. The charts below show how ～んです can be used.

Comment

	Verb (plain form)	
あまり	たべない	んですね。

You don't eat much.

Response

Topic		Adjective (plain form)	
にくは	あまり	好きじゃない	んですよ。

I don't like meat very much.

Although ～んです is used in many different situations, there are a few situations where ～んです is most commonly used. First, ～んです is used to invite additional information or explanations beyond the simple answer. For example, おんがくが好きなんですか indicates that the speaker not only wants to know whether the addressee likes music but also wants to learn more about it. On the other hand, おんがくが 好きですか merely asks the listener's likes and dislikes about music. This use of ～んです can express the speaker's interest to the addressee and friendliness. If overused, however, it sounds nosy or imposing.

水本(みずもと)： あのシャツ いいですね。
That shirt's nice.

田中： ええ、とても 好きなんですが、ちょっと 高いんですよ。
I really like it, but it's a bit expensive.

水本(みずもと)： そうですか。いくらぐらいですか。
Really? How much is it?

田中： セールで 二万円(にまんえん)です。
It's 20,000 yen on sale.

水本（みずもと）： 二万円（にまんえん）！ それは 高いですね。
20,000 yen! That's really expensive.

Notes

- 〜んです can be also used to make an excuse or to explain the reasons for a situation without indicating it explicitly. In the following example, Mr. Kim gives a vague excuse when Ms. Smith approaches him.

  スミス： あのう、すみませんが。
  Excuse me.

  キム： すみません。今 ちょっと いそがしいんです。
  Sorry, I'm tied up now.

- The 〜んです structure is also used for confirming the speaker's assumption, or giving and requesting an explanation or reason. For example, if the speaker assumes that the listener is going home, he/she would likely use かえるんですか instead of かえりますか.
- In addition, 〜んです can a imply surprise or irritation. In the following example, Ms. Lopez expresses her surprise by using 〜んですか in her second utterance.

  ロペス： どこに いくんですか。
  Where are you going?

  山田： びょういんです。
  To the hospital.

  ロペス： えっ、びょういんへ いくんですか。
  What? Are you going to the hospital?

- The structure 〜のです・のだ is used in writing instead of 〜んです. In casual speech, 〜んです becomes の in a question or statement. A male speaker may use 〜んだ・のだ in a statement as well.

  ロペス： どこに いくの？
  Where are you going?

  山田： びょういんに いくの。
  びょういんに いくんだ。
  To the hospital.

- The question word どうして (*why*) is frequently used with 〜んです, implying that an explanation is being asked for. The answer to such a question will also be given with 〜んです as well as ので indicating that the explanation is being given. どうしてですか means *why is that?* どうして tends to imply surprise about someone's response or behavior and the demand for an explanation, so it can sound rather aggressive or accusatory.

話(はな)してみましょう　Conversation Practice

Activity 1

You have heard various things about different people. Ask questions to confirm whether your understanding is correct.

Example: 大田さんは　新しいかれし (*boyfriend*) が　います。
<u>えっ、かれしが　いるんですか。</u>

1. 高山さんは　やさいを　たべません。
2. 古田(ふるた)さんの店(みせ)は　山の中に　あります。
3. サラさんは　パンツが　好きです。
4. ジョンさんは　ぜんぜん　りょうりをしません。
5. 大川さんのジーンズは　五万円(ごまんえん)です。
6. 高田さんのジーンズは　古いです。
7. ゆみさんは　スカートが　好きじゃありません。

Activity 2

Work with a classmate. Extend an invitation for this weekend. Your partner will refuse the invitation. Follow up by asking 何か　あるんですか (*Do you have something to do?*). Find out why your invitation was refused.

Example: A: 今週の週末に　あそびに　きませんか。
B: ありがとう。でも、ちょっと　つごうが　わるくて。
A: そうなんですか。何か　あるんですか。
B: ええ、月曜日に　テストが　あるんですよ。
A: そうですか。それは　大変(へん)ですね。

Activity 3

Work with a partner. You bump into each other on the street. Both of you are going shopping today. First decide the place, the item, and/or your reason for shopping. Then ask each other about your plans.

Example: A: おでかけですか (*Are you going out?*)
B: ええ、ちょっと　友達(だち)と　デパートまで。
A: そうですか。　おかいものですか。
（おかいもの is a polite form of かいもの）
B: ええ、今日は　セールが　あるんですよ。

II. Expressing desire using ほしい・ほしがっている and 〜たい・〜たがっている

Japanese has two ways to indicate desire. ほしい means *I want* something, and たい means *I want to do* something. ほしい and たい express only what you (the speaker) want. To talk about what someone else wants, ほしい and たい are attached to other expressions such as 〜がっている (*showing a sign that* 〜), 〜んです(*it is the case that* 〜), and 〜そうです (*I heard that* 〜).

A. ほしい　I want (something)

ほしい is an adjective that indicates the speaker wants something (a physical object). The subject of ほしい must be the speaker in a statement and either the speaker or the listener in a question. The object of ほしい takes the particle が.

Question

Topic (subject)		Noun (object)	Particle	い -adjective	
スミスさん	は	何	が	ほしいです	か。

What do you want, Ms. Smith?

Answer

Noun (object)	Particle	い -adjective
ジャケット	が	ほしいです。

I want a jacket.

おきゃくさん：　あのう、しろいブラウスが　ほしいんですが。
Excuse me, I want a white blouse.

店(みせ)の人：　はい、こちらに　ございますが。
Yes, they're right here.

As shown in the chart, ほしい is an い-adjective and takes が to mark the object, though が is often replaced by the contrastive marker は in negative form.

くろいきれいな　ストッキングが　ほしいです。
I want pretty black pantyhose.

ストッキングは　ほしくありません。／ほしくないです。
I don't want pantyhose.

B. ほしがっている　Someone else wants (something)

To express what someone else wants, ほしい is often followed by the suffix 〜がっている (*he/she is showing signs of* 〜). When the suffix 〜がっている is used, the object is marked by the particle を.

Topic (subject)		Noun (object)	Particle	い -adjective (stem)	Auxiliary verb
スミスさん	は	ジャケット	を	ほし	がっています。

Ms. Smith wants a jacket.

私の友達(だち)は　誕生日(たんじょうび)に　腕時計(うでどけい)を　ほしがっている。
My friend wants a wristwatch for his birthday.

This 〜がっている form is used because the Japanese language considers someone's emotional state to be known only by that person. Others can only guess about another person's feelings. For this reason, direct expressions of emotive states, such as 〜ほしい and 〜たい, are reserved for the speaker's feelings. To talk about other people's emotions, always use expressions that imply an understanding or a guess on the part of the speaker, such as 〜がっている (*showing a sign of*), 〜んです (*it is the case that* 〜), and そうです(*I heard*) (see chapter 12, grammar IV, on p. 500 for a detailed explanation). Note that with 〜んです and そうです, the direct object particle remains が, because the phrase 〜が ほしい is part of a clause embedded in the main clause with 〜んです and そうです.

山本さんは　しろいドレスが　ほしいそうです。

I heard that Ms. Yamamoto wants a white dress.

鈴(すず)木さんは　くろいコートが　ほしいんですよ。
It is the case that Mr. Suzuki wants a black coat.

C. 〜たい　I want (to do something)

Unlike ほしい, 〜たい indicates the speaker's wish to do something (an action). This is conveyed using verb-masu stem + たい. Compare these two examples.

このケーキが　ほしい。
I want this cake.

このケーキが／を　たべたい。
I want to eat this cake.

Topic (subject)		Direct object	Particle	Verb (stem)	Auxiliary (い -adjective)
私	は	コーヒー	が／を	のみ	たいです。

I want to drink some coffee.

山田： 日本で 何が したいですか。
What do you want to do in Japan?

トム： そうですね、富士山(ふじさん)が みたいですね。
Well, I want to see Mt. Fuji.

それから、きょうとにも いきたいですね。
I want to go to Kyoto, too.

Notes

- With たいです, the direct object marker を can be replaced with が. The first two sentences below are identical in meaning. Other particle usages remain unchanged.

  私は そのくつを かいたいです。
  I want to buy those shoes.

  私は そのくつが かいたいです。
  I want to buy those shoes.

  私は おふろに はいりたいです。
  I want to take a bath.

  私は ここで まちたいです。
  I want to wait here.

- It is impolite to use ～たいですか to your superior when asking if a superior wants to do something. Use ～ますか or ～いかがですか instead.

  ごはんを たべますか。
  Would you like to eat (rice/a meal)?

  ケーキは いかがですか。
  Would you like some cake?

As with ほしい, use ～たがっている to express what someone else wants to do, and use を for the direct object marker.

Topic (subject)		Direct object	Particle	Verb (stem)	たがっている (る -verb)
山田さん	は	スーツ	を	かい	たがっています。

Mr. Yamada wants to buy a suit.

キム： ジョンソンさんは 四月(しがつ)に 日本に いくんですか。
Is Ms. Johnson going to Japan in April?

高子(たかこ)： ええ、日本で 日本語を べんきょうしたがっているので。
Yes, because she wants to study Japanese in Japan.

You can also use ～たいんです and ～たいそうです. The direct object particle can be が or を.

> 田中さんは　その本が／を　かいたいんです。
> *It is that Mr. Tanaka wants to buy the book.*
>
> 田中さんは　その本が／を　かいたいそうです。
> *I heard that Mr. Tanaka wants to buy the book.*

話(はな)してみましょう　Conversation Practice

Activity 1

Each of the following people wants certain gifts for certain occasions. Assume the identity of each person to tell others what you would like. Use ほしい .

Example:　Assume you are Mr./Ms. Smith.

私は　誕生日(たんじょうび)に　いぬが　ほしいです。

	スミス	リー	ジョーンズ	キム
誕生日(たんじょうび)	いぬ	腕時計(うでどけい)	じてんしゃ	ジャケット
クリスマス／ハヌカ (*Hanukkah*)	ハンドバック	ネックレス	ぼうし	スーツ
バレンタインデー	イヤリング	ベルト	ネクタイ	ゆびわ

Activity 2

Now look at the chart again and use ほしがっている and/or ほしいんです to say what each person wants for the various occasions.

Example:　スミスさんは　誕生日(たんじょうび)に　いぬを　ほしがっています。
　　　　　スミスさんは　誕生日(たんじょうび)に　いぬが　ほしいんです。

Activity 3

Work with a partner. You are a customer and your partner is a salesperson in the clothing department of a department store. First think of a few clothing items you want. Then ask for his/her assistance.

Example: おきゃくさん：あのう、すみません。ジャケットが ほしいんですが。
店(みせ)の人：ジャケットですか。じゃあ、こちらは いかがですか。
おきゃくさん：ああ、いいですね。

Or おきゃくさん：ちょっと 小さいですね。もっと 大きいのが ほしいんですが。
店(みせ)の人：じゃあ、こちらは いかがですか。
おきゃくさん：ああ、いいですね。

Activity 4

Conjugate the verbs using the phrases 私は ～たいです and スミスさんは ～たがっています.

Example: うちに かえる
私は うちに かえりたいです。スミスさんは うちに かえりたがっています。

1. りょこうに いく
2. 新しいふくを かう
3. おちゃを のむ
4. 日本で べんきょうする
5. ゲームを する
6. おふろに はいる

Activity 5

In pairs, say what you want to do in each of the following situations. Note that だったら means *if* ～ *is* ～.

Example: A: お金持(かねも)ち (*rich person*) だったら、何が したいですか。
B: そうですね。大きい うちを かいたいですね。

1. 大学の先生だったら、何が したいですか。
2. おとこ (*male*) だったら／おんな (*female*) だったら、何が したいですか。
3. 日本人だったら、何が したいですか。
4. 有名人(ゆうめいじん) (*celebrity*) だったら、何が したいですか。
5. 明日(あした) 休みだったら、何が したいですか。

Activity 6

Work with the class. Ask your classmates what they want and what activities they want to do on their birthdays. Then decide which items or activities are most popular and which is the rarest.

Example: A: ～さんは 誕生日(たんじょうび)に どんなことが したいですか。

B: そうですね。うちで パーティが したいですね。

A: そうですか。いいですね。

じゃあ、プレゼント (*present*) は どんなものが いいですか。

B: そうですね。新しいくつが ほしいですね。

なまえ	したいこと	ほしいもの

III. Expressing quantities with numbers and the counters まい, 本, ひき, and さつ

You have already learned some expressions with numbers such as ～時, ～時間, and ～分. These are called counter expressions. In this chapter, you will learn more of them and how they work. In counting things, and even people, a counter must be attached to the number. Some English equivalents of Japanese counters are expressions such as "two *cups* of coffee" or "three *sheets* of paper." Japanese uses a number of different counters. The type, shape, and size of an object determines which counter should be used.

Counter	Object Type	Examples
～まい	thin objects	paper, plates, T-shirts, CDs, DVDs
～ひき	fish, small four-legged animals	dogs, cats, mice
～本	long cylindrical objects	pencils, pens, bottles, cans, belts, ties, trousers, movies/films
～さつ	bound objects	books, dictionaries, magazines

The following chart illustrates how to combine numbers with counters. As you have seen in 分, 百(ひゃく), and 千(せん), combining counters with numbers sometimes changes the pronunciation of both the numbers and the counters themselves. The underlined expressions in the chart are examples of these changes. Pronunciation changes for 本(ほん) and ひき follow the same pattern.

		Thin, flat objects ～まい	Cylindrical objects ～ほん（本）	Fish, animals ～ひき	Bound objects ～さつ
?	何	なんまい	※なんぼん	※なんびき	なんさつ
1	一	いちまい	※いっぽん	※いっぴき	※いっさつ
2	二	にまい	にほん	にひき	にさつ
3	三	さんまい	※さんぼん	※さんびき	さんさつ
4	四	よんまい	よんほん	よんひき	よんさつ
5	五	ごまい	ごほん	ごひき	ごさつ
6	六	ろくまい	※ろっぽん	※ろっぴき	ろくさつ
7	七	ななまい	ななほん	ななひき	ななさつ
8	八	はちまい	※はっぽん	※はっぴき	※はっさつ
9	九	きゅうまい	きゅうほん	きゅうひき	きゅうさつ
10	十	じゅうまい	※じゅっぽん	※じゅっぴき	※じゅっさつ

The counter expressions come immediately after the object and its particle.

Noun + Particle	Number + Counter	Verb	
セーターを	一(いち)まい	かいました。	*I bought one sweater.*
水を	四本(よんほん)	のみました。	*I drank four bottles of water.*
ねこが	十(じゅっ)ぴき	います。	*There are ten cats.*
そのざっしを	二(に)さつ	下さい。	*Give me two magazines.*
ベルトを	何本(ぼん)	かいますか。	*How many belts will you buy?*
本は	何さつ	ありますか。	*How many books are there?*

山田：このTシャツを 三(さん)まい 下さい。
Please give me these three T-shirts.

店(みせ)の人：三(さん)まいですね。かしこまりました。
Three of them. Certainly, sir.

田中：そこに えんぴつが 何本(ぼん) ありますか。
How many pencils are there?

スミス：六本(ろっぽん) あります。
There are six.

山田：ねこを 何びき みましたか。
How many cats did you see?

山本：二(に)ひき みました。
I saw two.

上田：としょかんには 日本語の本が たくさん ありますか。
Are there a lot of Japanese books in the library?

川口(かわぐち)：ええ。四千(よんせん)さつぐらい ありますよ。
Yes, there are about four thousand.

When talking about multiple items in a single sentence, the particle と comes after the counter expression.

大きいノートを 三(さん)さつと、小さいのを 二(に)さつ 下さい。
Please give me three large notebooks and two small ones.

そのシャツ 二(に)まいと、ベルトを はこに いれて下さい。
Please put two shirts and a belt in the box.

話(はな)してみましょう　Conversation Practice

Activity 1

Describe each picture using an appropriate counter expression.

Example:  ネクタイが　一本(いっぽん)　あります。

1　2　3　4　5

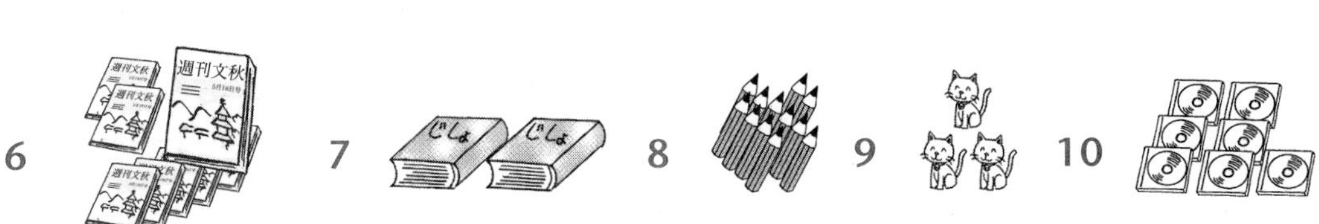

6　7　8　9　10

Activity 2

Work in groups of three or four. Ask your classmates how many of the following items they own. Find out who owns the most of each item. Then write down the name of that person and the number of items.

Example: A: 〜さんは　セーターが　何まい　ありますか。

B: そうですね。十(じゅう)まいぐらい　ありますね。

なまえ	私（　　　）			
セーター				
日本語の本				
ペット（いぬ／ねこ／*other*）				
ベルト				

Activity 3

Work with a partner. Ask what kind of clothing and how many items your partner would have if he/she were a famous movie star. Note that in this context, もっています means *to own*. Take turns.

Example: A: あのう、どんなふくを　もっていますか。

B: そうですね。パンツが　六十本(ろくじゅっぽん)と　シャツが　百(ひゃく)まいぐらい　ありますね。

A: すごいですね。(*Wow!*)

IV. Expressing quantities using Japanese-origin numbers

Numbers such as いち, に, and さん are Chinese-origin numbers. There is another series of numbers called *Japanese-origin numbers*. These numbers do not require counter expressions and are usually used for round, discrete objects, such as apples, oranges, or pebbles, or for objects that do not fit any specific category. Japanese-origin numbers only go up to ten. For numbers larger than ten, Chinese-origin numbers are used. The corresponding question word is いくつ.

		Japanese-origin numbers
1	一	ひとつ
2	二	ふたつ
3	三	みっつ
4	四	よっつ
5	五	いつつ
6	六	むっつ
7	七	ななつ
8	八	やっつ
9	九	ここのつ
10	十	とお

		Chinese-origin numbers
11	十一	じゅういち
12	十二	じゅうに
13	十三	じゅうさん
•	•	•
•	•	•
•	•	•
•	•	•
•	•	•
•	•	•
20	二十	にじゅう

		Chinese-origin numbers
30	三十	さんじゅう
45	四十五	よんじゅうご
100	百	ひゃく

タン：ぼうしは いくつ ありますか。
How many hats are there?

モリル：十二（じゅうに） あります。
There are twelve.

店（みせ）の人：いらっしゃいませ。
Welcome.

リー：あのう りんごを 五（いつ）つと バナナを 五本（ごほん） 下さい。
Could you give me five apples and five bananas, please?

店（みせ）の人：りんごを 五（いつ）つと バナナを 五本（ごほん）ですね。はい。
Five apples and five bananas. Here you are.

話(はな)してみましょう Conversation Practice

Activity 1

Describe the following pictures using the appropriate counter expression.

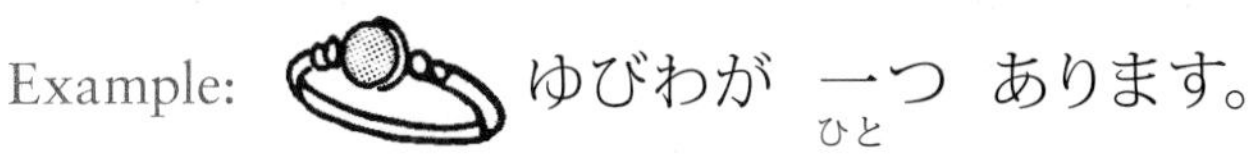

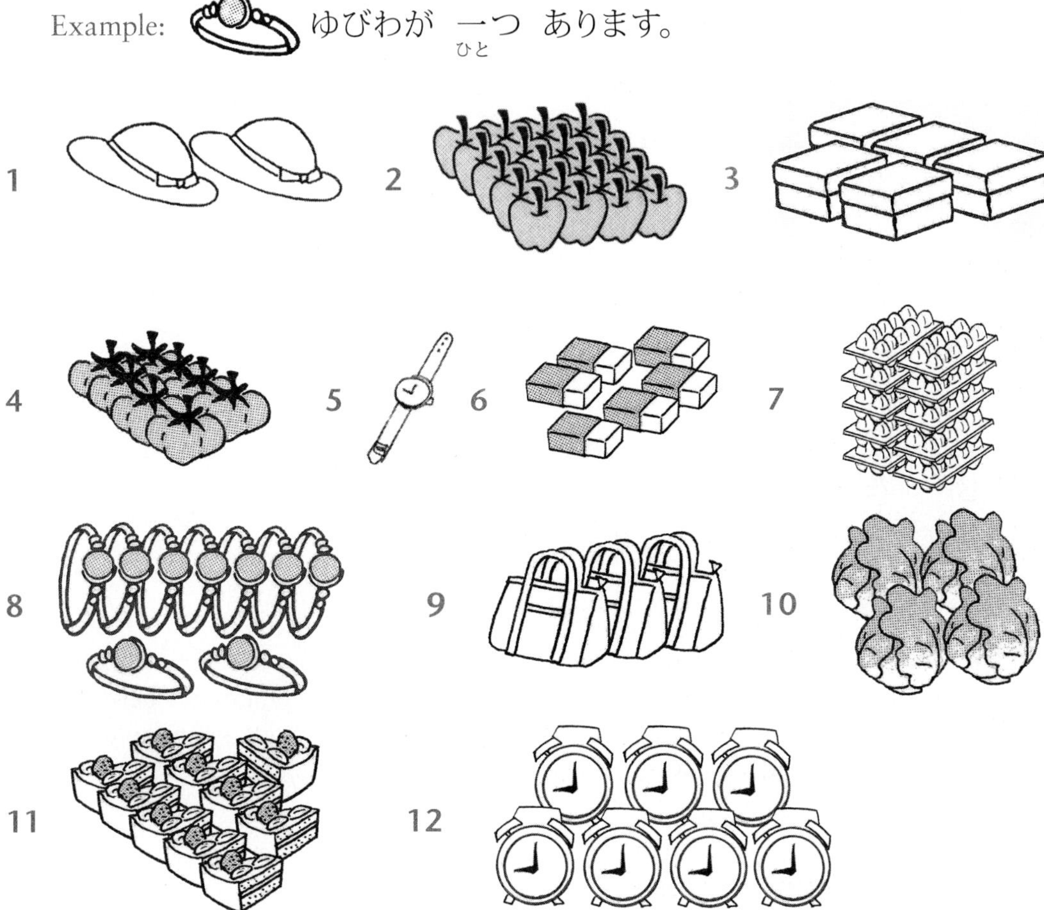

Activity 2

Classify the following words using the appropriate counter. Then make a sentence for each item with the counter.

えんぴつ、かばん、CD、きょうかしょ、けしゴム、じしょ、ノート、ペン、ボールペン、本、木、ねこ、いぬ、ざっし、コーラ、さかな、たまご、トマト、にんじん、セーター、バナナ、ビール、りんご、レタス、ワイン

Example: えんぴつ　　えんぴつを 十本(じゅっぽん) 下さい。

Counter	Item
まい	
さつ	
本	えんぴつ
ひき	
Japanese-origin numbers	

Activity 3

Work with a partner. You are going shopping and your partner is the clerk at each of the stores in the table below. First make out a shopping list. Then go to each store and ask for the items on your list. Your partner will ask how many you need of each item and write down your purchases.

Example:
店(みせ)の人：　いらっしゃいませ。
おきゃくさん：　あのう、りんごを 下さい。
店(みせ)の人：　いくつ さしあげましょうか。
おきゃくさん：　一(ひと)つ 下さい。

スーパー	デパート	コンビニ

Activity 4

Work with a different partner. Say what you bought in Activity 3, and compare your purchases. Follow the example.

Example: 私は スーパーで りんごを 二(ふた)つ かいました。
～さんは りんごを 二(ふた)つ かいました。

V. Talking about prices using 円(えん); indicating floor levels with かい

A. Asking about and stating prices with 円(えん)

You are probably familiar with the ¥ symbol for Japanese currency. *Yen* can also be written as 円(えん). Numbers that precede 円(えん) are pronounced in the same way as with the counter まい, except that *four yen* becomes よえん. The question word for price is いくら.

1（一）	いちえん	6（六）	ろくえん
2（二）	にえん	7（七）	ななえん
3（三）	さんえん	8（八）	はちえん
4（四）	＊よえん	9（九）	きゅうえん
5（五）	ごえん	10（十）	じゅうえん

上田：これは　いくらですか。
How much is this?

店(みせ)の人：百五十円(ひゃくごじゅうえん)です。
It is 150 yen.

スミス：きれいなイヤリングですね。
You have pretty earrings on.

田中：ありがとう。でも　安かったんですよ。
Thanks, but they were inexpensive.

スミス：そうですか。いくらだったんですか。
Really? How much were they?

田中：二千円(にせんえん)です。
2,000 yen.

スミス：それは　いい　かいものでしたね。
That's a good buy!

B. Indicating floor levels with かい

Numbers before the counter かい are pronounced in the same way as with the counter 本(ほん). Both さんかい (*third floor*) and なんかい (*what floor?*) can be pronounced as さんがい and なんがい, respectively. Use 地下(ちか)〜 (*underground*) to indicate a basement floor (地下(ちか)いっかい = B1).

?	なんかい なんがい		
1（一）	いっかい	6（六）	ろっかい
2（二）	にかい	7（七）	ななかい
3（三）	さんかい さんがい	8（八）	はちかい
4（四）	よんかい	9（九）	きゅうかい
5（五）	ごかい	10（十）	じゅっかい

Because floor levels indicate location, かい is used with a variety of location particles, such as に (place of existence), に (goal), で (place of action) , まで (*to*), and から (*from*).

リー：アクセサリーうりばは 何がいに ありますか。
Which floor is the accessory department on?

店(みせ)の人：一(いっ)かいに ございます。
It's on the first floor.

山本：すみません。ぶんぼうぐうりばは どこですか。
Excuse me. Where is the stationery section?

店(みせ)の人：六(ろっ)かいに ございます。
It's on the sixth floor.

二(に)かいまで あるいていきます。
I will walk up to the second floor.

三(さん)がいで あいませんか。
Why don't we meet on the third floor?

話(はな)してみましょう Conversation Practice

Activity 1

Look at the following pictures of Japanese currency and say how many yen each one is worth.

Example:  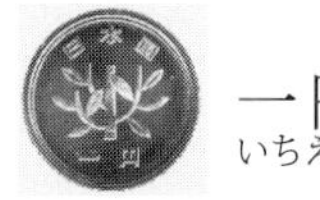 一円(いちえん)

1  2  3  4  5 

6 

7 

8 

Activity 2

Look at the following items and say how much each one costs.

Example:  

えんぴつは 二十五円(にじゅうごえん)です。

1 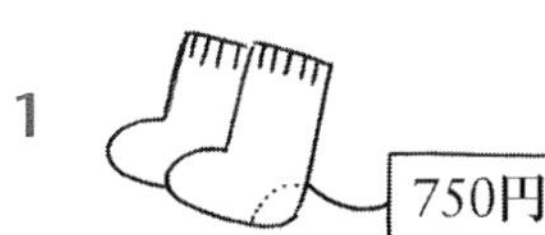

2  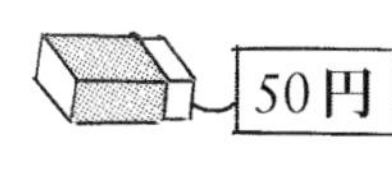

3 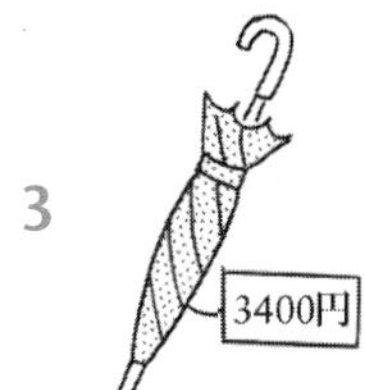

4 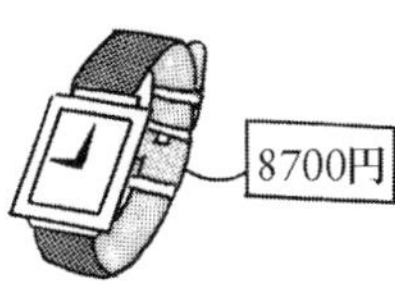

5 

6 

7 

8 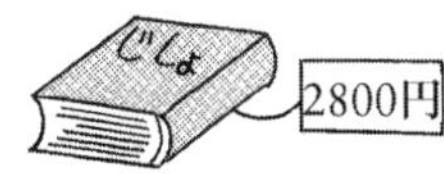

Activity 3

Work with a partner. You want to buy items in the chart and your budget is 20,000 yen. Your partner is a salesperson, and he/she decides on the price of each item. Ask your partner how much each item costs and say whether you will buy it. Make sure to stay within your budget!

Example: A: すみません、この靴下(くつした)は　いくらですか。
B: ～円(えん)です。
A: じゃ、これを　下さい。(*if buying*)
or そうですか。じゃ、また　きます。(*if not buying*)

	～円(えん)	かいますか。(はい　いいえ)
靴下(くつした)		
シャツ		
ジーンズ		
ジャケット		
ベルト		

Activity 4

Look at the floor directory below, and answer the following questions using ～かい.

Example: くつうりばは　何がいに　ありますか。
一(いっ)かいに　あります。

おくじょう (R)	ゆうえんち (*amusement center*)
8F	レストラン
7F	ぶんぼうぐ　本　CD ／ DVD　おもちゃ (*toys*)
6F	でんきせいひん (*electrical appliances*)
5F	かぐ (*furniture*)　しょっき　(*tableware*) だいどころようひん (*kitchenware*)
4F	こうげいひん (*traditional Japanese crafts and giftware*) きもの (*kimonos*)
3F	婦人服(ふじんふく)
2F	しんしふく
1F	ハンドバッグ　くつ ネクタイ　かばん アクセサリー けしょうひん (*cosmetics*)
B1	しょくひん

1. レストランは　何がいに　ありますか。
2. どこで　つくえを　かいますか。
3. どこで　パンツを　かいますか。
4. ぶんぼうぐうりばは　どこに　ありますか。
5. どこで　スカートを　かいますか。
6. 何がいで　にくを　かいますか。

Activity 5

Work with a partner. You are the customer and your partner works at the information desk on the first floor of a department store. Your partner will make a floor directory. Ask where the following sections or facilities are and write the information in the chart below.

Example: A: いらっしゃいませ。
B: すみませんが、かばんうりばは　どこですか。
A: かばんうりばは　一(いっ)かいに　ございます。
A: 一(いっ)かいですね。どうも　ありがとう。

1. かばんうりば
2. トイレ
3. CD うりば
4. レストラン
5. 婦人服(ふじんふく)うりば
6. しんしふくうりば
7. しょくひんうりば
8. アクセサリーうりば

8F	
7F	
6F	
5F	
4F	
3F	
2F	
1F	
B1	

聞く練習
き れんしゅう
Listening

上手な聞き方 Listening Strategy
じょうず き かた

Recognizing the characteristics of speech

Being aware of the characteristics of spoken language will help you to understand it better. Spoken language is highly redundant; that is, it repeats the same information more than once. It also contains hesitations, false starts, incomplete sentences, interruptions, and over-talk. These are all integral parts of authentic speech.

練習
れんしゅう

A. Listen to two conversations. For each one, write in English whether the customer is willing to buy the items. Then try to identify which characteristics of speech indicate the customer's intent.

1. ______________________________

2. ______________________________

B. 何を かいましたか。

You will hear three conversations. Listen to each one and list in Japanese the items the customer bought and the quantity of each item. Then write the total amount the customer paid.

	何	ねだん (*price per item*)	いくつ	ぜんぶで いくら
1				
2				
3				

聞き上手話し上手
Communication

上手な話し方 Communication Strategy

Asking for paraphrase and repetition

So far, you have learned some strategies for providing feedback to indicate that you are listening to the speaker and understanding what is being said. For example, you may nod your head and say はい or ええ. There will be times when you find yourself in situations where you don't understand what the speaker is saying and can't respond, because you don't know the words used or you didn't hear what was said. In these cases it is important to know how to ask for repetition or paraphrasing, and how to ask someone to speak more loudly or more slowly. Chapter 1 introduced these phrases using おねがいします, but you can also use ～てくれませんか (Chapter 6) to articulate your request even more clearly. The following is a list of some useful expressions to employ in these situations.

Asking for repetition:	もう一度 いってくれませんか。 *Please say it again.*
Asking for paraphrasing:	やさしいことばで いってくれませんか。 *Please say it in easier words.*
Asking someone to speak slowly:	ゆっくり いってくれませんか。 ゆっくり はなしてくれませんか。 *Please say it / speak slowly.*
Asking someone to speak more loudly:	大きいこえで いってくれませんか。 大きいこえで はなしてくれませんか。 *Please say it / speak more loudly.*

Also remember that it is a good strategy to add conversation fillers and phrases like あのう and すみませんが before making a request. These phrases not only soften a request—an essential part of communicating in Japanese—but give you time to think of what you will say next.

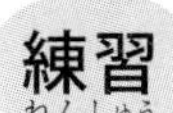

練習

Work with a partner. Imagine that you are a store clerk. Find polite expressions used by sales staff in this chapter. Say those expressions to your partner and have your partner respond with the expressions above.

漢字 (かんじ)
Kanji

Using kanji for numbers

Although you can write any number in **kanji**, you don't normally see numbers written in a long string of kanji, such as 六万三千五百二十二円 (¥63,522). In general, relatively simple numerical expressions are written in **kanji**, while long expressions are written in Arabic numerals.

The following are some common examples:

Prices with simple numbers such as 100, 1000, 2000, etc.: 百円 (ひゃくえん) 千円 (せんえん) 二千円 (にせんえん)

Counter expressions with single- or double-digit numbers: 三本 (さんぼん) 八階 (はっかい) 十二冊 (じゅうにさつ)

Dates: 六月二十五日 (ろくがつにじゅうごにち) 十二月三十日 (じゅうにがつさんじゅうにち)

Times: 一時 (いちじ) 三時二十分 (さんじにじゅっぷん)

Pronunciation changes for kanji with numbers

Pronunciations of **kanji** sometimes change slightly. For example, 一（いち）is pronounced いっ when it is used in the word 一本 (いっぽん). 本（ほん）in this example is pronounced ぽん.

えんぴつを 一本 (いっぽん) 下さい。

えんぴつを 二本 (にほん) 下さい。

When you read a sentence, you don't see any markings indicating such changes, because the reader makes the adjustment automatically. By the same token, you don't add any markings when you write them. (Note that the **furigana** accompanying new **kanji** is intended as a learning aid here.)

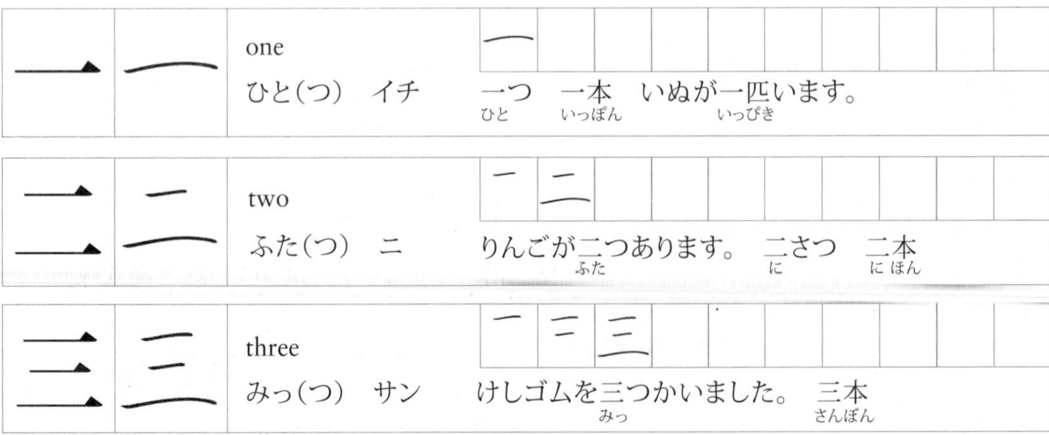

Kanji	Meaning / Readings	Examples
一	one ひと(つ) イチ	一つ (ひと) 一本 (いっぽん) いぬが一匹 (いっぴき) います。
二	two ふた(つ) ニ	りんごが二 (ふた) つあります。 二 (に) さつ 二本 (にほん)
三	three みっ(つ) サン	けしゴムを三 (みっ) つかいました。 三本 (さんぼん)

四	four	よ・よん・よっ(つ)　シ	四(よっ)つ　四時(よじ)　ビールが四本(よんほん)あります。
五	five	いつ(つ)　ゴ	五(いつ)つ　ベルトが五本(ごほん)あります。
六	six	むっ(つ)　ロク・ロッ	六(むっ)つ　六時(ろくじ)　えんぴつが六本(ろっぽん)あります。
七	seven	なな(つ)　シチ	七時(しちじ)　七本(ななほん)　オレンジが七(なな)つあります。
八	eight	やっ(つ)　ハチ・ハッ	八(やっ)つ　八時(はちじ)　ペンが八本(はっぽん)あります。
九	nine	ここの(つ)　キュウ・ク	九(ここの)つ　九時(くじ)　バナナが九本(きゅうほん)あります。
十	ten	とお　ジュウ・ジュッ	ぼうしが十(とお)あります。　十本(じゅっぽん)　十時(じゅうじ)
百	hundred	ヒャク・ビャク・ピャク	二百(にひゃく)　三百(さんびゃく)　六百(ろっぴゃく)
千	thousand	セン・ゼン	二千(にせん)　三千(さんぜん)　八千(はっせん)　千円(せんえん)
万	ten thousand	マン	一万円(いちまんえん)　百万円(ひゃくまんえん)
円	yen (Japanese currency)	エン	五十円(ごじゅうえん)　このセーターは、七千八百円(ななせんはっぴゃくえん)です。
店	store, shop	みせ　テン	大きい店(みせ)　店(みせ)の人　喫茶店(きっさてん)

読(よ)めるようになった漢字(かんじ) (**Kanji** and compounds you can now read)

一時　一本　一つ　一緒(いっしょ)に　もう一度(いちど)　二時　二本　二つ　三時
三本　三つ　四時　四本　四つ　五時　五本　五つ　六時　六本
六つ　七時　七本　七つ　八時　八本　八つ　九時　九本　九つ
十時　十本　十　百円　千円　一万円　店の人　喫茶店(きっさてん)　腕時計(うでどけい)
靴下(くつした)　誕生日(たんじょうび)　地下(ちか)　婦人服(ふじんふく)

日本人のなまえ：川口(かわぐち)　友田(ともだ)　古田(ふるた)　水本(みずもと)　高子(たかこ)

練習(れんしゅう)

Read the following sentences with numerical **kanji**.

1. 田中さんは十一時三十分に学生会館(かいかん)にきます。
2. としょかんには日本の本が四千五百さつぐらいあります。
3. 山川さんのつくえの上に二万八千九百円あります。
4. 私は六時にごはんをたべます。そして、七時に大学にいきます。
5. そこに小さい店があります。

読む練習
よ　れんしゅう
Reading Practice

上手な読み方　Reading Strategy
じょうず　よ　かた

Scanning

It is not always necessary to read an entire text when you are looking for specific information. For example, when you want to find out which floor of a department store sells food, you do not read the entire floor directory. You would look for a specific character such as the kanji 食 (*eat*). By employing this strategy, you will be able to find the information you need more quickly.

The same is true when you read a text looking for particular information. You can skip through the passage to find the specific information you need. This method of reading is called *scanning*.

練習
れんしゅう

Read the following advertisements and find out what is being sold in each ad.

1 
ふとんばさみ
4個組
天気がいい日は、ふとんをほす日。
きれいなふとんで、ぐっすり快眠。
ふところが深く、
しっかりはさめます。
バネを中心部に内蔵しているので、
ふとんを汚さずにはさめます。
4個組 680円
●サイズ / 約27X15.5X厚3cm●材質 / 本体：ポリプロピレン、バネ：鋼
●重量 / 約140g(1個)●耐熱温度 / 約100°C●中国製

Courtesy of Kazumi and Yukiko Hatasa

2 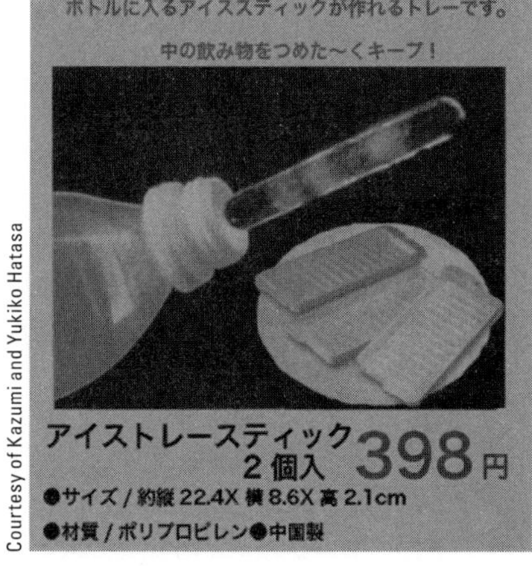
ボトルに入るアイススティックが作れるトレーです。
中の飲み物をつめた〜くキープ！
アイストレースティック
2個入 398円
●サイズ / 約縦22.4X横8.6X高2.1cm
●材質 / ポリプロピレン●中国製

Courtesy of Kazumi and Yukiko Hatasa

3 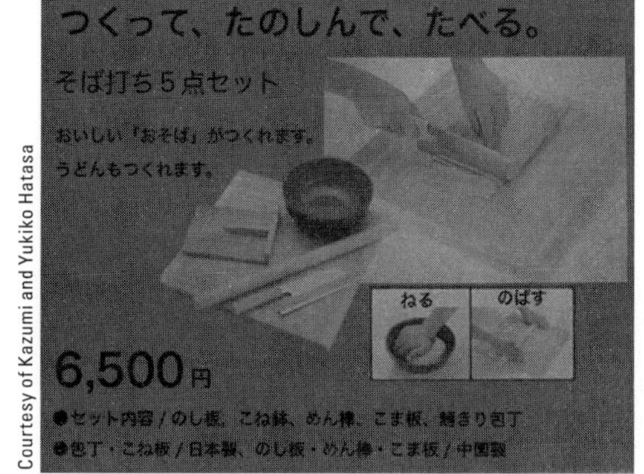
つくって、たのしんで、たべる。
そば打ち5点セット
おいしい『おそば』がつくれます。
うどんもつくれます。
ねる
のばす
6,500円
●セット内容 / のし板、こね鉢、めん棒、こま板、麺きり包丁
●包丁・こね鉢 / 日本製、のし板・めん棒・こま板 / 中国製

Courtesy of Kazumi and Yukiko Hatasa

4 
リントクリーナー
セーターの毛玉をきれいにカットしてリメイク。
ふるいセーターも、
あたらしいセーターみたい！
ソックス、ジャージ、ニット、
カーペットの毛玉もとれます。
1,480円
●サイズ / 約8X14X12cm●材質 / ポリスチレン、
ABC樹脂、ステンレス鋼●電池 / 単2電池X2(別売)
●台湾製

Courtesy of Kazumi and Yukiko Hatasa

きんじょのスーパー　Neighborhood supermarket

言葉(ことば)のリスト

スリッパ　slippers
洗剤(せんざい)　detergent
タオル　towel

私の家(うち)の近(ちか)くに大きいスーパーがあります。そのスーパーの一階(かい)には食品売(しょくひんう)り場(ば)があります。高いものはありませんが、私はそこでよく野菜(やさい)や魚(さかな)を買(か)います。二階(かい)は日用品売(にちようひんう)り場(ば)です。タオルやスリッパやシャンプーや洗剤(せんざい)があります。 三階(がい)には本や文房具(ぶんぼうぐ)があります。昨日(きのう)、私はこのスーパーでノートを三冊(さつ)とボールペンを五本買(か)いました。

読んだ後(あと)で　Comprehension

A. しつもんに　日本語で　こたえて下さい。Answer these questions in Japanese.

1. この人は　このスーパーで　何を　よく　かいますか。
2. このスーパーの　二階(かい)に　何が　ありますか。
3. 三階(がい)に　何が　ありますか。
4. 魚(さかな)は　何階(がい)に　ありますか。
5. 日用品(にちようひん)って　何ですか。
6. 昨日(きのう)　この人は　何を　かいましたか。それは　どこに　ありましたか。

B. Write a short passage about a department store you know. Use the following questions as a guide for what information to include.

1. デパートは　どこに　ありますか。
2. デパートは　大きいですか。小さいですか。
3. いいデパ トですか。
4. デパートに　どんなうりばが　ありますか。
6. いりぐち (*entrance*) のちかくに　何が　ありますか。
7. そのデパートで　何を　よく　かいますか。どうしてですか。

総合練習
そうごうれんしゅう
Integration

デパートのうりば Department Store Sections

The following is the floor directory of a full-scale department store in Tokyo. Work with a partner to describe the types of items available on different floors. Try to guess the meanings of the words written in **katakana**. Next, your instructor will give you a list of specific items to purchase. Figure out where each item would be located.

	東館(ひがしかん)	西館(にしかん)	
R/8	学生服(がくせいふく)/商品券(しょうひんけん) サービス/介護用品(かいごようひん)	屋上遊園(おくじょうゆうえん) 金魚(きんぎょ)・熱帯魚(ねったいぎょ)	R
7	呉服（ごふく）/宝飾品(ほうしょくひん) 時計(とけい)・メガネ・文具(ぶんぐ) レストラン	レストラン/催事場(さいじじょう)	7
6	催事場(さいじじょう)/婦人服(ふじんふく) [L サイズ]	こども服(ふく)・ベビー用品 (ようひん)/おもちゃ	6
5	婦人服(ふじんふく) [プレタポルテ&エレガンス]	リビング用品(ようひん)/タオル/ 寝具（しんぐ）/家具(かぐ) インテリア/美術画廊(びじゅつがろう)	5
4	婦人服(ふじんふく) [デザイナーズブティック&カジュアル] 婦人肌着(ふじんはだぎ)	リビング/和洋食器(わようしょっき)/ 調理(ちょうり)・日用品(にちようひん)/ ギフトサロン	4
3	婦人服(ふじんふく) [インポートブティック]	紳士服(しんしふく)/紳士用品(しんし ようひん)/紳士靴(しんしぐつ)	3
2	婦人服(ふじんふく) [キャリアブティック]	紳士服(しんしふく)/紳士用品(しんし ようひん)/ゴルフウェア/カバン	2
1	ハンドバッグ/婦人靴(ふじんぐつ) 婦人小物(ふじんこもの)/アクセサリー/ 化粧品(けしょうひん)	ファッション雑貨(ざっか)	1
B1	食品(しょくひん) [和洋菓子(わようがし)/のり/茶(ちゃ)/ 和洋酒(わようしゅ)・缶詰(かんづめ)] 地下鉄連絡口(ちかてつれんらくぐち)	食品(しょくひん)[鮮魚(せんぎょ) 精肉(せいにく)・野菜(やさい) 和洋中華惣菜(わようちゅうかそうざい)]	B1
		レストラン/喫茶(きっさ) 書籍(しょせき)	B2

ロールプレイ

1. Work in groups of six. Two people in each group take the role of customers in a department store with 50,000 yen each to spend. The rest play salesclerks in different departments, and your instructor will give them a price list of items for their department. Go to as many departments as you can, and make one or more purchases. Before leaving each department, note what you have bought and how much you paid. You must buy at least four different items. Try to spend all your money. Whoever is left with the smallest amount of change wins.

Examples:

店の人： いらっしゃいませ。
おきゃくさん： あのう、あかいハンドバッグが　ほしいんですが。
or そのあかいハンドバッグを　みせて下さい。
店の人： はい、どうぞ。
おきゃくさん： ちょっと小さいですね。もっと大きいのはありますか。
店の人： じゃあ、こちらはいかがですか。
おきゃくさん： ああ、いいですね。いくらですか。
店の人： 四万円です。
おきゃくさん： ああ、ちょっと高いですね。

店の人： いらっしゃいませ。
おきゃくさん： しろいシャツが　ほしいんですが。
店の人： こちらは　いかがですか。
おきゃくさん： いいですね。
or ちょっと高いですね。もうすこし　安いのはありますか。

2. You have run out of fruit and vegetables. Go to a market and buy the following items.

Item	Amount
レタス	1
トマト	3
にんじん	5
たまご	12
バナナ	6

Chapter 9

第九課（だいきゅうか）

レストランとしょうたい

Restaurants and Invitations

Objectives	Extending invitations, ordering at a restaurant
Vocabulary	Dishes, types of cuisine, food expressions
Dialogue	レストランで　*At a restaurant*
Japanese Culture	Eating habits in Japan, Japanese restaurants
Grammar	I. Indicating choices using ～にします; making requests using ～をおねがいします II. Eliciting and making proposals using ～ましょうか and ～ましょう III. Using question word + か + (particle) + affirmative and question word + (particle) + も + negative IV. Giving reasons using から; expressing opposition or hesitation using けど V. Making inferences based on direct observation using verb and adjective stems + そうだ
Listening	Using context
Communication	Introducing a new topic
Kanji	Creating inflectional endings with **okurigana** 行 来 帰 食 飲 見 聞 読 書 話 出 会 買 起 寝 作 入
Reading	Understanding Japanese e-mail formats

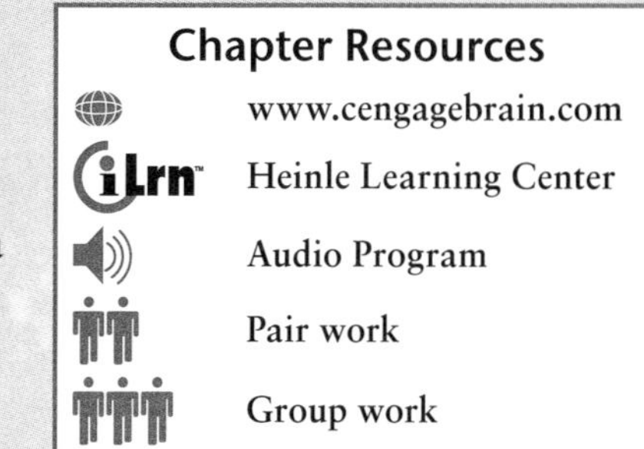

Chapter Resources

- www.cengagebrain.com
- Heinle Learning Center
- Audio Program
- Pair work
- Group work

単語 (たんご)

Nouns

アイスクリーム		ice cream
あぶら	油 (oil) ／脂 (fat)	oil あぶらが おおい fatty, oily
イタリア		Italy イタリアりょうり Italian cuisine
うどん		Japanese wheat noodles
カレーライス		Japanese curry and rice dish (abbreviation: カレー)
カロリー		calorie
クッキー		cookie
(お) さしみ	御刺身	sashimi (fillet of fresh raw fish, usually preceded by お)
サラダ		salad
サンドイッチ		sandwich
スープ		soup
(お) すし	御寿司／鮨	sushi (usually preceded by お)
ステーキ		steak
スパゲティ		spaghetti
セット		Western-style fixed menu, ハンバーガーセット hamburger set
(お) そば	蕎麦	Japanese buckwheat noodles
チーズ		cheese
チキン		chicken
チャーハン		Chinese-style fried rice
ちゅうかりょうり	中華料理	Chinese cuisine
ちゅうもん	注文	order ちゅうもんする to order
チョコレート		chocolate

ていしょく	定食	a Japanese or Asian-style dish set, さしみていしょく sashimi set
デザート		dessert
てんぷら	天ぷら / 天麩羅	tempura (fish, shrimp, and vegetables battered and deep-fried)
トースト		toast
ハンバーガー		hamburger
パン		bread
ビーフ		beef
ピザ		pizza
フライドチキン		fried chicken
ポーク		pork
ようしょく	洋食	Western-style cuisine
ライス		rice ライス is served on a plate, not in a bowl. ごはん is a generic term for cooked rice.
ラーメン		Chinese-style noodle soup
ランチ		lunch A ランチ lunch set A
わしょく	和食	Japanese cuisine (also 日本りょうり)

う -verbs

いる	要る	to need something ソースがいる It needs sauce.
たのむ	頼む	to order, to ask (someone to do ~)

い -adjectives

あたたかい	温かい	warm
あつい	熱い	hot
あまい	甘い	sweet
おおい	多い	a lot, much
かたい	固い	hard, tough

からい	辛い	spicy
しょっぱい／しおからい	塩辛い	salty
すくない	少ない	little (in number), few
すっぱい	酸っぱい	sour
つめたい	冷たい	cold
にがい	苦い	bitter
ひくい	低い	low, カロリーがひくい low in calories
やわらかい	柔らかい	soft

Prefix

ご〜	御〜	polite prefix ごちゅうもん, polite form of ちゅうもん (order)

Expressions

いいえ、どうぞおかまいなく。		Please do not bother/worry about it
〜に　します		to decide on 〜
〜を　おねがいします	〜をお願いします	I would like to have 〜

単語(たんご)の練習(れんしゅう)

A. りょうり Types of food

(お)すし
sushi

(お)さしみ
sashimi

てんぷら
tempura

うどん
udon noodles

(お)そば
buckwheat noodles

ラーメン
Chinese-style noodle soup

チャーハン
Chinese fried rice

カレーライス
Japanese curry and rice

スパゲティ
spaghetti

ステーキ
steak

サラダ
salad

フライドチキン
fried chicken

ハンバーガー
hamburger

サンドイッチ
sandwich

スープ
soup

チーズ
cheese

Aランチ
Lunch A (Western-style)

さしみ定食(ていしょく)
sashimi set (Japanese or Asian style)

デザート
dessert

アイスクリーム
ice cream

クッキー
cookies

おぼえていますか。 **Do you remember these words?**

さかな、にく、たまご、やさい、くだもの、レタス、トマト、にんじん、バナナ、オレンジ、りんご、ケーキ、おちゃ、ジュース、ミルク、(お)さけ、コーヒー、こうちゃ、ワイン、ビール、(お)水、コーラ

Activity 1

しつもんに日本語でこたえて下さい。

1. レストランでよく何をちゅうもんしますか。
2. あさは、よく何を食(た)べますか。よく何を飲(の)みますか。
3. おひるごはんには、よく何を食(た)べますか。よく何を飲(の)みますか。
4. ばんごはんはどうですか。
5. どんなりょうりをよく作(つく)りますか。
6. 今何が食(た)べたいですか。
7. あなたのくにには (*in your country*) どんなランチセットや定食(ていしょく)がありますか。

B. りょうりのタイプ Types of cuisine

Country names are often, but not always, used to identify types of dishes, as shown in the table below. スペインりょうり、メキシコりょうり、かんこくりょうり、インド (*Indian*) りょうり are commonly-used terms in Japanese, but Japanese has no specific terms for “American” or “Canadian” cuisine.

Activity 2

In the table below, write the names of some dishes that belong to each category and say them aloud.

タイプ	りょうり
和食(わしょく)/日本りょうり *Japanese cuisine*	
中華(ちゅうか)りょうり *Chinese cuisine*	
イタリアりょうり *Italian cuisine*	
フランスりょうり *French cuisine*	
そのほかの (*other*) 洋食(ようしょく)	

Activity 3

しつもんに日本語でこたえて下さい。

Example: A: (お) さしみは何りょうりですか。

B: 和食(わしょく)です。

1. どのくに (*country*) のりょうりが好きですか。
2. 何りょうりのレストランによく行(い)きますか。
3. どのくに (*country*) のりょうりは好きじゃありませんか。
4. ちかくにどんなレストランがありますか。

C. 食(た)べ物(もの)をせつめいすることば　Food expressions

あたたかい	warm	あつい	hot (temperature)
つめたい	cold	しょっぱい／しおからい	salty
あまい	sweet	からい	spicy
すっぱい	sour	にがい	bitter
かたい	hard, tough	やわらかい	soft
あぶらがおおい	oily, fatty	あぶらがすくない	not oily
カロリーが高い	high-calorie	カロリーがひくい	low-calorie

おぼえていますか。　おいしい

Activity 4

Work in groups of four. Discuss the dishes of the countries listed in the table, then fill in the right-hand column with the adjectives or expressions that you feel best describe the cuisine of each one.

〜のりょうり	どんなりょうりですか。
日本	
中国(ごく)	
かんこく	
イギリス	
フランス	
メキシコ	
アメリカ	
イタリア	

Activity 5

Ask a partner about his/her food preferences.

Example: あまい／からい

A: あまいものとからいものと、どちらの方が好きですか。

B: あまいものの方が好きです。

1. あまいもの／からいもの
2. あぶらがおおいもの／あぶらがすくないもの
3. つめたいスープ／あたたかいスープ
4. あたたかいコーヒー／つめたいコーヒー
5. あまいりんご／すっぱいりんご
6. からいカレー／あまいカレー
7. すっぱいもの／からいもの
8. すこししょっぱいチップス (*chips*)/ すこしにがいチョコレート
9. カロリーが高いもの／カロリーがひくいもの

ダイアローグ

はじめに　Warm-up

A. しつもんに日本語でこたえて下さい。

1. 週末に友達と何をよくしますか。
2. 和食のレストランにはどんな食べ物がありますか。
3. 中華りょうりのレストランにはどんな食べ物がありますか。
4. どんな洋食が好きですか。

B. Make a phone call inviting a partner out to eat somewhere. Remember to use ～ませんか and the expressions you've learned to identify yourself when calling and responding to a caller.

レストランで　*At a restaurant*

今日は土曜日です。石田さんと上田さんと山本さんはしぶやにあそびに来ました。

石田：　あのう、上田さん、山本さん。

上田と山本：　はい。

石田：　そろそろ十二時ですから、何か食べませんか。

山本：　いいですね。じゃあ、あそこはどうですか。

上田：　イタリアりょうりですね。いいですよ。

石(いし)田： じゃあ、あそこにしましょう。

石(いし)田さんと上田さんと山本さんはレストランでメニューを見ています。

上田： 何にしましょうか。

石(いし)田： そうですね。このピザはどうですか。

山本： おいしそうですね。上田さん、どうですか。

上田： ええ。私もピザは大好きです。

山本： じゃあ、そうしましょう。ほかに何かたのみますか。

上田： フライドチキンはどうですか。

石(いし)田： いいですね。じゃあ、飲(の)み物(もの)は？

山本： のどがかわきましたから、ぼくはビールにします。

石(いし)田： じゃあ、ぼくもそうします。上田さんはどうしますか。

上田： 私は何もいりません。水でいいです。

ウェイターが来(き)ました。

ウェイター： いらっしゃいませ。ごちゅうもんは。

石(いし)田： このピザとフライドチキンとビールをおねがいします。

ウェイター： ピザを一まいとフライドチキンをお一つですね。
ビールは何本にしましょうか。

石(いし)田： 二本おねがいします。

ウェイター： 二本ですね。かしこまりました。

上田： あ、それから、私はお水を下さい。

ウェイター： はい、かしこまりました。

Dialogue Phrase Notes

- そろそろ十二時です means *it's about 12 o'clock.*
- ほかに means *in addition.*
- のどがかわきました means *I am thirsty.*
- ごちゅうもんは? means *What would you like to order?"*
- かしこまりました (*Yes, I shall do as you say*) was introduced in the Japanese Culture section for Chapter 8. This phrase is used in restaurants as well as in shops.

ダイアローグの後(あと)で

A. Circle はい if the statement is true, or いいえ if it is false.

1. はい いいえ 上田さんは何か食(た)べたがっています。

2. はい いいえ 石(いし)田さんは山本さんとレストランに行(い)きました。

3. はい いいえ 石(いし)田さんと山本さんはレストランでビールを飲(の)みました。

4. はい いいえ 山本さんはピザとフライドチキンをちゅうもんしました。

5. はい いいえ 上田さんは何も飲(の)みませんでした。

B. Complete the following passage by filling in the appropriate particle for each blank.

石(いし)田さん____上田さん____山本さんは、土曜日____しぶや____あそび____行(い)きました。おなかがすきましたから (*they got hungry, so*)、イタリアりょうりのレストラン____行(い)って、ピザ____フライドチキン____食(た)べました。石(いし)田さん____山本さん____ビール____飲(の)みました。

日本の文化(ぶんか)

日本の食生活(しょくせいかつ) Eating habits in Japan

© Cengage Learning

A traditional Japanese breakfast consists of a bowl of rice, miso soup, a raw egg with some soy sauce, seaweed, pickles, and a small piece of fish. Western-style breakfasts consisting of buttered toast, an egg, green salad, and coffee or tea are very popular. Many restaurants and cafes offer special breakfast sets for commuters. These are called モーニングサービス, or モーニングセット, and the breakfast may be either Japanese- or Western-style.

At lunchtime, some people bring a box lunch (おべんとう), go to the company or university cafeteria, or eat at restaurants and cafes that offer a choice of special lunch sets of the day (日替(ひが)わりランチ). Popular lunches include noodles, Italian pasta, curried rice, fried rice, or bowls of rice topped with stewed beef, pork cutlet, and eggs, or tempura. Local eateries, convenience stores, supermarkets, and department stores also sell a variety of おべんとう. Most primary schools provide lunch for the children, while students at secondary schools usually bring their own.

For most Japanese people, dinner is the largest meal of the day, and is eaten around 6 or 7 p.m. A wide range of dishes, including tempura, sashimi, grilled fish, and sukiyaki, as well as foreign dishes, are cooked at home. Many local food shops offer a variety of prepared dishes for working mothers and businesspeople. Some local restaurants offer free delivery, so sushi, noodles, and Chinese dishes can be ordered by phone as well.

© Atsushi Sakai/MIXA/Alamy

The most popular international dishes are Chinese, Italian, and French. Some Indian and Korean dishes, such as curry or grilled beef, are also popular. Finally, American franchise stores like McDonald's bring Western fast food. Hamburgers, pizza, and fried chicken are popular, particularly among young people. Mexican cuisine is still not well known in Japan.

Before a meal, the Japanese say いただきます (literally, *I humbly receive this*). After the meal, they say ごちそうさまでした (literally, *It was a feast*). Both are expressions of gratitude to those who made the meal possible (farmers, fishermen, cooks), as well as for natural phenomena, like rain.

日本のレストラン

Restaurants in Japan range from very inexpensive to outrageously expensive places. Some restaurants display realistic-looking models of food in the front window to give an idea of the dishes they serve, and their prices. Moderately-priced restaurants tend to have free seating; that is, you don't have to wait to be seated. As soon as you are seated, a waiter or waitress often brings a steaming hot towel called おしぼり to wipe your hands and face. In some restaurants, you pay for the food at the cashier at the exit instead of at your table. In particular, payment for breakfast or lunch is almost always made at the cashier. Since the service charge is included in the bill, it is customary not to tip.

Courtesy Kazumi and Yukiko Hatasa

Dining out or going for drinks is very common among Japanese business people and students. Instead of hosting parties at home, Japanese people prefer to hold parties in restaurants, pubs, and hotels. The organizer often sets the menu and collects cash from the guests ahead of time. At the beginning of a party, it is customary to have a toast, or かんぱい. Pouring a drink into your own glass or drinking directly from a bottle is not polite. Instead, you should fill other people's glasses and let them fill yours.

If you are treated to a restaurant meal, thank the person after the meal (ごちそうさまでした), and again the next time you meet. You might say 昨日(きのう)／先日(せんじつ)はどうもごちそうさまでした. (*Thank you for the feast yesterday/the other day.*) And remember that the reciprocation of invitations and other favors plays a vital role in relationships among the Japanese.

文法（ぶんぽう）

I. Indicating choices using ～にします ; making requests using ～をおねがいします

When ordering something in a restaurant, you may say ～にします or ～をおねがいします as well as ～を下さい, as you learned in Chapter 8. しますin the ～にします construction does not mean *do* but something like *decide on* ～. It may also be used in other contexts, as in トヨタにします *(decide on a Toyota [when you buy a car]).*

ウェイター：お飲（の）みものは、何に　しますか。
What would you like to drink? (literally, *As for drinks, what will you decide on?*)

おきゃくさん：オレンジジュースに　します。
I will have orange juice. (literally, *I decide on juice.*)

オレンジジュースを　おねがいします。
I will have orange juice. (literally, *I request orange juice.*)

オレンジジュースを　下さい。
Please give me orange juice.

With ～をおねがいします and ～を下さい (but not with ～にします), you can use a number of quantity expressions depending on what it is you are asking. Use ～つ (Japanese origin number) to order dishes and drinks and ～本 for bottles. The quantity expression directly follows the particle を. When two or more items are listed, the sentence takes the form "X を Quantity Expression と Y を Quantity Expression . . . おねがいします。"

コーヒーを一つ下さい。
Please bring one coffee.

ビールを二本おねがいします。
Please bring two bottles of beer.

こうちゃを一つとコーヒーを一つおねがいします。
Please bring one tea and one coffee.

鈴木（すずき）：何、飲（の）みますか。
What would you like to drink?

リン：そうですね。鈴木（すずき）さんは？
Let's see. How about you, Mr. Suzuki?

鈴木（すずき）：ぼくはコーラにします。
I will have some cola.

リン： そうですか。じゃあ、私もコーラにします。
Well then, I will have cola, too.

鈴木(すず)： (to the waiter) すみません。コーラを二つおねがいします。
Excuse me. We will have two colas.

話(はな)してみましょう

Activity 1

Place an order using ～を おねがいします. Use すみません to get the server's attention.

Example: (お) そば／1

すみません。(お) そばを一つおねがいします。

1. コーラ／1
2. サンドイッチ／2
3. こうちゃ／1
4. ハンバーガー／3
5. ラーメン／5
6. A ランチ／1
7. (お) さしみ／4
8. うどん／2

Activity 2

Work with a partner. You are going to a restaurant with your partner. Think about a dish that you would like to order. Discuss with your partner and decide on the restaurant.

Example: A: 今、何が食(た)べたいですか。

B: そうですね。スパゲティが食(た)べたいですね。

A: そうですか。じゃあ、イタリアりょうりのレストランにしませんか。

B: あ、いいですね。

Activity 3

Work with a new partner. You are a customer and your partner is the waiter or waitress. Circle one item that you would like to have from each category in the table below. The waiter/waitress will ask for your order by saying ごちゅうもんは ? (Your order?). Place your order.

Example:

ウェイター： ごちゅうもんは？

おきゃくさん： こうちゃとサンドイッチとケーキを おねがいします。

ウェイター： こうちゃとサンドイッチとケーキですね。かしこまりました。

飲み物	ミルク オレンジジュース おちゃ 水 ワイン ビール コーヒー こうちゃ
食べ物	スープ サンドイッチ ハンバーガー サラダ スパゲティ ピザ (お)すし (お)さしみ てんぷら チャーハン カレーライス ステーキ
デザート	ケーキ アイスクリーム クッキー

Activity 4

Work in groups of three. One person is the waiter/waitress at a restaurant. The other two are customers. Look at the menu to decide what you are going to order. The waiter/waitress will ask ごちゅうもんは?, then write down your orders and confirm them by saying X と Y ですね。かしこまりました. Change roles and repeat the role play until everyone has had a turn taking orders.

Example:

ウェイター： ごちゅうもんは？

A: 飲み物はどうしますか。

B: ぼくはビールにします。

A: 私はオレンジジュースにします。じゃあ、ビールを一本とオレンジジュースを一つ おねがいします。

ウェイター： ビールを一本とオレンジジュース一つですね。かしこまりました。

メニュー

オードブル

オードブル取り合わせ	¥800
スモークサーモン	¥1,000
シュリンプ・カクテル	¥900

スパゲティ

スパゲティ・ナポリタン	¥900
スパゲティ・ミートソース	¥1,000

スープ

コンソメスープ	¥400
オニオングラタンスープ	¥600

サラダ

グリーンサラダ	¥500
ミックスサラダ	¥500
チキンサラダ	¥700

魚料理

エビフライ	¥1,200
エビグラタン	¥1,200
カニコロッケ	¥1,000

米飯料理

カレーライス	¥800
オムライス	¥900
エビピラフ	¥800

肉料理

サーロインステーキ	¥3,500
ビーフシチュー	¥3,000
ハンバーグステーキ	¥1,000
ポークソテー	¥1,200
チキンコロッケ	¥1,000

サンドイッチ

ハムサンド	¥600
タマゴサンド	¥500
やさいサンド	¥500
ミックスサンド	¥600

飲み物

ビール	¥500
オレンジジュース	¥400

II. Eliciting and making proposals using 〜ましょうか and 〜ましょう

In Chapter 6, the negative question form of a verb 〜ませんか is used for extending an invitation or making a suggestion. 〜ましょうか (*shall we*) and 〜ましょう (*let's* 〜) are used to elicit or make proposals.

Eliciting proposal	Making proposals
どこへ行(い)きましょうか。 *Where shall we go?*	きょうとへ行(い)きませんか。 *Why don't we go to Kyoto?* きょうとへ行(い)きましょう。 *Let's go to Kyoto.*
何を食(た)べましょうか。 *What shall we eat?*	和食(わしょく)にしませんか。 *Why don't we have Japanese food?* 和食(わしょく)にしましょう。 *Let's have Japanese food.*
どこで会(あ)いましょうか。 *Where shall we meet?*	えきで会(あ)いませんか。 *Why don't we meet at the station?* えきで会(あ)いましょう。 *Let's meet at the station.*

リー：上田さん、今週の金曜日にコンサートに行(い)きませんか。
Ms. Ueda, why don't we go to a concert together this Friday?

上田：ええ、ぜひ。何時にどこで会(あ)いましょうか。
Yes I'd love to. What time and where shall we meet?

リー：そうですね。三時十五分ごろに学生会館(かいかん)のまえはどうですか。
Let's see, how about around three fifteen in front of the student union?

上田：いいですね。じゃあ、三時十五分に学生会館(かいかん)のまえで。
That would be fine. Okay then, in front of the union at three fifteen.

話してみましょう

Activity 1

Work with a partner. Extend an invitation by rephrasing the following sentences with the ～ませんか form. Your partner will accept your invitation saying ええ、～ましょう. Then switch roles.

Example: A: ～さん、明日こうえんに行って、テニスをしませんか。
B: ええ、しましょう。

1. 木曜日に一緒にえいがを見る
2. アイスクリームを食べに行く
3. 明日一緒にべんきょうする
4. うちに来て、コーヒーを飲む
5. あのカフェに入る
6. 今日ばんごはんを一緒に食べる
7. 一緒に帰る

Activity 2

Invite a new partner to do the following activities. Then decide on the time and place together.

Example: A: 一緒に買い物に行きませんか。
B: ええ、いいですね。いつ行きましょうか。
A: 明日はどうですか。
B: いいですよ。どこに行きましょうか。
A: ～に行きませんか。
B: ええ、いいですよ。 じゃあ、～に行きましょう。

	いつ	どこ
1. 一緒に買い物に行く		
2. コンサートに行く		
3. 一緒にしゅくだいをする		
4. 一緒にばんごはんを作る		
5. おちゃを飲む		

読む練習

上手な読み方

Understanding Japanese e-mail formats

The format of Japanese e-mail programs for the PC is very similar to their counterparts in English, except that all of the labels are in Japanese. However, keyboard shortcuts remain in the menu as Roman letters in parentheses, such as (F) and (F), which will give you some clue as to what a menu is about. For example, (F) often represents File options and (E) usually stands for Editing options. So you can guess the contents of some of the fields using your knowledge of English software.

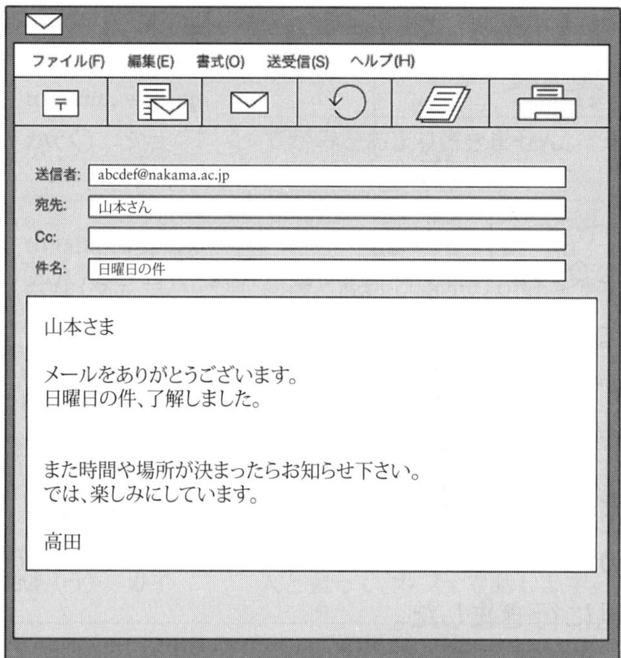

練習

Look at the e-mail screen above and try to guess the meaning of the following words.

書式（しょしき）
ファイル
ヘルプ
送信者（そうしんしゃ）
宛先（あてさき）
件名（けんめい）

E-メールが来ました

ファイル(F)　編集(E)　書式(O)　送受信(S)　ヘルプ(H)

送信者: 大木　高子　takako@westside.ac.jp

宛先: Sara Jones sjones@hotmail.com

Cc:

件名: パーティのこと

サラさん、

こんにちは。高子です。

来週の木曜日に山本さんの誕生日パーティがあるんですが、よかったら来ませんか。6時から、ぎんざのマルスというフランス料理のレストランでします。会費は一人5,000円です。

カードを買いましたから、あとで何か書いてくれませんか。

じゃあ、おへんじまっています。

読んだ後(あと)で　Comprehension

A. しつもんに日本語でこたえて下さい。

1. このメールはだれが書きましたか。
2. このメールはだれに書きましたか。
3. どうしてメールを書きましたか。
4. だれのパーティがありますか。
5. パーティはいつどこでありますか。
6. 一人 (*per person*) いくらかかりますか。

B. Imagine that you are the recipient of this e-mail, and write a response.

総合練習

そうごうれんしゅう

A. イベント・プランニング　Event Planning

Work in pairs. Plan an interesting event for the class. Once the plans are complete, each group gives a presentation inviting others to join their event. The pair with the most popular idea for an event wins.

Example: A: どんなイベントにしましょうか。
B: ピクニックはどうですか。
A: いいですね。いつにしましょうか。
B: 来週の土曜日にしませんか。

来週の土曜日にセントラルパークで日本語のクラスのピクニックがあります。ピクニックではいろいろなゲームをします。

B. いっしょに何かしませんか。

Your instructor will give you a card with a day of the week written on it to indicate which day you have off from class. On the card, write in Japanese an activity you'd like to do with someone. Your instructor will then divide the class into two groups. Everyone in the first group must find someone in the second group with a matching card and extend an invitation to do the activity. Together, negotiate the details, such as where to go and what time to meet. Remember to use the expressions and strategies you have learned in this chapter to introduce a topic and extend an invitation.

Example: You are free on: 水曜日
Activity: えいがを見る

ロールプレイ

1. You are with a friend at a Japanese department store and want to have lunch. You go up to the eighth floor, where there are a variety of restaurants (めいてんがい). Discuss your options (和食(わ)、洋食(よう)、中華(か)りょうり etc.) and decide where to eat.
2. You have gone out to eat with your friend. Place your orders and find out how long they will take. If any one of the dishes require more than 15 minutes to prepare, order something else.

Chapter 10

第(だい)十課(か)

私の家族(かぞく)
My family

Objectives Describing people, addressing family members

Vocabulary Kinship, parts of the body, physical appearance, personality, verbs of resultant states, age, number of people, and order in a family

Dialogue 私の家族(かぞく)は五人(ごにん)家族(かぞく)です。*There are five people in my family.*

Japanese Culture The Japanese family, insiders and outsiders

Grammar
- I. Stating the order within a family using 番(目(め))
- II. Describing a resultant state using verb て-form + いる
- III. Describing physical appearance and skills using ～は ～が
- IV. Describing people and things using nouns and modifying clauses
- V. Expressing opinions using ～とおもう

Listening Using one's background knowledge about a person

Communication Being modest about yourself and your family

Kanji **Kanji** derived from pictures (3)

男 女 目 口 耳 足 手 父 母 姉 兄 妹 弟
家 族 両 親 子

Reading Creating charts and figures

Chapter Resources

www.cengagebrain.com

Heinle Learning Center

Audio Program

Pair work

Group work

単語
たん

Nouns

あし	足	leg, foot
あたま	頭	head, あたまがいい smart, intelligent
あに	兄	older brother (the speaker's)
あね	姉	older sister (the speaker's)
いもうと	妹	younger sister (the speaker's)
いもうとさん	妹さん	younger sister (someone else's)
おかあさん	お母さん	mother (someone else's)
おくさん	奥さん	wife (someone else's)
おこさん	お子さん	child (someone else's)
おじいさん	お祖父さん	grandfather (someone else's)
おとうさん	お父さん	father (someone else's)
おとうと	弟	younger brother (the speaker's)
おとうとさん	弟さん	younger brother (someone else's)
おとこ	男	male, おとこの人 man
おにいさん	お兄さん	older brother (someone else's)
おねえさん	お姉さん	older sister (someone else's)
おばあさん	お祖母さん	grandmother (someone else's)
おんな	女	female, おんなの人 woman
かいしゃいん	会社員	businessperson
かお	顔	face
かぞく	家族	family, speaker's family
かみ	髪	hair (かみのけ is commonly used as well)
きょうだい	兄弟	sibling(s)
くち	口	mouth
けっこん	結婚	marriage, ～とけっこんする to marry ～, けっこんしている to be married
こ	子	child, おとこのこ boy, おんなのこ girl
ごかぞく	ご家族	family (someone else's)

～にん	～人	～ people
～ばん（め）	～番（目）	～th (ordinal suffix)

Conjunction

それに	in addition

Expressions

いいえ、そんなことはありません。	No, that's not the case.
いいえ、まだまだです。	No, I still have a long way to go.

単語の練習

A. 家族 Kinship terms

Japanese has two sets of kinship terms. One is used to refer to one's own family and the other is used to refer to someone else's.

	Your own family member (humble form)	Someone else's family member (polite form)
family	家族（かぞく）	ご家族（かぞく）
father	父（ちち）	お父（とう）さん
mother	母（はは）	お母（かあ）さん
parents	両親（りょうしん）	ご両親（りょうしん）
older brother	兄（あに）	お兄（にい）さん
older sister	姉（あね）	お姉（ねえ）さん
younger brother	弟（おとうと）	弟（おとうと）さん
younger sister	妹（いもうと）	妹（いもうと）さん
brothers and sisters	兄弟（きょうだい）	ご兄弟（きょうだい）
grandfather	祖父（そふ）	お祖父（じい）さん
grandmother	祖母（そぼ）	お祖母（ばあ）さん
husband	主人（しゅじん）	ご主人（しゅじん）
wife	つま	おくさん
child/children	子供（こども）	お子（こ）さん

Note that 子供(こども), 兄弟(きょうだい), 家族(かぞく) and 両親(りょうしん) can be used in general statements.

日本の子供(こども)はよくあそびます。 *Japanese children play a lot.*

ハワイには日本人の家族(かぞく)がたくさんいます。 *There are many Japanese families in Hawaii.*

Activity 1

Look at the family trees. Note that each family member is represented by a letter. Now, form groups of three. One of you will write the letters A through T in random order on a piece of paper and read a letter on the list. The other two will give the kinship term that corresponds to the letter. Remember to say 私の〜 or 山田さんの〜. Whoever calls out the correct term first gets a point. The person with the most points wins. Take turns reading the letters.

Example: The dealer says *H*. Player 1 says 私の 弟(おとうと) first. Player 1 gets a point.

私の家族(かぞく)　　山田さんのご家族(かぞく)

Supplementary Vocabulary: 親族(しんぞく) (Kinship terms)

	Your own family member (humble form)		Someone else's family member (polite form)	
cousin	いとこ	従兄弟	いとこさん	従兄弟さん
nephew	おい	甥	おいごさん	甥御さん
uncle	おじ	叔父／伯父	おじさん	叔父さん／伯父さん
aunt	おば	叔母／伯母	おばさん	叔母さん／伯母さん
relatives	しんせき	親戚	ごしんせき	ご親戚
niece	めい	姪	めいごさん	姪御さん
grandchild	まご	孫	おまごさん	お孫さん

B. からだのぶぶん Body Parts

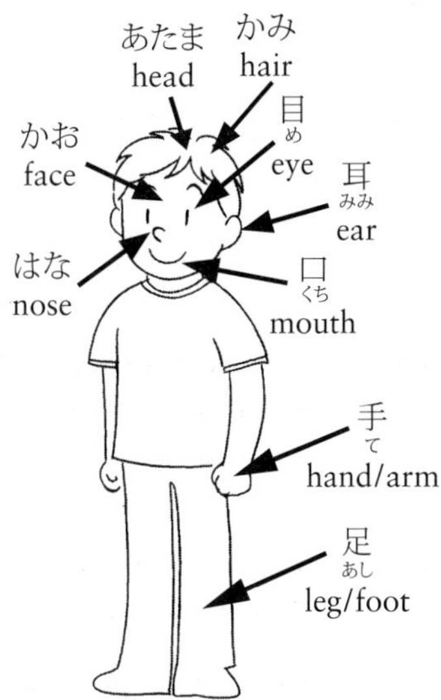

Activity 2

Work with the class. Everyone claps their hands twice and immediately after that, your instructor will say a body part in Japanese. Touch the part he/she says.

Activity 3

"Simon Says." Work with a partner. Using the vocabulary in this chapter, take turns calling out and identifying parts of the body in Japanese.

Supplementary Vocabulary: からだ The Body

あご	顎	chin
うで	腕	arm
おなか		belly
かた	肩	shoulder
からだ	体	body
くちびる	唇	lip(s)
くび	首	neck
こし	腰	waist
せなか	背中	back
つめ	爪	nail
のど	咽	throat
は	歯	tooth
ひげ	髭	mustache, beard
ほっぺた／ほお		cheek
まつげ	睫	eyelash
まゆげ	眉毛	eyebrow
ゆび	指	finger

C. からだのとくちょう Physical features

せが高い	tall (height)
せがひくい	short (height)
手(て)がながい	have a long reach
足(あし)がみじかい	have short legs
かおがまるい	have a round face
かおがほそながい	have a narrow face
かおが四角(しかく)い	have a square face
目(め)があおい	have blue eyes
口(くち)が小さい	have a small mouth
はなが高い	have a prominent nose
かっこいい	good-looking
かみがくろい	have black hair
ブロンド	blond hair
ふとっている	fat, chubby
やせている	thin

おぼえていますか。

あかい、きれい（な)、しろい、ちゃいろい、みどり

Activity 4

Write your guess for the opposite of each attribute listed below.

1. せがひくい ______________________
2. ふとっている ______________________
3. かみがくろい ______________________
4. かおが小さい ______________________
5. 足(あし)がみじかい ______________________
6. 手(て)がながい ______________________
7. 口(くち)が小さい ______________________
8. はなが高い ______________________
9. 耳(みみ)が大きい ______________________
10. あたまが小さい ______________________

Activity 5

Take a moment to think about your own physical features. Then state as many as you can in sixty seconds.

D. Verbs used with clothing and accessories

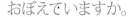

シャツをきる	put on a shirt
スカートをはく	put on a skirt
くつをはく	put on shoes
ぼうしをかぶる	put on a hat
めがねをかける	put on glasses
イヤリングをする	put on earrings
うでどけいをする	put on a wristwatch

おぼえていますか。

コート、ジャケット、シャツ、ジーンズ、スーツ、ストッキング、セーター、Tシャツ、ドレス、ネクタイ、ネックレス、パンツ、ふく、ベルト、ゆびわ

Activity 6

Classify the above articles of clothing and accessories that are used with the following verbs:

Verbs	Articles of clothing and accessories
きる	
はく	
する	

E. せいかくとのうりょく　Personality and ability

あかるい	cheerful
あたまがいい	smart, intelligent
かわいい	cute, adorable
親切(しんせつ)(な)	kind
スポーツが上手(じょうず)(な)	good at sports
日本語が分かる	understand Japanese

おぼえていますか。

いい、おもしろい、たのしい、つまらない、むずかしい、やさしい

げんき(な)、しずか(な)、にぎやか(な)、りっぱ(な)

Activity 7

しつもんに日本語でこたえて下さい。

1. お父(とう)さんはどんな人ですか。
2. お母(かあ)さんはどんな人ですか。
3. どんな人が好きですか。
4. 一番いい友達(だち)はどんな人ですか。

Supplementary Vocabulary: せいかく Personality

うちき（な）	内気（な）	shy, introverted
おだやか（な）	穏やか（な）	calm
きがつよい	気が強い	strong-minded
きがながい	気が長い	patient
きがはやい	気が早い	impatient, hasty, rash
きがみじかい	気が短い	short-tempered
きがよわい	気が弱い	weak-minded
くらい	暗い	somber, nerdy
たんき（な）	短気（な）	short-tempered
のんびりしている		easygoing, carefree
まじめ（な）	真面目（な）	serious, studious

F. しごととちい Work and social status

～と　けっこんする	to get married to
～に　すむ	to reside in
～に　つとめる	to get a job at
会社員(かいしゃいん)	business person
小学生(しょうがくせい)	elementary-school student
中学生(ちゅうがくせい)	middle-school student

おぼえていますか。

学生、高校、高校生、しごと、大学院(いん)生、大学生

Activity 8

しつもんに日本語でこたえて下さい。

1. 今、どこにすんでいますか。
2. どんなところにすみたいですか。
3. 日本の会社(かいしゃ)につとめたいですか。
4. どんなところにつとめたいですか。
5. けっこんしたいですか。いつけっこんしたいですか。
6. ご家族(かぞく)に小学生(しょうがくせい)／中学生(ちゅうがくせい)／高校生がいますか。
7. お父(とう)さんは／お母(かあ)さんはどこかにつとめていますか。

Supplementary Vocabulary: Occupations

いしゃ	医者	medical doctor
エンジニア		engineer
かんごし	看護師	nurse, medical assistant
きょうし／きょういん	教師／教員	teacher
こうむいん	公務員	government official
サラリーマン		white-collar worker (from the English term “salaried man”)
じえいぎょう	自営業	self-employed
だいがくきょうじゅ	大学教授	college professor
はいしゃ	歯医者	dentist
べんごし	弁護士	lawyer
マネージャー		manager

G. としと人数(にんずう) Age and number of people

	～人(にん) (～ people)	～さい (～ years old)
何	なんにん	（お）いくつ／なんさい
0		れいさい
一	※ ひとり	※ いっさい
二	※ ふたり	にさい
三	さんにん	さんさい
四	※ よにん	よんさい
五	ごにん	ごさい
六	ろくにん	ろくさい
七	※ しちにん	※ ななさい
八	はちにん	※ はっさい
九	きゅうにん	きゅうさい
十	じゅうにん	※ じゅっさい ※ じっさい
百	ひゃくにん	ひゃくさい
千	せんにん	
一万	いちまんにん	

Notes: An asterisk indicates an exception to some rule or a sound change.

四人家族(よにんかぞく) means *a family of four including yourself.* 兄弟(きょうだい)が二人(ふたり)います, however, means that you have two siblings, excluding yourself.

Activity 9

Sing a version of this popular counting rhyme in Japanese!

Allegro
ひ とり ふ たり さん にん いる よ よ にん ご にん ろく にん いる よ

しち にん はち にん きゅう にん い る よ じゅう にん のこ ども た

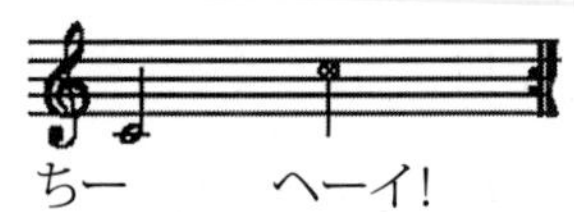
ちー ヘーイ!

Activity 10

Form groups of varying sizes according to the directions your instructor calls out. Try to join each group as quickly as possible so that you won't be left behind.

Example: 三人(にん)のグループを作って下さい。

Activity 11

Write down three numbers on a piece of paper. Your instructor will call out an age. Cross out a number if it corresponds to what you hear. Whoever crosses out all their numbers first wins.

Activity 12

しつもんに日本語でこたえて下さい。

1. この大学には学生が何人(にん)ぐらいいますか。
2. この大学には先生が何人(にん)ぐらいいますか。
3. 日本語の先生は何人(にん)いますか。
4. 日本語の学生が何人(にん)ぐらいいますか。
5. 今、きょうしつにクラスメートが何人(にん)いますか。
6. ご兄弟(きょうだい)がいますか。何人(にん)いますか。
7. 何人(にん)家族(かぞく)ですか。

Activity 13

Work in groups of five or six. Make up a number representing a classmate's age, write it down on a piece of paper, and tape it to the back of someone else in your group. Take turns asking about your ages. Then line up in order from "youngest" to "oldest."

Activity 14

The following table lists typical age ranges for children and young adults who attend school or day care in Japan. The information about Japan is provided. Fill in the information about your country and compare the two.

Example: 日本ではれいさいから三さいの子供(こども)がたくじしょに行きます。

アメリカでは／も、～さいから～さいの子供(こども)がたくじしょに行きます。

	日本	私の国(くに) (*country*)
たくじしょ (*nursery*)	0 さいから　3 さい	(　　) さいから　(　　) さい
ほいくえん (*day-care center*)	0 さいから　6 さい	(　　) さいから　(　　) さい
ようちえん (*kindergarten*)	3 さいから　6 さい	(　　) さいから　(　　) さい
小学校(しょうがっこう)	6 さいから　12 さい	(　　) さいから　(　　) さい
中学校(ちゅうがっこう)	12 さいから　15 さい	(　　) さいから　(　　) さい
高校	15 さいから　18 さい	(　　) さいから　(　　) さい
大学	18 さいから　22 さい	(　　) さいから　(　　) さい

Activity 15

しつもんに日本語でこたえて下さい。

1. お父(とう)さんはおいくつですか。
2. お母(かあ)さんはおいくつですか。
3. ～さんは、今何さいですか。
4. ～さんの一番いい友達(だち)は、今何さいですか。

ダイアローグ

はじめに　Warm-up

しつもんに日本語でこたえて下さい。

1. 何人家族ですか。
2. お兄さんがいますか。お姉さんはどうですか。
3. 妹さんがいますか。弟さんはどうですか。

私の家族は五人家族です。 *There are five people in my family.*

上田さんの友達の川口さんがあそびに来ています。上田さんと川口さんは、上田さんのへやにいます。

川口：　あ、あのしゃしん、上田さんのご家族ですか。

上田：　ええ、そうです。これが父で、これが母です。

川口：　かっこいいお父さんですね。それにとてもきれいなお母さんですね。

上田：　ああ、でも、父も母も四十九さいなんですよ。

川口：　そうですか。とてもわかく見えますけど。

上田：　父はくるまの会社(かいしゃ)につとめていて、母(はは)は英(えい)語の先生なんです。

川口：　すてきですね。じゃあ、この帽子(ぼうし)をかぶっている男(おとこ)の子(こ)は弟(おとうと)さんですか。

上田：　ええ、そうです。なまえはデービッドで、今、小学(しょうがく)三年生です。

川口：　かわいいですね。じゃあ、この人はお姉(ねえ)さんですか。

上田：　いいえ、それは妹(いもうと)のパムです。パムはまだ十七さいなんですが、パムのほうが私よりせが高くて大きいから、よく年上(としうえ)に見られるんですよ。

川口：　そうなんですか。

Dialogue Phrase Notes

- It is rude to refer to people using これ, それ, あれ, but you can do so when you talk about a person in a photograph or drawing, because pictures are not actual human beings.
- わかく見えます means *look young*. わかい means *young*, and it is usually used for teenagers or adults but not for children.
- 年上(としうえ)に見られる means *to be mistaken for an older (sibling)*.

ダイアローグの後(あと)で

A. Look at the pictures of family trees on page 386. Using them as examples, draw Ms. Ueda's family tree.

B. Based on the dialogue, complete the following paragraphs using appropriate words and phrases.

上田さんの家族(かぞく)は五人家族(にんかぞく)です。お父(とう)さんとお母(かあ)さんと＿＿＿＿＿＿と＿＿＿＿＿＿がいます。上田さんの＿＿＿＿＿＿は四十九さいで、くるまの会社(かいしゃ)につとめています。上田さんの＿＿＿＿＿＿＿＿＿も四十九さいです。＿＿＿＿＿＿＿＿は　英(えい)語の先生です。上田さんの＿＿＿＿＿＿のなまえは＿＿＿＿＿で、高校生ですが、せがとても高いです。上田さんの＿＿＿＿＿＿のなまえはデービッドで、小学校(しょうがっこう)の＿＿＿＿＿＿です。とてもかわいいです。

日本の文化

日本の家族

According to a 2012 government survey, 58.3% of Japanese families fall under the category of nuclear families, and 32.4% are single-person households. Only 10.2% are three-generation families.

Since the end of World War II, the number of children in a Japanese family has decreased substantially. The average for 2012 was only 1.39 children per household, compared with 2.1 for the same year in the U.S.; Japan is ranked 175th of 193 countries in the WHO's 2012 World Health Statistics. Some reasons for the decline are economic; others are social, such as later marriages and a lack of support for women to continue to work after having children. According to 2010 statistics from the Japanese Ministry of Health, Labor and Welfare, the average age for a man to marry was 30.5 years. For a woman, it was 28.8 years. 88.1% of women work before getting married, but only 61% continue to work after marriage. After a child is born, the percentage plummets to 38%. The Global Gender Gap Report 2012 (World Economic Forum, 2012) ranked Japan 101st out of 135 countries in gender equality because Japanese women do not receive the same status as men in terms of economic, political, or education- or health-based criteria. Traditionally, wives are expected to take care of the house and children even while holding down a job. Despite recent efforts to update traditional roles, the current support infrastructure, such as day-care facilities and baby-sitting services, is still inadequate to allow many women to work.

© Joeri DeRocker/Photo Japan

© VStock BR/Agency

Conversely, Japanese husbands are expected to support the family financially, and tend to work long hours. Although some companies offer parental leave for men in addition to maternity leave, new fathers rarely take advantage of this benefit, as it would lower their income significantly, could inconvenience their co-workers, and might even affect chances for promotion.

Despite these pressures, the divorce rate in Japan is extremely low. Until 1972, it was less than one percent. After climbing to a high of 2.3 percent in 2002, the rate as of 2005 declined to under 2.1 percent.

ウチとソト **Insiders and Outsiders**

The Japanese rarely praise members of their own family when they are talking to someone outside the family. They are very conscious of the distinction between “in-group” (ウチ) and “out-group” (ソト). It is very important to be polite to those who are not in one’s in-group, and praising members of your own family—the primary in-group—is considered impolite. Accordingly, you may often hear a Japanese man complaining that his wife is not good at cooking when in fact she is an excellent cook, or you may hear a woman say that her husband is impractical and inept at household matters. Similarly, boasting about yourself is considered socially inappropriate.

Within one’s own family, お父さん, お母さん, お兄さん, お姉さん and similar terms are used to address senior members. First names are used only to address younger members. A daughter or son would address their mother as お母さん, お母ちゃん (ちゃん being the more familiar form), or ママ (*Mama, Mommy*); older brothers as お兄さん or お兄ちゃん; and a younger sister named Michiko as みち子ちゃん. Senior members tend to refer to themselves using their kinship terms when talking to a younger member of the family. Instead of using their first names in front of their children, parents usually call each other お父さん／パパ (*Papa, Daddy*) and お母さん／ママ (Mom, Mommy).

In addition, Japanese forms of address do not distinguish between biological parents and stepparents. Using the Japanese equivalent of terms such as *stepfather* and *stepmother* can imply a distant relationship between the stepchild and the stepparents, so both biological and step-parents are addressed in the same way.

文法(ぶんぽう)

I. Stating the order within a family using 番(目(め))

Expressing the order within a family using 番(目(め))

番(目(め)) converts cardinal numbers into ordinal numbers, and is used to describe one's standing in one's family, as in:

一番上	oldest (*literally*, the first from the top, the highest)
上から二番目(め)	second oldest (*literally*, the second from the top, the second highest)
真ん中(まんなか)	right in the middle
下から二番目(め)	second youngest (*literally*, the second from the bottom, the second lowest)
一番下	youngest (*literally*, the first from the bottom, the lowest)

The pronunciation of numbers preceding ばん(め) is regular and follows the same pattern as the pronunciaiton for counter 〜まい.

	〜番(目(め)) (ordinal, 〜 th)		
何	なんばん(め)	六	ろくばん(め)
一	いちばん(め)	七	ななばん(め)
二	にばん(め)	八	はちばん(め)
三	さんばん(め)	九	きゅうばん(め)
四	よんばん(め)	十	じゅうばん(め)
五	ごばん(め)	百	ひゃくばん(め)

川中：私の家族(かぞく)は五人家族(にんかぞく)です。
My family consists of five members.

小山(こやま)：そうですか。ゆみ子(こ)さんは何番目(め)ですか。
Where do you come in the family (literally, *what order are you*), *Yumiko?*

川中：一番上です。
I am the oldest.

小山(こやま)：そうですか。じゃあ、一番下はだれですか。
I see. Who is the youngest?

川中：妹(いもうと)のみかです。みかは、今、十五さいです。
My younger sister Mika. She is fifteen years old now.

Note that the term for *only child* is 一人(ひとり)っ子(こ).

話してみましょう

Activity 1

Take turns asking your classmates how many people are in their families. Then compare the results. Whose family is the largest? Whose is the smallest? Discuss the advantages and disadvantages of coming from a large or small family.

Example: A: ～さんのご家族(かぞく)は何人家族(にんかぞく)ですか。
B: 四人家族(にんかぞく)です。
or 母(はは)と私と妹(いもうと)が二人(ふたり)います。

Activity 2

Work in groups of four or five. Take turns asking your classmates how many siblings they have and their order in the family. Then compare the results. Who is the oldest or the youngest?

Example: A: ～さんはご兄弟(きょうだい)がいますか。
B: はい、二人(ふたり)います。
A: ～さんは何番目(め)ですか。
B: 私は一番上です。

Activity 3

Work with a partner. Take turns describing your family members in terms of name and age, and fill in the table below with your partner's descriptions.

Example: 私の家族(かぞく)は三人家族(にんかぞく)です。兄(あに)が一人(ひとり)います。なまえはトーマスで、二十五さいです。父(ちち)のなまえはジョンです。今、五十二さいです。

～さんのご兄弟(きょうだい)	おなまえ	～さい

～さんのご両親(りょうしん)	おなまえ	～さい

II. Describing a resultant state using verb て-form + いる

The verb て-form + いる describes a state (of being) that is the result of a past action. For example, めがねをかける means *to put on* (*glasses*), and めがねをかけている means *as the result of putting glasses on, the person is now wearing them.*

めがねをかける

めがねをかけている

Similarly, けっこんする means *to get married* whereas けっこんしている means *to be married.*

Action: けっこんする (*get married*)	**Resultant state: けっこんしている (*is married*)**

Action: ふとる (*gain weight*)	**Resultant state: ふとっている (*is fat*)**

山本：　田中さんはめがねをかけていますか。
Does Ms. Tanaka wear glasses?

チョイ：　いいえ、めがねはかけていませんが、イヤリングをしていますよ。
No, she doesn't, but she wears earrings.

Notes

- The past form ～ていました describes a (resultant) state at a specified time in the past.

  たくさん食べて、ふとりました。
  I ate a lot and gained some weight.

  私は小さい時(とき)、ふとっていました。
  I was fat (chubby) when I was small.

- ～ている can be used to describe a person who wears something habitually.

  田中さんはよくジーンズをはいています。
  Mr. Tanaka often wears jeans.

  山田さんはいつもネクタイをしています。
  Mr. Yamada always wears a tie.

- The verbs すむ and つとめる are usually used with ～ている. The particle に is used to indicate a location, company or organization.

  私はとうきょうにすんでいます。
  I live in Tokyo.

  山田さんはアパートにすんでいました。
  Mr. Yamada used to live (was living) in an apartment.

  ぼくはじょうとう大学につとめています。
  I work for Joto University.

話してみましょう

Activity 1

Describe what each person is wearing, using the verb with ている.

Example: さとうさんはスーツをきています。そして、ネクタイをしています。

さとうさん　　山本さん　　こんどうさん　　木村(むら)さん

Activity 2

Work with a partner. Pick a classmate and have your partner guess who it is by asking what the person is wearing, using はい／いいえ questions.

Example: A: その人は帽子(ぼうし)をかぶっていますか。
B: いいえ、かぶっていません。
A: その人はスカートをはいていますか。
B: はい、はいています。

Activity 3

Your instructor will ask the students to walk around the classroom observing what others are wearing. When he/she tells the class to stop, each student will stand back to back with the person who is closest and describe his/her clothing. How many items can you describe correctly?

Example: 〜さんはあかいセーターをきていて、ジーンズをはいています。

Activity 4

Work with a series of partners. Take turns finding out where your classmates have lived up until now. Note that 〜の時(とき) means *at the time of* 〜 or *when I was / am* 〜 .

Example: A: 〜さんは、今、どこにすんでいますか。

B: ハリソン・ホールにすんでいます。

A: ずっと (*for a long time*) そこにすんでいますか。

B: いいえ、高校の時(とき)は両親(りょうしん)とすんでいました。

A: そうですか。ご両親(りょうしん)はどこにすんでいますか。

B: バーリントンにすんでいます。

III. Describing physical appearance and skills using ～は ～が

The ～は ～が construction is used to describe the characteristics of a variety of things such as people, places, and other physical objects. This chapter introduces how ～は ～が can be used to describe people's physical appearance, skills, and personality.

A. Describing physical appearance

The construction "person は body parts が adjectives" is used to describe a person's physical appearance.

山下さんは　はなが　高いです。　*Mr. Yamashita has a prominent nose.*

リーさんは　目(め)が　ちゃいろいです。　*Ms. Li has brown eyes.*

上田さんは　かみが　ながいです。　*Ms. Ueda has long hair.*

キムさんは　かおが　四角(しかく)いです。　*Mr. Kim has a square face.*

本木(もとき)：　あの人はせが高くて、足(あし)がながくて、かっこいいですね。
That person over there is good-looking. She is very tall, and has long legs.

山口(やまぐち)：　ああ、あの人はモデルですからね。
Oh yes, that's because she is a model.

B. Describing skills and ability

～は ～が can be used with other personal traits such as personality and ability. In the following example, いい and 上手(じょうず) are adjectives and 分かる is an intransitive verb. Unlike a transitive verb, an intransitive verb does not take a direct object or the direct object marker を. Instead, the particle が is used.

チョイさんは　あたまが　いいです。　*Mr. Choi is smart.*

石(いし)田さんは　テニスが　上手(じょうず)です。　*Mr. Ishida is good at tennis.*

山田さんは　フランス語が　分かります。　*Mr. Yamada understands French.*

田口(たぐち)：　あの人は日本語が分かりそうですね。
That person over there appears to understand Japanese.

三上(みかみ)：　ええ、でも、あまり上手(じょうず)じゃなさそうです。
Yes, but it does not look like he is good at it.

NOTES

- Like 好き and きらい, the plain present affirmative form of a verb + の can be used with 上手(じょうず).

  アリソンさんはうたをうたうのが上手(じょうず)です。
  Allison is good at singing songs.

話してみましょう

Activity 1

Using the following chart listing various physical characteristics, describe the persons named.

Example: 私

私はせがひくいですが、手(て)と足(あし)はながいです。

かおがまるくて、かみがながいです。そして、目(め)もはなも口(くち)も小さいです。

からだ	大きい　小さい
せ	高い　ひくい
手(て)	ながい　みじかい　きれい
足(あし)	ながい　みじかい　きれい
かお	まるい　四角(しかく)い　ほそながい　たまごがた (*egg-shaped*)
かみ	ながい　みじかい　くろい　あかい　ちゃいろい　ブロンド
目(め)	大きい　小さい　あおい　ちゃいろい　くろい　みどり
はな	大きい　小さい　高い　ひくい
口(くち)	大きい　小さい

1. 私
2. 父(ちち)
3. 母(はは)
4. 一番いい友達(だち)
5. Other members of your family

Activity 2

Work with a partner. Pick one face in the drawing and describe it to your partner. Have him/her identify the face by the number on the illustration.

Example: この人はかおがまるいです。

この人は目(め)が大きいです。

Activity 3

Work with a partner. Draw a person's face. Then, describe the face to your partner. Your partner will try to draw the face according to your description. Compare the two faces.

Example: この人はかおがほそながくて、目(め)が小さいです。

Activity 4

Work with the class. Find out which languages your classmates can speak, who knows the most languages, and other talents they may have. List the information you obtain in the chart.

Example:

1. A: ～さんはどんなことば (*language*) が分かりますか。
   B: かんこく語が分かります。
   A: そうですか。かっこいいですね。

2. A: ～さんはどんなことをするのが上手(じょうず)ですか。
   B: かんじを書くのが上手(じょうず)です。
   A: そうですか。いいですね。私はかんじを書くのは、あまり上手(じょうず)じゃないんです。

クラスメートのなまえ	ことば (*language*)	上手(じょうず)なこと

IV. Describing people and things using nouns and modifying clauses

A noun may be modified by another noun, an adjective, or a modifying clause. The modifier always comes before the noun. In a noun-modifying clause, the verb must be in the plain form. The negative forms of adjectives and the copula verb must be in the plain form as well.

ブロンドの	かみ	*blond hair*
日本のくるまじゃない	くるま	*a car that is not a Japanese car*
きれいな	家(うち)	*a clean house*
きれいじゃない	家(うち)	*a house that is not clean*
りょうりが上手(じょうず)な	人	*a person who is good at cooking*
そうじが上手(じょうず)じゃない	人	*a person who is not good at cleaning*
小さい	くつ	*small shoes*
小さくない	くつ	*not-so-small shoes*
かみがながい	人	*a person who has long hair*
かみがながくない	人	*a person who does not have long hair*
英(えい)語が分かる	人	*a person who understands English*
新聞をよく読む	人	*a person who often reads the paper*
けっこんしている	人	*a person who is married*
けっこんしていない	人	*a person who is not married*

ホン： 田中さんのお母(かあ)さんはどの方(かた)ですか。
Which (person) is Mr. Tanaka's mother?

木村(むら)： あそこにいる人ですよ。せが高くてかみがながい人です。
(She is) the person over there—the tall person with long hair.

ホン： ああ、 あの方(かた)ですか。とてもきれいな方(かた)ですね。
Oh, that person? She's very beautiful, isn't she?

木村(むら)： 本当(ほんとう)にそうですね。
Indeed.

話してみましょう

Activity 1

Look at the drawings and answer the questions using a noun-modifying clause wherever appropriate.

さとうさん

山本さん

こんどうさん

木村(むら)さん

Example: さとうさんはどの人ですか。
スーツをきている人です。

1. さとうさんはどの人ですか。
2. こんどうさんはどの人ですか。
3. 木村(むら)さんはどの人ですか。
4. 山本さんはどの人ですか。
5. ジーンズをはいている人は木村(むら)さんですか。
6. ネックレスをしている人はどの人ですか。
7. めがねをかけている人はこんどうさんですか。

Activity 2

Fruit Basket. The class arranges its chairs in a circle so that all but one person has a place to sit. That person stands in the center of the circle and calls out a physical descriptor. Anyone who fits the description must move to another seat, and the one in the center may try to sit down in an open seat. Whoever is left without a seat then takes the center and calls out another descriptor.

Example: The person in the center says: めがねをかけている人
People who wear glasses must move to another seat.

Activity 3

Take turns finding out how many in the class fall into the categories listed in the chart. Then check your answers with each other. Note that 私のデータでは means *according to my data*.

Example:
1. A: ～さんは、りょうにすんでいますか。
   B: いいえ、すんでいません。
2. A: りょうにすんでいる人は何人(にん)いますか。
   B: 二人(ふたり)います。／ぜんぜんいません。
   A: そうですか。私のデータでは一人(ひとり)です。

	はい	いいえ
りょうにすんでいる		
お姉(ねえ)さんがいる		
妹(いもうと)さんがいる		
一人(ひとり)っ子(こ)だ		
スポーツが上手(じょうず)だ		
スペイン語が分かる		

Activity 4

Work in groups of four. One student thinks of a classmate but does not say his/her name. The other members ask questions about his/her characteristics to find out who he or she is. They can ask up to six questions. Anyone who guesses the answer after the first question receives six points. After the second question, he/she receives five points. If no one is able to get the correct answer after the sixth question, the person who has chosen the name receives six points. The person who earns the most points wins.

Example: A: 女(おんな)の人ですか。
B: はい。
C: かみがながい人ですか。
B: いいえ、かみはみじかいです。
D: じゃあ、ブロンドですか。
B: いいえ、ちゃいろいかみの人です。

Activity 5

With a partner, take turns asking what kind of person appeals to each of you. Have your partner describe the person in terms of physical appearance, personality, interests, and ability, using noun modifiers. Take turns. Take detailed notes on the information that your partner gives you.

Example: A: スミスさんはどんな人が好きですか。
B: せが高くて、かみがブロンドの人が好きです。
そして、やきゅうが上手(じょうず)な人がいいですね。
おいしいものを食べるのが好きな人もいいですね。
A: せいかくはどんな人がいいですか。
B: そうですね。あたまがよくて、やさしい人がいいですね。

Activity 6

You are a dating consultant looking for the best match for your partner from the previous activity. Take turns asking about your classmates' favorite types. They will give information about their previous partner's preferences.

Example: A: どの人のデータ (*data*) がありますか。
B: スミスさんのデータがあります。
A: スミスさんはどんな人が好きなんですか。
B: せが高くて、かみがブロンドの人が好きです。
そして、あたまがよくて、やさしい人が好きです。

V. Expressing opinions using 〜とおもう

〜とおもう expresses the speaker's opinion about things or events. The subject of おもう, the speaker, is often deleted. The clause before とおもう must end in the plain form.

Copula verb	
ご主人(しゅじん)は　会社員(かいしゃいん) だと　おもいます。	*I think her husband is a businessman.*
ご主人(しゅじん)は　日本人じゃないと　おもいます。	*I think her husband is not Japanese./ I don't think her husband is Japanese.*
い - adjectives	
上田さんは　かわいいと　おもいます。	*I think Ms. Ueda is cute.*
このテストは　むずかしくないと　おもいます。	*I think this test isn't difficult./ I don't think this test is difficult.*
な - adjectives	
先生は　とても親切(しんせつ)だと　おもいます。	*I think my teacher is very kind.*
弟(おとうと)は　さしみが好きじゃないと　おもいます。	*I think my younger brother doesn't like sashimi./ I don't think my younger brother likes sashimi.*
Verbs	
友田さんは　けっこんしていると　おもいます。	*I think Mr. Tomoda is married.*
山田さんは　明日(あした)来ないと　おもいます。	*I think Ms. Yamada is not coming tomorrow./I don't think Ms. Yamada is coming tomorrow.*

The speaker can be specified for emphasis to clarify the context.

私はアリソンさんは明日(あした)来るとおもいます。
I think Allison is coming tomorrow.

私はこの本はいいとおもいます。
I think this book is good.

When the subject of the main clause is someone other than the speaker, the form おもっている is used instead of おもう.

トムさんは足(あし)がながいと　おもっています。

Tom thinks he has long legs.

トムさんは足(あし)がながいと　おもいます。

I think Tom has long legs.

木村(むら)さんはふとっていないと　おもっています。

Mr. Kimura thinks he isn't fat.

木村(むら)さんはふとっていないと　おもいます。

I think Mr. Kimura isn't fat.

ペギーさんは和(わ)食は高いと　おもっています。

Peggy thinks Japanese food is expensive.

私も和(わ)食は高いと　おもいます。

I also think that Japanese food is expensive.

To form an information question, use a question word and end the sentence and か. To ask for a general impression or opinion, use ～をどうおもいますか, what do you think of ～.

高田：　このクラスでだれが一番せが高いとおもいますか。
Who do you think is the tallest in this class?

キム：　イアンさんが一番高いとおもいます。
I think Ian is the tallest.

さとう：　どの新聞がいいとおもいますか。
Which newspaper do you think is good?

もり：　朝日(あさひ)新聞がいいとおもいます。
I think the Asahi Newspaper *is good.*

ゆみ：　田中さんをどうおもいますか。
What do you think of Ms. Tanaka?

トム：　ちょっとしずかだけど、いい人だとおもいます。
I think she's rather quiet but a nice person.

石(いし)田：　この本、どうおもいますか。
What do you think of this book?

大川：　むずかしくて、あまりおもしろくないとおもいます。
I think it's difficult and not very interesting.

石(いし)田：　ぼくもそうおもうんですよ。
I think so, too!

Notes

- The plain form とおもう cannot express the speaker's wish or intention without an additional suffix attached to the verb. You will learn how to express intentions in Nakama 2.

  日本に行くとおもいます。
  I think (someone, in context) is going to Japan.

  キムさんは日本に行くとおもいます。
  I think Ms. Kim is going to Japan.

- ～たいとおもいます to express a wish is often used instead of たいです in conversation, because it sounds softer and more polite.

  私は日本に行きたいとおもいます。
  I would like to go to Japan.

  キムさんは日本に行きたいとおもっています。
  Ms. Kim would like to go to Japan.

- そうおもいます expresses agreement. It is equivalent to "(I) think so."

話してみましょう

Activity 1

A friend of Mr. Ishida is thinking about applying to your school. Answer his/her questions using plain form +とおもう.

Example: ～さんの大学は大きいですか。
いいえ、あまり大きくないとおもいます。

1. ～さんの大学は、どんな大学ですか。
2. 大学には日本人がたくさんいますか。
3. 大学のじゅぎょうは大変(へん)ですか。
4. 大学があるまちはどんなまちですか。
5. 大学があるまちには日本のレストランがありますか。

Activity 2

Work with a partner. Look at the following pictures and guess what kind of people they show.

Example: A: この男(おとこ)の子(こ)はどんな子供(こども)だとおもいますか。
B: げんきな子供(こども)だとおもいます。
or げんきそうな子供(こども)だとおもいます。

Activity 3

Work with a partner. Think about the strengths (ちょうしょ) of each one of your classmates and write down your opinions using ～とおもう.

Example: A: スミスさんのちょうしょは何だとおもいますか。
B: そうですね。スミスさんはかんじがとても上手(じょうず)だとおもいますね。
A: ええ、私もそうおもいます。

Activity 4

Work with the class. Think of a famous person or cartoon figure, and write out a description, including your opinion of the person or character. After reading your description to the class, have them guess who it is.

Example: A: この人は高いところが好きだとおもいます。そして、スポーツが上手(じょうず)だとおもいます。あかいマスク (*mask*) をしていて、あかくてかっこいいスーツをきています。
B: スパイダーマンですか。
A: はい、そうです。

聞く練習
れんしゅう

上手な聞き方
じょうず　かた

Using one's background knowledge about a person

Besides visual cues, background knowledge about a person such as his/her age, sex, and occupation can help you to understand better what is being said or asked.

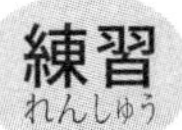

Look at the photo below. Then listen to each question and circle the letter of the answer you think is correct. The questions will be repeated.

© Bruce Weaver/AFP/Getty Images

1.	a	b	c	d
2.	a	b	c	d
3.	a	b	c	d

私たちの家族 Our family

CDを聞いて、家系図 (*family tree*) を書いて下さい。そして、「はい」か「いいえ」にまるをつけて下さい。(Then circle はい if a statement below is true or いいえ if it is false.)

A. 中山あやかさんの家族

家系図

1. はい　いいえ　　中山さんはお兄さんがいます。
2. はい　いいえ　　中山さんの弟さんはせが高いです。
3. はい　いいえ　　中山さんのお母さんはびょういんにつとめています。
4. はい　いいえ　　中山さんのお姉さんは大学生です。

B. 吉田けい子さんの家族

家系図

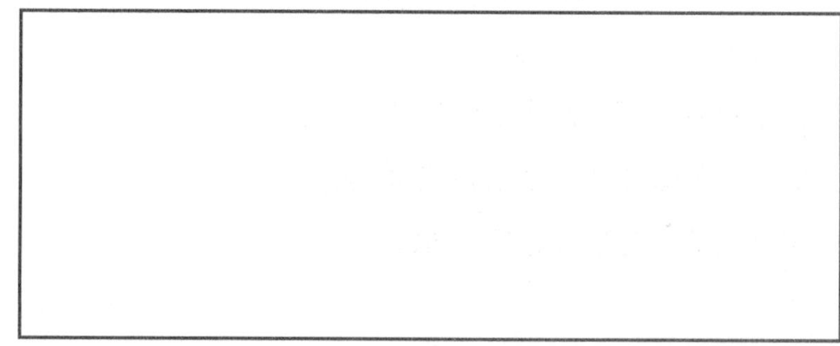

1. はい　いいえ　　けい子さんは兄弟がいます。
2. はい　いいえ　　けい子さんのお祖父さんは七十五さいです。
3. はい　いいえ　　けい子さんのお父さんはふとっています。

聞き上手話し上手

上手な話し方

Being modest about yourself and your family

As noted earlier in this chapter, the Japanese generally refrain from praising or bragging about their families. In addition, if someone praises a member of their family, they usually deny the compliment or try to steer the conversation in another direction. For example, when someone says to a Japanese person that his mother is beautiful, he will say something like *No, she isn't.* or *Do you really think so?* This is not an attempt to milk the compliment, and may seem strange to people from cultures where praise is received in a straightforward manner. In Japan, however, it is best to observe this protocol. If you receive a compliment in Japanese, try using the following standard replies:

いいえ、そんなことありません／ないですよ。
No, that isn't the case.

いいえ、まだまだです。
No, I still have a long way to go.

練習

Work with a partner. Respond to each compliment appropriately. Ask your instructor to check your manner of delivery.

1. ～さんは日本語が上手ですね。
2. ～さんのお母さんはとてもきれいな方ですね。
3. ～さんはあたまがいいですね。
4. ～さんは足がながくて、かっこいいですね。
5. ～さんのおじいさんはりっぱな方ですね。
6. ～さんの家は大きくてりっぱですね。

漢字(かんじ)

Kanji derived from pictures (3)

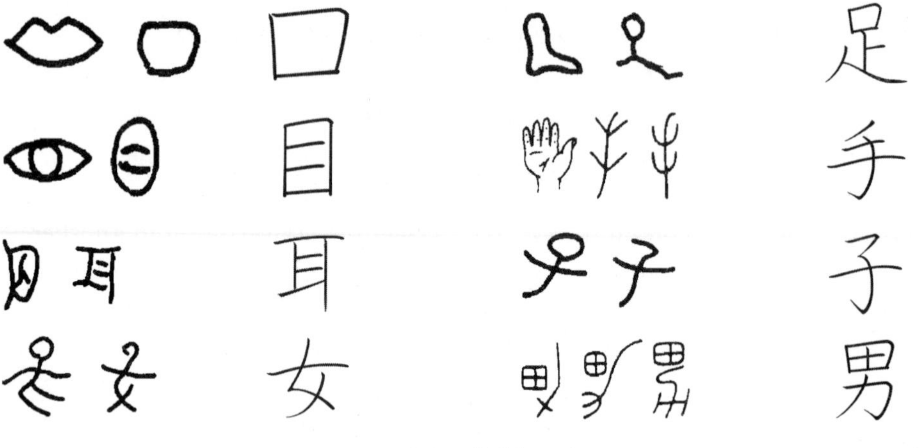

(Rice field and a strong arm came to mean *male*.)

(女, "female" with breasts came to mean *mother*.)

(An axe and a strong hand → *man* → *father*)

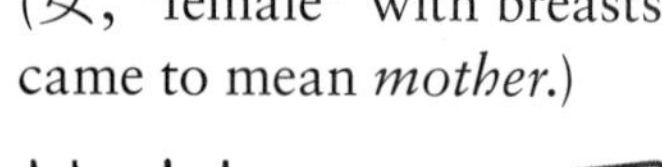

(A person with a big head → *bigger brother*)

(A pig under a roof. → *house*. Pigs were important livestock.)

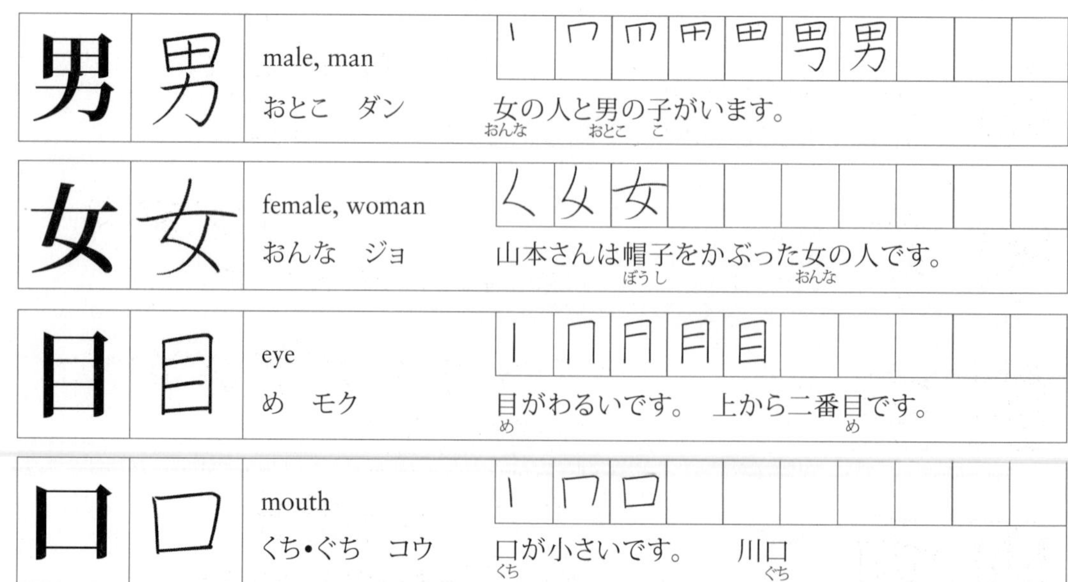

Kanji		Meaning / Readings	Stroke order / Examples
男	男	male, man おとこ　ダン	女(おんな)の人と男(おとこ)の子(こ)がいます。
女	女	female, woman おんな　ジョ	山本さんは帽子(ぼうし)をかぶった女(おんな)の人です。
目	目	eye め　モク	目(め)がわるいです。　上から二番目(め)です。
口	口	mouth くち・ぐち　コウ	口(くち)が小さいです。　川口(ぐち)

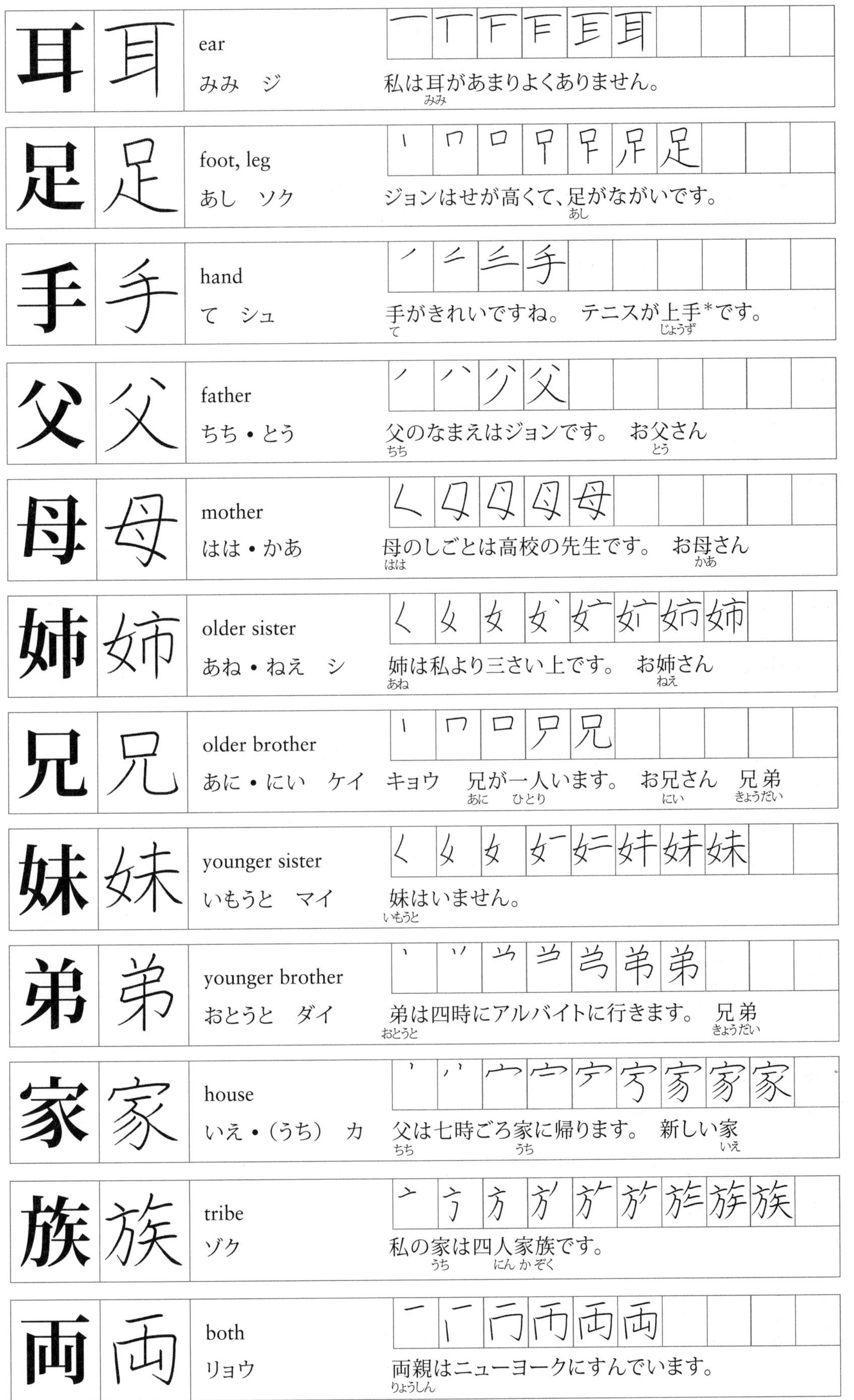

耳	ear	みみ　ジ	私は耳(みみ)があまりよくありません。
足	foot, leg	あし　ソク	ジョンはせが高くて、足(あし)がながいです。
手	hand	て　シュ	手(て)がきれいですね。　テニスが上手(じょうず)*です。
父	father	ちち・とう	父(ちち)のなまえはジョンです。　お父(とう)さん
母	mother	はは・かあ	母(はは)のしごとは高校の先生です。　お母(かあ)さん
姉	older sister	あね・ねえ　シ	姉(あね)は私より三さい上です。　お姉(ねえ)さん
兄	older brother	あに・にい　ケイ　キョウ	兄(あに)が一人(ひとり)います。　お兄(にい)さん　兄弟(きょうだい)
妹	younger sister	いもうと　マイ	妹(いもうと)はいません。
弟	younger brother	おとうと　ダイ	弟(おとうと)は四時にアルバイトに行きます。　兄弟(きょうだい)
家	house	いえ・(うち)　カ	父(ちち)は七時ごろ家(うち)に帰ります。　新しい家(いえ)
族	tribe	ゾク	私の家(うち)は四人家族(にんかぞく)です。
両	both	リョウ	両親(りょうしん)はニューヨークにすんでいます。

親	親	parent おや　シン	亠	亣	立	辛	亲	亲	新	親	親	
			両親(りょうしん)はアメリカが好きです。　親切(しんせつ)な人									
子	子	child こ　シ	乛	了	子							
			男(おとこ)の子(こ)が三人(さんにん)います。　母(はは)のなまえは「よし子(こ)」です。									

An asterisk (*) indicates an irregular reading.

読めるようになった漢字(かんじ)

男の人　男の子　女の人　女の子　目　番目　口　耳　足　手　手紙(てがみ)
上手(じょうず)　父　お父さん　祖父(そふ)　母　お母さん　祖母(そぼ)　姉　お姉さん　兄
お兄さん　妹　弟　兄弟　家族　私の家　両親　親切(しんせつ)　子供(ども)
お子さん　一人(ひとり)っ子(こ)　帽子(ぼうし)　いい方(かた)　一人(ひとり)　二人(ふたり)　三人(にん)　何人(にん)
ご主人(しゅじん)　会社員(かいしゃいん)　真(ま)ん中(なか)　四角(しかく)い　小学生(しょうがくせい)　小学校(しょうがっこう)　中学生(ちゅうがくせい)　中学校(ちゅうがっこう)
日本人のなまえ：小山(こやま)　田口(たぐち)　三上(みかみ)　本木(もとき)　山口(やまぐち)　吉田(よしだ)　ゆみ子(こ)　けい子(こ)

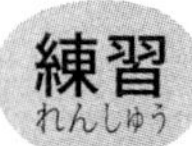

練習(れんしゅう)

Read the following sentences.

1. 父は先週の月曜日に川につりに行きました。弟はえいがを見に行きました。私と母は家にいました。
2. 中山さんのお父さんはせが高くて、目が大きいですね。
3. 妹は小学生で、弟は中学一年生です。
4. 高田:「ご兄弟は何人いますか。」
   川口:「三人います。」
5. めがねをかけている女の人が山田さんのお姉さんで、スーツをきている人がお兄さんです。
6. 山本:「川口さんは何人家族ですか。」
   川口:「両親と弟の四人家族です。」
7. 田中さんのお子さんは目が大きくて、口が小さくて、とてもかわいいですよ。
8. 私は上から三番目で、姉が二人います。
9. A:「あの男の人は手と足がながくて、スタイルがいいですねえ。」
   B:「そうですか。あれは、私の兄なんですよ。」
10. 祖(そ)父のいぬは耳がながくて足がみじかいです。

読む練習

上手な読み方

Creating charts and figures

People usually read with a purpose in mind, such as to gather specific information or to skim for the main ideas in a text. When reading an assignment, you might jot down only the information that you need. If you organize your notes systematically, you may understand the assignment better and retain the information longer. One way to organize material is to make charts or tables.

練習

A. Review the dialogue on pages 394–395 and complete the following table.

上田さんの家族	なまえ	しごと	Physical appearance

B. Now read the following passage. It was written by Ms. Ueda, but some of the information is different from what the dialogue contains on pages 394–395. Circle the discrepancies or write them on a separate piece of paper. Don't worry about any unfamiliar words or **kanji** you may encounter.

上田さんの家族

私の家族は五人家族です。父は四十五歳の会社員で、銀行に勤めています。父は目があまりよくないので、たいていめがねをかけています。ゴルフが大好きで、日曜日にはよくゴルフに行きます。母は四十三歳で、大学で英語を教えています。背があまり高くないので、たいていハイヒールの靴を履いています。母はとても優しくて明るい人です。弟のトムは十三歳で、中学生です。背が高くて、目がとても大きいです。スポーツは好きなんですが、勉強がきらいなので、こまります。そして、妹の名前はパムです。パムは背は高くありませんが、とてもかわいいです。頭がよくて、勉強もスポーツも大好きな高校一年生です。

C. Underline all the sentence and clause connectors in the above passage.

D. Describe your ideal family (りそうの家族). Use the following questions as cues.

1. 何人家族がいいですか。
2. 子供(ども)は何人がいいですか。
3. どんな子供(ども)がいいですか。
4. お父さんとお母さんはどんな人ですか。
5. どんなところにすみたいですか。
6. お父さん／お母さんはどんなしごとをしますか。

総合練習（そうごうれんしゅう）

Work with the class. Your instructor will give you a card similar to the one in the example below. It will have a description of two people, A and B. You are A. You are looking for B. Go around the class and ask your classmates questions using B's description. After you find B, check his/her identity card against yours.

Example:

Features	A Your identity	B The person you are looking for
かみ	ながい	くろい
目	あおい	みどり
すんでいる	とうきょう	ニューヨーク
上手	日本語	英語（えい）

A: その人はかみがくろいですか。

B: はい、くろいです。

A: その人は目があおいですか。

B: いいえ、あおくありません。

A: そうですか。それじゃあ、また。

(Go to a different person.)

ロールプレイ

1. You are introducing a member of your family to your instructor. Your instructor will praise the person. Respond appropriately.
2. You are looking for a new roommate. Tell your partner what type of person you are looking for and ask for help.

Nouns

あき
あめ
おんど
かぜ
きおん
きこう
きせつ
きた
きょねん
くも
くもり
けさ
ことし
さいきん
しつど
たいふう
つゆ
(お)てんき
てんきよほう
なつ
なんせい
なんとう
にし
にわかあめ
はる
はれ
ひがし
ふゆ

むしあつい	蒸し暑い	humid
よわい	弱い	weak
わるい	悪い	bad

な-adjectives

いや(な)	嫌(な)	unpleasant, yuck
きゅう(な)	急(な)	sudden, きゅうに suddenly

Suffixes

～がつ	～月	month
～ど	～度	degree, temperature

Expressions

～のち～	～後～	after, あめのちはれ clear skies after rain
ほんとう(に) / ほんと(に)	本当(に)	truly, really, indeed ほんと(に) is more conversational than ほんとう(に)

単語の練習

A. 天気予報 Weather forecast

晴れ
sunny/clear

くもり
cloudy

雨
rain/rainy

雪
snow/snowy

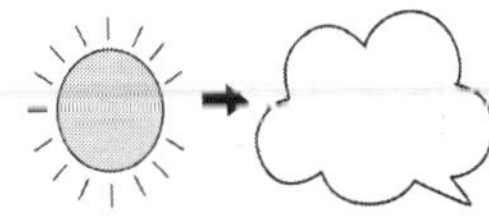

晴れのちくもり
sunny/clear, then cloudy

くもり時々雨
cloudy with occasional rain

Activity 1

Write the readings of the following weather symbols.

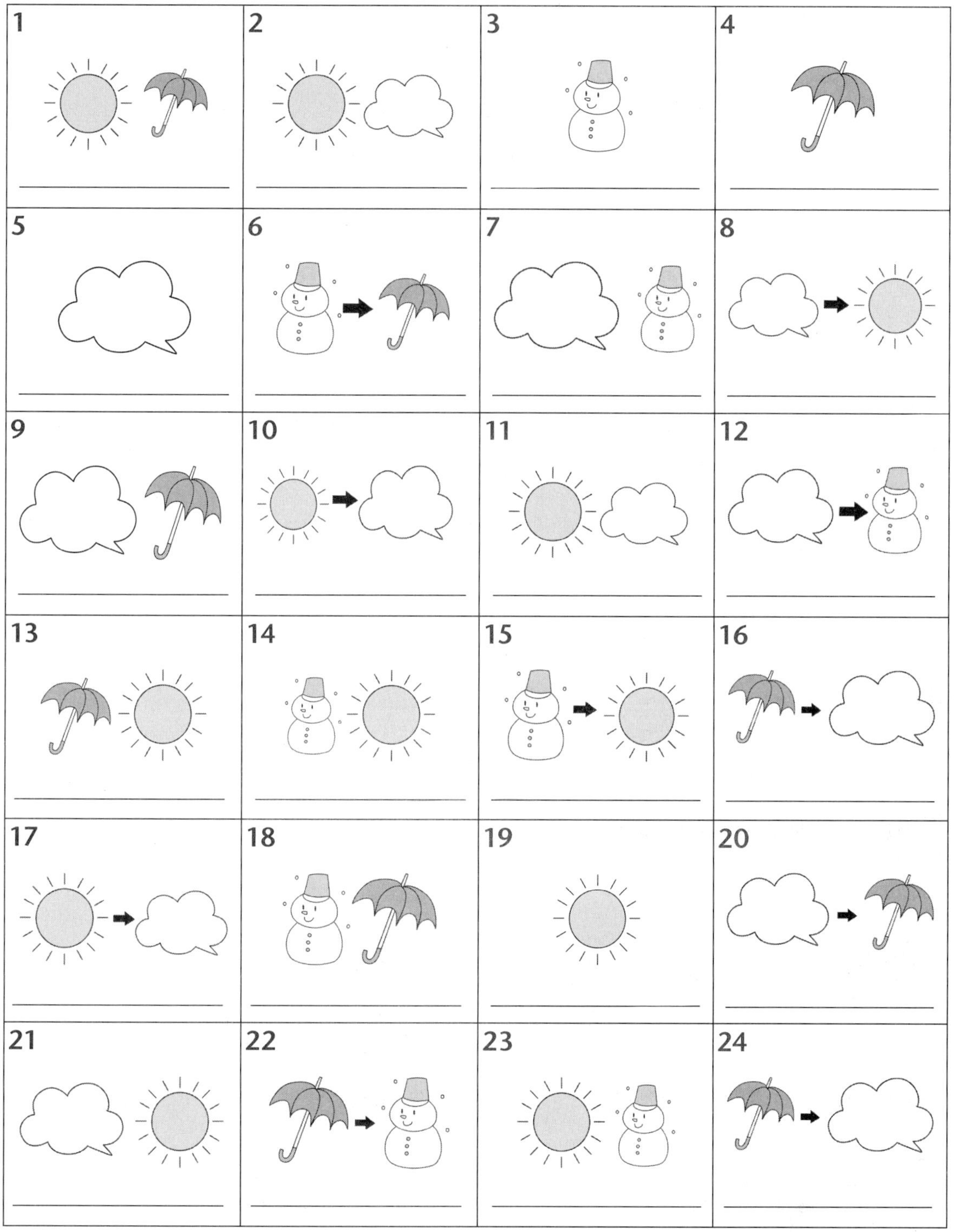

1	2	3	4
5	6	7	8
9	10	11	12
13	14	15	16
17	18	19	20
21	22	23	24

Supplementary Vocabulary: Nouns to indicate regions

たいへいようがわ	太平洋側	Pacific Ocean side (east side) of Japan
にほんかいがわ	日本海側	Sea of Japan side (west side) of Japan
さんがくぶ	山岳部	mountainous area (in any country)
にしかいがん	西海岸	West coast region (USA)
ちゅうせいぶ	中西部	Midwest region (USA)
なんぶ	南部	South region (USA)
なんせいぶ	南西部	Southwest region (USA)
ひがしかいがん	東海岸	East coast region (USA)

Supplementary Vocabulary: Nouns expressing weather

かし	華氏	Fahrenheit
きあつ	気圧	air pressure
こうすいりょう	降水量	amount of precipitation
さいこうきおん	最高気温	highest temperature
さいていきおん	最低気温	lowest temperature
せっし	摂氏	Celsius
てんきず	天気図	weather map

B. 天気(てんき) Weather

暑(あつ)い	hot	晴(は)れる	to clear up
寒(さむ)い	cold	くもる	to become cloudy
すずしい	cool	風(かぜ)がふく	wind blows
あたたかい	warm	雨(あめ)がふる	to rain
むし暑(あつ)い	humid	雪(ゆき)がふる	to snow
雪(ゆき)が積(つ)もる	snow accumulates	雨(あめ)がやむ	rain stops
天気(てんき)がいい	good weather	にわか雨(あめ)がふる	sudden showers
天気(てんき)がわるい	bad weather	台風(たいふう)が来る	a typhoon comes
くもが多(おお)い	cloudy	梅雨(つゆ)になる	the rainy season comes
風(かぜ)がつよい	strong winds	大雨(おおあめ)がふる	heavy rain falls
風(かぜ)がよわい	mild winds	大雪(おおゆき)がつづく	heavy snow continues

おぼえていますか。

多(おお)い、少(すく)ない、少(すこ)し、高い、冷(つめ)たい、ひくい

Notes

- Both 寒い(さむ) and 冷たい(つめ) mean *cold*, but 寒い(さむ) refers to cold temperatures, as in 今日は寒い(さむ) (*It is cold today*). On the other hand, 冷たい(つめ) refers to objects that are cold, e.g., 水が冷たい(つめ), 風(かぜ)が冷たい(つめ).
- 梅雨(つゆ) refers specifically to Japan's rainy season. It usually starts in early June and ends in mid-July. 雨期(うき) is the general term used for the rainy season in tropical climates.

Supplementary Vocabulary: 天気(てんき)の言葉(ことば)

あらし	嵐	storm
あられ		hail
いなびかり	稲光り	lightening
かみなり	雷	thunder
きり	霧	fog
けいほう	警報	warning
こうずい	洪水	flood
こさめ	小雨	light rain
たつまき	竜巻	tornado
ちゅういほう	注意報	alert
つなみ	津波	tidal wave, tsunami
どしゃぶり	どしゃ降り	downpour
ハリケーン		hurricane
ひでり	日照り	drought
ふぶき	吹雪	snowstorm
みぞれ		sleet
ゆうだち	夕立ち	evening shower

Activity 2

Imagine that the following chart shows tomorrow's weather in some of the major cities in the world. そして、下のしつもんに日本語でこたえて下さい。

Example: 明日(あした)、カイロの天気(てんき)はいいですか。
ええ、明日(あした)は晴(は)れますよ。

まち	東京(とうきょう)	ニューヨーク	モスクワ	シドニー	カイロ
天気(てんき)					
気温(きおん)	61.9/48.9° F 16.6/9.4° C	49.8/39.0° F 9.9/3.9° C	34.7/26° F 1.5/-3.3° C	75.2/58.1° F 24/14.5° C	98.2/60.3° F 36.8/15.7° C
風(かぜ)	SW 5 mph	NE 20 mph	NE 15 mph	SE 10 mph	E 3 mph

1. 明日(あした)、モスクワは天気(てんき)がいいですか。
2. 東京(とうきょう)は明日(あした)晴(は)れますか。ニューヨークはどうですか。
3. 明日(あした)、どこで雨(あめ)がふりますか。
4. シドニーとカイロとどちらの方が暑(あつ)いですか。
5. ニューヨークと東京(とうきょう)とどちらの方が寒(さむ)いですか。
6. どこがあたたかいですか。
7. どこがすずしいですか。
8. 明日(あした)、東京(とうきょう)は風(かぜ)がつよいですか。ニューヨークはどうですか。
9. カイロは風(かぜ)がつよいですか。よわいですか。
10. モスクワではつよい風(かぜ)がふきますか。

Activity 3

Select the item that describes recent weather in your area.

1. 寒(さむ)い／すずしい／あたたかい／暑(あつ)い／むし暑(あつ)い
2. 天気(てんき)がいい／天気(てんき)がよくない
3. いやな天気(てんき)がつづく／いい天気(てんき)がつづく
4. 雨(あめ)がぜんぜんふらない／雨(あめ)があまりふらない／雨(あめ)が時々(ときどき)ふる
5. 雨(あめ)がよくふる／毎日雨(あめ)がふる／雨(あめ)はふるが、すぐやむ
6. にわか雨(あめ)が多(おお)い／にわか雨(あめ)が少(すく)ない
7. 雪(ゆき)がぜんぜんふらない／雪(ゆき)があまりふらない／雪(ゆき)が時々(ときどき)ふる
8. 雪(ゆき)がよくつもる／雪(ゆき)がふるが、つもらない
9. 大雪(おおゆき)になる／大雪(おおゆき)にはならない
10. よく風(かぜ)がふく／あまり風(かぜ)がふかない
11. 風(かぜ)がつよい／風(かぜ)がよわい

Activity 4

Describe the recent weather in your area using your answers from Activity 2. It is unnecessary to use all of your responses, but make sure that your description is cohesive.

Example: このへんは、さいきんいい天気(てんき)がつづいて、むし暑(あつ)いです。
雨(あめ)はぜんぜんふりません。そして、風(かぜ)もあまりありません。

C. きせつ　Seasons

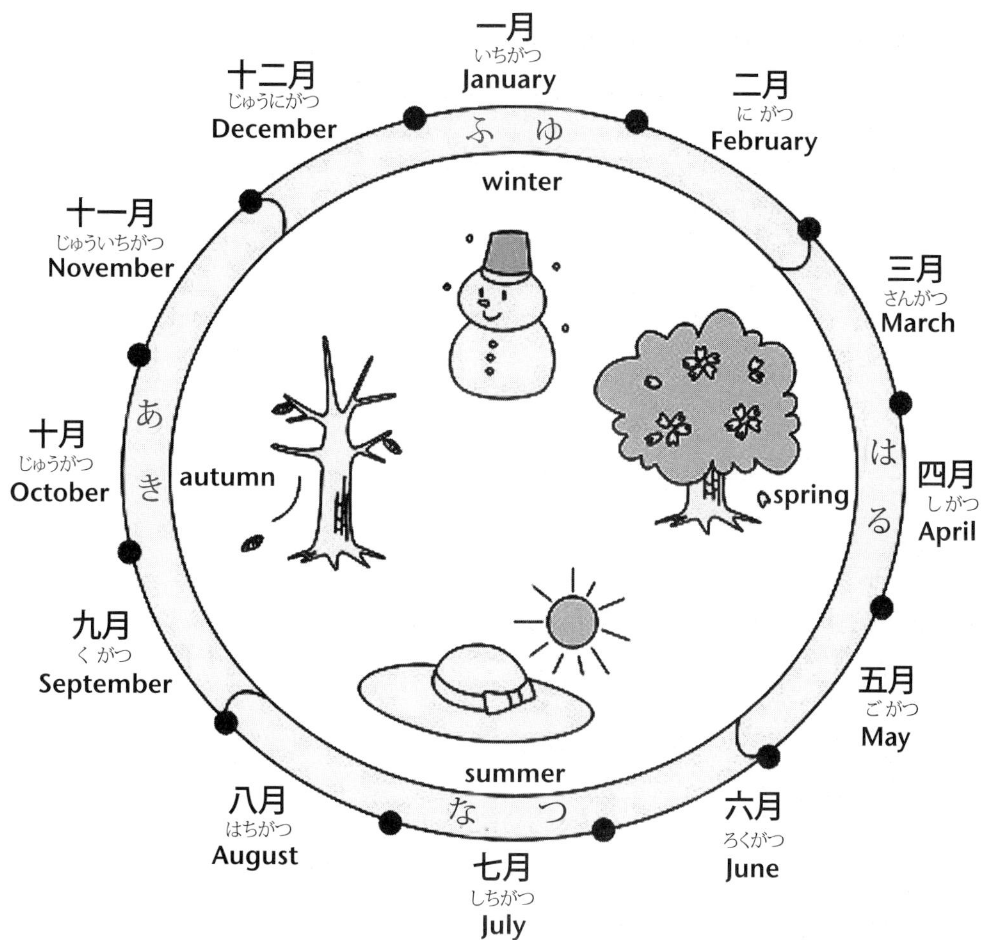

Activity 5

Complete the following statements about seasons in Japan and where you live.

Example: 日本では、六月に梅雨（つゆ）がはじまって、七月におわります。

1. 日本では＿＿＿＿＿にはるがはじまって、＿＿＿＿＿におわります。
2. 日本では＿＿＿＿＿になつがはじまって、＿＿＿＿＿におわります。
3. 日本では＿＿＿＿＿にあきがはじまって、＿＿＿＿＿におわります。
4. 日本では＿＿＿＿＿にふゆがはじまって、＿＿＿＿＿におわります。
5. このへんは＿＿＿＿＿にはるがはじまって、＿＿＿＿＿におわります。
6. このへんは＿＿＿＿＿になつがはじまって、＿＿＿＿＿におわります。
7. このへんは＿＿＿＿＿にあきがはじまって、＿＿＿＿＿におわります。
8. このへんは＿＿＿＿＿にふゆがはじまって、＿＿＿＿＿におわります。

Activity 6

For each season, write five things that describe where you live.

Example: このへんは　ふゆに雪(ゆき)がたくさんふります。

はる	
なつ	
あき	
ふゆ	

D. 気温(きおん)　Air temperature

気温(きおん)が下(さ)がる　air temperature falls

気温(きおん)が上(あ)がる　air temperature rises

何度	なんど
−１度	マイナスいちど
０度	れいど
１度	いちど
２度	にど
３度	さんど
４度	よんど
５度	ごど
６度	ろくど
７度	ななど、しちど
８度	はちど
９度	きゅうど、くど
１０度	じゅうど

Japan uses the Celsius scale for temperature, and the metric system for other measurements. The following table shows equivalent temperatures for Celsius and Fahrenheit.

せっし (Celsius)	かし (Fahrenheit)
０℃	３２℉
１０℃	５０℉
２０℃	６８℉
３０℃	８６℉
４０℃	１０４℉

Activity 7

しつもんに日本語でこたえて下さい。

1. 今の気温(きおん)は何度(ど)ぐらいですか。
2. 今朝(けさ)の気温(きおん)は何度(ど)ぐらいでしたか。
3. あさから何度(ど)ぐらい気温(きおん)が上(あ)がりましたか。
4. 今晩(ばん)、何度(ど)ぐらいまで気温(きおん)が下(さ)がるとおもいますか。
5. 寒(さむ)い日は何度(ど)ぐらいまで気温(きおん)が下(さ)がりますか。
6. 暑(あつ)い日は何度(ど)ぐらいまで気温(きおん)が上(あ)がりますか。
7. せっし (*Celsius*) 0 度(ど)はかし (*Fahrenheit*) 何度(ど)ですか。
8. かし (*Fahrenheit*) 0 度(ど)はせっし (*Celsius*) 何度(ど)ですか。

Activity 8

Using your answers from Activity 5, give a short description of your town in its four seasons.

E. 方角(ほうがく) Compass directions

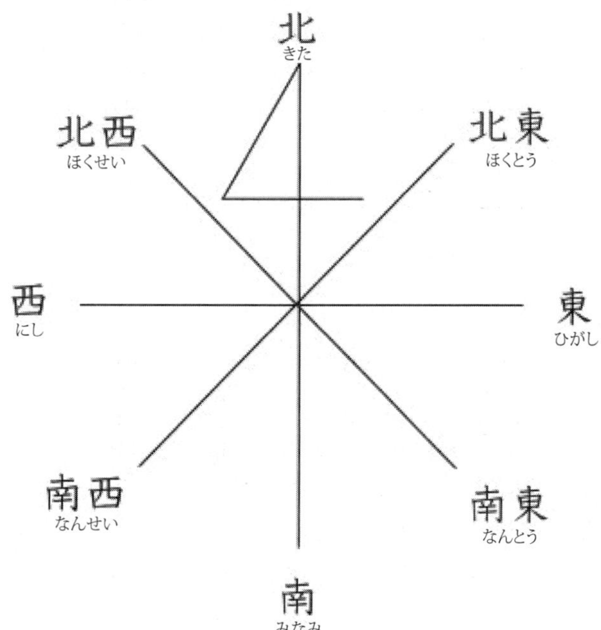

～の方(ほう)	toward ～
北(きた)の方(ほう)	to the north

Activity 9

Write the appropriate direction word in each blank.

Example: オーストラリアは日本の__南(みなみ)__にあります。

1. カナダはアメリカの________にあります。
2. 日本はかんこくの________にあります。
3. メキシコはアメリカの________にあります。
4. フランスはスペインの________にあって、ドイツの______にあります。
5. 中国(ごく)はかんこくの________にあります。

Activity 10

えを見て、しつもんに日本語でこたえて下さい。

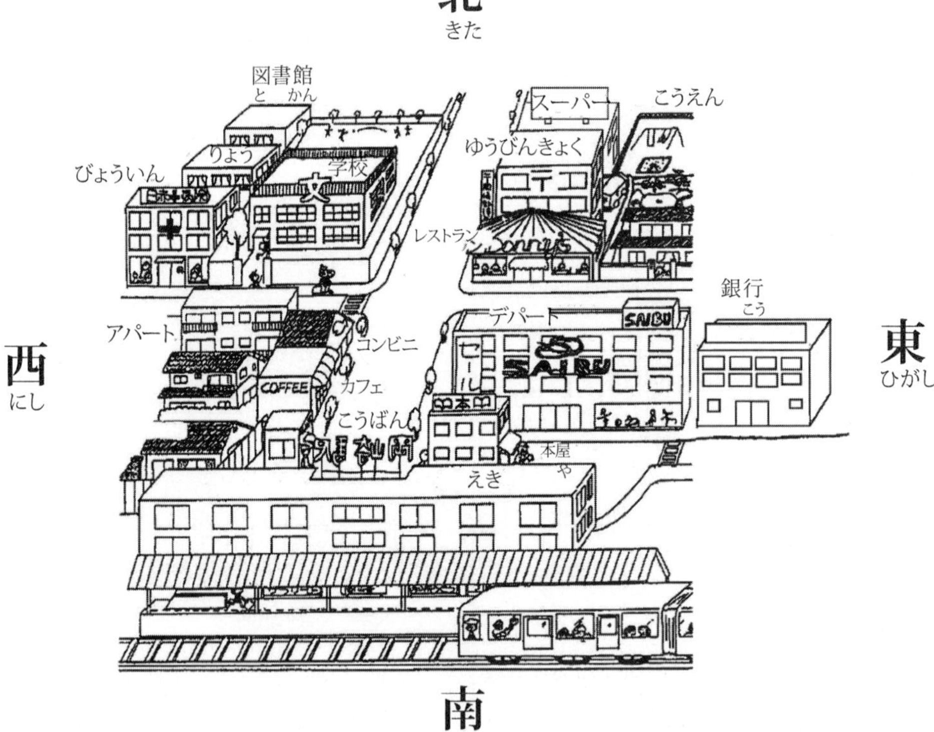

1. このまちの北(きた)の方(ほう)には何がありますか。南(みなみ)の方(ほう)には何がありますか。
2. 学校はどこにありますか。
3. 学校の東(ひがし)の方(ほう)に何がありますか。西(にし)の方(ほう)に何がありますか。
4. こうえんはどこにありますか。
5. 図(と)書館(かん)はどこにありますか。
6. えきの北(きた)には何がありますか。

ダイアローグ

はじめに

しつもんに日本語でこたえて下さい。

1. 今日のお天気(てんき)はどうですか。
2. ふゆの寒(さむ)い日の気温(きおん)は何度(ど)ぐらいですか。
3. ふゆのあたたかい日の気温(きおん)は何度(ど)ぐらいですか。

寒(さむ)いですね。 *It's cold.*

鈴木道子(すずみちこ)さんは石田(いし)さんにきょうしつで会いました。

鈴木(すず)： あ、石田(いし)さん。おはよう。
石田(いし)： あ、鈴木(すず)さん。寒(さむ)いね。
鈴木(すず)： ええ、今日は風(かぜ)がつよいから。
石田(いし)： たしかに。今晩(ばん)は雪(ゆき)かな。
鈴木(すず)： そうね。くもってるから、ふるかもしれないね。
石田(いし)： でも、まだ十一月だよ。
鈴木(すず)： そうね。今年(ことし)はいつもよりはやく寒(さむ)くなりそうね。ざんねんだけど。
石田(いし)： いやだなあ。

先生がきょうしつにいらっしゃいました。
(*The professor has come to the classroom.*)

鈴木(すず)： あ、先生。おはようございます。
先生： あ、鈴木(すず)さん、石田(いし)くん。おはよう。寒(さむ)いね。
石田(いし)： ええ、それにくもっていますね。
先生： そうだね。雪(ゆき)がふりそうな天気(てんき)だね。

鈴木(すず)さんはまどのそとを見ました。雪(ゆき)がふっています。

鈴木(すず)： あ、先生、雪(ゆき)がふっていますよ。
先生： 本当(ほんとう)だね。みんな風邪(かぜ)ひかないように気(き)をつけるんだよ。

Dialogue Phrase Notes

- たしかに means *certainly.*
- いつもより means ～ *than usual.*
- いやだなあ means *unpleasant.*
- みんな風邪(かぜ)をひかないように気(き)をつけるんだよ means *Everybody, take care so you don't catch cold.* 風邪(かぜ) means *cold.* Note that the **kanji** is different from 風(かぜ), wind.

ダイアローグの後(あと)で

A. The following manga frames are scrambled—they are not in the order described in the dialogue. Read the dialogue and unscramble the frames by writing their correct order in the box located in the upper right corner of each frame.

B. しつもんに日本語でこたえて下さい。

1. 今、何月ですか。何時ごろですか。
2. 今どんな天気(てんき)ですか。
3. 今日の天気(てんき)はどうですか。
4. 石(いし)田さんはふゆが好きだとおもいますか。

C. Work with a partner. The following conversation is a simplified version of the dialogue. You meet each other in the classroom in the morning. Decide on a season and the weather, and complete the following conversation using appropriate phrases.

A: あ、__________さん。おはよう。

B: あ、_________さん。今日は_________________ね。

A: ええ、_________________ね。

B: _________________かもしれないね。

A: そうだね。

日本の文化 (ぶんか)

© Cengage Learning

気候 (きこう) Climate

Japan lies in the temperate zone and has four distinct seasons. The climate is predominantly temperate, but it varies from subarctic to subtropical because the country extends so far from north to south. Southeast winds blow across Japan from the Pacific in the summer, bringing humidity to the Pacific side of the country (たいへいようがわ). Northwest winds blow across Japan from continental Asia in the winter, bringing sunny and dry weather to the Pacific Ocean side but heavy snow to the Japan Sea side (日本海側 (にほんかいがわ)).

© Kenneth Hamm/Photo Japan

Between June and July, there is a period of predominantly rainy weather, called *tsuyu* (梅雨 (つゆ)), in all parts of Japan except the northernmost island, 北海道 (ほっかいどう). Typhoons (台風 (たいふう)) occur most frequently from August through October.

Japan's climate is further divided into six principal zones because of its geographical features. On 北海道 (ほっかいどう), spring and summer are short, and it is cool with little rain throughout the year. Although precipitation is not heavy, winters are severe with deep snow banks from November through April.

The Japan Sea side of the northern main island, such as the 北陸 (ほくりく) region and the west coast of 東北 (とうほく), experiences heavy snowfall in the winter,

© Kenneth Hamm/Photo Japan

but it is cooler than the Pacific Ocean side in the summer. Areas on the Pacific Ocean side, such as 関東(かんとう), 東海(とうかい), and きんき, are generally sunny, cold, and dry in winter, but experience summers which are hot and humid.

Temperatures in the central highland region, 中部(ちゅうぶ), range widely between summer and winter, and between day and night, although precipitation is generally light.

Southwestern regions such as 四国(しこく), 中国(ちゅうごく), and 九州(きゅうしゅう) tend to have mild weather throughout the year, especially in the せとないかい (Seto Inland Ocean) area, which is surrounded by these three regions.

The southern islands, おきなわ and いしがきじま, have a subtropical climate and are known for high temperatures and precipitation throughout the year. The rainfall is heavy during 梅雨(つゆ), and 台風(たいふう) are very common.

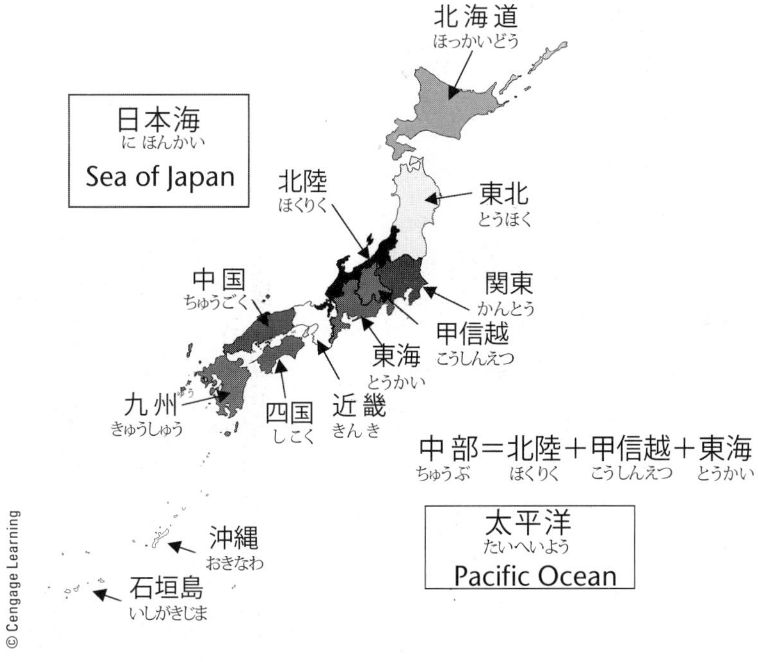

文法(ぶんぽう)

I. Expressing ongoing and repeated actions using the て-form of verbs + いる

In Chapter 10, you learned the verb て-form + いる, which expresses resultant state. This interpretation is common for verbs used to express wearing clothes or accessories.

田中さんはめがねをかけている。 *Mr. Tanaka has glasses on.*

田中さんはネクタイをしている。 *Mr. Tanaka is wearing a tie.*

Also, if the verb indicates an instantaneous change of state or transfer (e.g., 行く, けっこんする), then the verb て-form + いる will express a resultant state.

田中さんはけっこんしている。 *Mr. Tanaka is married.*

田中さんは高校につとめている。 *Mr. Tanaka works for a high school.*

田中さんは学校に行っている。 *Mr. Tanaka has gone to school and is there.*

田中さんはここに来ている。 *Mr. Tanaka has come here and is here now.*

田中さんはその人をしっている。 *Mr. Tanaka knows that person.*

今日は晴(は)れている。 *It is sunny today.*

くもっている。 *It is cloudy.*

In the above example, the て-form of the verb しる (*to come to know*) , しっている (*to know*), expresses the result of one's discovery of information.

In addition to this usage, the verb て-form + いる can express ongoing action and repeated action. This chapter introduces these two usages of the verb て-form + いる.

A. Ongoing action

The verb て-form + いる can express ongoing action when used with certain action verbs. The verbs indicate activities that take place for a period of time. For example, the act of eating, drinking, raining, etc., can take place for a long time.

石(いし)田さんはおすしを食べている。 *Mr. Ishida is eating sushi.*

石(いし)田さんはおちゃを飲んでいる。 *Mr. Ishida is drinking tea.*

石(いし)田さんは本を読んでいる。 *Mr. Ishida is reading.*

雨(あめ)がふっている。 *It is raining.*

風(かぜ)がふいている。 *The wind is blowing.*

The verb て-form + いる is often contracted to the verb て-form + る in conversation (in both formal and casual styles).

ドレスを<u>きています</u>。	ドレスを<u>きてます</u>。
けっこん<u>しています</u>。	けっこん<u>してます</u>。
しゅくだいを<u>しています</u>。	しゅくだいを<u>してます</u>。
さとみさんを<u>しっている</u>。	さとみさん、<u>しってる</u>。
ごはんを<u>食べている</u>。	ごはん、<u>食べてる</u>。

かおり：何、してるの。　*What are you doing?*

まさお：しゅくだい、してるんだ。　*I am doing homework.*

リン：どうしたんですか。
What's wrong?

鈴木(すず)：雨(あめ)がふっているんですが、かさがないんです。
It's raining but I don't have an umbrella.

リン：そうですか。じゃあ、私のくるまで行きませんか。
I see. Well, why don't we take my car?

鈴木(すず)：いいんですか。
Is that okay?

リン：ええ、どうぞ。
Yeah, sure.

B. Repeated action

Many verbs, including both action verbs and change-of-state verbs, can be used to express habitual action with the verb て-form + いる.

鈴木(すず)さんはよくあかいジャケットをきている。
Ms. Suzuki often wears a red jacket.

田中さんは時々(ときどき)バスでびょういんへ行っています。
Mr. Tanaka sometimes goes to hospital by bus.

毎週土曜日にテニスをしています。
I play tennis every Saturday.

健一(けんいち)：ブラウンさんはよくサングラスをかけてるけど、どうして？
Ms. Brown often wears sunglasses, but why?

道子(みちこ)：サラは目がよわいからよ。
Because Sarah has weak eyes.

健一(けんいち)：そうなんだ。
Oh, I see.

話してみましょう

Activity 1

Make sentences from the following expressions using the verb て-form +いる. Then say whether the sentence indicates an ongoing action or a resultant state.

Example: ごはんを食べる

ごはんを食べています。 Ongoing action

1. 大雨（おおあめ）がふる
2. くもる
3. 気温（きおん）が下（さ）がる
4. 雪（ゆき）がつもる
5. 風（かぜ）がやむ
6. つよい風（かぜ）がふく
7. 大雨（おおあめ）がつづく
8. 気温（きおん）が三十度（ど）まで上（あ）がる

Activity 2

Work with a partner. Your partner will write a name for each person in the picture. Ask your partner who is who by describing what the people are doing.

Example: A: コーヒーを飲んでいる人はだれですか。

B: スミスさんです。

Activity 3

Work with a partner. Think of five actions, then act them out and have your partner guess what you are doing by asking questions using ～ている.

Example: You act as though you are drinking coffee.

A: おちゃを飲んでいるんですか。

B: いいえ。

A: コーヒーを飲んでいるんですか。

B: はい。

Activity 4

Work as a class. Ask your classmates what kinds of things they practiced or learned recently for fun or personal improvement.

Example: A: さいきん、どんなことをよくしていますか。

B: テニスをよくしています。

なまえ	さいきんよくしていること

II. Plain past forms and casual speech

The plain forms are used in a variety of structures and contexts in Japanese. For example, they are used in the structure ので (*because*) in Chapter 7, ～んです in Chapter 8, から and けど in Chapter 9, and とおもう and noun modification in Chapter 10. So far the plain present forms have been used with these structures, but the plain past forms can be used with all of them. This chapter introduces the plain past forms of verbs and adjectives. It also introduces another usage of the plain form, namely casual and self-directed speech.

Plain past forms

1. Plain past affirmative form

The plain past affirmative form of the verbs is formed by taking the て-form of a verb and replacing it with た (or だ).

Verb types	Dictionary form	て -form	Plain past affirmative form
う -verb	つづく (*to continue*)	つづいて	つづいた (*continued*)
	読む (*to read*)	読んで	読んだ (*read*)
る -verb	晴れる (*to clear up*)	晴れて	晴れた (*became clear*)
	食べる (*to eat*)	食べて	食べた (*ate*)
Irregular verb	する (*to do*)	して	した (*did*)
	来る (*to come*)	来て	来た (*came*)

The plain past affirmative form of い-adjectives is formed by deleting です from the polite past affirmative form.

Dictionary form	Polite past affirmative form	Plain past affirmative form
暑い (*hot*)	暑かったです	暑かった (*was hot*)
いい (*good*)	よかったです	よかった (*was good*)

The plain past affirmative form of な-adjectives and the copula verb is formed by adding った to the plain present affirmative form.

	Dictionary form	Plain present affirmative form	Plain past affirmative form
な -adjective	好き (*like*)	好きだ	好きだった (*liked*)
	元気 (*healthy*)	元気だ	元気だった (*was healthy*)
Noun + copula	台風 (*typhoon*)	台風だ	台風だった (*was typhoon*)
	くも (*cloud*)	くもだ	くもだった (*was a cloud*)

2. Plain past negative form

The plain past negative form of the verbs and adjectives of all types is formed by replacing the plain present negative ending ない with なかった.

	Dictionary form	Plain present negative form	Plain past negative form
う-verb	行く (*to go*)	行かない	行かなかった (*didn't go*)
	飲む (*to drink*)	飲まない	飲まなかった (*didn't drink*)
	ある (*to exist*)	ない	なかった (*didn't exist*)
る-verb	起きる (*to get up*)	起きない	起きなかった (*didn't get up*)
	食べる (*to eat*)	食べない	食べなかった (*didn't eat*)
Irregular verb	する (*to do*)	しない	しなかった (*didn't do*)
	来る (*to come*)	来(こ)ない	来(こ)なかった (*didn't come*)
い-adjective	わるい (*bad*)	わるくない	わるくなかった (*wasn't bad*)
	いい (*good*)	よくない	よくなかった (*wasn't good*)
な-adjective	元気(げんき) (*healthy*)	元気(げんき)じゃない	元気(げんき)じゃなかった (*wasn't healthy*)
	きれい (*pretty*)	きれいじゃない	きれいじゃなかった (*wasn't pretty*)
Noun + Copula	雪(ゆき) (*snow*)	雪(ゆき)じゃない	雪(ゆき)じゃなかった (*wasn't snow*)
	南(みなみ) (*south*)	南(みなみ)じゃない	南(みなみ)じゃなかった (*wasn't south*)

梅雨(つゆ)がながかったので、今年(ことし)のなつはむし暑(あつ)いとおもいます。

Because the rainy season was long, I think this summer will be humid.

いい天気(てんき)がつづかなかったので、ざんねんでした。

I was disappointed because the nice weather did not last long.

風(かぜ)が冷(つめ)たかったから、ジャケットをきました。

I put on a jacket because the wind was cold.

天気(てんき)がよくなかったから、家にいました。

I stayed home because the weather was not good.

お母さんは親切(しんせつ)だったけど、お父さんはあまり話しませんでした。

The mother was kind but the father did not talk much.

そのアパートはきれいじゃなかったけど、安かったです。

The apartment was not very clean, but it was cheap.

元気(げんき)そうだったけど、本当(ほんとう)は病気(びょうき)でした。

(He) looked healthy, but was actually sick.

去年(きょねん)の三月はあたたかかったとおもいます。

I think March was warm last year.

図(と)書館(かん)はまちの北(きた)の方(ほう)にあったとおもいます。

I think the library was on the north side of the town.

今年(ことし)の梅雨(つゆ)はあまりながくなかったんです。

This year's rainy season was not very long.

あれは台風(たいふう)じゃなかったんです。

That was not a typhoon.

昨日(きのう)ふった大雪(おおゆき)ででんしゃがストップしました。

The train stopped because of the heavy snow that fell yesterday.

日本へ帰った友達(だち)にメールを書きました。

I wrote a letter to a friend who went back to Japan.

Plain forms in casual conversation

Plain forms are used in conversations among close friends and family members, because the plain forms indicate closeness, intimacy, and carefree attitudes. On the other hand, です／ます indicates that the speaker is more aware of the listener's presence and intends to maintain a proper social distance.

The use of plain and polite forms is not always determined by the degree of formality. For example, in relatively casual situations such as a home party and going out after work, a person may use です／ます toward someone who holds a higher social status or someone who is much older, in order to show respect. In this situation, です／ます signals that the speaker is aware of the social difference and does not consider his/her interlocutor a mere equal. Conversely, the social superior may use the plain form toward the junior interlocutor in order to show a close or carefree attitude. Also, it is very common for two people of the same age group who meet for the first time to start conversation in です／ます forms but switch to plain forms as the conversation progresses. In other words, the choice between です／ます and the plain form depends on the speaker's perception about his/her social relationship with his/ her interlocutor. For this reason, it is common for a teacher to use the plain form to show familiarity to his/her students while the students use です／ます toward the teachers to show respect in the same conversational context.

子供(ども)：お母さん、かさ、いるよ。 *Mom, I need an umbrella.*
お母さん：え、どうして？ *Why?*
子供(ども)：雨(あめ)、ふってるよ。 *It's raining.*
お母さん：ええっ！ *Oh, really?*

In answering a yes-no question, use うん (the casual form of はい or ええ) or ううん (the casual form of いいえ).

Mr. Li and Ms. Ueda are friends:

リー：ねえ、上田さん、今日いそがしい？
Hey, Ms. Ueda, are you busy today?

上田：ううん、ひまだけど。
No, not really.

学生：先生、少(すこ)し寒(さむ)くありませんか。 *Professor, isn't it a bit cold here?*
先生：うん、ほんとに寒(さむ)いね。 *Yeah, it's really cold.*
学生：ヒーター、入(い)れましょうか。 *Shall I turn on the heater?*
先生：うん、そうして。 *Yes, please.*

Notes

- The thematic particle は、the subject particle が, and the direct object particle を are not used in conversations often.

  今日、すずしいね。 *It's cool today.*
  あ、雪(ゆき)、ふってる。 *Gee, it's snowing.*
  雨(あめ)、ふった。 *It rained.*

- In casual conversation, the question marker か is often omitted in questions. It is replaced with a rising intonation.

  リー：寒(さむ)い？ *Are you cold?*
  上田：うん、ちょっと寒(さむ)い。 *Yes, a little bit.*
  リー：これ、きる？ *Do you want to put this on?*
  上田：ありがとう。 *Thank you.*

- The copular verb だ and the だ in な - adjectives are also deleted in questions. Deleting だ before particles like ね and よ makes the speech sound feminine.

  リー：大丈夫(じょうぶ)？ *Are you OK?*
  上田：うん、大丈夫(じょうぶ)（だ）よ。 *Yes, I am.*
  リー：あの人、学生？ *Is he a student?*
  上田：うん、学生（だ）よ。 *Yes, he is.*

- The plain form of んです is んだ or の. In questions の is usually used. In statements, both の and んだ can be used.

  上田：昨日(きのう)どうしたの？ *What happened yesterday?*
  リー：あ、病気(びょうき)で寝てたんだ。 *I got sick and stayed in bed.*

- ～てください is ～て:

  リー：わるいけど、あれとって。 *Sorry, but can you take that?*
  上田：ああ、いいよ。 *Sure.*

話してみましょう

Activity 1

The following conversations take place between two acquaintances. Change the style so that the conversation takes place between close friends.

Example: A: 昨日(きのう)はすずしかったですね。
B: ええ。

A: 昨日(きのう)はすずしかったね。
B: ええ／うん。

1. A: 先週の火曜日は休みでしたか。
   B: いいえ、じゅぎょうはありましたよ。
2. A: 昨日(きのう)は本当(ほんとう)に暑(あつ)かったですね。
   B: ええ、気温(きおん)が三十五度(ど)まで上(あ)がりましたからね。
3. A: 今朝(けさ)、雨(あめ)がふっていましたか。
   B: いいえ、ふりませんでしたよ。昨日(きのう)のばん、雪(ゆき)がふっていましたけど。
4. A: 去年(きょねん)のはるは寒(さむ)い日がつづきましたけど、今年(ことし)はあたたかい日が多(おお)くていいですね。
   B: そうですね。去年(きょねん)の三月と四月は気温(きおん)がぜんぜん上(あ)がりませんでしたから、寒(さむ)かったですね。
5. A: 昨日(きのう)の台風(たいふう)は大きかったですね。
   B: ええ、雨(あめ)はあまり多くありませんでしたけど、風(かぜ)がとてもつよかったですね。

Activity 2

Work with a partner. One person restates the following questions using the plain form, and the other person responds to them using ～とおもう.

Example: 日本のなつをどうおもいますか。

A: 日本のなつ（を）どうおもう。

B: そう（だ）ね。アメリカよりむし暑(あつ)いとおもう。

1. 今朝(けさ)の気温(きおん)は何度(ど)ぐらいでしたか。
2. 今日は気温(きおん)が何度(ど)ぐらいまで上(あ)がりますか。
3. 昨日(きのう)のばんは気温(きおん)が何度(ど)ぐらいまで下(さ)がりましたか。
4. 昨日(きのう)と今日とどちらの方があたたかいですか。
5. 昨日(きのう)と一昨日(おととい)とどちらの方があたたかかったですか。

Activity 3

Work with partner. Ask and answer questions using the sentences provided.

Example: 今までいろいろなえいがを見ましたが、～が一番おもしろかったです。
(いろいろな = *various*)

A: 今まで見たえいがの中で何が一番おもしろかったですか。

B: ～です。

1. 今までいろいろなところに行きましたが、～が一番たのしかったです。
2. 今までいろいろなりょうりを食べましたが、～が一番おいしかったです。
3. 今までいろいろな本を読みましたが、～が一番おもしろかったです。
4. 今までいろいろな先生に会いましたが、～先生が一番よかったです。
5. 今までいろいろなアルバイトをしましたが、～が一番大変(へん)でした。

	パートナーのこたえ
一番たのしかったところ	
一番おいしかったりょうり	
一番おもしろかった本	
一番よかった先生	
一番大変(へん)だったアルバイト	

III. Describing characteristics of places, objects, and time using ～は～が

In addition to describing physical appearance, as you learned in Chapter 10, ～は～が is used to describe other characteristics or to comment on things and concepts. The particle は indicates what the rest of the sentence is going to be about. You can interpret ～は as *as for* ～.

十二月は雨(あめ)が少(すく)ない。	*We have little rain in December.*
あきは食べものがおいしい。	*Food tastes good in fall.*
ふゆは水が冷(つめ)たい。	*Water is cold in winter.*
ハワイは気候(きこう)がいい。	*Hawaii has a nice climate.*
東京(とうきょう)はものが高い。	*Things are expensive in Tokyo.*
日本は山が多(おお)い。	*Japan is mountainous.*
まどは南(みなみ)の方(ほう)がいい。	*The south (side) is good for a window.*
和食(わ)は天(てん)ぷらがおいしい。	*When it comes to Japanese food, tempura is good.*
山は富士山(ふじさん)が一番だ。	*Mt. Fuji is No.1 of all mountains.*
ここは水がきれいだ。	*The water is clean here.*

リー：今日は風(かぜ)がつよいね。	*The wind is strong today.*
上田：ほんと。	*Indeed.*

山中：このへんはどのきせつがいいですか。
Which season is the best around here?

高山：はるが一番きれいですね。
Spring is the nicest.

話してみましょう

Activity 1

しつもんに日本語でこたえて下さい。

Example: アメリカはどのまちが一番好きですか。
ニューヨークが一番好きです。

1. ～さんの大学は何がゆうめいですか。
2. ～さんは何が上手ですか。
3. ～さんのまちはどのきせつが一番いいですか。
4. アメリカはどの大学が一番大きいですか。
5. 先生はどんな人がいいですか。
6. 日本語は何が大変(へん)ですか。むずかしいですか。

Activity 2

The following charts indicate average temperature or precipitation in various cities. Describe the climate in each city, using ～は～が. Find similarities among various cities.

Example: 東京(とうきょう)は八月が暑(あつ)いです。　シンガポールは雨(あめ)が多(おお)いです。

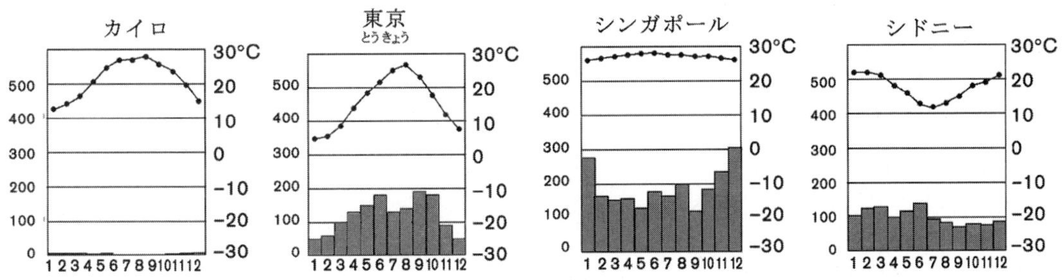

Activity 3

Work with a partner. Choose a town you like. One person will ask the following questions about his/her partner's favorite town and take notes. Then write a short description about the partner's favorite town using the ～は～ が forms. Speak casually.

Example: A: ～さん、どのまちが好き？

B: メルボルンが好きだね。

A: そう。メルボルンのどんなところが好きなの？

B: メルボルンはこうえんが多(おお)くてきれいだから。

A: いいねえ。じゃあ、気候(きこう)はどう？

B: そう（だ）ね。なつは暑(あつ)いけど、ふゆはあまり寒(さむ)くないよ。

～さんが好きなまちはメルボルンです。メルボルンはこうえんがたくさんあって、きれいです。なつは暑(あつ)いですが、ふゆは寒(さむ)くありません。

1. ～さんはどのまちが好きですか。
2. どうしてそのまちが好きなんですか。
3. そのまちの気候(きこう)はどうですか。
4. そのまちはどのきせつがいいですか。どうしてですか。
5. そのまちは何がゆうめいですか。どこがおもしろいですか。

Activity 4

Work in groups of three or four. One person will select a city in the box without telling the rest of the group. The others will take turns asking questions about various characteristics of the city to find out which it is.

ニューヨーク	シカゴ	アンカレッジ
ホノルル	デンバー	ロサンゼルス
アテネ	ローマ	シドニー
東京(とうきょう)	きょうと	ロンドン

Example: A: そのまちは古いたてものが多(おお)いですか。

B: いいえ。

C: くるまや人が多(おお)いですか。

B: ええ、多(おお)いです。

D: そのまちは日本にありますか。

B: ええ。

C: 東京(とうきょう)ですか。

B: はい、そうです。

Activity 5

Work with a partner. The following chart shows information about food available at each of three restaurants. テンホー is a Chinese restaurant, コナ is a café, and みよしや serves Japanese food. Make a dialogue, using ～は～が and casual speech.

Example: A: テンホーは何がおいしいの。

B: チャーハンがおいしいんだよ。

	テンホー	コナ	みよしや
ゆうめいなもの	ギョーザ	コーヒー	さかなりょうり
おいしいもの	チャーハン	カレーライス	みそしる
安いもの	ラーメン	サンドイッチ	定食(てい)
高いもの	飲みもの	デザート	天(てん)ぷら

IV. Expressing manner of action or outcome of a change using the adverbial forms of adjectives and noun + に

The く-form of い-adjectives and the に-form of な-adjectives modify verbs. They are called adverbial forms.

Adjective type	Dictionary form	Adverbial form
い -adjective	おもしろい	おもしろく
な -adjective	きれい	きれいに

The adverbial forms modify a verb indicating how an action takes place.

元気(げんき)に あるいて下さい。 *Please walk cheerfully.*
かんじを 上手に 書いた。 *I wrote kanji skillfully (beautifully).*
雨(あめ)が しずかに ふっている。 *It is quietly raining.*
雪(ゆき)が きゅうに つもった。 *The snow piled up suddenly.*
あかるく わらう。 *to smile brightly (cheerfully)*
今日は はやく 起きた。 *I woke up early (or quickly) today.*
風(かぜ)が やさしく ふいていた。 *The wind was blowing gently.*

They are also used to express change of state or outcome. The adverbial form + する means "to make something/someone into ～," and the adverbial form + なる means "to become ～."

子供(ども)を 先生に する *(Parents) make a child into a teacher.*
子供(ども)が 先生に なる *A child becomes a teacher.*

しずかに する *to make (something/someone) quiet*
しずかに なる *to become quiet*

じゅぎょうを おもしろく する *(A teacher) makes the class interesting.*
じゅぎょうが おもしろく なる *A class becomes interesting.*

お母さん： へや、きれいにしてね。 *Clean this room.*
子供(ども)： は～い。 *Okay./Yes.*

川田(かわだ)： くるまを新しくしたんですよ。
I got a new car.

山下： ええっ、新しいくるまを買ったんですか。
What? You bought a brand-new car?

川田(かわだ)： いいえ。くるまは古いんですけど、さいきん買ったんです。
No, the car is old, but I got it recently.

話してみましょう

Activity 1

しつもんに日本語でこたえて下さい。

Example: なつはあさ何時ごろあかるくなりますか。
五時ごろあかるくなります。

1. なつは何時ごろくらくなりますか。
2. ふゆは何時ごろあかるくなりますか。
3. ふゆは何時ごろくらくなりますか。
4. このへんはいつごろ寒(さむ)くなりますか。
5. このへんはいつごろあたたかくなりますか。
6. ふゆの気温(きおん)は何度(ど)ぐらいになりますか。
7. なつの気温(きおん)は何度(ど)ぐらいになりますか。

Activity 2

Describe the following pictures using the adverbial forms of adjectives.

Example: 風(かぜ)がつよくふいています。

Example 1 2 3 4 5 6

Activity 3

Work with a partner. Your partner first draws a face without showing it to you, then gives you instructions on how to draw this face. Compare the two faces when you are done. Use casual speech.

Example: A: かおを大きくかいて。まるくかいて。

B draws a big round face.

A: そして、目を小さくかいて。はなはひくくかいて。

B draws small eyes and a short nose.

Activity 4

A home remodeling expert is trying to make suggestions to make a room more comfortable. Help the expert make suggestions by completing the sentences using the adverbial form of adjective + する or noun + にする.

Example: かべ (*wall*) がきれいじゃないから、きれいにしましょう。

1. 押(お)し入れがせまいから、______________________。
2. このへやは小さいから、______________________。
3. まどが少(すく)ないから、______________________。
4. ドアが古いから、______________________。
5. トイレがくらいから、______________________。

Activity 5

Discuss the results of the remodeling performed in Activity 4.

Example: かべ (*wall*) をきれいにしたので、へやがあかるくなりました。

V. Expressing uncertainty using ～でしょう , ～かもしれない , and ～かな

～でしょう, ～かもしれない, and ～かな express the speaker's conjecture, but they vary in degree of certainty and the intended recipient. All of these expressions are preceded by the plain form of verbs and adjectives. However, with な-adjectives and the copula verb, だ is deleted.

Verb くもる (*to become cloudy*)

	Probably	Maybe	I wonder
Present affirmative	くもるでしょう	くもるかもしれない	くもるかな
Present negative	くもらないでしょう	くもらないかもしれない	くもらないかな
Past affirmative	くもったでしょう	くもったかもしれない	くもったかな
Past negative	くもらなかったでしょう	くもらなかったかもしれない	くもらなかったかな

い -adjective 寒い (*cold*)

	Probably	Maybe	I wonder
Present affirmative	寒いでしょう	寒いかもしれない	寒いかな
Present negative	寒くないでしょう	寒くないかもしれない	寒くないかな
Past affirmative	寒かったでしょう	寒かったかもしれない	寒かったかな
Past negative	寒くなかったでしょう	寒くなかったかもしれない	寒くなかったかな

な-adjective いや (*unpleasant*)

	Probably	Maybe	I wonder
Present affirmative	いやでしょう	いやかもしれない	いやかな
Present negative	いやじゃないでしょう	いやじゃないかもしれない	いやじゃないかな
Past affirmative	いやだったでしょう	いやだったかもしれない	いやだったかな
Past negative	いやじゃなかったでしょう	いやじゃなかったかもしれない	いやじゃなかったかな

Noun + copula verb

	Probably	Maybe	I wonder
Present affirmative	風(かぜ)でしょう	風(かぜ)かもしれない	風(かぜ)かな
Present negative	風(かぜ)じゃないでしょう	風(かぜ)じゃないかもしれない	風(かぜ)じゃないかな
Past affirmative	風(かぜ)だったでしょう	風(かぜ)だったかもしれない	風(かぜ)だったかな
Past negative	風(かぜ)じゃなかったでしょう	風(かぜ)じゃなかったかもしれない	風(かぜ)じゃなかったかな

～でしょう／だろう **probably, I suppose**

～でしょう indicates probability or conjecture. It can be used for future and past events or actions. The probability expressed by でしょう ranges from *probably* to *must be/must have been*. ～でしょう is often used in weather forecasts.

いい天気(てんき)でしょう。 *It will probably be good weather.*
にぎやかでしょう。 *It will probably be lively.*
東京(とうきょう)はくもり時々(ときどき)雨(あめ)でしょう。 *It will be cloudy with occasional rain in Tokyo.*
よこはまは雨(あめ)でしょう。 *It will be rainy in Yokohama.*

In addition, ～でしょう can be used with a rising intonation to ask for confirmation. This usage of ～でしょう is rather casual and should not be used toward someone in a superior status.

そとはむし暑(あつ)いでしょう。 *It is humid outside, don't you think?*
あの人は上田さんでしょう。 *That's Ms. Ueda over there, isn't it?*

The question form of ～でしょう, ～でしょうか is used for questions that are more polite than those ending in ～ですか.

あのう、えきはどこでしょうか。 *Excuse me, but where is the station? (more polite)*
あのう、えきはどこですか。 *Excuse me, but where is the station?*
今、何時でしょうか。 *Do you have the time? (more polite)*
今、何時ですか。 *What time is it now?*

田中：明日(あした)の天気(てんき)はどうでしょうか。 *How will tomorrow's weather be?*
川口：さあ、よく分かりませんが。 *Well, I'm not sure.*

鈴(すず)木：田中さんは来ますか。 *Is Mr. Tanaka coming?*
川口：雨(あめ)だから、たぶん来ないでしょう。 *It's raining, so he probably won't come.*

Notes

- でしょう is sometimes used with たぶん (*perhaps*).

  たぶん雨(あめ)でしょう。 *It will probably rain.*

- The plain form of でしょう is だろう . When ～だろう is used in a question such as あの人は日本人だろうか , it can be interpreted as a self-directed question: *I wonder if that person is Japanese*. The polite speech version, あの人は日本人でしょうか , would be consistently interpreted as being a polite question.

～かもしれない **might**

～かもしれない also indicates probability or conjecture and can be used for future and past events or actions. The probability expressed by かもしれない is about 50% or lower.

石田(いし)： にわか雨(あめ)がふりそうですね。
It looks like we will have a shower.

チョイ： そうですね。くもが多(おお)いから、ふるかもしれませんね。
I agree. It's very cloudy, so it might rain.

イアン： あの人は山田先生でしょうか。
Is that person (perhaps) Professor Yamada?

本田： さあ、どうでしょうね。Tシャツ、きてるから、学生かもしれませんよ。
Well, I am not sure. He is wearing a T-shirt, so he may be a student.

～かな **I wonder ～ (Casual speech)**

～かな is used when the speaker asks himself/herself about something. Since it expresses the speaker's monologue question, *I wonder* ～, it cannot be used as someone else's monologue questions such as *he/she wonders* ～. Also, it indicates present tense and cannot be used in cases such as *I wondered* ～ or *he/she wondered* ～.

台風(たいふう)かな。	*I wonder if it is a typhoon.*
そとは寒(さむ)いかな。	*I wonder if it is cold outside.*
今晩(ばん)は気温(きおん)が下(さ)がるかな。	*I wonder if the temperature will fall tonight.*

～かな is not used as a straightforward question to others like ～でしょうか but can be used to solicit the listener's answer indirectly. However, it should not be used toward someone of superior status, because it is used in fairly informal speech.

アリス：今日も雨(あめ)かな。
I wonder if it will rain today, too.

健一(けんいち)：ううん。昨日(きのう)のばん、ふったから、今日は大丈夫(じょうぶ)だよ。
No. It won't because we had rain last night.

道子(みちこ)：これは石(いし)田さんのかな。リーさんのかな。
I wonder if this is Mr. Ishida's or Mr. Li's.

ふみえ：さあ、よく分からないけど。イニシャルがT.I.だから、石(いし)田さんのかもしれないね。
Well, I don't know, but it might be Mr. Ishida's because the initials are T.I.

古田：上田さんは来るかな。 *I wonder if Ms. Ueda is coming.*

山下：さあ、どうかな。 *Well, I wonder that, too.*

Notes

- In feminine speech 〜かしら is used instead of かな.

大雪(おおゆき)になるかしら。 *I wonder if the snow will get heavy* (feminine).

話してみましょう

Activity 1

Convert the following questions into monologue questions using 〜かな.

Example: 今年(ことし)のなつは暑(あつ)いですか。
今年(ことし)のなつは暑(あつ)いかな。

1. 去年(きょねん)の八月は暑(あつ)い日が多(おお)かったですか。
2. 今年(ことし)のふゆは寒(さむ)いでしょうか。
3. 去年(きょねん)は雨(あめ)がたくさんふりましたか。
4. 去年(きょねん)のふゆは雪(ゆき)が少なかったでしょうか。
5. 一昨年(おととし)のふゆはあまり寒(さむ)くありませんでしたか。
6. 今年(ことし)のなつは暑(あつ)くなりますか。

Activity 2

Work with a partner. The following chart shows today's weather forecast for various cities. One person asks a question using the words in 1-8 and ～でしょう. The other person answers the questions, using ～でしょう or ～かもしれません.

Example: 東京(とうきょう)／いい天気(てんき)

A: 東京(とうきょう)はいい天気(てんき)でしょうか。

B: いいえ、天気(てんき)はあまりよくないでしょう。

東京(とうきょう)／雨(あめ)

A: 今日東京(とうきょう)は雨(あめ)がふるでしょうか。

B: そうですね。東京(とうきょう)は雨(あめ)がふるかもしれませんね。

	東京(とうきょう)	アラスカ	ニューヨーク	シドニー	ロサンゼルス
天気(てんき)	くもり	雪(ゆき)	くもりのち雨(あめ)	晴(は)れ	くもり時々(ときどき)晴(は)れ
気温(きおん)	59° F 15° C	-4° F -20° C	41° F 5° C	91.4° F 33° C	77° F 25° C
雨(あめ)	50%	0%	80%	0%	30%
雪(ゆき)	0%	100%	15%	0%	0%

1. 東京(とうきょう)／あたたかい
2. アラスカ／雪(ゆき)
3. ニューヨーク／寒(さむ)い
4. ニューヨーク／雨(あめ)
5. シドニー／晴(は)れる
6. ロサンゼルス／あたたかい
7. ロサンゼルス／雨(あめ)
8. シドニー／むし暑(あつ)い

Activity 3

Work with a partner. One of you plays the role of a psychic, the other is a customer who is a bit skeptical. The customer asks questions and the pyschic attempts to answer them convincingly.

Example: A: 私のしゅみは何でしょうか。

B: そうですね。本を読むのが好きでしょう。それから、おんがくも好きでしょう。

A: そうですか。じゃあ、今週の週末、私は何をするでしょうか。

B: ～さんは友達(だち)の家のパーティに行くでしょう。そこで、かっこいい人に会うでしょう。

A: え、本当(ほんとう)ですか。

Activity 4

Using the state of Illinois (イリノイしゅう, しゅう = *state*) as a reference point, ask your classmates where other states are in respect to Illinois. Your classmates will answer using direction words and ～でしょう, ～かもしれない, or ～とおもう depending on their level of certainty. Tally the results.

Example: A: イリノイしゅうの北(きた)に何(なに)しゅうがありますか。

B: ウィスコンシンしゅうがあります／あるでしょう／あるかもしれません／あるとおもいます。

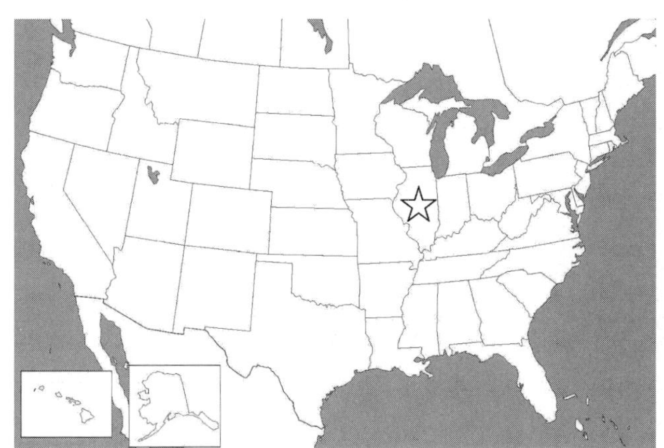

Activity 5

Work with a partner. Look at the following weather map and say what seems to be happening weather-wise in various places. Use casual speech.

Example: 今日、テキサスはいい天気(てんき)になるとおもう／なるかもしれない。

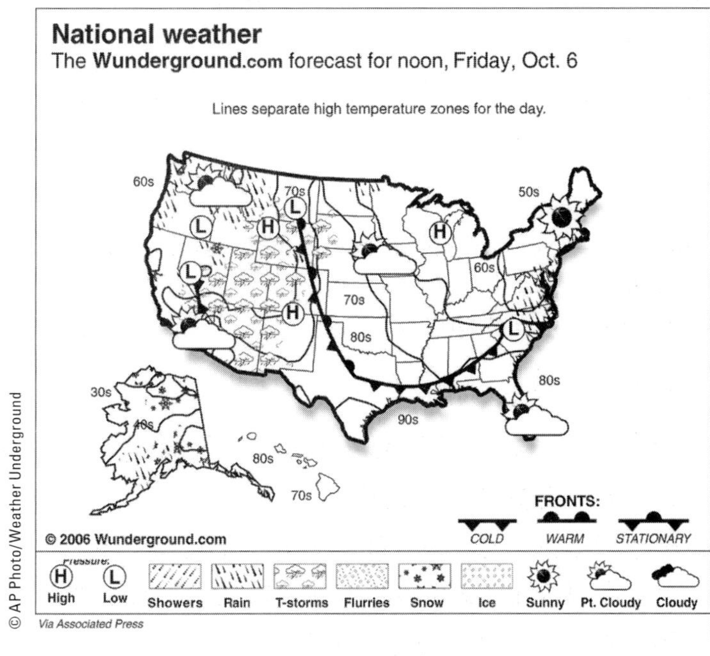

聞く練習(れんしゅう)

上手な聞き方(かた)

Understanding the organization of prepared speech

Unlike face-to-face conversations, news reports and weather forecasts are based on prepared text and hence do not have much redundant information. It is thus very important to understand the information the first time. Luckily, prepared speech usually has a set pattern. Being aware of the organization of speech helps you to identify when to pay attention and to what. For example, news reports usually start with what happens, to whom, where, and when. The details come later.

聞く前(まえ)に

Write an outline of the organization of a weather report. Include the types of information provided and their order.

天気予報(てんきよほう)を聞く **Listening to weather forecasts**

Listen to the following weather forecasts. Then complete the chart, in English, by writing in the weather as well as high and low temperatures for each city listed.

言葉(ことば)のリスト

最高気温(さいこうきおん) highest temperature さいてい気温(きおん) lowest temperature

	天気予報(てんきよほう) (Example)	天気予報(てんきよほう) 1	天気予報(てんきよほう) 2	天気予報報(てんきよほう) 3
まち	きょうと	東京(とうきょう)	よこはま	きょうと
天気(てんき)	雪(ゆき)			
気温(きおん)	1度(ど)／ -1度(ど)			

聞いた後(あと)で

しつもんに日本語でこたえて下さい。

1. 天気予報(てんきよほう)1のきせつはいつですか。
2. そのきせつの東京(とうきょう)と～さんのまちとどちらの方が寒(さむ)いですか。
3. 天気予報(てんきよほう)2のきせつはいつですか。
4. そのきせつのよこはまと～さんのまちとどちらの方があたたかいですか。
5. 天気予報(てんきよほう)3のきせつはいつですか。
6. ～さんのまちでは、そのきせつに雨(あめ)がたくさんふりますか。

聞き上手話し上手

上手な話し方(かた)

Expressing agreement and solidarity using ね and も

To facilitate conversation, it is important to give feedback and show a willingness to participate in the conversation.

Expressing agreement or emphasizing similarity is one way to show your support to the listener. This will help to create a sense of sharing or solidarity. In Japanese, two particles, ね and も, are often used to show agreement. For example, the particle ね in Ms. Suzuki's speech below indicates that she is requesting a confirmation of her impression about the weather. The particle ね in Mr. Yamamoto's speech indicates that he agrees with Ms. Suzuki's assertion that it is humid today.

鈴木(すず)：今日はむし暑(あつ)いですね。 *It's humid today, isn't it?*
山本：ええ、本当(ほんとう)に暑(あつ)いですね。 *It certainly is.*

Similarly, the particle も in the following example emphasizes agreement between Ms. Suzuki and Mr. Yamamoto and indicates what they have in common.

鈴木(すず)：私はいぬが好きです。 *I like dogs.*
山本：そうですか。ぼくもいぬが好きなんですよ。 *Really? So do I.*

Even if you disagree with a person, it is good to start off by agreeing about something before stating a disagreement. Starting a conversation with a disagreement often sounds rude or cold.

鈴木(すず)：今年(ことし)は雪(ゆき)が多(おお)いですね。 *It has snowed a lot this year.*

山本：本当(ほんとう)にそうですね。でも、去年(きょねん)はもっと多(おお)かったですよ。
It has, hasn't it? But there was more snow last year.

練習(れんしゅう)

1. You will hear six people expressing their opinions. First express your agreement using ね and も. Then express your disagreement, but (1) show your support by using ね and も, and (2) articulate the point on which you disagree.
2. Work with a partner. Your partner will express opinions about class, school, weather, a particular hobby, parents. Agree with him/her using ね and も.
3. Work with a partner. Your partner will again express opinions about class, school, weather, a hobby or parents, but this time, show your support for his/her opinion using ね and も, and then express your disagreement.
4. The following conversation is unnatural. Make it more natural by using ね and も.

A: こんにちは。暑(あつ)いです。おでかけですか。
B: ああ、こんにちは。およぎに行くんです。
A: いいです。私はおよぎに行きたいです。明日(あした)は暑(あつ)いでしょうか。
B: むし暑(あつ)いから、よるは雨(あめ)がふるかもしれません。
A: そうですか。じゃあ、少(すこ)しすずしくなります。

漢字

かんじ

Component shapes of kanji 1 – Introduction

Many **kanji** consist of more than one component. Certain components appear in many different **kanji**. Some of them are **kanji** by themselves while others are not. Since the number of these component shapes is much smaller than the number of **kanji**, approximately 300 in total, they serve as organizers and aid in memorizing.

The term *radical* (部首 ぶしゅ) is traditionally used to refer to components of characters. The concept of radicals was developed to classify and index a large number of **kanji**. In modern Japanese, a little over 200 radicals are used to index **kanji**. A radical is assigned to every **kanji**. Although radicals are very useful in studying **kanji**, they are sometimes deceptive. For example, the radical of 家 is 宀, but the radical of 字 is 子.

In this book, we use the term *component shape* to refer to any shape that repeatedly appears as part of **kanji** (e.g., 寸, 口, 又, 月, 宀, etc.). Some component shapes can be **kanji** by themselves, while others only appear inside of larger **kanji**. There are about 300 such shapes, which include all of the shapes used as radicals. Some of the component shapes indicate the meaning (or meaning category) of **kanji**. For example, if a **kanji** contains 日, it is likely that the meaning of the **kanji** is related to day or sun. Some other component shapes may indicate an on-reading of the **kanji**.

Component shapes appear in various places within **kanji**, but some shapes have a strong tendency to appear in fixed locations such as the left, the right, the top, or the bottom of the character. The following is a list of major types of component shapes based on where they are found within the character.

Type *	Example		Use Example
へん (left side)	亻	meaning: person	休 体 住
つくり (right side)	冓	on-reading: /kou/	講 構 購
かんむり (top)	宀	meaning: roof	家 寒
あし (bottom)	儿	meaning: leg	兄 見 先 元
たれ (top to left)	疒	meaning: sickness	病 痛 疲
かまえ (enclosure)	門	meaning: gate	間 聞 閉
くにがまえ (enclosure)	囗	meaning: border	回 国
にょう (left to bottom)	辶	meaning: walk, round	週 道 進 近

* These names are used to label radicals.

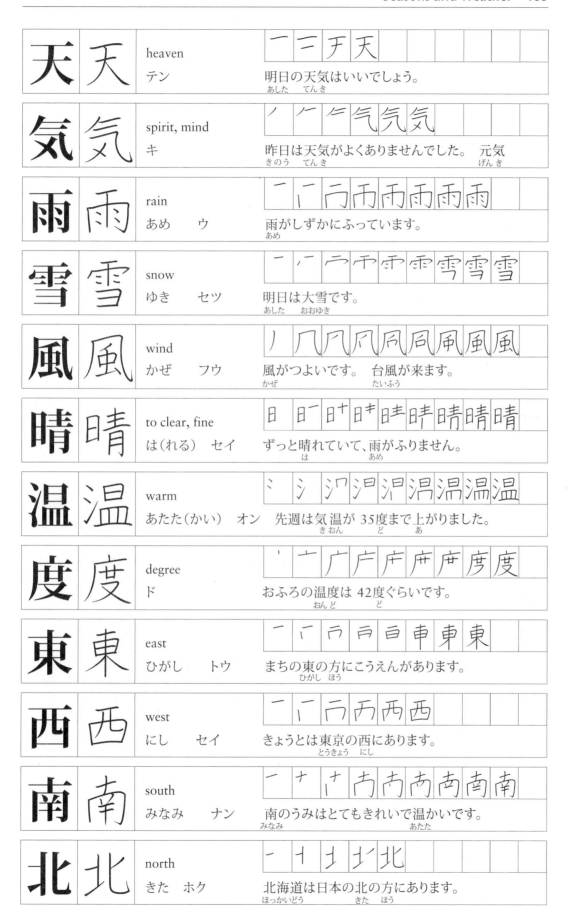

Kanji	Handwritten	Meaning / Readings	Example
天	天	heaven テン	明日の天気はいいでしょう。 あした　てんき
気	気	spirit, mind キ	昨日は天気がよくありませんでした。　元気 きのう　てんき　げんき
雨	雨	rain あめ　ウ	雨がしずかにふっています。 あめ
雪	雪	snow ゆき　セツ	明日は大雪です。 あした　おおゆき
風	風	wind かぜ　フウ	風がつよいです。　台風が来ます。 かぜ　たいふう
晴	晴	to clear, fine は(れる)　セイ	ずっと晴れていて、雨がふりません。 は　あめ
温	温	warm あたた(かい)　オン	先週は気温が 35度まで上がりました。 きおん　ど　あ
度	度	degree ド	おふろの温度は 42度ぐらいです。 おんど　ど
東	東	east ひがし　トウ	まちの東の方にこうえんがあります。 ひがし　ほう
西	西	west にし　セイ	きょうとは東京の西にあります。 とうきょう　にし
南	南	south みなみ　ナン	南のうみはとてもきれいで温かいです。 みなみ　あたた
北	北	north きた　ホク	北海道は日本の北の方にあります。 ほっかいどう　きた　ほう

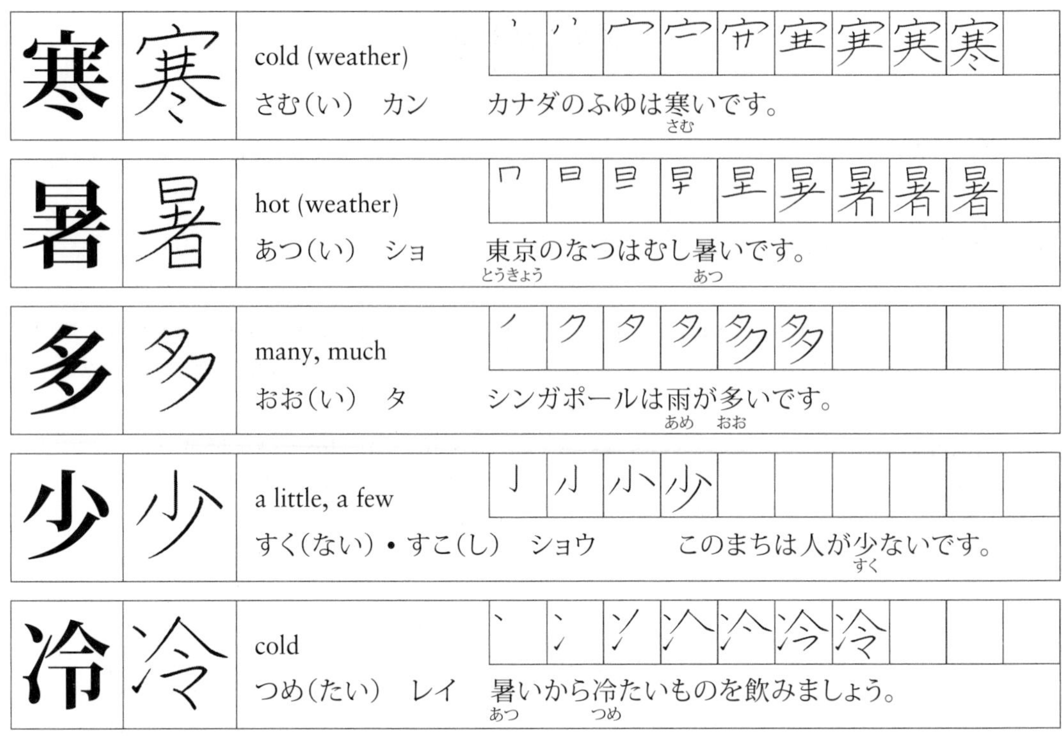

Kanji	Handwritten	Meaning / Readings	Example
寒	寒	cold (weather) さむ(い)　カン	カナダのふゆは寒(さむ)いです。
暑	暑	hot (weather) あつ(い)　ショ	東京(とうきょう)のなつはむし暑(あつ)いです。
多	多	many, much おお(い)　タ	シンガポールは雨(あめ)が多(おお)いです。
少	少	a little, a few すく(ない)・すこ(し)　ショウ	このまちは人が少(すく)ないです。
冷	冷	cold つめ(たい)　レイ	暑(あつ)いから冷(つめ)たいものを飲みましょう。

読めるようになった漢字(かんじ)

天気　天気予報(よほう)　天ぷら　気温　気候(きこう)　雨　梅雨(つゆ)　にわか雨　雪　風
台風(たいふう)　晴れる　温かい　温度　何度　東　西　南　南東　南西　北
北東　北西　寒い　暑い　多い　少ない　冷(つめ)たい　上がる　下がる
去年(きょねん)　今朝(けさ)　今年(ことし)　方(ほう)　夕方(ゆうがた)　本当(ほんとう)に　少し

日本人のなまえ：川田(かわだ)　道子(みちこ)　健一(けんいち)

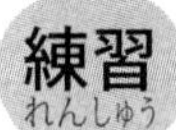

練習(れんしゅう)

Read the following sentences.

1. 東京(とうきょう)の天気は雨のち晴れです。ごごには気温が二十五度まで上がるでしょう。
2. 今晩(ばん)は北の風がつよいですが、明日(あした)は南の風になって、よわくなるでしょう。
3. 西の方が暗(くら)いですから、晴れないでしょう。
4. なつは暑くて、ふゆは寒いです。雪もたくさんふります。
5. ひるごはんの時は人が多いですが、そのあとは少なくなります。
6. 大阪(おおさか)は東京(とうきょう)の西にあります。せんだいは東京(とうきょう)の北です。
7. 今日はあたたかかったけど、明日(あした)は雨がふるそうだから、気温が下がって、寒くなるかもしれないね。

読む練習(れんしゅう)

上手な読み方(かた)

Getting used to vertical writing

Japanese text can be written either horizontally or vertically. In vertical writing, text is read from top to bottom, right to left. Japanese newspaper articles are written vertically, including the weather forecast. Popular magazines and literary works are also usually written vertically. Texts requiring scientific symbols, equations, formulas, and foreign words, such as science textbooks, language texts, and computer magazines, tend to be written horizontally.

練習(れんしゅう)

1. Mark the beginning and end of each of the following short paragraphs.

メルボルンに給水制限？

メルボルンでは十三年ぶりに給水制限がしかれる可能性が高いと見られている。

一五〇年ぶりの低雨量を記録したメルボルン供給ダムの水量は七二%と、去年の同時期の九五%を大幅に下回り、関係者もこの状態を深刻に受け止めている様子。

メルボルン水道局のベイリー氏は、市民に対し節水に協力してくれるよう積極的に呼びかけている。

ちなみに、年間平均降雨量六三九ミリに対し、去年の降雨量はわずか三五九ミリだった。

2. Rewrite the following text vertically in two or more lines.

東京(とうきょう)は今日は晴れ時々(ときどき)くもりで、ごぜんちゅうは少し寒いですが、ごごには十度ぐらいになるでしょう。よるになって、雨がふるでしょう。この雨はあしたのごごまでつづくでしょう。

読む前(まえ)に

1. The numbers in the following map represent various regions in Japan. Read the description of each region below and write the number that matches the description. Note that しま means *island*.

山陰(さんいん)	本州(ほんしゅう)にあります。大阪(おおさか)の西で、四国(しこく)の北です。かんこくにちかいです。
北海道(ほっかいどう)	日本で一番北にあるしまです。
関東(かんとう)	本州(ほんしゅう)にあります。東京(とうきょう)と東京(とうきょう)のちかくです。
近畿(きんき)	本州(ほんしゅう)にあります。東京(とうきょう)の西です。大阪(おおさか)やきょうとがあります。四国(しこく)にちかいです。
九州(きゅうしゅう)	四国(しこく)の南西にあるしまです。
北陸(ほくりく)	本州(ほんしゅう)にあります。東京(とうきょう)の北西の方です。
本州(ほんしゅう)	日本で一番大きいしまです。
東北(とうほく)	本州(ほんしゅう)にあります。東京(とうきょう)の北の方です。
東海(とうかい)	本州(ほんしゅう)にあります。東京(とうきょう)の少し南西の方です。
四国(しこく)	日本にある四つの大きいしまの中で一番小さいしまです。
沖縄(おきなわ)	日本の一番南にあるしまです。

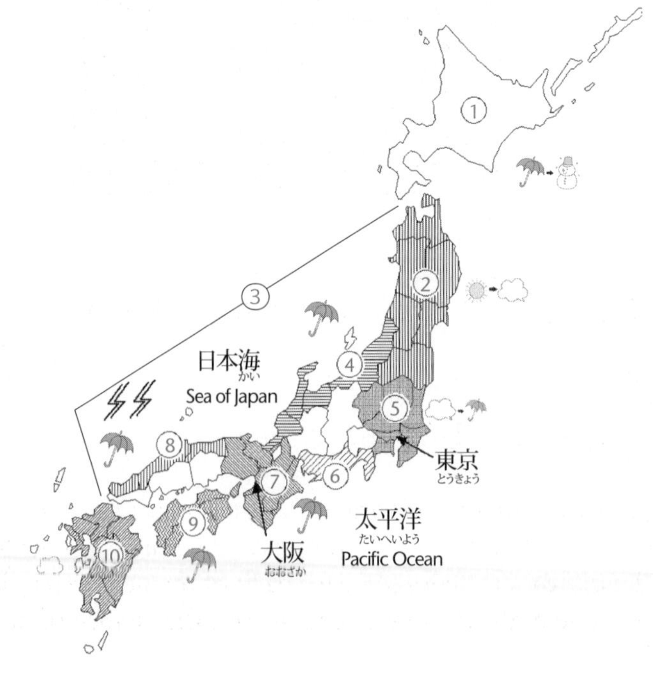

新聞の天気予報(よほう) A weather forecast in a newspaper

前線を伴った低気圧が日本海から東北東に進み、全国的に天気はくずれる。本州の日本海側や四国、九州は朝から雨、関東、東北、北陸も午後から雨になる。山陰地方の海岸では所々で雷雨を伴い風も強まる。北海道は雪か雨、沖縄も晴れ後曇りで、昼過ぎから雨。

読んだ後(あと)で

A. After reading the above weather forecast, choose the weather map that corresponds to the forecast.

1 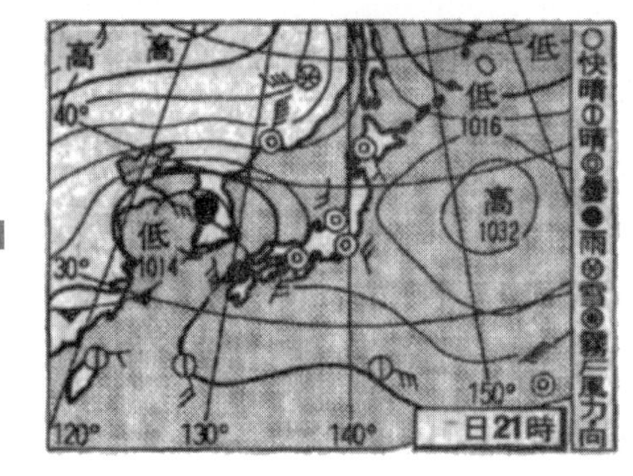

2 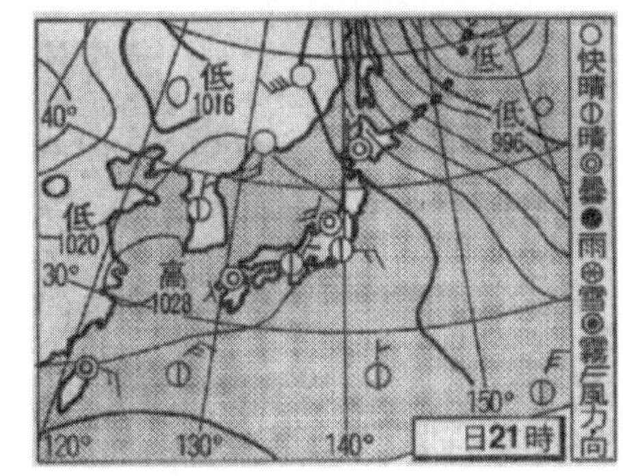

3 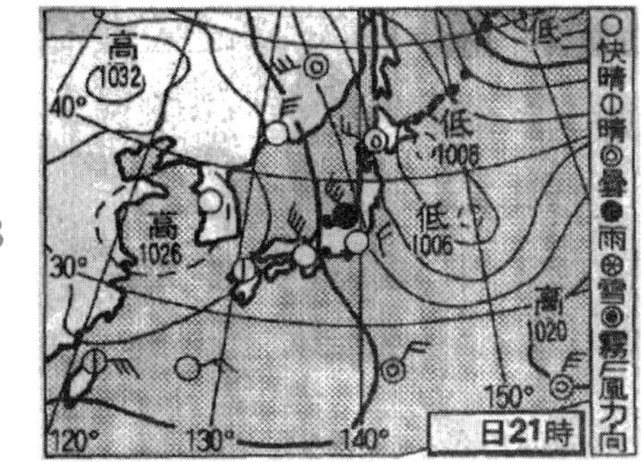

B. しつもんに日本語でこたえて下さい。

1. 四国(しこく)にすんでいる人は今日はかさがいりますか。
2. 北海道(ほっかいどう)はあたたかいですか。
3. 沖縄(おきなわ)のあさの天気はどうですか。

C. An out-of-town friend is planning to visit you for a week and has asked what the weather is like now. Compose an e-mail message to your friend giving details about the forecast for each of the next seven days. Information should include high and low temperatures, the chance of precipitation, and so forth.

単語(たんご)

Nouns

うみ	海	ocean, sea
おととし	一昨年	the year before last
おもいで	思い出	memories
がいこく	外国	foreign countries
がっき	学期	semester, quarter いちがっき one semester はるがっき spring semester/quarter
かぶき	歌舞伎	kabuki (Japanese traditional performing art)
きもの	着物	traditional Japanese clothes, kimono
キャンプ		camping
きょうかい	教会	church
クリスマス		Christmas
けんか		fight, quarrel けんかをする to fight
こんげつ	今月	this month
しょうがつ	正月	the New Year (often used as おしょうがつ)
じんじゃ	神社	Shinto shrine
すいぞくかん	水族館	aquarium
せんげつ	先月	last month
ちゅうがく	中学	junior high school (shortened form of 中学校)
デート		dating, デートする to go out on a date
てら	寺	Buddhist temple (often used as おてら)
どうぶつえん	動物園	zoo
とき	時	when, at the time of ～ (子供(ども)の時 when I was a child)
なつやすみ	夏休み	summer holidays, summer break はるやすみ spring break, ふゆやすみ winter break
はくぶつかん	博物館	museum
バレンタインデー		St. Valentine's Day
ハロウィン		Halloween
はんとし	半年	a half-year
ひこうき	飛行機	airplane

びじゅつかん	美術館	art museum
プレゼント		present, gift
まつり	祭り	festival (often used as おまつり)
ミュージカル		musical
やまのぼり	山登り	mountain climbing
ゆうえんち	遊園地	amusement park
らいげつ	来月	next month

う -verbs

なく	泣く	to cry
のる	乗る	to get on, to ride (ひこうきにのる to get on a plane)
もらう		to receive, to get

Irregular verb

しつれんする	失恋する	to be disappointed in love

Adverb

はじめて	初めて	for the first time

Particle

なあ		A particle of exclamation to express desires or feelings without addressing anyone in particular. Used in casual speech.

Suffixes

～かい	～回	～ times
～かげつ	～か月	counter for months
～ご	～後	from ～, after ～ (三年ご three years from now)
～しゅうかん	～週間	for ～ weeks
～ど	～度	～ times
～にち	～日	day
～ねん	～年	specific year (1996 年), counter for year (十年)
～まえ	～前	～ ago (一年まえ one year ago)

Expressions

えーと		Well, let's see . . .
あけましておめでとうございます。	明けましておめでとうございます。	Happy New Year!

単語の練習
たん　れんしゅう

A. 日にち　Days of the month

日	月	火	水	木	金	土
		一日 ついたち	二日 ふつか	三日 みっか	四日 よっか	五日 いつか
六日 むいか	七日 なのか (なぬか)	八日 ようか	九日 ここのか	十日 とおか	十一日 じゅういち にち	十二日 じゅうに にち
十三日 じゅうさん にち	十四日 じゅう よっか	十五日 じゅうご にち	十六日 じゅうろく にち	十七日 じゅうしち にち	十八日 じゅうはち にち	十九日 じゅうく にち
二十日 はつか	二十一日 にじゅう いちにち	二十二日 にじゅうに にち	二十三日 にじゅう さんにち	二十四日 にじゅう よっか	二十五日 にじゅうご にち	二十六日 にじゅう ろくにち
二十七日 にじゅう しちにち	二十八日 にじゅう はちにち	二十九日 にじゅうく にち	三十日 さんじゅう にち	三十一日 さんじゅう いちにち		

NOTE

- いちにち means *one day*; ついたち means the *first of the month.* Both are written as 一日 in **kanji** but the context makes the reading clear. The other date expressions can be used for durations of time. For example, ふつか may mean the *second day of the month* or *two days*, depending on context.

おぼえていますか。

何月、一月、二月、三月、四月、五月、六月、七月、八月、九月、十月、十一月,,、十二月

Activity 1

Work with the class. Ask your classmates about their birthdays, and put them in the following charts.

Example: A: スミスさんのお誕生(たんじょう)日はいつですか。

B: 一月一日(ついたち)です。

月	日にちと名前(なまえ)
一月	一日(ついたち)　スミスさん
二月	
三月	
四月	
五月	
六月	
七月	
八月	
九月	
十月	
十一月	
十二月	

B. とくべつな日　Special days

お正月(しょうがつ)	New Year's Day
クリスマス	Christmas
バレンタインデー	Valentine's Day
ハロウィン	Halloween

Supplementary Vocabulary: アメリカの休日(きゅうじつ) US holidays

マーティン・ルーサー・キング・デー	Martin Luther King, Jr. Day
プレジデンツ・デー	President's Day
イースター	Easter
どくりつきねんび　独立記念日	Independence Day
メモリアルデー	Memorial Day
レーバーデー	Labor Day
コロンブス・デー	Columbus Day
ハヌカ	Hanukkah

Activity 2

Work with a partner. Ask your partner about the dates of holidays this year.

Example: A: 今年のハヌカ (*Hanukkah*) はいつですか。

B: 十二月十一日です。

C. ほかの時間のいい方 Other time expressions

	日	週	月	年
〜 before last 〜	1 day before yesterday	N/A	N/A	一昨年(おととし) year before last
Last	2 Yesterday	5	先月(せんげつ) last month	8
This	3 Today	6	今月(こんげつ) this month	9
Next	4 Tomorrow	7	来月(らいげつ) next month	来年 next year

Activity 3

Fill in the blanks in the above table with appropriate time expressions that you have learned in previous chapters.

Activity 4

しつもんに日本語でこたえて下さい。

1. 今月(こんげつ)は何月ですか。
2. 来月は何月ですか。
3. 先月(せんげつ)は何月でしたか。
4. 今年は何年ですか。
5. 来年は何年ですか。
6. 一昨年(おととし)は何年でしたか。
7. 去年(きょ)は何年でしたか。

D. 時間のながさ Duration of time

～度／回(かい) (times)	～週間(しゅうかん) (for ～ week)	～か月(げつ) (for ～ month)	～年 (year)
いちど／いっかい	いっしゅうかん	いっかげつ	いちねん
にど／にかい	にしゅうかん	にかげつ	にねん
さんど／さんかい	さんしゅうかん	さんかげつ	さんねん
よんかい	よんしゅうかん	よんかげつ	よねん
ごかい	ごしゅうかん	ごかげつ	ごねん
ろっかい	ろくしゅうかん	はんとし ／ろっかげつ	ろくねん
ななかい	ななしゅうかん	ななかげつ	しちねん
はちかい ／はっかい	はっしゅうかん	はちかげつ ／はっかげつ	はちねん
きゅうかい	きゅうしゅうかん	きゅうかげつ	きゅうねん ／くねん
じゅっかい ／じっかい	じゅっしゅうかん ／じっしゅうかん	じゅっかげつ ／じっかげつ	じゅうねん

Notes

- ～度 refers to both frequency (*times*) and temperature (*degrees*) up to 3. Beyond that, it usually refers to temperature only.
- ～年 indicates both the specific point of time, as in 2008 年 (*the year 2008*), and the duration of time as in 八年 (*for 8 years*).
- When ～かい is written as the **kanji** 階(かい), it refers to *floor levels*, as in Chapter 8, but when it is written as 回(かい), it refers to *frequency*. There are some differences between them in terms of pronunciation as well. For example, the first mora is pronounced with a low pitch and the following morae all have high pitch when the expression refers to a floor level, such as いっかい, にかい, and さんかい, but not for frequency, as in いっかい, にかい, さんかい. Also, *3rd floor* can be pronounced either さんがい or さんかい, but *3 times* is さんかい. On the other hand, *8th floor* is usually pronounced はちかい but *8 times* can be はちかい or はっかい.
- Instead of the western (Gregorian) calendar, Japanese people and documents frequently use the current Emperor's era to refer to a certain year. For example, へいせい五年 is 1993. Recent eras are: 明治(めいじ) (1868–1912), 大正(たいしょう) (1912–1926), しょうわ (1926–1989), and へいせい (1989–).

Activity 5

Say what year the following events occurred. If you do not know the answer, ask your classmates.

1. コロンブス (*Columbus*) がアメリカに来た。
2. アメリカがイギリスからどくりつした (*became independent*)。
3. アメリカで夏(なつ)のオリンピックがあった。
4. アメリカで冬(ふゆ)のオリンピックがあった。
5. 第二次世界大戦(だいにじせかいたいせん) (*WWII*) がはじまった。
6. 第二次世界大戦(だいにじせかいたいせん) (*WWII*) がおわった。
7. ベトナムせんそう (*the Vietnam War*) がおわった。
8. イラクせんそう (*the Iraq War*) がはじまった。

Activity 6

しつもんに日本語でこたえて下さい。

1. 夏休(なつやす)みは何か月ありますか。冬休(ふゆやす)みはどうですか。春休(はるやす)みは？
2. 一学期(がっき)は何週間ありますか。
3. 今週は何度学校に来ますか。
4. 今年、何度えいがを見ましたか。
5. 今学期(こんがっき)、何度じゅぎょうを休みましたか。

E. めいしょとレジャー Attractions and leisure activities

Activity 7

Identify the picture that depicts each of the buildings and activities in the list by writing the number corresponding to the picture.

1.	はくぶつかん	museum	__.	ゆうえんち	amusement park
__.	ミュージカル	musical	__.	教会 (きょうかい)	church
__.	水族館 (すいぞくかん)	aquarium	__.	うみ	sea
__.	山のぼり	mountain climbing	__.	(お)てら	temple
__.	旅行 (りょ)	travel	__.	じんじゃ	Shinto shrine
__.	びじゅつかん	art museum	__.	(お)まつり	festival
__.	かぶき	kabuki	__.	キャンプ	camping
__.	がいこく	foreign country	__.	どうぶつえん	zoo

おぼえていますか。

えいが、こうえん、コンサート、たいいくかん、図書館(とかん)、パーティ、ピクニック、休みの日

Activity 8

Work with a partner. Ask each other whether you have been to any of the places or attractions or have participated in them this year.

Example: A: 今年、はくぶつかんに行きましたか。
B: ええ、行きました。
A: 何度ぐらい行きましたか。
B: 一度／一回(かい)行きました。

	今年行った／見に行った／した	～度／回(かい)
はくぶつかん		
びじゅつかん		
水族館(すいぞくかん)		
どうぶつえん		
ゆうえんち		
教会(きょうかい)		
(お)てら		
じんじゃ		
うみ		
がいこく		
ミュージカル		
(お)まつり		
山のぼり		
かぶき		
旅行(りょ)		
キャンプ		

F. 思(おも)い出(で) Memories

きものをきる
to wear a kimono

飛行機(ひこうき)にのる
to get on a plane

プレゼントをもらう
to receive a present

デートする
to go on a date

けんかをする
to have a fight, a quarrel

しつれんする
to be disappointed in love

なく
to cry

おぼえていますか。

おふろに入る、およぐ、出かける、和(わ)食を食べる

Activity 9

Work in a group of three or four. One person acts out an activity from the list, and the rest of the group try to guess which it is.

Activity 10

Complete the following statements using ～さいの時(とき) (*when I was ～ years old*).

1. ____________________の時(とき)、はじめて人を好きになりました。
2. ____________________の時(とき)、はじめて外国人(がいこくじん)と話しました。
3. ____________________の時(とき)、はじめて飛行機(ひこうき)にのりました。
4. ____________________の時(とき)、はじめてデートをしました。
5. ____________________の時(とき)、はじめて友達(だち)とけんかしました。
6. ____________________の時(とき)、しつれんしました。
7. ____________________の時(とき)、高いプレゼントをもらいました。

ダイアローグ

はじめに

A. しつもんに日本語でこたえて下さい。

1. 子供(ども)の時(とき)、どんな子供(ども)でしたか。
2. 小学校の時(とき)、よくどんなことをしましたか。
3. 中学の時(とき)、よくどんなことをしましたか。
4. 高校の時(とき)、よくどんなことをしましたか。

B. Work with a partner. Ask your partner about his/her childhood memories.

Example: A: ～さんは子供(ども)の時(とき)、どんな子供(ども)だったの？

B: そう（だ）ね。とても元気(げん)だったけど、よくなく子供(ども)だったんだ／だったの。

子供(ども)の時(とき)の上田さん *Ms. Ueda as a child*

道子(みち)さんはたんすの上のしゃしんを見ています。

道子(みち)： あら、これ、アリス？

上田： ええ、そうよ。

道子(みち)： かわいい。何さい？

上田： そうね。それは、七さいの誕生(たんじょう)日の時(とき)にとったしゃしんなの。

道子(みち)： そう、アリスはどんな子供(ども)だったの？

上田： そうね。父や母によると、明(あか)るくて元(げん)気な子供(ども)だったそうよ。

道子(みち)： へえ、そうなんだ。

上田： ええ、スポーツが好きだったから、いつもそとであそんでた。

道子(みち)： そうなの。

上田： で、道(みち)子はどんな子供(ども)だったの？

道子(みち)： そうね。私も小さい時(とき)は、よくうみにあそびに行ったり、山にハイキングに行ったりしてたから、けっこうかっぱつだったかな。けど、中学や高校の時(とき)は、いつもべんきょうしてた。

上田： そうか。日本はじゅけんがあるからね。

道子(みち)： え、ないの、アメリカじゃ。

上田： SAT や ACT はあるけど、じゅけんはないのよ。だから、じゅけんべんきょうもしたこと、ないの。

道子(みち)： そう。いいなあ。

上田： だから、高校の時(とき)は、よくパーティに行ったり、友達(だち)とえいがを見たりしたんだ。

道子(みち)： いいなあ。私もアメリカの学校に行きたかった。

上田： でも、大学はアメリカの方がずっと大変(へん)だよ。

道子(みち)： あ、そうか。じゃあ、おなじことね。

Dialogue Phrase Notes

- けっこう means *quite* and かっぱつ means *active.*
- ないの、アメリカじゃ。This is an inverted formation of アメリカじゃないの , but it does not mean *it is not America*. In this sentence, じゃない is not the negative form of だ. Instead, it consists of じゃ and ない. じゃ is a contraction of では, where で refers to the place of action and は is a topic marker. ない is the negative form of ある. Therefore the sentence means: *Don't they have that* (i.e. entrance exams) *in the U.S.?*
- じゅけん means" entrance examination."
- 私もアメリカの学校に行きたかった。 Literally, *I wanted to go to a U.S. school*, and in this context, it means *I wish I had gone to a U.S. school.*
- おなじ means *same*, and おなじこと means *the same thing.*

ダイアローグの後で(あと)

Complete the chart with information about Ms. Ueda's and Michiko's childhoods.

	どんな子供(ども)でしたか。	よくどんなことをしましたか。
アリス		
道子(みち)		

文法(ぶんぽう)

I. Talking about time using noun/adjective + 時(とき), duration + 前(まえ)／後(ご)

When you want to express a period of time in your life rather than a date, a day of the week, or a specific time, you can create a phrase using 時(とき) (*when*), 前(まえ) (*before*) or 後(ご) (*after*). Grammatically these are nouns, so they can be modified by a noun, adjective, or clauselike noun modification. This chapter introduces 時(とき) with respect to nouns and adjectives and 前(まえ)／後(ご) in relation to counterexpressions.

A. Noun/adjectives + 時(とき) (*when, at the time of*～)

時(とき) can be modified by a noun in the form of noun の noun (時(とき)) or adjective + noun. The particle に for a time expression can be used with ～時(とき).

子供(こども)の時(とき)	*When I was a child*
小学校の時(とき)	*When I was in elementary school*
十一さいの時(とき)	*When I was eleven*
ひまな時(とき)	*When I have free time*
いやな時(とき)	*When I am annoyed*
元気(げんき)な時(とき)	*When I am healthy*
いそがしい時(とき)	*When I am busy*
寒い時(とき)	*When I am cold*
小さい時(とき)	*When I was small*

The negative ending ない is grammatically an い-adjective, so it can be combined with 時(とき) just like other い-adjectives.

病気(びょうき)じゃない時(とき)	*When I am not sick*
ひまじゃない時(とき)	*When I do not have free time*
いそがしくない時(とき)	*When I am not busy*

ウィル：いつアメリカに来たんですか。
When did you come to the United States?

あつ子(こ)：高校の時(とき)に来ました。
It was when I was in high school.

キム： ひまな時(とき)はよくいぬのさんぽをします。
I often walk my dog when I am free.

スミス： そうですか。どんないぬですか。
I see. What kind of dog do you have?

B. Duration + 前(まえ)／後(ご)

Duration + 前(まえ) indicates *ago* or *before*; it is used with the particle of time, に.

三年前(まえ)に日本に行きました。 *I went to Japan three years ago.*
一か月前(まえ)にけっこんしました。 *I got married a month ago.*

Duration + 後(ご) indicates *later* or *after*, and it can be used with に.

三日(みっか)後(ご)に会いましょう。 *I will see you three days from now.*
一年後(ご)に日本に行きました。 *I went to Japan a year later.*

ジョン： ホンコンへはいつ行ったの？
When did you go to Hong Kong?

ひろし： 二か月ぐらい前(まえ)。
About two months ago.

ジョン： どうだった？
How was it?

ひろし： おもしろかったけど、ちょっと暑くて大変(へん)だった。
It was fun, but it was a bit too hot and that was hard to take.

ジョン： 今度はいつ行くの。
When are you going again?

ひろし： 半年(はんとし)後(ご)だと思(おも)う。
I think it will be six months from now.

ジョン： そうか。いいなあ。
I see. That is nice.

Note

- ぐらい can be used with 前(まえ) and 後(ご). It is used right after the duration and before 前(まえ) or 後(ご). When ぐらい used with 後(ご), the pronunciation of the **kanji** 後 becomes あと.

その人に四日(よっか)ぐらい前(まえ)に会った。 *I met the person about four days ago.*
その人に一年ぐらい後(あと)に会った。 *I met the person about a year later.*

話してみましょう

Activity 1

Answer the following questions using 〜 時(とき).

Example: どんな時(とき)にセーターをきますか。
寒い時(とき)にきます。

1. どんな時(とき)に家でゆっくりしますか。
2. どんな時(とき)になきますか。
3. どんな時(とき)に友達(だち)にメールを書きますか。
4. どんな時(とき)は時間がありませんか。
5. どんな時(とき)にびょういんへ行きますか。

Activity 2

Work with a partner. Ask what he/she does on the occasions listed below.

Example: A: ひまな時(とき)に何をしますか。
B: 家でテレビを見ます。
A: 〜さんはひまな時(とき)に何をしますか。
B: たいてい友達(だち)と電(でん)話で話します。

	すること
ひまな時(とき)	
暑い時(とき)	
寒い時(とき)	
うれしい時(とき)	
かなしい時(とき)	
さびしい時(とき)	

Activity 3

Work with a partner. Your partner is a psychic. Ask him/her about your future.

Example: A: 私はこれから何をするでしょうか。

B: 二か月後(ご)に、だれかを好きになるでしょう。

そして、半年後(はんとしご)にけっこんするでしょう。

Activity 4

Work with a partner. Ask your partner about places where he/she visited in the past six months and for how long.

Example: A: どんなところに行きましたか。

B: シカゴに行きました。

A: そうですか。いいですね。いつ行ったんですか。

B: 三週間前(まえ)です。

A: そうですか。何日ぐらいシカゴにいましたか。

B: えーと、二日(ふつか)いました。

どこ	いつ	どのくらい

II. Talking about past experiences using ～たことがある; listing representative activities using ～たり～たりする

The plain past affirmative form ～た can be used in various structures in Japanese. This chapter introduce two commonly used structures, namely ～たことがある and ～たり～たりする.

A. Talking about past experiences using ～たことがある

The construction ～たことがある is used to express an experience one has had in the past. In contrast, ～ました simply expresses a past action. The absence of any experience is expressed by ～たことが／はない.

私はミュージカルを見たことがあります。
I have seen a musical.

私はミュージカルを見たことがありません。
I have never seen a musical.

私はミュージカルを見ました。
I saw a musical.

私はミュージカルを見ませんでした。
I did not see a musical.

The construction ～たことがある is usually used to talk about experiences in the not-so-recent past, not about things as recent as 昨日(きのう) or 一昨日(おととい).

二年前(まえ)、中国(ごく)に行ったことがあります。
I had the experience of going to China two years ago.

一昨日(おととい)、中国(ごく)に行きました。
I went to China the day before yesterday.

チョイ：田中さんは英(えい)語が上手ですね。
Mr. Tanaka is good at English, isn't he?

山本：ああ、田中さんは小さい時(とき)、がいこくにすんでいたことがあるそうですよ。
Well, I heard that he lived in a foreign country when he was small.

チョイ：ああ、それで、上手なんですね。
I see, that's why he is so good.

To answer questions using the pattern ～たことがありますか, say either はい、あります or いいえ、ありません。

川口：日本へ行ったことがありますか。
Have you ever been to Japan?

キム：はい、あります／いいえ、ありません。
Yes, I have./No, I haven't.

B. Listing representative activities using ～たり～たりする

The construction ～たり～たりする is used to list representative activities. It is similar to や in Chapter 7, which is used with nouns and noun phrases.

食べたり飲んだりしました。
I ate and drank. (Literally, *I did things like eating and drinking.*)

新聞を読んだり、ざっしを見たりします。
I do things like reading newspapers and browsing through magazines.

新聞やざっしを読みます。
I read things, like newspapers and magazines. (*etc.*)

川口：きょうとに行ったことがありますか。
Have you ever to Kyoto?

ワット：ええ、ありますよ。じつは、先月(せんげつ)行ったんです。
Yes, I have. In fact, I went there last month.

川口：そうなんですか。どうでしたか、きょうとは？
Is that so? How was it?

ワット：とてもたのしかったですよ。おてらやじんじゃを見たり、買いものをしたりしました。
It was really fun. I saw temples and shrines and did some shopping.

キム：子供(こども)の時(とき)、よく何したの？
What kinds of things did you do when you were a child?

一也(かずや)：どうぶつえんに行ったり、ゆうえんちであそんだりしたよ。
I did things like going to the zoo and playing at the amusement park.

話してみましょう

Activity 1

Look at the drawings on the following page and make up questions asking whether someone has ever done these things.

IV. Expressing hearsay using the plain form + そうだ

A construction using the stem of the verb + そうだ was introduced in Chapter 9; it expresses the speaker's conjecture based on a direct observation.

おまつりは　おもしろ　そうだ。　*The festival looks interesting.*
おまつりは　おもしろくなさ　そうだ。　*The festival does not look interesting.*

This chapter introduces a different type of そうだ, which takes the plain form of verbs and adjectives. It expresses hearsay and it means *I heard* or *I have heard.*

おまつりは　おもしろい　そうだ。　*I've heard that the festival is interesting.*
おまつりは　おもしろくない　そうだ。　*I've heard the festival is not interesting.*

In addition to the present form, ～そうだ for hearsay is used with the plain past forms.

おまつりは　おもしろかった　そうだ。　*I've heard that the festival was interesting.*
おまつりは　おもしろくなかった　そうだ。　*I've heard the festival was not interesting.*

Also, ～そうだ in this usage is often used with ～によると (*according to* ～).

スミスさんによると、ハロウィンはアメリカのおまつりだそうだ。
According to Mr. Smith, (I heard that) Halloween is an American festival.

田中さんによると、キムさんは来年けっこんするそうです。
According to Mr. Tanaka, (I heard that) Mr. Kim is getting married next year.

木村(むら)：冬休(ふゆやす)みにハワイ旅行(りょ)に行ったそうですね。
I heard that you went on trip to Hawaii during winter vacation.
リー：ええ、二十三日から五日(いつか)行きました。
Yes. I went there for five days, starting on the 23rd.
木村(むら)：いいですね。私はハワイへは行ったことがないんですよ。
Nice. I've never been to Hawaii.

Note

- It may be difficult to distinguish the そうだ meaning *it looks like* from the そうだ indicating hearsay with い -adjectives, because they can sound very similar. So it is essential to pay attention to pronunciation.

おいしそうですね。	*It looks delicious.*
おいしいそうですね。	*I heard that it is delicious.*

話してみましょう

Activity 1

You heard some things about Ms. Tanaka. Make a sentence that reports what you have heard.

Example: 田中さんは小さい時(とき)よく寝る子供(ども)でした。
田中さんは小さい時(とき)よく寝る子供(ども)だったそうです。

1. 田中さんは大学院(いん)の学生です。
2. 田中さんは中学の時(とき)よく山のぼりをしました。
3. 田中さんはしゃしんをとるのが好きです。
4. 田中さんはがいこくにすんでいたことがあります。
5. 田中さんは先週かぶきを見に行きました。
6. かぶきは少しむずかしかったけど、おもしろかったです。

Activity 2

Work in a group of four or five, and form a line. The instructor tells something to the front member of each team. These members then go back to their respective teams and each person on the team whispers the information to the next person in line. The last person on each team, when they get the information, goes to the board and writes what they heard.

Example: 〜さんから本をもらいました。
先生は〜さんから本をもらったそうです。

2. Write summer and New Year's greeting cards to your friends, following the examples on the previous page.

総合練習 (そうごうれんしゅう)

私はだれですか

1. Work in a group of three or four. First, complete the following paragraph with your own information as in the example. Then, interview each other and write memos about other members of your group.

Example: 私の名(な)前はスーザン・ロスです。私はシカゴから来ました。誕生(たんじょう)日は六月二十五日です。私は子供の時はしずかな子供でした。そして、よく本を読んだり、おんがくを聞いたりしました。それから、一か月に一度ピアノのレッスンに行きました。私はフランスに行ったことがあります。十五さいの時でした。フランスに友達(だち)がいたからです。

私の名(な)前は＿＿＿＿＿＿＿＿＿＿です。私は＿＿＿＿＿＿＿＿＿＿から来ました。誕生(たんじょう)日は＿＿＿＿＿＿＿＿＿です。私は子供の時＿＿＿＿＿＿＿＿＿＿子供でした。そして、＿＿＿＿＿＿＿＿＿＿たり、＿＿＿＿＿＿＿＿＿＿＿＿＿＿＿たりしました。それから、＿＿＿＿＿＿に＿＿＿＿＿＿＿＿＿＿＿＿＿＿＿＿＿＿ました。＿＿＿＿＿＿＿＿＿＿＿＿＿＿＿＿＿＿＿＿＿＿＿＿＿＿ことがあります。＿＿＿＿＿＿＿＿＿＿時でした。＿＿＿＿＿＿＿＿＿＿＿＿＿＿＿＿からです。

Sample interview questions

Q: どこから来ましたか。

Q: 子供の時、どんな子供でしたか。

Q: 子供の時、どんなことをしましたか。

Q: どんなことをしたことがありますか。何さいの時でしたか。
どうしてしたんですか。

APPENDIX C

ADJECTIVE AND COPULA CONJUGATIONS

			い - adjective おおきい (*big*)	な - adjective しずか（な） (*quiet*)	Copula だ / です (*be*)
Plain	Present	Affirmative	おおきい	しずかだ	N だ
		Negative	おおきくない	しずかじゃない	N じゃない
	Past	Affirmative	おおきかった	しずかだった	N だった
		Negative	おおきくなかった	しずかじゃなかった	N じゃなかった
Polite	Present	Affirmative	おおきいです	しずかです	N です
		Negative	おおきくないです / おおきくありません	しずかじゃないです / しずかじゃありません	N じゃないです / N じゃありません
	Past	Affirmative	おおきかったです	しずかでした	N でした
		Negative	おおきくなかったです / おおきくありませんでした	しずかじゃなかったです / しずかじゃありませんでした	N じゃなかったです / N じゃありませんでした
		Prenominal	おおきい（だいがく）	しずかな（ひと）	N の
		Conditional	おおきければ	しずかなら / しずかだったら	N なら /N だったら
		て - form	おおきくて	しずかで	N で
Adverbial			おおきく	しずかに	N/A

APPENDIX D

COUNTERS AND TIME EXPRESSIONS

Common Counters				
	General Counter 〜つ	People 〜にん	Bound Objects (book, magazine, etc.) 〜さつ	Cylindrical Objects (pen, umbrella, etc.) 〜ほん
1	ひとつ	ひとり	いっさつ	いっぽん
2	ふたつ	ふたり	にさつ	にほん
3	みっつ	さんにん	さんさつ	さんぼん
4	よっつ	よにん	よんさつ	よんほん
5	いつつ	ごにん	ごさつ	ごほん
6	むっつ	ろくにん	ろくさつ	ろっぽん
7	ななつ	しちにん	ななさつ	ななほん
8	やっつ	はちにん	はっさつ	はっぽん
9	ここのつ	きゅうにん / くにん	きゅうさつ	きゅうほん
10	とお	じゅうにん	じゅっさつ / じっさつ	じゅっぽん / じっぽん
11	じゅういち	じゅういちにん	じゅういっさつ	じゅういっぽん
12	じゅうに	じゅうににん	じゅうにさつ	じゅうにほん
	いくつ	なんにん	なんさつ	なんぼん

Specific Time				
	Month ～がつ	Day ～にち	Time (o'clock) ～じ	Time (minute) ～ふん
1	いちがつ	ついたち	いちじ	いっぷん
2	にがつ	ふつか	にじ	にふん
3	さんがつ	みっか	さんじ	さんぷん
4	しがつ	よっか	よじ	よんぷん / よんふん
5	ごがつ	いつか	ごじ	ごふん
6	ろくがつ	むいか	ろくじ	ろっぷん
7	しちがつ	なのか	しちじ	ななふん / しちふん
8	はちがつ	ようか	はちじ	はっぷん / はちふん
9	くがつ	ここのか	くじ	きゅうふん
10	じゅうがつ	とおか	じゅうじ	じゅっぷん / じっぷん
11	じゅういちがつ	じゅういちにち	じゅういちじ	じゅういっぷん
12	じゅうにがつ	じゅうににち	じゅうにじ	じゅうにふん
14		じゅうよっか		
20		はつか		にじゅっぷん / にじっぷん
24		にじゅうよっか		

	Extent				
	Year 〜ねん	Month 〜かげつ	Week 〜しゅうかん	Day 〜にち	Hour 〜じかん
1	いちねん	いっかげつ	いっしゅうかん	いちにち	いちじかん
2	にねん	にかげつ	にしゅうかん	ふつか（かん）	にじかん
3	さんねん	さんかげつ	さんしゅうかん	みっか（かん）	さんじかん
4	よねん	よんかげつ	よんしゅうかん	よっか（かん）	よじかん
5	ごねん	ごかげつ	ごしゅうかん	いつか（かん）	ごじかん
6	ろくねん	ろっかげつ	ろくしゅうかん	むいか（かん）	ろくじかん
7	しちねん ななねん	ななかげつ	ななしゅうかん	なのか（かん）	しちじかん
8	はちねん	はちかげつ / はっかげつ	はっしゅうかん	ようか（かん）	はちじかん
9	きゅうねん / くねん	きゅうかげつ	きゅうしゅうかん	ここのか（かん）	くじかん
10	じゅうねん	じゅっかげつ / じっかげつ	じゅっしゅうかん / じっしゅうかん	とおか（かん）	じゅうじかん
11	じゅういちねん	じゅういっかげつ	じゅういっしゅうかん	じゅういちにち（かん）	じゅういちじかん
12	じゅうにねん	じゅうにかげつ	じゅうにしゅうかん	じゅうににち（かん）	じゅうにじかん
14				じゅうよっか（かん）	
20				はつか（かん）	
24				にじゅうよっか（かん）	

APPENDIX E

DEMONSTRATIVE WORDS（こそあど）

	こ series	そ series	あ series	ど series
	Close to both speaker and listener	Closer to listener than to speaker; moderately far away from both	Away from both speaker and listener	Interrogative
Adjective	この～ (*this* ～)	その～ (*that* ～)	あの～ (*that* ～)	どの～ (*which* ～)
Pronoun	これ (*this thing*)	それ (*that thing*)	あれ (*that thing*)	どれ (*which thing*)
Location	ここ (*this place*)	そこ (*that place*)	あそこ (*that place*)	どこ (*where*)
Direction	こちら (*this way*)*	そちら (*that way*)	あちら (*that way*)	どちら (*which way*)
Manner	こう (*this way*)	そう (*that way*)	ああ (*that way*)	どう (*how*)

* こちら can be used for "this person" (polite)

APPENDIX F

KANJI LIST

No.	Kanji	Ch.	Kun-reading	On-reading	Examples
1	大	4	おお（きい）	ダイ	大学／大きい／大学院／大学院生 だいがく　おお　だいがくいん　だいがくいんせい
2	学	4	まな（ぶ）	ガク・ガッ	学生／学校／～学 がくせい　がっこう　がく
3	校	4		コウ	学校／高校 がっこう　こうこう
4	先	4	さき	セン	先生／先週 せんせい　せんしゅう
5	生	4	なま・う（まれる）	セイ	学生／先生／一年生／留学生／生活 がくせい　せんせい　いちねんせい　りゅうがくせい　せいかつ
6	山	5	やま	サン・ザン	山田さん／富士山／山の上 やまだ　ふじさん　やま　うえ
7	川	5	かわ・がわ	セン	小川さん／川中さん／ミシシッピ川 おがわ　かわなか　がわ
8	田	5	た・だ	デン	上田さん／田中さん うえだ　たなか
9	人	5	ひと	ジン・ニン	日本人／あの人 にほんじん　ひと
10	上	5	うえ・かみ	ジョウ	テーブルの上 うえ
11	中	5	なか	チュウ	へやの中／中国 なか　ちゅうごく
12	下	5	した・くだ（さい）	カ・ゲ	まどの下／いって下さい した　くだ
13	小	5	ちい（さい）	ショウ	小さいへや／小学生 ちい　しょう
14	日	5	ひ・び	ニチ・ニ・ジツ・カ	日本／昨日／今日／明日 にほん　きのう　きょう　あした
15	本	5	もと	ホン・ボン・ポン	山田さんの本／日本／山本さん やまだ　ほん　にほん　やまもと
16	今	6	いま	コン	今、何時ですか。／今週／今日 いま　なんじ　こんしゅう　きょう
17	私	6	わたし・わたくし	シ	私は日本人です。 わたし
18	月	6	つき	ゲツ・ガツ	月曜日／四月／毎月 げつようび　しがつ　まいつき

No.	Kanji	Ch.	Kun-reading	On-reading	Examples
19	火	6	ひ	カ	火曜日（かようび）
20	水	6	みず	スイ	水曜日（すいようび）
21	木	6	き	モク	木曜日（もくようび）
22	金	6	かね	キン	金曜日（きんようび）
23	土	6	つち	ト・ド	土曜日（どようび）
24	曜	6		ヨウ	日曜日（にちようび）
25	何	6	なに・なん		何曜日（なんようび）／何（なん）ですか。／何時（なんじ）ですか。
26	週	6		シュウ	今週（こんしゅう）の週末（しゅうまつ）／先週（せんしゅう）
27	末	6	すえ	マツ	週末（しゅうまつ）
28	休	6	やす（む）	キュウ	休（やす）みの日（ひ）
29	時	7	とき	ジ	一時（いちじ）／二時半（にじはん）／五時間（ごじかん）べんきょうします。／その時（とき）
30	間	7	あいだ	カン	時間（じかん）がありません。
31	分	7	わ（ける）・わ（かる）	フン・ブン・プン	二十分（にじゅっぷん）／分（わ）かりました。
32	半	7		ハン	毎日六時半（まいにちろくじはん）におきます。
33	毎	7		マイ	毎週（まいしゅう）シカゴにいきます。／毎日（まいにち）／毎月（まいつき）
34	年	7	とし	ネン	三年生（さんねんせい）／毎年（まいとし）
35	好	7	す（き）	コウ	テニスが好（す）きです。
36	語	7	かた（る）	ゴ	日本語（ご）／フランス語（ご）ではなします。
37	高	7	たか（い）	コウ	古（ふる）い高校（こうこう）／高（たか）い山
38	番	7		バン	やさいが一番（いちばん）好きです。
39	方	7	かた	ホウ	サッカーの方（ほう）がフットボールより好（す）きです。
40	新	7	あたら（しい）	シン	新（あたら）しいレストラン
41	古	7	ふる（い）	コ	カラオケで古（ふる）いうたをうたいます。

No.	Kanji	Ch.	Kun-reading	On-reading	Examples
42	安	7	やす（い）	アン	今日はやさいが安(やす)いです。
43	友	7	とも	ユウ	友達(ともだち)とかいものにいくのが好(す)きです。
44	一	8	ひと（つ）	イチ	一(ひと)つ／一本(いっぽん)／もう一度(いちど)いって下さい。
45	二	8	ふた（つ）	ニ	りんごが二(ふた)つあります。／二(に)さつ／二本(にほん)
46	三	8	みっ（つ）	サン	けしゴムを三(みっ)つかいました。／三本(さんぼん)
47	四	8	よ・よん・よっ（つ）	シ	四(よっ)つ／四時(よじ)／ビールが四本(よんほん)あります。
48	五	8	いつ（つ）	ゴ	五(いつ)つ／ベルトが五本(ごほん)あります。
49	六	8	むっ（つ）	ロク・ロッ	六(むっ)つ／六時(ろくじ)／えんぴつが六本(ろっぽん)あります。
50	七	8	なな（つ）	シチ	七時(しちじ)／七本(ななほん)／オレンジが七(なな)つあります。
51	八	8	やっ（つ）	ハチ・ハッ	八(やっ)つ／八時(はちじ)／ペンが八本(はっぽん)あります。
52	九	8	ここの（つ）	キュウ・ク	九(ここの)つ／九時(くじ)／バナナが九本(きゅうほん)あります。
53	十	8	とお	ジュウ・ジュッ	靴下(くつした)が十(とお)あります。／十本(じゅっぽん)／十時(じゅうじ)
54	百	8		ヒャク・ビャク・ピャク	二百(にひゃく)／三百(さんびゃく)／六百(ろっぴゃく)
55	千	8		セン・ゼン	二千(にせん)／三千(さんぜん)／八千(はっせん)／千円(せんえん)
56	万	8		マン	一万円(いちまんえん)／百万円(ひゃくまんえん)
57	円	8		エン	五十円(ごじゅうえん)／このセーターは 7,800 円(えん)です。
58	店	8	みせ	テン	大きい店(みせ)／店(みせ)の人(ひと)／喫茶店(きっさてん)
59	行	9	い（く）	コウ	来年(らいねん)日本に行(い)きます。
60	来	9	く（る）	ライ	いつアメリカに来(き)ますか。／来週(らいしゅう)は来(こ)ない。
61	帰	9	かえ（る）	キ	たいてい七時(しちじ)にうちに帰(かえ)ります。
62	食	9	た（べる）	ショク	あさごはんを食(た)べて下さい。／学食(がくしょく)
63	飲	9	の（む）	イン	ビールを二本飲(の)みました。

No.	Kanji	Ch.	Kun-reading	On-reading	Examples
64	見	9	み（る）	ケン	えいがを見(み)に行(い)きませんか。
65	聞	9	き（く）	ブン	インターネットでラジオを聞(き)く。／新聞(しんぶん)
66	読	9	よ（む）	ドク	本を読(よ)むのが好きです。
67	書	9	か（く）	ショ	手紙(てがみ)をあまり書(か)きません。
68	話	9	はな（す）	ワ	友達(だち)と日本語で話(はな)すのが好きです。
69	出	9	で（る）・で（かける）・だ（す）	シュッ	銀座(ぎんざ)に出(で)かけます。
70	会	9	あ（う）	カイ	人と会(あ)って、カフェで話(はなし)をします。
71	買	9	か（う）	バイ	買(か)い物(もの)が好きです。
72	起	9	お（きる）	キ	毎朝(まいあさ)六時に起(お)きます。
73	寝	9	ね（る）	シン	十二時ごろ寝(ね)ます。
74	作	9	つく（る）	サク	ばんごはんはカレーを作(つく)りましょう。
75	入	9	はい（る）・い（れる）	ニュウ	はこに入(い)れます。／店に入(はい)ります。
76	男	10	おとこ	ダン	女(おんな)の人と男(おとこ)の子(こ)がいます。
77	女	10	おんな	ジョ	山本さんは帽子(ぼうし)をかぶった女(おんな)の人です。
78	目	10	め	モク	目(め)がわるいです。／上から二番目(め)です。
79	口	10	くち・ぐち	コウ	口(くち)が小さいです。／川口(かわぐち)
80	耳	10	みみ	ジ	私は耳(みみ)があまりよくありません。
81	足	10	あし	ソク	ジョンはせが高くて、足(あし)がながいです。
82	手	10	て	シュ	手(て)がきれいですね。／テニスが上手(じょうず)です。
83	父	10	ちち・とう	フ	父(ちち)のなまえはジョンです。／お父(とう)さん
84	母	10	はは・かあ	ボ	母(はは)のしごとは高校の先生です。／お母(かあ)さん
85	姉	10	あね・ねえ	シ	姉(あね)は私より三さい上です。／お姉(ねえ)さん

No.	Kanji	Ch.	Kun-reading	On-reading	Examples
86	兄	10	あに・にい	ケイ・キョウ	兄(あに)が一人います。／お兄(にい)さん／兄弟(きょうだい)
87	妹	10	いもうと	マイ	妹(いもうと)はいません。
88	弟	10	おとうと	ダイ	弟(おとうと)はアルバイトにいきます。／兄弟(きょうだい)
89	家	10	いえ・うち	カ	父(ちち)は七時ごろ家(うち)に帰ります。
90	族	10		ゾク	私の家(うち)は四人家族(かぞく)です。
91	両	10		リョウ	両親(りょうしん)はニューヨークにすんでいます。
92	親	10	おや	シン	両親(りょうしん)はアメリカが好きです。／親切(しんせつ)な人
93	子	10	こ	シ	男(おとこ)の子(こ)が三人います。／母(はは)のなまえは「よし子(こ)」です。
94	天	11		テン	明日(あした)の天気(てんき)はいいでしょう。
95	気	11		キ	昨日(きのう)は天気(てんき)がよくありませんでした。
96	雨	11	あめ	ウ	雨(あめ)がしずかにふっています。
97	雪	11	ゆき	セツ	明日(あした)は大雪(おおゆき)です。
98	風	11	かぜ	フウ	風(かぜ)がつよいです。／台風(たいふう)が来ます。
99	晴	11	は（れる）	セイ	ずっと晴(は)れていて、雨(あめ)がふりません。
100	温	11	あたた（かい）	オン	先週は気温(きおん)が３５度(ど)まで上(あ)がりました。
101	度	11		ド	おふろの温度(おんど)は４２度(ど)ぐらいです。
102	東	11	ひがし	トウ	まちの東(ひがし)の方にこうえんがあります。
103	西	11	にし	セイ	きょうとは東京(とうきょう)の西(にし)にあります。
104	南	11	みなみ	ナン	南(みなみ)のうみはとてもきれいで温(あたた)かいです。
105	北	11	きた	ホク	ほっかいどうは日本の北(きた)にあります。
106	寒	11	さむ（い）	カン	カナダのふゆは寒(さむ)いです。
107	暑	11	あつ（い）	ショ	東京(とうきょう)のなつはむし暑(あつ)いです。

No.	Kanji	Ch.	Kun-reading	On-reading	Examples
108	多	11	おお（い）	タ	シンガポールは雨(あめ)が多(おお)いです。
109	少	11	すく（ない）・すこ（し）	ショウ	このまちは人が少(すく)ないです。
110	冷	11	つめ（たい）	レイ	暑(あつ)いから冷(つめ)たいものを飲みましょう。
111	春	12	はる	シュン	春(はる)は雨が多いです。
112	夏	12	なつ	カ	日本の夏(なつ)は暑いです。
113	秋	12	あき	シュウ	秋(あき)の山はとてもきれいです。
114	冬	12	ふゆ	トウ	冬(ふゆ)は寒いから、時々(ときどき)雪がふります。
115	朝	12	あさ	チョウ	日曜日の朝(あさ)、おそくまで寝るのが好きです。
116	昼	12	ひる	チュウ	母が昼御飯(ひるごはん)を作りました。
117	晩	12		バン	明日の晩御飯(ばんごはん)は天ぷらです。
118	午	12		ゴ	月曜日の午後(ごご)、両親と家族が来ます。／午前(ごぜん)
119	前	12	まえ	ゼン	午前(ごぜん)中にしゅくだいをします。／中学の前(まえ)／名前(なまえ)
120	後	12	あと・のち・うし（ろ）	ゴ	午後(ごご)は暑かったです。／一か月ぐらい後(あと)／つくえの後(うし)ろ
121	去	12	さ（る）	キョ	去年(きょねん)南アメリカに行きました。
122	昨	12		サク	一昨年(おととし)日本に行きました。／昨日(きのう)
123	供	12	とも・ども	キョウ	子供(ども)が二人います。
124	元	12	もと	ゲン	父は元気(げんき)です。
125	思	12	おも（う）	シ	昨日(きのう)の朝(あさ)は風がつよかったと思(おも)います。
126	明	12	あか（るい）	メイ	明(あか)るいへや／明日(あした)
127	回	12	まわ（る）	カイ	私の弟は一か月に十回(かい)ぐらいラーメンを食べます。

JAPANESE-ENGLISH GLOSSARY

This glossary contains all Japanese words that appear in the chapter vocbulary lists. They are listed according to **gojuuon-jun** (Japanese alphabetical order). Each entry follows this format: word written in kana, word written in kanji (if appropriate), part of speech, English meaning, and the number of the chapter where it first appears. Note that some words may be supplementary vocabulary, and not appear in the chapter's main list. In general, abbreviations and labels are as used in each chapter's list. When verbs are listed in the polite form, the English translation "to" is in parentheses, "(to)~." This is not done when verbs are listed in dictionary form.

adv.	adverb	*conj.*	conjunction	*q. word*	question word
い*-adj.*	い-adjective	*inter.*	interjection	*pref.*	prefix
な*-adj.*	な-adjective	*count.*	counter	*suf.*	suffix
う*-v.*	う-verb	*n.*	noun	*part.*	particle
る*-v.*	る-verb	*exp.*	expression	*cop. v.*	copula verb
irr. v.	irregular verb	*demo.*	demonstrative	*number*	number
aux.v.	auxiliary verb	*loc.n.*	location noun		

あ

アイスクリーム *n.* ice cream, 9
あいます (会います) う*-v.* (to) meet (dictionary form is あう), 6
あおい (青い) い*-adj.* blue, 4
あかい (赤い) い*-adj.* red, 4
あがってください。(上がって下さい。) *exp.* Please come in., 5
あがる (上がる) う*-v.* to rise; to go up, 11
あかるい (明るい) い*-adj.* bright, 5
あかるい (明るい) い*-adj.* cheerful, 10
あき (秋) *n.* fall, autumn, 11
アクセサリー *n.* accessories, 8
アクセサリーうりば (アクセサリー売り場) *n.* accessory department/section, 8
あけましておめでとうございます。(明けましておめでとうございます。) *exp.* Happy New Year, 12
あさ (朝) *n.* morning, 3
あさごはん (朝御飯) *n.* breakfast, 3
あさって (明後日) *n.* the day after tomorrow, 3
あし (足) *n.* leg, foot, 10
アジアけんきゅう (アジア研究) *n.* Asian studies, 2
あした (明日) *n.* tomorrow, 3
あそこ *demo.* over there, that place (far away from both speaker and listener), 4
あそびます (遊びます) う*-v.* (to) play (dictionary form is あそぶ), 6
あたたかい (暖かい) い*-adj.* warm (air temperature), 11
あたたかい (温かい) い*-adj.* warm (object temperature, mood, etc.), 9
あたま (頭) *n.* head, あたまがいい smart, intelligent, 10
あたらしい (新しい) い*-adj.* new, 4
あつい (暑い) い*-adj.* hot (air temperature), 11
あつい (熱い) い*-adj.* hot (object temperature, mood, etc.), 9

あに（兄） *n.* older brother (the speaker's), 10
あね（姉） *n.* older sister (the speaker's), 10
あの *demo.* that [+ noun] over there, 5
あのう *inter.* uh, well... 2
アパート *n.* apartment, 4
あびます（浴びます） る-*v.* (to) take (a shower) (dictionary form is あびる), 3
　シャワーをあびます (to) take a shower.
あぶら（油 oil/ 脂 fat） *n.* fat, oil あぶらがおおい fatty, oily, 9
あまい（甘い） い-*adj.* sweet, 9
あまり *adv.* not very often (used with negative verb forms), 3
あめ（雨） *n.* rain, 11
アメリカ *n.* America, the United States, 2
ありがとう　ございます。 *exp.* Thank you., 1
あります う-*v.* (to) be held, (to) have (dictionary form is ある), 3
あるいて（歩いて） *exp.* on foot , 5
あるきます（歩きます） う-*v.* (to) walk (dictionary form is あるく)., 6
アルバイト *n.* part-time job (バイト can be used in casual speech), 6
あれ *demo.* that object over there, that, 4
あれは　にほんごで　なんと　いいますか。 *exp.* How do you say that (over there) in Japanese?, 1

い

いい い-*adj.* good, 4
いいえ *inter.* no, don't mention it, you're welcome, 2
いいえ、そうじゃありません／そうじゃないです。 *exp.* No, that's not so., 2
いいえ、そんなことはありません。 *exp.* No, that's not the case., 10
いいえ、どうぞおかまいなく。 *exp.* Please do not bother/worry about it., 9
いいえ、まだまだです。 *exp.* No, I still have a long way to go., 10
いいえ、わかりません。*exp.* No, I don't understand (it)., 1
いいます（言います） う-*v.* (to) say (dictionary form is いう), 6
いかが *q. word* how (polite form of どう), 8
いきます（行きます） う-*v.* (to) go (dictionary form is いく), 3
イギリス *n.* England, 2
いくつ *q. word* how many, 8
いくつ *q. word* How old ～？おいくつ polite form of いくつ, 10
いくら *q. word* how much (money), 8
いす（椅子） *n.* chair, 5
いそがしい（忙しい） い-*adj.* busy, 6
イタリア *n.* Italy, 9
いち（一） *number* one, 3
いちじ（一時） *time exp.* one o'clock, 2
いちねんせい（一年生） *n.* freshman, first-year student (the suffix せい may be dropped), 2
いつ *q. word* when, 3
いっしょに（一緒に） *adv.* together, 6
いって ください。 *exp.* Please say ~. / Repeat after me., 1
いつも *adv.* always, 3
いぬ（犬） *n.* dog, 5

いま (今) *n.* now, 2
います る-*v.* (to) be, (to) exist (used for animate beings) (dictionary form is いる), 4
いもうと (妹) *n.* younger sister (the speaker's), 10
いもうとさん (妹さん) *n.* younger sister (someone else's), 10
いや (な) (嫌 (な)) な -*adj.* unpleasant, yuck, 11
イヤリング *n.* earring, 8
いらっしゃい。 *exp.* Welcome! Come in., 5
いらっしゃいませ。 *exp.* Welcome, 8
いる (要る) う -*v.* to need something, 9
いれる (入れる) る -*v.* to put, 8

う

うえ (上) *loc. n.* on, above, over, 5
うしろ (後ろ) *loc. n.* behind, in back of, 5
うた (歌) *n.* song, 7
うたう (歌う) う -*v.* to sing, 7
うち (家) *n.* home, 3
うでどけい (腕時計) *n.* wristwatch, 8
うどん *n.* Japanese wheat noodles, 9
うみ (海) *n.* ocean, sea, 12
うりば (売り場) *n.* department, section (of a store), 8
うれしい (嬉しい) い -*adj.* happy, 6
うんどう (運動) *n.* (physical) exercises うんどう (を) します (to) exercise, 6

え

え (絵) *n.* picture, 5
えいが (映画) *n.* movie, 3
えいご (英語) *n.* English, 2
ええ *inter.* yes, 2
ええ、そうです。 *exp.* Yes, that's so., 2
えーと *exp.* Well, Let's see. . . , 12
えき (駅) *n.* (train) station, 4
〜えん (〜円) *count.* Yen, counter for Japanese currency, 8
えんぴつ (鉛筆) *n.* pencil, 4

お

お (御) 〜 *pref.* polite prefix おなまえ polite form of なまえ (name), 2
おいしい い -*adj.* delicious, good, tasty, 7
おおい (多い) い -*adj.* a lot, much, 9
おおきい (大きい) い -*adj.* big, 4
おおきい こえで いってください。*exp.* Please speak loudly. (instructor request), 1
おおきい こえで おねがいします。*exp.* Please speak loudly. (student request), 1
オーストラリア *n.* Australia, 2
おかあさん (お母さん) *n.* mother (someone else's), 10
おきます (起きます) る -*v.* (to) get up, (to) wake up (dictionary form is おきる), 3
おきゃくさん (お客さん) *n.* customer, guest, 8

おくさん（奥さん） *n.* wife (someone else's), 10
おこさん（お子さん） *n.* child (someone else's), 10
おじいさん（お祖父さん） *n.* grandfather (someone else's), 10
おしいれ（押し入れ） *n.* Japanese-style closet, storage space, 5
おじゃまします。（お邪魔します。） *exp.* Thank you. (literally, *I will intrude on you*) (said before going inside someone's house or apartment), 5
おちゃ（お茶） *n.* tea, green tea, 7
おとうさん（お父さん） *n.* father (someone else's), 10
おとうと（弟） *n.* younger brother (the speaker's), 10
おとうとさん（弟さん） *n.* younger brother (someone else's), 10
おとこ（男） *n.* male, おとこの人 man, 10
おととい（一昨日） *n.* the day before yesterday, 3
おととし（一昨年） *n.* the year before last, 12
おにいさん（お兄さん） *n.* older brother (someone else's), 10
おねえさん（お姉さん） *n.* older sister (someone else's), 10
おばあさん（お祖母さん） *n.* grandmother (someone else's), 10
おはよう。 *exp.* Good morning. / Hello. (casual), 1
おはようございます。 *exp.* Good morning. / Hello. (polite), 1
おふろ（お風呂） *n.* bath, 3
おもいで（思い出） *n.* memories, 12
おもう（思う） う*-v.* to think, 10
おもしろい（面白い） い*-adj.* interesting, 6
およぎます（泳ぎます） う*-v.* (to) swim (dictionary form is およぐ), 6
オレンジ *n.* orange, 7
おわる（終わる） う*-v.* (for something) to end, 7
おんがく（音楽） *n.* music, 6
おんど（温度） *n.* temperature, 11
おんな（女） *n.* female (human) おんなの人 woman, 10

か

か *part.* question marker, 2
～かい（～階） *count.* counter for floors of a building, 8
～かい（～回） *suf.* times, 12
がいこく（外国） *n.* foreign countries, 12
かいしゃいん（会社員） *n.* businessperson, 10
かいて ください。 *exp.* Please write., 1
かいもの（買い物） *n.* shopping かいもの（を）します (to) go shopping, 6
かえります（帰ります） う*-v.* (to) return, (to) go home (dictionary form is かえる), 3
かう（買う） う*-v.* to buy, 8
かお（顔） *n.* face, 10
かかります う*-v.* (to) take (time), it costs (dictionary form is かかる), 5
かきます（書きます） う*-v.* (to) write (dictionary form is かく), 6
がくしょく（学食） *n.* school cafeteria (a shortened form of 学生しょくどう), 5
がくせい（学生） *n.* student, 2
がくせいかいかん（学生会館） *n.* student union, 5
～かげつ（～か月） *suf.* counter for months, 12

かけます る-*v.* (to) make (a phone call) (dictionary form is かける) でんわをかけます, 6
かける る-*v.* to put on (glasses), 10
かさ(傘) *n.* umbrella, 8
かぜ(風) *n.* wind, 11
かぞく(家族) *n.* family, speaker's family, 10
〜かた(〜方) *suf.* person (polite form of 人) いいかた (nice person), 10
かたい(固い) い-*adj.* hard, tough, 9
〜がつ(〜月) *suf.* month, 11
がっき(学期) *n.* semester, quarter いちがっき one semester はるがっき spring semester, 12
かっこいい い-*adj.* good-looking, cool, neat, 10
がっこう(学校) *n.* school, 3
かなしい(悲しい) い-*adj.* sad, 6
カナダ *n.* Canada, 2
かばん(鞄) *n.* luggage, bag, 4
カフェ *n.* coffee shop, café (recent term), 4
かぶき(歌舞伎) *n.* kabuki (Japanese traditional performing art), 12
かぶる う-*v.* to put on (on the head, e.g. hat, cap), 10
かみ(髪) *n.* hair, 10
かようび(火曜日) *n.* Tuesday, 3
から *part.* from, 5
〜から きました。 *exp.* came from 〜 (casual), 2
からい(辛い) い-*adj.* spicy, 9
カラオケ *n.* Karaoke, sing-along, 7
カレーライス *n.* Japanese curry and rice dish. An abbreviated form is カレー, 9
カロリー *n.* calorie, 9
かわ(川) *n.* river, 5
かわいい(可愛い) い-*adj.* cute, adorable, 10
かんこく(韓国) *n.* South Korea, 2

き

き(木) *n.* tree, 5
きいて ください。 *exp.* Please listen., 1
きいろい(黄色い) い-*adj.* yellow, 4
きおん(気温) *n.* air temperature, 11
ききます(聞きます) う-*v.* (to) ask, (to) listen to (dictionary form is きく), 6
ききます(聴きます) う-*v.* (to) listen to (dictionary form is きく), 6
きこう(気候) *n.* climate, 11
きせつ(季節) *n.* season, 11
きた(北) *n.* north, 11
きっさてん(喫茶店) *n.* coffee shop (traditional term), 4
きのう(昨日) *n.* yesterday , 3
きます(来ます) *irr. v.* (to) come (dictionary form is くる), 3
きもの(着物) *n.* traditional Japanese clothes, kimono, 12
キャンプ *n.* camping, 12
きゅう(九) *number* nine, 3
きゅう(な)(急(な)) な-*adj.* sudden きゅうに suddenly, 11

ぎゅうにゅう (牛乳) *n.* cow milk, 7
きょう (今日) *n.* today, 3
きょうかい (教会) *n.* church, 12
きょうかしょ (教科書) *n.* textbook, 4
きょうしつ (教室) *n.* classroom, 5
きょうだい (兄弟) *n.* sibling(s), 10
きょねん (去年) *n.* last year, 11
きらい (な)(嫌い (な)) な *-adj.* dislike, hate, 7
きる (着る) る *-v.* to put on (on the upper body, e.g. sweater, shirt, jacket), 10
きれい (な) (綺麗 (な)) な*-adj.* clean, pretty, neat, 4
ぎんこう (銀行) *n.* bank, 4
きんようび (金曜日) *n.* Friday, 3

く

く (九) *number* nine, 3
くじ (九時) *time exp.* nine o'clock, 2
くだもの (果物) *n.* fruit, 7
くち (口) *n.* mouth, 10
くつ (靴) *n.* shoe(s), 8
クッキー *n.* cookie, 9
くつした (靴下) *n.* sock(s), 8
くも (雲) *n.* cloud, 11
くもり (曇り) *n.* cloudy, 11
くもる (曇る) う *-v.* to become cloudy, 11
くらい (暗い) い*-adj.* dark, 5
〜ぐらい／〜くらい *suf.* about 〜 (duration or quantity), 5
クラシック *n.* classical music, 7
クラス *n.* class, 3
クリスマス *n.* Christmas, 12
くるま (車) *n.* car, 5
くろい (黒い) い*-adj.* black, 4

け

けいえいがく (経営学) *n.* management, business administration, 2
けいたい (でんわ) (携帯 (電話)) *n.* cell phone, mobile phone (note スマホ smartphone), 5
ケーキ *n.* cake, 7
ゲーム *n.* game, 6
けさ (今朝) *n.* this morning, 11
けしゴム (消しゴム) *n.* eraser, 4
けっこん (結婚) *n.* marriage, 〜とけっこんする to marry 〜, けっこんしている to be married, 10
げつようび (月曜日) *n.* Monday, 3
けんか *n.* fight, quarrel けんかをする to fight, 12
げんき (な) (元気 (な)) な*-adj.* healthy, cheerful, lively (person), 6

こ

こ (子) *n.* child, おとこのこ boy, おんなのこ girl, 10
〜ご (〜語) *suf.* language にほんご Japanese language, 2
〜ご (〜後) *suf.* from 〜, after 〜 (三年ご three years from now/later), 12
ご〜 (御〜) *pref.* polite prefix ごちゅうもん, 9
ご (五) *number* five, 3
こうえん (公園) *n.* park, 4
こうがく (工学) *n.* engineering, 2
こうこう (高校) *n.* high school, 2
こうちゃ (紅茶) *n.* black tea, 7
コート *n.* coat, 8
こうばん (交番) *n.* police box, 4
コーヒー *n.* coffee, 3
コーラ *n.* cola, 7
ごかぞく (ご家族) *n.* family (someone else's), 10
ごきょうだい (ご兄弟) *n.* sibling(s) (someone else's), 10
こくばん (黒板) *n.* chalkboard, 5
ここ *demo.* here, this place, 4
ごご (午後) *n.* p.m., afternoon, 2
ごじ (五時) *time exp.* five o'clock, 2
ごしゅじん (ご主人) *n.* husband (someone else's), 10
ごぜん (午前) *n.* a.m., morning, 2
こちら *n.* this person, this way (polite), 2
こちらこそ。 *exp.* It is I who should be saying that. Thank you., 2
こと *n.* thing (intangible), 7
ことし (今年) *n.* this year, 11
こども (子供) *n.* child, 10
この *demo.* this [+ noun], 5
このへん (この辺) *n.* this area, 4
ごはん (御飯) *n.* meal, cooked rice, 3
ごめんください。(御免下さい。) *exp.* Excuse me., Is anyone home?, 5
ゴルフ *n.* golf, 7
これ *demo.* this (object), 4
これは にほんごで なんと いいますか。*exp.* How do you say this in Japanese?, 1
〜ごろ *suf.* about 〜 (used only with time expressions), 3
こん〜 (今〜) *pref.* this [time unit] こんしゅう this week, こんばん tonight, 3
こんげつ (今月) *n.* this month, 12
コンサート *n.* concert, 6
こんしゅう (今週) *n.* this week, 3
こんど (今度) *n.* next time, 6
こんにちは。 *exp.* Good afternoon. / Hello., 1
こんばん (今晩) *n.* tonight, 3
こんばんは。 *exp.* Good evening. / Hello., 1
コンビニ *n.* convenience store, 4
コンピュータ *n.* computer, 5

さ

～さい（～歳／才） *suf.* ～ years old, 10
さいきん（最近） *n.* recent, recently, 11
さかな（魚） *n.* fish, 7
さがる（下がる） う*-v.* to fall, to go down, 11
さけ（酒） *n.* rice wine, alcoholic beverage (often with お at the beginning, i.e. おさけ), 7
さしみ（刺身） *n.* sashimi (fillet of fresh raw fish) (usually with お at the beginning, i.e. おさしみ), 9
～さつ（～冊） *count.* counter for bound objects (e.g. books, magazines), 8
ざっし（雑誌） *n.* magazine, 6
さびしい（寂しい） い*-adj.* lonely, 6
さむい（寒い） い*-adj.* cold (air temperature), 11
サラダ *n.* salad, 9
さようなら。／さよなら。 *exp.* Good-bye., 1
～さん *suf.* Mr./Mrs./Miss/Ms. ～, 1
さん（三） *number* three, 3
さんじ（三時） *time exp.* three o'clock, 2
サンドイッチ *n.* sandwich, 9
ざんねん（な）（残念（な）） な*-adj.* sorry, regrettable, 6
さんねんせい（三年生） *n.* junior, third-year student (The suffix せい may be dropped.), 2
さんぽ（散歩） *n.* walk, stroll さんぽ（を）します (to) take a walk, 6

し

し（四） *number* four (also, commonly, よん), 3
～じ（～時） *suf.* ～ o'clock, 2
CD/DVD うりば (CD/DVD 売り場) *n.* CD/DVD department/section, 8
ジーンズ *n.* jeans, 8
しおからい（塩辛い） い*-adj.* salty, 9
しかくい（四角い） い*-adj.* square, 10
～じかん *suf.* （～時間）～ hours, 5
しごと（仕事） *n.* job, work, 6
じしょ（辞書） *n.* dictionary, 4
しずか（な）（静か（な）） な*-adj.* quiet, 5
した（下） *loc. n.* under, beneath, 5
しち（七） *number* seven (less common than なな), 3
しちじ（七時） *time exp.* seven o'clock, 2
しつど（湿度） *n.* humidity, 11
しつもん（質問） *n.* question しつもん（を）します (to) ask a question, 6
しつれいします。 *exp.* Good-bye. / Excuse me., 1
しつれんする（失恋する） *irr.v.* to be disappointed in love, 12
じてんしゃ（自転車） *n.* bicycle, 5
します *irr. v.* (to) do (dictionary form is する), 3
じゃあ、また。 *exp.* See you later. (literally, *Well then, again.*), 1
ジャケット *n.* jacket, 8
しゃしん（写真） *n.* photograph, 5
ジャズ *n.* jazz, 7

シャツ *n.* shirt, 8
シャワー *n.* shower, 3
じゅう（十） *number* ten, 3
じゅういちじ（十一時） *time exp.* eleven o'clock, 2
〜しゅうかん（〜週間） *suf.* (for) 〜 weeks, 12
じゅうじ（十時） *time exp.* ten o'clock, 2
ジュース *n.* juice, 7
じゅうにじ（十二時） *time exp.* twelve o'clock, 2
しゅうまつ（週末） *n.* weekend, 3
じゅぎょう（授業） *n.* class, course, 3
しゅくだい（宿題） *n.* homework, 3
しゅじん（主人） *n.* husband (the speaker's), 10
しゅみ（趣味） *n.* hobby, 7
しょう〜（小〜） *pref.* elementary, 小学生 elementary school student, 小学校 elementary school, 10
しょうがつ（正月） *n.* the New Year (usually with お at the beginning, i.e. おしょうがつ), 12
じょうず（な）（上手（な）） な*-adj.* good at, skillful, 10
ジョギング *n.* jogging, 6
しょくじ（食事） *n.* dining, しょくじする to dine, 7
しょくひん（食品） *n.* food, 8
しょくひんうりば（食品売り場） *n.* foodstuffs department/section, food court, 8
しょっぱい い*-adj.* salty, 9
しる（知る） う*-v.* to come to know, しっている to know, しらない don't know, 11
しろい（白い） い*-adj.* white, 4
〜じん（〜人） *suf.* 〜 nationality indicator アメリカじん American, 2
しんしふく（紳士服） *n.* menswear, 8
しんしふくうりば（紳士服売り場） *n.* menswear department/section, 8
じんじゃ（神社） *n.* Shinto shrine, 12
しんせつ（な）（親切（な）） な*-adj.* kind, 10
しんぶん（新聞） *n.* newspaper, 6

す

すいぞくかん（水族館） *n.* aquarium, 12
すいようび（水曜日） *n.* Wednesday, 3
スーツ *n.* suit, 8
スーパー *n.* supermarket, 4
スープ *n.* soup, 9
スカート *n.* skirt, 8
すき（な）（好き（な）） な*-adj.* like, 7
スキー *n.* skiing, ski, 7
すきでもきらいでもありません。（好きでも嫌いでもありません。） *exp.* I neither like nor dislike it, 7
すくない（少ない） い*-adj.* little (in number), few, 9
すこし（少し） *adv.* a little, a few, 8
すし（寿司／鮨） *n.* sushi (usually with お at the beginning, i.e. おすし), 9
すずしい（涼しい） い*-adj.* cool, 11

すっぱい（酸っぱい） い-*adj.* sour, 9
ステーキ *n.* steak, 9
ストッキング *n.* stockings, pantyhose, 8
スパゲティ *n.* spaghetti, 9
スペイン *n.* Spain, 2
スポーツ *n.* sport, 7
（あのう、）すみません。 *exp.* (Um,) Excuse me., 1
すみません。 *exp.* I am sorry. / Excuse me., 1
すむ（住む） う-*v.* to reside, ～にすんでいる to live in ～, 10
する *irr. v.* to do (plain form of します, used in many compound verbs), 3
する *irr. v.* to put on (accessories), 10

せ

せ（背） *n.* back (part of the body), height (of a person), 10
～せい（～生） *suf.* ～ student だいがくせい college student いちねんせい freshman, 2
せいかく（性格） *n.* personality, 10
せいかつ（生活） *n.* life, living, 3
セーター *n.* sweater, 8
セール *n.* sale, 8
セット *n.* Western-style fixed meal, 9
ぜひ（是非） *adv.* I'd love to., By all means., 6
せまい（狭い） い-*adj.* cramped, narrow, 5
ゼロ *number* zero, 3
せん（千） *number* thousand, 8
せんげつ（先月） *n.* last month, 12
せんこう（専攻） *n.* major (course of study), 2
せんしゅう（先週） *n.* last week, 3
せんせい（先生） *n.* teacher, 1
～せんせい（先生） *suf.* Professor ～, 1
ぜんぜん（全然） *adv.* not at all (used with negative form of verbs), 3
せんたく（洗濯） *n.* laundry ～のせんたくをします or ～をせんたくします (to) do laundry, 6
ぜんぶで（全部で） *exp.* all together, 8

そ

そうじ（掃除） *n.* cleaning ～のそうじをします or ～をそうじします (to) clean up, 6
そうじゃないです *exp.* No, that's not so., 2
そうですか *exp.* Is that so? I see., 2
そこ *demo.* there, that place (close to the listener or slightly removed from both speaker and listener), 4
そして *conj.* and, 6
そと（外） *loc. n.* outside, 5
その *demo.* that [+ noun], 5
そば（蕎麦） *n.* Japanese buckwheat noodles (often with お at the beginning, i.e. おそば), 9
そふ（祖父） *n.* grandfather (the speaker's), 10
ソファ *n.* sofa, 5
そぼ（祖母） *n.* grandmother (the speaker's), 10
それ *demo.* that (object) (close to the listener or slightly removed from both speaker and listener), 4

それから　*conj.* and, in addition, then, 7
それに *conj.* in addition, 10
それは　にほんごで　なんと　いいますか。 *exp.* How do you say that in Japanese?, 1

た

だい～ (大～)　*pref.* very much, 大すき like very much, 7
たいいくかん (体育館) *n.* gym, 5
だいがく (大学) *n.* college, university, 2
だいがくいんせい (大学院生) *n.* graduate student, 2
だいがくせい (大学生) *n.* college student, 2
だいじょうぶ (な) (大丈夫 (な)) な-*adj.* all right, no problem, OK, 6
たいそう (体操) *n.* calisthenics, physical exercise, 7
たいてい *adv.* usually, 3
たいふう (台風) *n.* typhoon, 11
たいへん (な)(大変 (な)) な-*adj.* tough, 6
たいわん (台湾) *n.* Taiwan, 2
たかい (高い) い-*adj.* tall, high, 4
たかい (高い) い-*adj.* expensive, 7
たくさん *adv.* a lot, many, much, 8
たてもの (建物) *n.* building, structure, 4
たとえば (例えば) *conj.* for example, 7
たのしい (楽しい) い-*adj.* fun, 6
たのむ (頼む) う-*v.* to order, to ask (someone to do something), 9
たべます (食べます) る-*v.* (to) eat (dictionary form is たべる), 3
たべもの (食べ物) *n.* food, 7
たまご (卵 / 玉子) *n.* egg, 7
だれ *q. word* who, 4
たんじょうび (誕生日) *n.* birthday, 8
たんす (箪笥) *n.* chest, drawers, 5

ち

ちいさい (小さい) い-*adj.* small, 4
チーズ *n.* cheese, 9
ちか (地下) *n.* basement, underground　ちかいっかい B1, 8
ちかく (近く) *loc. n.* near, in the vicinity of, 5
チキン *n.* chicken meat (the live animal is とり or にわとり), 9
ちち (父) *n.* father (the speaker's), 10
チャーハン *n.* Chinese-style fried rice, 9
ちゃいろい (茶色い) い-*adj.* brown, 4
ちゅう～ (中～) *pref.* middle, 中学生 middle school student, 中学校 middle school, junior high school, 10
ちゅうがく (中学) *n.* junior high school (shortened form of 中学校), 12
ちゅうかりょうり (中華料理) *n.* Chinese cuisine, 9
ちゅうごく (中国) *n.* China, 2
ちゅうもん (注文) *n.* order, ちゅうもんする to order, 9
チョコレート *n.* chocolate, 9

ちょっと　*adv.* a little, a few (more casual than すこし), 8
(は)ちょっと *exp.* ~is a bit, 7
ちょっと　つごうが　わるくて。(ちょっと都合が悪くて。) *exp.* I'm a little busy. (literally, *Sorry, it's a little inconvenient.*), 6
ちょっと　ようじが　あって。(ちょっと用事があって。) *exp.* Sorry, I have some errands/business to attend to., 6

つ

～つ　*count.* general counter (Japanese-origin numbers), 8
つぎ(次) *n.* next, 3
つくえ(机) *n.* desk, 5
つくる(作る)　う-*v.* to make, 7
つづく(続く)　う-*v.* to continue, 11
～って　なんですか。*exp.* What does ～ mean?, 1
～って　いいます。 *exp.* colloquial version of ～と　いいます。, 2
つとめる(勤める)　る-*v.* to become employed, ～につとめている to be employed at, work for ～, 10
つま(妻) *n.* wife (the speaker's), 10
つまらない　い-*adj.* boring, 6
つめたい(冷たい)　い-*adj.* cold (object temperature, mood, etc.), 9
つもる(積もる)　う-*v.* to accumulate, 11
つゆ(梅雨)　*n.* rainy season, 11
つよい(強い)　い-*adj.* strong, 11
つり(釣り)　*n.* fishing, 7

て

て(手)　*n.* hand, 10
で　*part.* at, in, on, etc. (location of action or event)　としょかんで　べんきょうします。, 3
で　*part.* by means of, by, with, 5
Tシャツ　*n.* T-shirt, 8
デート　*n.* date, デートする to go out on a date, 12
テーブル　*n.* table, 5
ていしょく(定食)　*n.* Japanese or Asian-style set meal, 9
～ている　*aux. v.* resultant state, 10
でかけます(出かけます)　る-*v.* (to) go out (dictionary form is でかける), 6
てがみ(手紙)　*n.* letter (postal), 6
デザート　*n.* dessert, 9
です　*cop. v.* (to) be, 2
テスト　*n.* test, 4
テニス　*n.* tennis テニスをします (to) play tennis, 6
デパート　*n.* department store, 4
でも　*conj.* but, 5
てら(寺)　*n.* Buddhist temple (often used as おてら), 12
テレビ　*n.* television, TV, 3
てんき(天気)　*n.* weather (often used as おてんき), 11
てんきよほう(天気予報)　*n.* weather forecast, 11

てんぷら（天麩羅 / 天ぷら） *n.* tempura (fish, shrimp, and vegetables battered and deep-fried), 9
でんわ（電話） *n.* telephone, 5
でんわばんごう（電話番号） *n.* telephone number, 3

と

と *part.* with, together with (association), 6
と *part.* and (exhaustive listing), 6
～と　いいます。／～って　いいます。 *exp.* You say ～. / You call it ～, 1
～ど（～度） *suf.* degree, temperature, 11
～ど（～度） *suf.* ~times, 12
ドア *n.* door, 5
トイレ *n.* toilet; restroom, 5
どう *q. word* how, 6
どういたしまして。 *exp.* You are welcome., 1
どうして *q. word* why, 8
トースト *n.* toast, 9
（～は）どうですか。 *exp.* How about ～?, 7
どうぶつえん（動物園） *n.* zoo, 12
どうも *adv.* very どうも　すみません。I'm very sorry., 4
どうも　ありがとう　ございます。 *exp.* Thank you very much., 2
とき（時） *n.* when, at the time of ～ （子供の時 when I was a child), 12
ときどき（時々） *adv.* sometimes, 3
とけい（時計） *n.* clock, watch, 5
どこ *q. word* where, 2
どこから　きましたか。 *exp.* Where are you from?, 2
ところ（所） *n.* place, 5
とし（年） *n.* age, としうえ elder, older, としした younger, 10
としょかん（図書館） *n.* library, 3
どちら *q. word* where (more polite than どこ), which way, 2
どちらから　いらっしゃいましたか。 *exp.* Where are you from? (polite version of どこから　きましたか), 2
とても *adv.* very (always used with an affirmative form), 4
となり（隣） *loc. n.* next to, 5
どの *demo.* which [+ noun]?, 5
どのぐらい／どのくらい *exp.* how long, how much, how many, 5
トマト *n.* tomato, 7
ともだち（友達） *n.* friend, 6
どようび（土曜日） *n.* Saturday, 3
ドライブ *n.* driving (for pleasure), 7
とる（撮る） う*-v.* to take (a photograph) しゃしんをとる, 7
とる（取る） う*-v.* to take, 8
どれ *q. word* which one, 4
ドレス *n.* dress, 8
どんな *q. word* what kind of, 4

な

なあ *part.* A particle of exclamation to express desires or feelings without addressing anyone in particular. Used in casual speech, 12
なか (中) *loc. n.* in, inside, 5
ながい (長い) い *-adj.* long, 10
なく (泣く) う *-v.* to cry, 12
なつ (夏) *n.* summer, 11
なつやすみ (夏休み) *n.* summer vacation, summer break, 12
なな (七) *number* seven, 3
なに／なん (何) *q. word* what, 2
なまえ (名前) *n.* name, 2
なんせい (南西) *n.* southwest, 11
なんとう (南東) *n.* southeast, 11

に

に (二) *number* two, 3
に *part.* at, on, in (point in time) 10じにねます。, 3
に *part.* to (goal, activity + に) クラスにいきます。, 3
に *part.* in order to, for (purpose), 6
に *part.* to (goal, receiver), 6
〜に します *exp.* to decide on 〜, 9
にがい (苦い) い *-adj.* bitter, 9
にぎやか (な) (賑やか (な)) な *-adj.* lively (place or event), 6
にく (肉) *n.* meat, 7
にし (西) *n.* west, 11
にじ (二時) *time exp.* two o'clock, 2
〜にち (〜日) *suf.* day (of the month), 12
にちようび (日曜日) *n.* Sunday, 3
にねんせい (二年生) *n.* sophomore, second-year student (The suffix せい may be dropped.), 2
にほん (日本) *n.* Japan, 2
にほんりょうり (日本料理) *n.* Japanese cuisine, 2
にわかあめ (にわか雨) *n.* shower (rain), 11
〜にん (〜人) *suf.* 〜 people, 10
にんじん *n.* carrot, 7

ね

ネクタイ *n.* tie, 8
ねこ (猫) *n.* cat, 5
ネックレス *n.* necklace, 8
ねます (寝ます) る *-v.* (to) go to bed (dictionary form is ねる), 3
〜ねん (〜年) *suf.* year いちねん first year, 2
〜ねん (〜年) *suf.* specific year (1996 年), counter for years (十年), 12

の

の *part.* noun modifier marker (of, 's), 2
ノート *n.* notebook, 4

のち (後) *n.* after, 11
〜のち〜 *exp.* after あめのちはれ clear skies after rain, 11
のみます (飲みます) う-*v.* (to) drink (dictionary form is のむ), 3
のみもの (飲み物) *n.* beverage, drink, 7
のる (乗る) う-*v.* to get on, to ride ひこうきにのる to get on a plane, 12

は

は *part.* topic marker, 2
〜は ありませんか。 *exp.* Do you have ~ ?, Do you carry ~ ? (lit, *Isn't there ~ ?*), 8
〜は にほんごで なんと いいますか。 *exp.* How do you say 〜 in Japanese?, 1
パーティ *n.* party パーティをします (to) host a party, 6
はい *inter.* yes, 2
はい、そうです。 *exp.* Yes, that's so., 2
はい、わかりました。 *exp.* Yes, I understand it., 1
ハイキング *n.* hiking, 7
はいります (入ります) う-*v.* (to) take (a bath), (to) enter (dictionary form is はいる)
 おふろに はいります (to) take a bath, 3
はく う-*v.* to put on (skirt, pants, socks, shoes), 10
はくぶつかん (博物館) *n.* museum, 12
はこ (箱) *n.* box, 8
はじまる (始まる) う-*v.* (for something) to begin, 7
はじめまして。〜です。どうぞ よろしく。 *exp.* How do you do? I am 〜. Pleased to meet you., 1
はじめて (初めて) *adv.* for the first time, 12
バス *n.* bus, 5
バスケットボール *n.* basketball (abbreviated as バスケット or バスケ), 7
はち (八) *number* eight, 3
はちじ (八時) *time exp.* eight o'clock, 2
はな (鼻) *n.* nose, 10
はなします (話します) う-*v.* (to) talk (dictionary form is はなす), 6
バナナ *n.* banana, 7
はは (母) *n.* mother (the speaker's), 10
はやい (速い) い-*adj.* fast, quick, 5
はやい (早い) い-*adj.* early, 11
はる (春) *n.* spring, 11
はれ (晴れ) *n.* clear skies, 11
はれる (晴れる) る-*v.* to become sunny, 11
バレンタインデー *n.* Valentine's Day, 12
ハロウィン *n.* Halloween, 12
はん (半) *time exp.* half past いちじはん 1:30, 2
ばん (晩) *n.* night, evening, 3
パン *n.* bread, 9
〜ばん (め)(〜番 (目)) *suf.* 〜 th (ordinal suffix), 10
ばんごはん (晩御飯) *n.* supper, dinner, 3
パンツ *n.* trousers, shorts, 8
はんとし (半年) *n.* half a year, 12
ハンドバッグ *n.* handbag, 8

ハンバーガー *n.* hamburger, 9

ひ

ビーフ *n.* beef, 9
ビール *n.* beer, 7
ひがし(東) *n.* east, 11
〜ひき(〜匹) *count.* counter for fish and small four-legged animals, 8
ひくい(低い) い*-adj.* low, カロリーがひくい low in calories, 9
ピクニック *n.* picnic, 6
ひこうき(飛行機) *n.* airplane, 12
ピザ *n.* pizza, 9
びじゅつかん(美術館) *n.* art museum, 12
ビジネス *n.* business, 2
ひだり(左) *loc. n.* to the left, left side, 5
ヒップホップ *n.* hip-hop music, 7
ビデオ *n.* video, 5
ひと(人) *n.* person, 5
ひとりっこ(一人っ子) *n.* only child, 10
ひま(な)(暇(な)) な*-adj.* free, idle, unscheduled, 6
ひゃく(百) *number* hundred, 8
びょういん(病院) *n.* hospital, 4
ひる(昼) *n.* afternoon, 3
ビル *n.* (office) building, 4
ひるごはん(昼御飯) *n.* lunch, 3
ひろい(広い) い*-adj.* spacious, wide, 5

ふ

プール *n.* pool, 6
ふく(服) *n.* clothing, 8
ふく(吹く) う*-v.* to blow, 11
ふじんふく(婦人服) *n.* woman's clothing, 8
ふじんふくうりば(婦人服売り場) *n.* women's clothing department/section, 8
フットボール *n.* (American) football (also, contracted as アメフト), 7
ふとる(太る) う*-v.* to gain weight, ふとっている to be fat, 10
ふとん(布団) *n.* futon, 5
ふゆ(冬) *n.* winter, 11
フライドチキン *n.* fried chicken, 9
ブラウス *n.* blouse, 8
フランス *n.* France, 2
ふる(降る) う*-v.* to fall (as precipitation), 11
ふるい(古い) い*-adj.* old (of non-living things), 4
プレゼント *n.* present, gift, 12
ブロンド *n.* blond(e), 10
〜ふん(〜分) *count.* 〜 minute(s), (for) 〜 minute(s), 3
ぶんがく(文学) *n.* literature, 2
ぶんぼうぐ(文房具) *n.* stationery, 8

ぶんぼうぐうりば (文房具売り場) *n.* stationery department/section, 8

へ

へ *part.* to (direction) がっこうへ　いきます。, 3
ベッド *n.* bed, 5
へや (部屋) *n.* room, 5
ベルト *n.* belt, 8
ペン *n.* pen, 4
べんきょう (勉強) *n.* study, 3
べんきょうします (勉強します) *irr. v.* (to) study (dictionary form is べんきょうする), 3

ほ

ほう (方) *n.* direction, 11
ぼうし (帽子) *n.* hat, cap, 8
ポーク *n.* pork, 9
ボールペン *n.* ballpoint pen, 4
ぼく (僕) *pron.* I (normally used by males), 2
ほくせい (北西) *n.* northwest, 11
ほくとう (北東) *n.* northeast, 11
ほそながい (細長い) い *-adj.* long and thin, elongated, 10
ポップス *n.* pop music, 7
〜ほん (〜本) *count.* counter for long, cylindrical objects (e.g. bottles, films, pens, pencils), 8
ほん (本) *n.* book, 3
ほんだな (本棚) *n.* bookshelf, 5
ほんとうに / ほんとに (本当に) *adv.* truly, really, indeed (ほんとに is more conversational than ほんとうに), 11
ほんや (本屋) *n.* bookstore, 4

ま

〜まい (〜枚) *count.* counter for thin objects (e.g. paper, shirts, plates), 8
まい〜 (毎〜) *pref.* every まいしゅう、まいあさ、まいばん、まいにち, 3
まいあさ (毎朝) *n.* every morning, 3
まいしゅう (毎週) *n.* every week, 3
マイナス *n.* minus, 11
まいにち (毎日) *n.* every day, 3
まいばん (毎晩) *n.* every night, 3
まえ (前) *loc. n.* in front of, in the front, 5
〜まえ (〜前) *suf.* 〜 ago (一年まえ one year ago), 12
まち (町) *n.* town, 4
まちます (待ちます) う *-v.* (to) wait (dictionary form is まつ), 6
まつり (祭り) *n.* festival (often used as おまつり), 12
まで *part.* until, to, 5
まど (窓) *n.* window, 5
まるい (丸い) い *-adj.* round, 10
まん (万) *number* ten thousand, 8
まんなか (真ん中) *n.* center, middle, middle child, 10

at, on, in (point in time)　に　10じにねます I sleep at 10:00　*part.*, 3
at the time of ～　とき (時)　*n.*, 12
Australia　オーストラリア　*n.*, 2

B

back (part of the body)　せ (背)　*n.*, 10
bad　わるい (悪い)　い*-adj.*, 11
ballpoint pen　ボールペン　*n.*, 4
banana　バナナ　*n.*, 7
bank　ぎんこう (銀行)　*n.*, 4
baseball　やきゅう (野球)　*n.*, 7
basement　ちか (地下)　*n.*, 8
basketball　バスケットボール (also バスケット or バスケ)　*n.*, 7
bath　おふろ (お風呂)　*n.*, 3
(to) be　です　*cop. v.*, 2
(to) be, (to) exist (animate beings)　います (dictionary form is いる) る*-v.*, 4
(to) be held, (to) have　あります (dictionary form is ある) う*-v.*, 3
(to) become cloudy　くもる (曇る)　う*-v.*, 11
(to) become employed　つとめる (勤める)　る*-v.*, 10
(to) become sunny　はれる (晴れる)　る*-v.*, 11
bed　ベッド　*n.*, 5
beef　ビーフ　*n.*, 9
beer　ビール　*n.*, 7
(to) begin　はじまる (始まる)　う*-v.*, 7
behind, in back of　うしろ (後ろ)　*loc. n.*, 5
belt　ベルト　*n.*, 8
beneath, under　した (下)　*loc. n.*, 5
beverage　のみもの (飲み物)　*n.*, 7
bicycle　じてんしゃ (自転車)　*n.*, 5
big　おおきい (大きい)　い*-adj.*, 4
birthday　たんじょうび (誕生日)　*n.*, 8
bitter　にがい (苦い)　い*-adj.*, 9
black　くろい (黒い)　い*-adj.*, 4
black tea　こうちゃ (紅茶)　*n.*, 7
blond(e)　ブロンド　*n.*, 10
blouse　ブラウス　*n.*, 8
(to) blow　ふく (吹く)　う*-v.*, 11
blue　あおい (青い)　い*-adj.*, 4
book　ほん (本)　*n.*, 3
bookshelf　ほんだな (本棚)　*n.*, 5
bookstore　ほんや (本屋)　*n.*, 4
boring　つまらない　い*-adj.*, 6
box　はこ (箱)　*n.*, 8
boy　おとこのこ (男の子)　*n.*, 10
bread　パン　*n.*, 9
breakfast　あさごはん (朝御飯)　*n.*, 3

bright あかるい (明るい) い-*adj.*, 5
brown ちゃいろい (茶色い) い-*adj.*, 4
(Japanese) buckwheat noodles そば (蕎麦) (often おそば) *n.*, 9
Buddhist temple (often おてら) てら (寺) *n.*, 12
(office) building ビル *n.*, 4
building, structure たてもの (建物) *n.*, 4
bus バス *n.*, 5
business ビジネス *n.*, 2
business administration, management けいえいがく (経営学) *n.*, 2
businessperson かいしゃいん (会社員) *n.*, 10
busy いそがしい (忙しい) い-*adj.*, 6
but でも *conj.*, 5
(to) buy かう (買う) う-*v.*, 7
by means of, by, with で *part.*, 5

C

cake ケーキ *n.*, 7
(to) call (someone), (to) invite よびます (呼びます) (dictionary form is よぶ) う-*v.*, 6
calisthenics, physical exercise たいそう (体操) *n.*, 7
calorie カロリー *n.*, 9
came from ～ (casual) ～から きました。 *exp.*, 2
camping キャンプ *n.*, 12
Canada カナダ *n.*, 2
car くるま (車) *n.*, 5
carrot にんじん *n.*, 7
cat ねこ (猫) *n.*, 5
cell phone けいたい (でんわ) (携帯 (電話)) (note スマホ smartphone) *n.*, 5
center, middle, middle child まんなか (真ん中) *n.*, 10
chair いす (椅子) *n.*, 5
chalkboard こくばん (黒板) *n.*, 5
cheerful あかるい (明るい) い-*adj.*, 10
cheese チーズ *n.*, 9
chest, drawers たんす (箪笥) *n.*, 5
chicken チキン *n.*, 9
child こ (子)/ こども (子供) *n.*, 10
child (someone else's) おこさん (お子さん) *n.*, 10
China ちゅうごく (中国) *n.*, 2
Chinese cuisine ちゅうかりょうり (中華料理) *n.*, 9
chocolate チョコレート *n.*, 9
Christmas クリスマス *n.*, 12
church きょうかい (教会) *n.*, 12
class クラス *n.*, 3
class, course じゅぎょう (授業) *n.*, 3
classical music クラシック *n.*, 7
classroom きょうしつ (教室) *n.*, 5
clean, pretty, neat きれい (な) な-*adj.*, 4

(to) clean up ～のそうじをします、～そうじします *irr. v.*, 6
cleaning そうじ (掃除) *n.*, 6
clear skies はれ (晴れ) *n.*, 11
climate きこう (気候) *n.*, 11
clock, watch とけい (時計) *n.*, 5
closet (Japanese style) おしいれ (押し入れ) *n.*, 5
clothing ふく (服) *n.*, 8
cloud くも (雲) *n.*, 11
cloudy くもり (曇り) *n.*, 11
coat コート *n.*, 8
coffee コーヒー *n.*, 3
coffee shop (traditional term) きっさてん (喫茶店) *n.*, 4
coffee shop, café (recent term) カフェ *n.*, 4
cola コーラ *n.*, 7
cold (air temperature) さむい (寒い) い *-adj.*, 11
cold (objects, mood, etc.) つめたい (冷たい) い *-adj.*, 9
college student だいがくせい (大学生) *n.*, 2
college, university だいがく (大学) *n.*, 2
(to) come きます (来ます) (dictionary form is くる) *irr. v.*, 3
(to) come to know しる (知る) う *-v.*, 11
computer コンピュータ *n.*, 5
concert コンサート *n.*, 6
(to) continue つづく (続く) う *-v.*, 11
convenience store コンビニ *n.*, 4
cookie クッキー *n.*, 9
cooking, cuisine りょうり (料理) *n.*, 6
cool (air temperature) すずしい (涼しい) い *-adj.*, 11
cool, good looking, neat かっこいい い *-adj.*, 10
counter for bound objects (e.g. books, magazines) ～さつ (～冊) *count.*, 8
counter for fish and small four-legged animals ～ひき (～匹) *count.*, 8
counter for floors of a building ～かい (～階) *count.*, 8
counter for Japanese currency ～えん (～円), *count.*, 8
counter for long, cylindrical objects (e.g. bottles, films, pens, pencils) ～ほん (～本) *count.*, 8
counter for months ～かげつ (～か月) *count.*, 12
counter for people ～にん (～人) *count.*, 10
counter for thin objects (e.g. paper, shirts, plates) ～まい (～枚) *count.*, 8
counter for years ～ねん (～年) *count.*, 12
counter, general (Japanese-origin numbers) ～つ *count.*, 8
cramped, narrow せまい (狭い) い *-adj.*, 5
(to) cry なく (泣く) う *-v.*, 12
(Japanese) curry and rice カレーライス *n.*, 9
customer, guest おきゃくさん (お客さん) *n.*, 8
cute, adorable かわいい (可愛い) い *-adj.*, 10

D

dark くらい (暗い) い *-adj.*, 5

dating デート *n.*, 12
(the) day after tomorrow あさって (明後日) *n.*, 3
(the) day before yesterday おととい (一昨日) *n.*, 3
day (of the month) ～にち (～日) *suf.*, 12
day (of the week) ～ようび (～曜日) *suf.*, 3
day off, holiday やすみのひ (休みの日) *n.*, 6
(to) decide on ～. ～に します *exp.*, 9
degree, temperature ～ど (～度) *suf.*, 11
delicious, good, tasty おいしい い -*adj.*, 7
department うりば (売り場) *n.*, 8
department store デパート *n.*, 4
desk つくえ (机) *n.*, 5
dessert デザート *n.*, 9
dictionary じしょ (辞書) *n.*, 4
difficult むずかしい (難しい) い -*adj.*, 6
(to) dine しょくじする (食事する) *irr. v.*, 7
dining しょくじ (食事) *n.*, 7
dinner, supper (evening meal) ばんごはん (晩御飯) *n.*, 3
direct object marker を ほんをよみます。I read a book. *part.*, 3
direction ほう (方) *n.*, 11
(to be) disappointed in love しつれんする (失恋する) *irr.v.*, 12
dish set (Japanese or Asian style) ていしょく (定食) *n.*, 9
dislike, hate きらい (な)(嫌い (な)) な -*adj.*, 7
(to) do します (dictionary form is する) *irr. v.*, 3
Do you have ～ ? / Do you carry ～ ? (lit., *Isn't there ～ ?*) ～は ありませんか。 *exp.*, 8
Do you understand it? わかりましたか。 *exp.*, 1
dog いぬ (犬) *n.*, 5
door ドア *n.*, 5
dormitory りょう *n.*, 4
dress ドレス *n.*, 8
(to) drink のみます (飲みます) (dictionary form is のむ) う -*v.*, 3
drink, beverage のみもの (飲み物) *n.*, 7
(a) drive (for pleasure) ドライブ *n.*, 7

E

ear みみ (耳) *n.*, 10
early はやい (早い) い -*adj.*, 11
earring イヤリング *n.*, 8
east ひがし (東) *n.*, 11
easy やさしい (易しい) い -*adj.*, 6
(to) eat たべます (食べます) (dictionary form is たべる) る -*v.*, 3
egg たまご (卵 / 玉子) *n.*, 7
eight はち (八) *number*, 3
eight o'clock はちじ (八時) *time exp.*, 2
elementary しょう～ (小～) 小学校、小学生 *pref.*, 10
eleven o'clock じゅういちじ (十一時) *time exp.*, 2

e-mail　メール *n.*, 6
(to be) employed at, to work for　〜につとめている　る-*v.*, 10　(see also つとめる to become employed)
(to) become employed　つとめる（勤める）る-*v.* 10
(to) end　おわる（終わる）　う-*v.*, 7
engineering　こうがく（工学）*n.*, 2
England　イギリス *n.*, 2
English　えいご（英語）*n.*, 2
(to) enter　はいります（入ります）(dictionary form is はいる）う-*v.*, 3
eraser　けしゴム（消しゴム）*n.*, 4
evening　ゆうがた（夕方）*n.*, 11
every　まいしゅう（毎〜）　まいあさ、まいばん、まいにち *pref.*, 3
every day　まいにち（毎日）*n.*, 3
every morning　まいあさ（毎朝）*n.*, 3
every night　まいばん（毎晩）*n.*, 3
every week　まいしゅう（毎週）*n.*, 3
(Um,) Excuse me.（あのう、）すみません。*exp.*, 1
Excuse me., Is anyone home?　ごめんください。（御免下さい。）*exp.*, 5
(particle of) exclamation　なあ　*part.*, 12
exercise (physical)　うんどう（運動）*n.*, 6
(to) exist (animate beings)　います (dictionary form is いる）る-*v.*, 4
expensive (cf. Chapter 4: high, tall)　たかい（高い）　い-*adj.*, 7
eye　め（目）*n.*, 10

F

face　かお（顔）*n.*, 10
(to) fall (as precipitation)　ふる（降る）　う-*v.*, 11
fall, autumn　あき（秋）*n.*, 11
(to) fall, (to) go down　さがる（下がる）　う-*v.*, 11
family (someone else's)　ごかぞく（ご家族）*n.*, 10
family, the speaker's family　かぞく（家族）*n.*, 10
famous　ゆうめい（な）(有名（な）)　な-*adj.*, 4
fast, quick　はやい（速い）い-*adj.*, 5
father (someone else's)　おとうさん（お父さん）*n.*, 10
(to be) fat　ふとっている (see also ふとる to gain weight) 10
father (the speaker's)　ちち（父）*n.*, 10
female　おんな（女）*n.*, 10
festival (often used as おまつり)　まつり（祭り）*n.*, 12
fight, quarrel　けんか *n.*, 12
(to) fight　けんかする　*irr. v.*, 12
fine, splendid, nice　りっぱ（な）(立派（な）)　な-*adj.*, 4
fish　さかな（魚）*n.*, 7
fishing　つり（釣り）*n.*, 7
five　ご（五）*number*, 3
five o'clock　ごじ（五時）*time exp.*, 2
(to) fix a meal　りょうりをします, *irr. v.*, 6

food　しょくひん (食品)　*n.*, 8
food　たべもの (食べ物)　*n.*, 7
foot (and leg)　あし (足)　*n.*, 10
(on) foot　あるいて (歩いて) *exp.*, 5
(American) football (アメフト)　フットボール　*n.*, 7
for ～ weeks　～しゅうかん (～週間)　*suf.*, 12
for example　たとえば (例えば)　*conj.*, 7
for the first time　はじめて (初めて)　*adv.*, 12
foreign countries　がいこく (外国)　*n.*, 12
four　よん／し (四)　*number*, 3
four o'clock　よじ (四時)　*time exp.*, 2
France　フランス *n.*, 2
free, idle, unscheduled (of a person's time)　ひま (な)(暇 (な))　な*-adj.*, 6
freshman, first-year student (the suffix せい may be dropped)　いちねんせい (一年生) *n.*, 2
Friday　きんようび (金曜日)　*n.*, 3
fried chicken　フライドチキン　*n.*, 9
(Chinese-style) fried rice　チャーハン　*n.*, 9
friend　ともだち (友達)　*n.*, 6
from　から *part.*, 5
from ～, after ～　～ご (～後)　*suf.*, 12
fruit　くだもの (果物)　*n.*, 7
fun　たのしい (楽しい)　い*-adj.*, 6
futon　ふとん (布団)　*n.*, 5

G

(to) gain weight　ふとる (太る)　う *-v.*, 10
game　ゲーム *n.*, 6
(to) get　もらう う *-v.*, 12
(to) get on, to ride　のる (乗る)　う *-v.*, 12
(to) get up, (to) wake up　おきます (起きます) (dictionary form is おきる)　る*-v.*, 3
gift　プレゼント　*n.*, 12
girl　おんなのこ (女の子) *n.*, 10
glasses　めがね (眼鏡)　*n.*, 10
(to) go　いきます (行きます) (dictionary form is いく)　う*-v.*, 3
(to) go out　でかけます (出かけます) (dictionary form is でかける)　る*-v.*, 6
(to) go out on a date　デートする　*irr. v.*, 12
(to) go to bed　ねます (寝ます) (dictionary form is ねる)　る*-v.*, 3
golf　ゴルフ　*n.*, 7
good　いい い*-adj.*, 4
Good afternoon. / Hello.　こんにちは。 *exp.*, 1
good at, skillful　じょうず (な) (上手 (な))　な*-adj.*, 10
Good evening. / Hello.　こんばんは。　*exp.*, 1
good-looking, cool, neat　かっこいい い*-adj.*, 10
Good morning. / Hello. (polite)　おはようございます。 *exp.*, 1
Good morning. / Hello. (casual)　おはよう。 *exp.*, 1
Good-bye.　さようなら。／さよなら。 *exp.*, 1

Good-bye. / Excuse me. しつれいします。 *exp.*, 1
graduate student だいがくいんせい (大学院生) *n.*, 2
grandfather (someone else's) おじいさん (お祖父さん) *n.*, 10
grandfather (the speaker's) そふ (祖父) *n.*, 10
grandmother (someone else's) おばあさん (お祖母さん) *n.*, 10
grandmother (the speaker's) そぼ (祖母) *n.*, 10
gym たいいくかん (体育館) *n.*, 5

H

hair かみ (髪)(かみのけ is also commonly used) *n.*, 10
half past はん (半) いちじはん 1:30 *time exp.*, 2
half-year はんとし (半年) *n.*, 12
Halloween ハロウィン *n.*, 12
hamburger ハンバーガー *n.*, 9
hand て (手) *n.*, 10
handbag ハンドバッグ *n.*, 8
happy うれしい (嬉しい) い-*adj.*, 6
Happy New Year あけましておめでとうございます。(明けまして …。) *exp.*, 12
hard, tough かたい (固い) い -*adj.*, 9
hat, cap ぼうし (帽子) *n.*, 8
head あたま (頭) *n.*, 10
healthy, cheerful, lively (person) げんき (な) (元気 (な)) な-*adj.*, 6
height (of a person) せ (背) *n.*, 10
Hello. おはよう (ございます)。 morning, こんにちは。 midday, こんばんは。 evening *exp.*, 1
here, this place ここ *demo.*, 4
high たかい (高い) い -*adj.*, 4
high school こうこう (高校) *n.*, 2
hiking ハイキング *n.*, 7
hip-hop music ヒップホップ *n.*, 7
history れきし (歴史) *n.*, 2
hobby しゅみ (趣味) *n.*, 7
holiday, day off やすみのひ (休みの日) *n.*, 6
home うち (家) *n.*, 3
homework しゅくだい (宿題) *n.*, 3
hospital びょういん (病院) *n.*, 4
hot (air temperature) あつい (暑い) い -*adj.*, 11
hot (objects, mood, etc.) あつい (熱い) い -*adj.*, 9
～ hours ～じかん (～時間) *suf.*, 5
how どう *q. word*, 6
how いかが (polite form of どう) *q. word*, 8
How about ～ ? (～は) どうですか。 *exp.*, 7
How do you do? I am ～. Pleased to meet you. はじめまして。～です。どうぞよろしく。 *exp.*, 1
How do you say ～ in Japanese? ～は にほんごで なんと いいますか。 *exp.*, 1
How do you say that (over there) in Japanese? あれは にほんごで なんと いいますか。 *exp.*, 1
How do you say that in Japanese? それは にほんごで なんと いいますか。 *exp.*, 1

How do you say this in Japanese? これは　にほんごで　なんと　いいますか。 *exp.*, 1
how long, how much, how many　どのぐらい／どのくらい　*exp.*, 5
how many　いくつ　*q. word*, 8
how much (money)　いくら　*q. word*, 8
How old ～？　いくつ　*q. word*, 10
humid　むしあつい（蒸し暑い）　い *-adj.*, 11
humidity　しつど（湿度） *n.*, 11
hundred　ひゃく（百） *number*, 8
husband (someone else's)　ごしゅじん（ご主人）　*n.*, 10
husband (the speaker's)　しゅじん（主人）　*n.*, 10

I

I (normally used by males)　ぼく（僕） *pron.*, 2
I (used by both males and females)　わたし（私） *pron.*, 2
I'd love to., By all means.　ぜひ（是非） *adv.*, 6
I'm a little busy. (literally, *Sorry, it's a little inconvenient.*)　ちょっと　つごうが　わるくて。（ちょっと都合が悪くて。）*exp.*, 6
I'm sorry. / Excuse me. すみません。 *exp.*, 1
I'm very sorry　どうも　すみません　*adv.*, 4
I see.　そうですか　*exp.*, 2
I neither like nor dislike it.　すきでもきらいでもありません。（好きでも嫌いでも ...。） *exp.*, 7
I would like to have ～.　～を　おねがいします。（～をお願いします。）　*exp.*, 9
ice cream　アイスクリーム　*n.*, 9
in, inside　なか（中） *loc. n.*, 5
in addition　それに　*conj.* 10
in front of, in the front　まえ（前） *loc. n.*, 5
in order to, for (purpose)　に　*part.*, 6
inexpensive　やすい（安い）　い *-adj.*, 7
interesting　おもしろい（面白い）　い*-adj.*, 6
international student　りゅうがくせい（留学生） *n.*, 2
Is that so? I see.　そうですか　*exp.*, 2
It is I who should be saying that. Thank you. こちらこそ。 *exp.*, 2
Italy　イタリア　*n.*, 9

J

jacket　ジャケット　*n.*, 8
Japan　にほん（日本） *n.*, 2
Japanese cuisine　わしょく（和食）／にほんりょうり（日本料理）　*n.*, 9
jazz　ジャズ　*n.*, 7
jeans　ジーンズ　*n.*, 8
job　しごと（仕事） *n.*, 6
jogging　ジョギング　*n.*, 6
juice　ジュース　*n.*, 7
junior, third-year student (The suffix せい may be dropped.) さんねんせい（三年生） *n.*, 2
junior high school (shortened form of 中学校）　ちゅうがく（中学）　*n.*, 12

K

kabuki (Japanese traditional performing art) かぶき (歌舞伎) *n.*, 12
Karaoke, sing-along カラオケ *n.*, 7
kind やさしい (優しい) い *-adj.*, 6
kind しんせつ (な)(親切 (な)) な *-adj.*, 10
(to) know しっている (知っている) (see also しる to come to know) (the negative form is しらない)

L

language にほんご Japanese language 〜ご (〜語) *suf.*, 2
last month せんげつ (先月) *n.*, 12
last week せんしゅう (先週) *n.*, 3
last year きょねん (去年) *n.*, 11
laundry せんたく (洗濯) *n.*, 6
(to do) laundry 〜のせんたくをします／〜をせんたくします *irr. v.*, 6
(to the) left, left side ひだり (左) *loc. n.*, 5
leg, foot あし (足) *n.*, 10
letter (postal) てがみ (手紙) *n.*, 6
lettuce レタス *n.*, 7
library としょかん (図書館) *n.*, 3
life, living せいかつ (生活) *n.*, 3
like すき (な) (好き (な)) な *-adj.*, 7
(to) listen (to something) ききます (聞きます / 聴きます) (dictionary form is きく) う *-v.*, 6
literature ぶんがく (文学) *n.*, 2
(a) little ちょっと *adv.*, 8
(to) live in (a place) 〜にすんでいる (see also すむ to reside), 10
lively (person), healthy, cheerful げんき (な) (元気 (な)) な *-adj.*, 6
lively (place or event) にぎやか (な) (賑やか (な)) な *-adj.*, 6
lonely さびしい (寂しい) い *-adj.*, 6
long ながい (長い) い *-adj.*, 10
long and thin, elongated ほそながい (細長い) い *-adj.*, 10
(to) lose weight やせる る *-v.*, 10
low ひくい (低い) い *-adj.*, 9
luggage, bag かばん (鞄) *n.*, 4
lunch ひるごはん (昼御飯) *n.*, 3
lunch, luch set ランチ *n.*, 9

M

magazine ざっし (雑誌) *n.*, 6
major (course of study) せんこう (専攻) *n.*, 2
(to) make つくる (作る) う *-v.*, 7
(to) make (a phone call) かけます (dictionary form is かける) でんわをかけます る *-v.*, 6
male (human) おとこ (男) *n.*, 10
management, business administration けいえいがく (経営学) *n.*, 2
marriage けっこん (結婚) *n.*, 10
(to) marry 〜 (〜と) けっこんする (結婚する) (けっこんしている) married *irr.v.*, 10

meal, cooked rice ごはん (御飯) *n.*, 3
meal (Western-style entree with side dishes at restaurants) セット *n.*, 9
meat にく (肉) *n.*, 7
(to) meet あいます (会います) (dictionary form is あう) う-*v.*, 6
memories おもいで (思い出) *n.*, 12
menswear しんしふく (紳士服) *n.*, 8
Mexico メキシコ *n.*, 2
middle ちゅう〜 (中〜) 中学校、中学生 *pref.*, 10
milk ミルク *n.*, 7
minus マイナス *n.*, 11
〜 minute(s), (for) 〜 minute(s) 〜ふん (〜分) *count.*, 3
Monday げつようび (月曜日) *n.*, 3
month 〜がつ (〜月) *suf.*, 11
more もっと *adv.*, 7
more, another もう *adv.*, 8
morning あさ (朝) *n.*, 3
morning, a.m. ごぜん (午前) *n.*, 2
mother (someone else's) おかあさん (お母さん) *n.*, 10
mother (the speaker's) はは (母) *n.*, 10
mountain やま (山) *n.*, 5
mountain climbing やまのぼり (山登り) *n.*, 12
mouth くち (口) *n.*, 10
movie えいが (映画) *n.*, 3
Mr./Mrs./Miss/Ms. 〜 〜さん *suf.*, 1
museum はくぶつかん (博物館) *n.*, 12
music おんがく (音楽) *n.*, 6
musical ミュージカル *n.*, 12

N

name なまえ (名前) *n.*, 2
〜 nationality アメリカじん 〜じん (〜人) *suf.*, 2
near, vicinity ちかく (近く) *loc. n.*, 5
necklace ネックレス *n.*, 8
necktie ネクタイ *n.*, 8
(to) need something いる (要る) う-*v.*, 9
new あたらしい (新しい) い-*adj.*, 4
newspaper しんぶん (新聞) *n.*, 6
(the) New Year しょうがつ (正月) (often おしょうがつ) *n.*, 12
next つぎ (次) *n.*, 3
next month らいげつ (来月) *n.*, 12
next time こんど (今度) *n.*, 6
next to となり (隣) *loc. n.*, 5
next to, at the side of よこ (横) *loc. n.*, 5
next year らいねん (来年) *n.*, 2
night, evening ばん (晩) *n.*, 3
night よる (夜) *n.*, 11

nine きゅう／く（九） *number*, 3
nine o'clock くじ（九時） *time exp.*, 2
no, don't mention it, you're welcome いいえ *inter.*, 2
No, I don't understand it. いいえ、わかりません。 *exp.*, 1
No, I still have a long way to go. いいえ、まだまだです。 *exp.*, 10
No, that's not so. いいえ、そうじゃありません／そうじゃないです。 *exp.*, 2
No, that's not the case. いいえ、そんなことはありません。 *exp.*, 10
north きた（北） *n.*, 11
northeast ほくとう（北東） *n.*, 11
northwest ほくせい（北西） *n.*, 11
nose はな（鼻） *n.*, 10
not at all (used with the negative form of verbs) ぜんぜん（全然） *adv.*, 3
not very often (used with the negative form of verbs) あまり *adv.*, 3
notebook ノート *n.*, 4
noun modifier marker (of), ('s) の *part.*, 2
now いま（今） *n.*, 2

O

ocean, sea うみ（海） *n.*, 12
～ o'clock ～じ（～時） *suf.*, 2
often, well よく *adv.*, 3
oil あぶら（油／脂） *n.*, 9
old (of non-living things) ふるい（古い） い*-adj.*, 4
older brother (someone else's) おにいさん（お兄さん） *n.*, 10
older brother (the speaker's) あに（兄） *n.*, 10
older sister (someone else's) おねえさん（お姉さん） *n.*, 10
older sister (the speaker's) あね（姉） *n.*, 10
on, above, over うえ（上） *loc. n.*, 5
one いち（一） *number*, 3
one o'clock いちじ（一時） *time exp.*, 2
only child ひとりっこ（一人っ子） *n.*, 10
orange オレンジ *n.*, 7
(to) order, (to) ask (someone to do something) たのむ（頼む） う*-v.*, 9
order ちゅうもん（注文） *n.*, 9
(to) order ちゅうもんする（注文する） *irr. v.*, 9
outside そと（外） *loc. n.*, 5
over there, that place (far away from both speaker and listener) あそこ *demo.*, 4

P

p.m., afternoon ごご（午後） *n.*, 2
parents (both) りょうしん（両親） *n.*, 6
park こうえん（公園） *n.*, 4
part-time job アルバイト／バイト *n.*, 6
party パーティ *n.*, 6
pen ペン *n.*, 4
pencil えんぴつ（鉛筆） *n.*, 4

person ひと(人) (see "counters" for *people*) *n.*, 5
person (polite form of 人) ～かた(～方) *suf.*, 10
personality せいかく(性格) *n.*, 10
photograph しゃしん(写真) *n.*, 5
picnic ピクニック *n.*, 6
picture え(絵) *n.*, 5
pizza ピザ *n.*, 9
place ところ(所) *n.*, 5
(to) play あそびます(遊びます) (dictionary form is あそぶ) う-*v.*, 6
Please come in. あがってください。(上がって下さい。) *exp.*, 5
Please do not bother/worry about it. いいえ、どうぞおかまいなく。 *exp.*, 9
Please give me ～. ～を ください。(～を下さい。) *exp.*, 8
Please listen. きいて ください。 *exp.*, 1
Please look at it. みて ください。 *exp.*, 1
Please read. よんで ください。 *exp.*, 1
Please say ～. / Repeat after me. いって ください。 *exp.*, 1
Please say it again. (student request) もう いちど おねがいします。 *exp.*, 1
Please say it again. (instructor request) もう いちど いってください。 *exp.*, 1
Please say it in easier words. やさしい ことばで いってください。(やさしい 言葉で 言って下さい。) *exp.*, 8
Please say it slowly. もう すこし ゆっくり おねがいします。 *exp.*, 1
Please speak loudly. (student request) おおきい こえで おねがいします。 *exp.*, 1
Please speak loudly. (instructor request) おおきい こえで いってください。 *exp.*, 1
Please write. かいて ください。 *exp.*, 1
p.m., afternoon ごご(午後) *n.*, 2
police box こうばん(交番) *n.*, 4
polite prefix お～(御～) *pref.*, 2
polite prefix ご～(御～) *pref.*, 9
pool プール *n.*, 6
pop music ポップス *n.*, 7
pork ポーク *n.*, 9
post office ゆうびんきょく(郵便局) *n.*, 4
present, gift プレゼント *n.*, 12
pretty, clean, neat きれい(な) (綺麗(な)) な-*adj.*, 4
Professor ～ ～せんせい(～先生) *suf.*, 1
(to) put いれる(入れる) る-*v.*, 8
(to) put on (top of head, e.g. hat, cap) かぶる う-*v.*, 10
(to) put on (accessories) する irr-*v.*, 10
(to) put on (glasses) かける る-*v.*, 10
(to) put on (lower body, e.g. skirt, pants, socks) はく う-*v.*, 10
(to) put on (upper body, e.g. sweater, shirt, jacket) きる(着る) る-*v.*, 10

Q

question しつもん(質問)*n.* しつもん(を)します (to) ask a question, 6
question marker か *part.*, 2
quiet しずか(な)(静か(な)) な-*adj.*, 5

R

rain あめ (雨) *n.*, 11
rainy season つゆ (梅雨) *n.*, 11
ramen, Chinese noodles in soup ラーメン *n.*, 9
rap music ラップ *n.*, 7
(to) read よみます (読みます) (dictionary form is よむ) う-*v.*, 3
(to) receive, (to) get もらう う-*v.*, 12
recent, recently さいきん (最近) *n.*, 11
red あかい (赤い) い-*adj.*, 4
regrettable ざんねん (な) (残念 (な)) な-*adj.*, 6
(to) relax, (to) take it easy ゆっくりする *irr. v.*, 6
(to) reside すむ (住む) う-*v.*, 10
rest, absence, day off やすみ (休み) *n.*, 6
restaurant レストラン *n.*, 4
restroom, toilet トイレ *n.*, 5
resultant state 〜ている *aux. v.*, 10
(to) return, (to) go home かえります (帰ります) (dictionary form is かえる) う-*v.*, 3
rice (cooked, served as part of Japanese cuisine) ごはん (御飯) *n.*, 3
rice (in foreign dishes; see also *curry and rice*) ライス *n.*, 9
rice wine, alcoholic beverage さけ (酒) (often おさけ) *n.*, 7
(to the) right, right side みぎ (右) *loc. n.*, 5
ring ゆびわ (指輪) *n.*, 8
river かわ (川) *n.*, 5
(to) rise; to go up あがる (上がる) う-*v.*, 11
rock and roll ロック *n.*, 7
room へや (部屋) ／ルーム コンピュータ・ルーム computer room, computer lab *n.*, 5
round まるい (丸い) い-*adj.*, 10

S

sad かなしい (悲しい) い-*adj.*, 6
salad サラダ *n.*, 9
sale セール *n.*, 8
salty しょっぱい／しおからい い-*adj.*, 9
sandwich サンドイッチ *n.*, 9
sashimi さしみ (刺身) (often お (御) さしみ) *n.*, 9
Saturday どようび (土曜日) *n.*, 3
(to) say いいます (言います) (dictionary form is よむ) う-*v.*, 6
school がっこう (学校) *n.*, 3
school cafeteria がくしょく (学食) (a shortened form of 学生しょくどう) *n.*, 5
season きせつ (季節) *n.*, 11
See you later. (literally, *Well then, again.*) じゃあ、また。*exp.*, 1
(to) see, (to) watch みます (見ます) (dictionary form is みる) る-*v.*, 3
semester, quarter がっき (学期) *n.*, 12
senior, fourth-year student (The suffix せい may be dropped.) よねんせい (四年生) *n.*, 2
seven なな、しち (七) *number*, 3

seven o'clock しちじ (七時) *time exp.*, 2
Shinto shrine じんじゃ (神社) *n.*, 12
shirt シャツ *n.*, 8
shoe(s) くつ (靴) *n.*, 8
shop [see *store*]
shopping かいもの (買い物) *n.*, 6
short (length) みじかい (短い) い *-adj.*, 10
(to) show みせる (見せる) る *-v.*, 8
shower シャワー *n.*, 3
shower (rain) にわかあめ (にわか雨) *n.*, 11
sibling(s), (the speaker's) きょうだい (兄弟) *n.*, 10
sibling(s) (someone else's) ごきょうだい (ご兄弟) *n.*, 10
(to) sing うたう (歌う) う *-v.*, 7
six ろく (六) *number*, 3
six o'clock ろくじ (六時) *time exp.*, 2
skiing, ski スキー *n.*, 7
skillful じょうず (な) (上手 (な)) な *-adj.*, 10
skirt スカート *n.*, 8
slowly ゆっくり *adv.* (to) relax ゆっくりします *irr. v.*, 6
small ちいさい (小さい) い *-adj.*, 4
smart, intelligent あたまがいい *exp.*, 10
snow ゆき (雪) *n.*, 11
sock(s) くつした (靴下) *n.*, 8
sofa ソファ *n.*, 5
soft やわらかい (柔らかい) い *-adj.*, 9
sometimes ときどき (時々) *adv.*, 3
song うた (歌) *n.*, 7
sophomore, second-year student (The suffix せい may be dropped.) にねんせい (二年生) *n.*, 2
sorry, regrettable ざんねん (な)(残念 (な)) な *-adj.*, 6
Sorry, I have some errands/business to attend to. ちょっとようじ (用事) があって。 *exp.*, 6
soup スープ *n.*, 9
sour すっぱい (酸っぱい) い *-adj.*, 9
south みなみ (南) *n.*, 11
South Korea かんこく (韓国) *n.*, 2
southeast なんとう (南東) *n.*, 11
southwest なんせい (南西) *n.*, 11
spacious, wide ひろい (広い) い *-adj.*, 5
spaghetti スパゲティ *n.*, 9
Spain スペイン *n.*, 2
spicy からい (辛い) い *-adj.*, 9
sport スポーツ *n.*, 7
spring はる (春) *n.*, 11
square しかくい (四角い) い *-adj.*, 10
station (for trains) えき (駅) *n.*, 4
stationery ぶんぼうぐ (文房具) *n.*, 8

steak ステーキ *n.*, 9
stockings, pantyhose ストッキング *n.*, 8
(to) stop やむ (止む) う *-v.*, 11
storage space (Japanese style) おしいれ (押し入れ) *n.*, 5
〜 store, 〜 shop 〜や (〜屋) (e.g. ほんや bookstore) *suf.*, 4
store, shop みせ (店) *n.*, 8
stroll, walk さんぽ (散歩) さんぽ (を) します to take a walk *n.*, 6
strong つよい (強い) い *-adj.*, 11
student がくせい (学生) *n.*, 2
Student union がくせいかいかん (学生会館) *n.*, 5
〜 student 〜せい (〜生) だいがくせい college student いちねんせい freshman *suf.*, 2
study べんきょう (勉強) *n.*, 3
(to) study べんきょうします (勉強します) (dictionary form is べんきょうする) *irr. v.*, 3
sudden きゅう (な) (急 (な)) きゅうに suddenly な *-adj.*, 11
suit スーツ *n.*, 8
summer なつ (夏) *n.*, 11
summer holidays, summer break なつやすみ (夏休み) *n.*, 12
Sunday にちようび (日曜日) *n.*, 3
supermarket スーパー *n.*, 4
supper, dinner (evening meal) ばんごはん (晩御飯) *n.*, 3
sushi すし (寿司／鮨)(usually おすし) *n.*, 9
sweater セーター *n.*, 8
sweet あまい (甘い) い *-adj.*, 9
(to) swim およぎます (泳ぎます) (dictionary form is およぐ) う *-v.*, 6

T

table テーブル *n.*, 5
Taiwan たいわん (台湾) *n.*, 2
(to) take とる (取る) う *-v.*, 8
(to) take (a bath) (おふろに) はいります (入ります) (dictionary form is はいる) う *-v.*, 3
(to) take (a photograph) とる (撮る) しゃしんをとる う *-v.*, 7
(to) take (a shower) (シャワーを) あびます (浴びます) (dictionary form is あびる) る *-v.*, 3
(to) take (time), it costs かかります (dictionary form is かかる) う *-v.*, 5
(to) talk はなします (話します) (dictionary form is はなす) う *-v.*, 6
tall, high たかい (高い) い *-adj.*, 4
tea, green tea おちゃ (お茶) *n.*, 7
teacher せんせい (先生) *n.*, 1
telephone でんわ (電話) *n.*, 5
telephone number でんわばんごう (電話番号) *n.*, 3
television, TV テレビ *n.*, 3
temperature おんど (温度) *n.*, 11
tempura (fish, shrimp, vegetables; battered and deep-fried) てんぷら (天麩羅 / 天ぷら) *n.*, 9
ten じゅう (十) *number*, 3
ten o'clock じゅうじ (十時) *time exp.*, 2
ten thousand まん (万) *number*, 8
tennis テニス *n.* テニスをします to play tennis, 6

test テスト *n.*, 4
textbook きょうかしょ（教科書） *n.*, 4
～th (ordinal suffix) ～ばん（め）(～番（目）) *suf.*, 10
Thank you. ありがとうございます。*exp.*, 1
Thank you. (literally, *I will intrude on you*) (said before going inside someone's house or apartment)
おじゃまします。（お邪魔します。）*exp.*, 5
Thank you very much どうも ありがとうございます。*exp.*, 2
that [+ noun] その [+ noun] *demo.*, 5
that [+ noun] over there あの [+ noun] *demo.*, 5
that (object over there) あれ *demo.*, 4
that (object) (close to the listener or slightly removed from both speaker and listener) それ *demo.*, 4
the year before last year おととし（一昨年） *n.*, 12
there, that place (close to listener or slightly removed from both speaker and listener) そこ *demo.*, 4
(to be) thin やせている
thing (intangible) こと *n.*, 7
thing (tangible) もの（物） *n.*, 5
(to) think おもう（思う） う*-v.*, 10
this ～ こん～（今～） こんしゅう this week, こんばん tonight *pref.*, 3
this area このへん（この辺） *n.*, 4
this month こんげつ（今月） *n.*, 12
this morning けさ（今朝） *n.*, 11
this [+ noun] この [+ noun] *demo.*, 5
this (object) これ *demo.*, 4
this person, this way こちら *n.*, 2
this week こんしゅう（今週） *n.*, 3
this year ことし（今年） *n.*, 11
thousand せん（千） *number*, 8
three さん（三） *number*, 3
three o'clock さんじ（三時） *time exp.*, 2
Thursday もくようび（木曜日） *n.*, 3
tie ネクタイ *n.*, 8
times ～ど（～度）/ ～かい（～回） *suf.*, 12
to, until まで *part.*, 5
to (direction) がっこうへ いきます。 へ *part.*, 3
to (goal, activity + に) クラスに いきます。 に *part.*, 3
to (goal, receiver) に *part.*, 6
toast トースト *n.*, 9
today きょう（今日） *n.*, 3
together いっしょに（一緒に） *adv.*, 6
together with (association) と *part.*, 6
toilet, restroom トイレ *n.*, 5
tomato トマト *n.*, 7
tomorrow あした（明日） *n.*, 3
tonight こんばん（今晩） *n.*, 3
too ("similarity marker") も *part.*, 2

topic marker　は *part.*, 2
tough (situation)　たいへん（な）（大変（な））　な-*adj.*, 6
town　まち（町）　*n.*, 4
traditional Japanese clothes, kimono　きもの（着物）　*n.*, 12
travel　りょこう（旅行）　*n.*, 7
(to) travel　りょこうする（旅行する）　*irr. v.*, 7
tree　き（木）　*n.*, 5
trousers, shorts　パンツ　*n.*, 8
truly, really, indeed　ほんとうに / ほんとに（本当に）　*adv.*, 11
T-shirt　T シャツ　*n.*, 8
Tuesday　かようび（火曜日）　*n.*, 3
TV, television　テレビ　*n.*, 3
twelve o'clock　じゅうにじ（十二時）　*time exp.*, 2
two　に（二）　*number*, 3
two o'clock　にじ（二時）　*time exp.*, 2
typhoon　たいふう（台風）　*n.*, 11

U

uh, well...　あのう　*inter.*, 2
umbrella　かさ（傘）　*n.*, 8
under, beneath　した（下）　*loc. n.*, 5
underground　ちか（地下）　*n.*, 8
(to) understand　わかる（分かる）　う-*v.*, 10
(the) United States of America　アメリカ　*n.*, 2
unpleasant, yuck　いや（な）（嫌（な））　な-*adj.*, 11
until, to　まで　*part.*, 5
usually　たいてい　*adv.*, 3

V

Valentine's Day　バレンタインデー　*n.*, 12
vegetable　やさい（野菜）　*n.*, 7
very　どうも　*adv.*, 4
very (as in *not very*; always used with a negative form)　あまり　*adv.*, 4
very (always used with an affirmative form)　とても　*adv.*, 4
very much　だい～（大～）　大すき like very much　*pref.*, 7
video　ビデオ　*n.*, 5

W

(to) wait　まちます（待ちます）(dictionary form is まつ）　う-*v.*, 6
(to) walk　あるきます（歩きます）(dictionary form is あるく）　う-*v.*, 6
walk, stroll　さんぽ（散歩）　さんぽ（を）します　to take a walk　*n.*, 6
walking, on/by foot　あるいて（歩いて）　*exp.*, 5
warm (air temperature)　あたたかい（暖かい）　い-*adj.*, 11
warm (objects, mood, etc.)　あたたかい（温かい）　い-*adj.*, 9
watch, clock　とけい（時計）　*n.*, 5
(to) watch　みます（見ます）(dictionary form is みる）　る-*v.*, 3

water みず (水) (often おみず) *n.*, 7
weak よわい (弱い) い *-adj.*, 11
weather てんき (天気) *n.*, 11
weather forecast てんきよほう (天気予報) *n.*, 11
Wednesday すいようび (水曜日) *n.*, 3
weekend しゅうまつ (週末) *n.*, 3
Welcome. いらっしゃいませ。 *exp.*, 8
Welcome! Come in. いらっしゃい。 *exp.*, 5
well, often よく *adv.*, 3
Well, let's see. . . えーと *exp.*, 12
west にし (西) *n.*, 11
Western-style cuisine ようしょく (洋食) *n.*, 9
what なに／なん (何) *q. word*, 2
What does ～ mean? ～って なんですか。 *exp.*, 1
what kind of どんな *q. word*, 4
(Japanese) wheat noodles うどん *n.*, 9
when いつ *q. word*, 3
when, at the time of ～ とき (時) *n.*, 12
where どこ *q. word*, 2
where (more polite than どこ), which way どちら *q. word*, 2
Where are you from? どこから きましたか。(polite どちらから いらっしゃいましたか。) *exp.*, 2
which [+ noun] どの [+ noun] *demo.*, 5
which one どれ *q. word*, 4
white しろい (白い) い*-adj.*, 4
who だれ *q. word*, 4
why どうして *q. word*, 8
wide, spacious ひろい (広い) い *-adj.*, 5
wife (someone else's) おくさん (奥さん) *n.*, 10
wife (the speaker's) つま (妻) *n.*, 10
wind かぜ (風) *n.*, 11
window まど (窓) *n.*, 5
wine ワイン *n.*, 7
winter ふゆ (冬) *n.*, 11
with, together with (association) と *part.*, 6
women's clothing ふじんふく (婦人服) *n.*, 8
wristwatch うでどけい (腕時計) *n.*, 8
(to) write かきます (書きます) (dictionary form is かく) う*-v.*, 6

Y

year ～ねん (～年) (for specific years, e.g. 1996 年) *suf.*, 12
(～ th) year ～ねん (～年) いちねん first year *suf.*, 2
～ years old ～さい (～歳 / 才) *suf.*, 10
yellow きいろい (黄色い) い*-adj.*, 4
Yen (counter for Japanese currency) ～えん (～円) *count.*, 8

yes　はい／ええ *inter.*, 2
Yes, I understand (it).　はい、わかりました。 *exp.*, 1
Yes, that's so.　はい／ええ、そうです。 *exp.*, 2
yesterday　きのう (昨日) *n.*, 3
You are welcome.　どういたしまして。 *exp.*, 1
You call it ～/You say ～　～と　いいます。／～って　いいます。 *exp.*, 1
younger brother (someone else's)　おとうとさん (弟さん) *n.*, 10
younger brother (the speaker's)　おとうと (弟) *n.*, 10
younger sister (someone else's)　いもうとさん (妹さん) *n.*, 10
younger sister (the speaker's)　いもうと (妹) *n.*, 10

Z

zero　ゼロ／れい (ゼロ／零) *number*, 3
zoo　どうぶつえん (動物園) *n.*, 12

INDEX

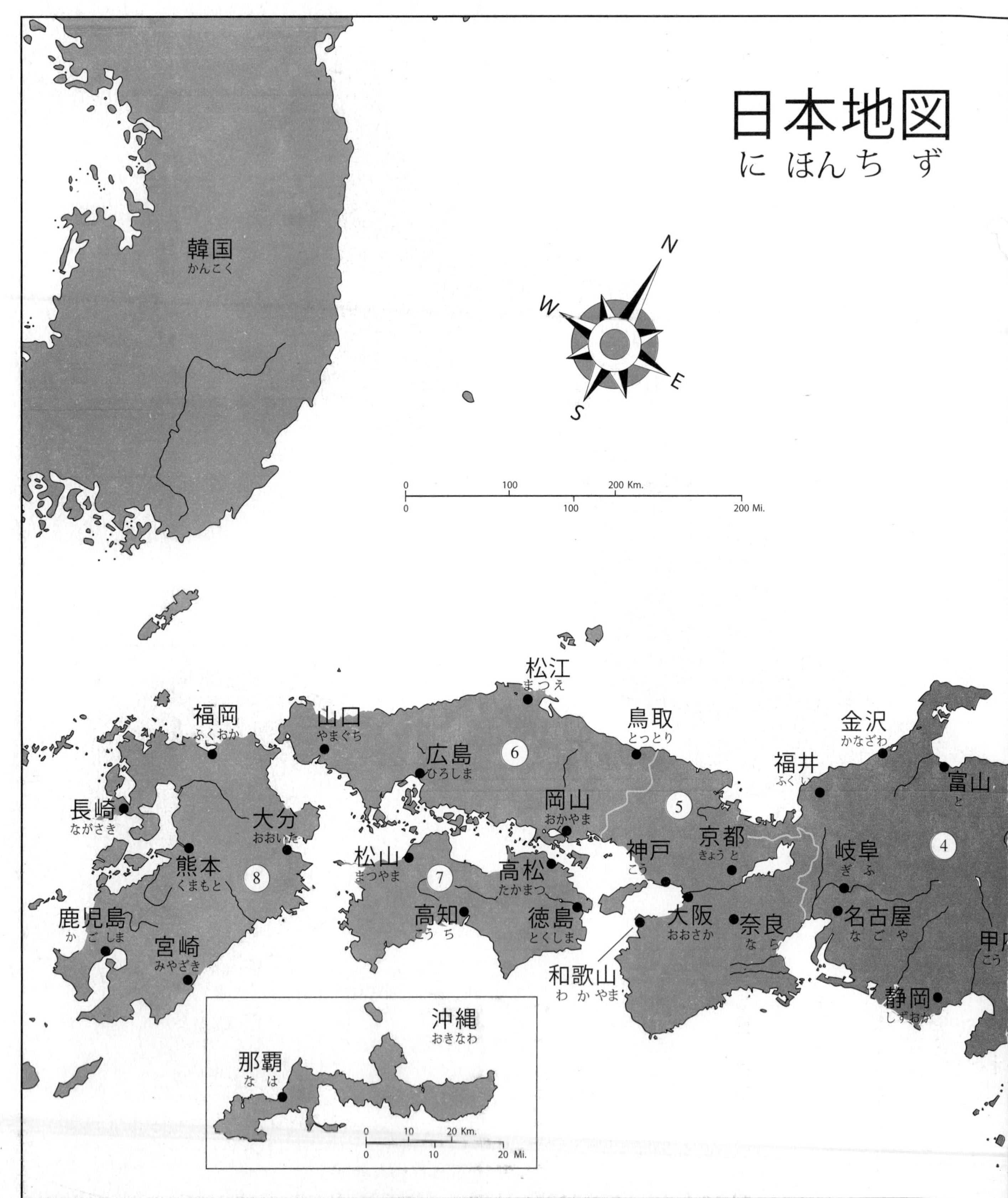

日本地図
にほんちず
韓国
かんこく
N
W
E
S
0 100 200 Km.
0 100 200 Mi.
松江
まつえ
鳥取
とっとり
金沢
かなざわ
福岡
ふくおか
山口
やまぐち
広島
ひろしま
6
福井
富山
長崎
ながさき
大分
岡山
おかやま
5
京都
きょうと
神戸
岐阜
ぎふ
4
熊本
くまもと
8
松山
まつやま
7
高松
たかまつ
高知
こうち
徳島
とくしま
大阪
おおさか
奈良
名古屋
なごや
鹿児島
かごしま
宮崎
みやざき
和歌山
わかやま
静岡
しずおか
沖縄
おきなわ
那覇
なは
0 10 20 Km.
0 10 20 Mi.